PERFORMANCE IN AMERICA

PERVERSE MODERNITIES

A series edited by Judith Halberstam and Lisa Lowe

DUKE UNIVERSITY PRESS   **DURHAM AND LONDON 2005**

PERFORMANCE IN AMERICA

CONTEMPORARY U.S. CULTURE AND THE PERFORMING ARTS

David Román

THE DISTRIBUTION OF THIS BOOK IS
SUPPORTED BY A GENEROUS GRANT FROM
THE GILL FOUNDATION.

Designed by Rebecca Giménez

Typeset in Minion and Meta by Tseng Information Systems

Library of Congress Cataloging-in-Publication Data and complete
republication information appear following the
index.

FOR SUE-ELLEN CASE

CONTENTS

ILLUSTRATIONS

ACKNOWLEDGMENTS

The book is a result of the many conversations I had with friends and colleagues about the status of the performing arts in contemporary American culture. I've been writing the book since 1998—and thus have many people to thank for helping me along the way. First and foremost I want to acknowledge Richard Meyer, my partner for the past ten years, who I love dearly and deeply. We share perhaps too many things, but I am so delighted that we share what matters most, which is to say our lives. His care for my work and my well-being deserves much more thanks than I can offer here. Richard has read every word in this book more times than I should have asked, and, truth be told, he's written a few as well. He believes in me in ways I've never experienced. He gives me the gift of confidence. Let it suffice to say that he is everywhere in this book, and that I could not have imagined writing it without him by my side.

There are many friends who have engaged my work over the years and whose hard questioning has pushed me to think differently and more imaginatively about this project. Jill Dolan, José Muñoz, Karen Shimakawa, and Josh Kun have entertained most of these ideas since the beginning of this project, and I love having them as my primary readers and close friends. Their contributions are too numerous to detail and, at this point, so completely integrated into the book itself that I couldn't even begin to untangle them. But I must report that it was José who dared me to write about cabaret performance and whose own audacious thinking inspired me to do so. Others, too, have read and engaged these ideas; at the University of Southern California (USC), where I teach, I have the following colleagues in the Department of English and in the Program in American Studies to thank for reading and commenting on my early drafts: Joe Boone, Leo Braudy, Judith Halberstam, Jane Iwamura, Carla Kaplan, Jim Kincaid, Dorinne Kondo, Rebecca Lemon, and Viet Nguyen. Leo Braudy deserves special mention for his consistently generous engagement with my work and career. Carol Bunch was my main research assistant on this book, and her support has been invaluable. Jesús Hernández served as my research assistant more recently, and for this I am extremely grateful. His commitment to this project and to our friendship made the final stages of the book's production joyful and rewarding. Thanks also to the following USC graduate students for helping me out with their research and technical skills: Teresa Lee, Tiffany Knight, Wendy Cheng, and Viet Le. My thanks to Nellie Ayala-Reyes, who makes my life in the English Department easier and more enjoyable, and Sandra Jones, who makes walking into the office of the Program in American Studies and Ethnicity something I want to keep doing. Thanks also to my other enduring allies at USC, especially Meiling Cheng, Pierrette Hondagneu-Sotelo, Ruthie Gilmore, Nancy Troy, Tara McPherson, and Cynthia Young. Laura Pulido, Teresa McKenna, Roberto Lint-Sagarena, Ricardo Ramirez, Macarena Gomez-Barris, and George Sanchez, my trusted cohorts in the Chicano/Latino faculty cluster, allow me to do my own version of Latino Studies, something for which I am extremely grateful. George Sanchez, the director of American Studies and Ethnicity at USC, ranks among the most generous people I know, and among the most visionary; he has offered me tangible material support and the remarkable gift of intellectual community. I am indebted to Beth Meyerowitz, the dean of faculty of USC's College of Letters, Arts and Sciences, who offered me the means to write the book I wanted to write from the start, and who trusted I could do so. My thanks also to Joseph Aoun, dean at the college, for his decade-long support of my career.

I am lucky to have a diverse and expansive intellectual community outside of my home institution. My thanks to Carolyn Dinshaw, David Halperin, Andrea Most, Deborah Paredez, Janelle Reinelt, Alberto Sandoval, Shannon Steen, and Stacy Wolf for reading and commenting on sections of this book and for encouraging me along the way. Thanks also to Una Chaudhuri, Kandice Chuh, Elin Diamond, Harry Elam, Susan Foster, Gayatri Gopinath, George Haggerty, Kathleen McHugh, Chon Noriega, Ricardo Ortiz, Diana Paulin, Ann Pellegrini, Joe Roach, Bob Vorlicky, and Bill Worthen, dear friends and respected colleagues all. I would like to acknowledge Judith Butler, David Halperin, and Susan Jeffords who, when I first started in this profession, offered me unexpected kindness and support. Dwight Conquergood's enthusiasm for my work helped me keep at it. His untimely death remains a major loss for the field of performance studies and to all who knew and cared for him. Jennifer Brody offered me useful comments that literally changed the book as I was writing it. Her thoughtful engagement pushed me to clarify more forcefully my ideas and dig deeper into my archive. But it is Lisa Lowe to whom I owe the most gratitude in shaping the book's intellectual scope. Simply put, this has become a better book because of her consistent critical engagement and her belief in my work and career. Lisa's intellectual rigor is matched only by her generosity; I have been tremendously fortunate to have been offered both over the years.

I am grateful to Lisa Lowe and Judith Halberstam for inviting me to be a part of their series. Among other things, they provided me with the extraordinary opportunity to work with Ken Wissoker. Everything I've read about Ken in all my Duke University Press books is true. His touch is firm and kind, his sense of purpose clear and honest. From our first conversation, Ken's support and encouragement have been consistent and invaluable. And thanks to Courtney Berger and Christine Dahlin, who have helped usher the book through the editorial process. Kate Lothman oversaw the book's production, and for that I am also enormously grateful. I was also very lucky to have Rebecca Giménez serve as the book's designer. The entire experience with Duke has been simply amazing and one of the most satisfying of my academic career.

Many of the ideas in this book have been presented at the annual conferences of the American Studies Association, the Modern Language Association, the Association for Theatre in Higher Education, and the International Federation of Theatre Research. I wrote this book as a bridge project between American Studies and Theatre and Performance Studies, the two main fields in which I work. My colleagues in these fields have been wonderfully supportive, inviting me to present my scholarship on their campuses. Audiences at Bowling Green State University; Brown University; California State University, Los Angeles; Duke University; East Los Angeles College; New York University; Northwestern University; Oberlin College; Pomona College; Stanford University; University of California, Berkeley; University of California, Davis; University of California, Riverside; University of California, San Diego; University of California, Santa Cruz; University of Colorado, Boulder; University of Guelph; University of Oregon; University of Texas, Austin; University of Toronto; Vassar College; and the University of Wisconsin, Madison provided me an invaluable critical engagement for which I am very thankful. I need to single out the Latino and queer undergraduate student organizations at Duke University and at Oberlin College for inviting me to visit their campuses. Their commitments to cultural diversity, curricular reform, and progressive cultural politics in general offer me the gift of inspiration. Here, too, let me acknowledge the undergrads at USC, who continue to impress me even though I know well enough to anticipate their brilliance and warmth. Thanks especially to Kevin Reynard, and also the various students in the "AIDS and the Arts in America" classes, for teaching me how to listen differently.

The book is indebted to the artists whose work I discuss, and to the vibrant and inviting performance communities in which it is in conversation. These performance worlds offer me the gift of intimacy and immediacy. This book is written out of a deep love for the performing arts and for many of the people who have devoted their lives to it. I spend an inordinate amount of my life in the theatre. The archive in this book stands as the evidence of this passion, but in many ways it is a random one. I could have easily written about any number of the hundreds of performances I have seen over the years.

In Los Angeles, where I have been living since 1995, the Mark Taper Forum and Highways Performance Space frame my performance community. My thanks to Luis Alfaro, Brian Freeman, Diane Rodriguez, and Chay Yew at the Taper for always inviting me to be a part of whatever they do, and to Tim Miller and Danielle Brazell, the former artistic directors of Highways. These artists believe that my role as a scholar is vital to the mission of their artistic homes. At USC, I have had the privilege to host a number of artists, many of them friends whose work has had a profound impact on my worldview, artists such as Coco Fusco, the late Spalding Gray, Neil Greenberg, Danny Hoch, Holly Hughes, Michael Kearns, Suzan-Lori Parks, Reno, Peggy Shaw, Alina Troyano (aka Carmelita Tropicana), Paula Vogel, and Chay Yew. Some of these artists are discussed in this book, others I have written about elsewhere; all of them are remarkable people. Let me also thank the artists discussed in *Performance in America* whose openness to my engagement with their work enriched my project immeasurably: Cornerstone Theatre, Neil Greenberg, Mary Cleere Haran, Bill T. Jones, John Kelly, Reno, and Chay Yew.

In New York, my home away from home, I should begin by thanking my friends at the former Paramount, a group of people who looked out for me and whose hospitality was most appreciated: Loida Martinez, Celso Moreira, Christopher Roche, Justin Yatwa, and especially Patricia Herrera. And thanks to Sherry Meyer and Gladys Eisenstadt for the endless encouragement and boundless affection; Terrence Kissack and everyone at the Gay, Lesbian, Bisexual, and Transgender Historical Society of Northern California; the librarians and staff of the Library of the Performing Arts at Lincoln Center; and all of the photographers who gave me permission to use their amazing images in this book. My thanks to Chris Bennion, Tom Brazil, Paula Court, Michal Daniel, Johan Elbers, Alice Garik, Joan Marcus, Mike Martin, Beatriz Schiller, Craig Schwartz, Lisa Silvestri, Martha Swope, and Richard Termine for their support of my project and for their ongoing belief in the importance of the performing arts. I couldn't imagine my book without their visual documentation of its archive. Martha Swope deserves special mention for sharing with me—and the readers of this book—her historical images of the original Broadway cast of *A Chorus Line*.

And here's to the people who don't easily fit in any of the categories above. My thanks and love to Holly Hughes and Esther Newton and all the living creatures they nurture; to my friend Matt Garcia who on first meeting jumped into my heart; to Michael Mayer who has held residence there since the late 1970s; to Joe Boone, Dustin Shell, and Tim Miller, who have known me longest and best; to Ira Sachs, Glenn Ligon, and Connie Wolf, for being my friend too; to Catherine Lord and Kim Thomsen for inviting me in; to Susan Foster for the chickens and the love; to Myriam Román, my mother, for being my friend for over forty years; to Chay Yew, who I rarely see but still feel is near; to Jesús Hernández, who more and more belongs here too; to Teresa McKenna, for taking a chance on me many years ago and for continuing to give me the benefit of the doubt; to David Joselit because when he laughs the room fills up; to David Rousseve and Conor McTeague with whom I share the big moments and the big feelings; to Richard, because once is not enough; to Jenny, our dog, who showed up unannounced and stayed knowing our home might be a place for those seeking alternative belonging; to Anthony Rapp, for turning me on to *Survivor*, for asking me to tell the stories of my life that I had nearly forgotten, and for bringing along Rodney—Anthony's sweet voice is for me the sound of friendship; and to Cris Rivera, my most cherished friend, who fills my world with the force of life. These are the people who occupy my heart and who embody all that I hold dear.

Finally, I want to acknowledge Sue-Ellen Case, to whom I dedicate this book with love. She broke down the doors that then opened up a space for people like me. Thank you, Sue-Ellen, for everything.

Here and Now

Performance in America argues for the significance of the performing arts in contemporary U.S. culture by challenging the conventional wisdom that performance is marginal to the national imaginary. The book takes seriously the role that the performing arts play in shaping American culture, especially around ideologies of race, citizenship, and national identity. Through a series of case studies drawn from contemporary culture, the book demonstrates the vitality of theatre, performance, and dance to local, regional, and national communities and poses the question: What might be gained by placing performance at the center of current national inquiries and debates?

In order to begin answering this question, the book proposes a way of thinking about performance as a practice that both shapes and informs a space that I call the "contemporary." I here understand the contemporary as a critical temporality that engages the past without being held captive to it and that instantiates the present without defining a future. Performance proves an especially effective means to engage the contemporary in that artists and audiences are constituted and composed as a provisional collective in a particular temporal moment and in a specific localized space. They may or may not share the same history or future, but in the moment during which they compose a group, they enact and perform a temporary and conditional we. Performance's liveness and impermanence allow for a process of exchange—between artists and audiences, between the past and the present—where new social formations emerge. These new social formations constitute a counterpublic that offers both respite and change from normative structures of being and belonging assumed both in the national culture and in the subcultural worlds that form a part of it. While *Performance in America* is especially drawn to understanding how performance critically reinvents what is meant by "America," it is equally committed to understanding how the contemporary engages with the histories that precede and help produce it. The book understands the contemporary as that which both carries and reinvents particular moments and performances from the past.

The three keywords of my project—*performance, America,* and *contemporary*—converge in the book's various case studies. While drawn from contemporary American performance, each case study holds a different set of relations to, and investments in, these three terms. Rather than attempt to unify these keywords in such a way as to prescribe the work that contemporary performance in America enacts, I wish to open up interpretive possibilities, rather than foreclose them. Although the book is organized under a central theme that showcases performance's critical engagement with contemporary American culture, my consideration of the contemporary results in retrieving previous historical moments and performances that might seem anachronistic to the book's mission: *Performance in America*'s archive is expansive without being exhaustive, and it includes unlikely sources and events.

The primary archive consists of work performed between 1994 and 2004, a ten-year period during which dramatic and unanticipated events unfolded throughout the nation and the world. From the profound results of innovative HIV/AIDS treatments introduced in the United States in the mid-1990s to the changing demographics of the American population at the end of the twentieth century, from the immediate aftermath of 9/11 to the ongoing effects of the second Iraqi war, performance engages the contemporary as a dialogue about the country, its people, and its history. In staging these conversations, performance creates its audiences as critical subjects of this now; the provisional gathering that characterizes performance opens up a space in the public sphere that might challenge or refute local or national sentiments prioritized by other media. This moment, although local and temporal, should not be underestimated: not only does it rehearse new forms of sociality but those involved experience it in the process of the event itself.[1]

Yet not all of the performances examined here engage the national culture with equal force or overtness. While this book mostly preoccupies itself with performances that address many of the pressing issues of our times, it also is interested in considering performances with less explicitly global implications. The focus in these moments rests on performances emerging out of particular communities or demographics and those exploring and mining questions of identity and affiliation. I am especially interested in the ways certain artists mark themselves as historical subjects whose genealogies might be found outside of traditional systems of identification and belonging. The performances I address here are located in critically undervalued genres such as cabaret, female impersonation, and Broadway entertainment. These performances also tell us much about contemporary American culture, even if their political themes appear less transparent than those more directly aligned with national political issues. As much as they engage contemporary matters, they also enable a reimagination of history and genealogy, both individual and communal, and demonstrate how performance functions as an archive itself. Throughout the book I thus explore the various connections that the contemporary makes with the past, not as a means to anchor the contemporary within an accepted tradition that needs to be either rescued or upheld, but as a means to trace the remains of history within our present moment so as to better understand that present. My project constitutes as much a historicization of the contemporary as a reflection on the relationship between the past and the present, thus exploring the dynamic relationship between performance, history, and contemporary U.S. culture.

Performance in America imagines performance as relevant and meaningful, and as fully capable of enacting cultural critique within multiple public spheres. It refutes the notion that the advocacy of performance is something merely romantic, as if a belief in the arts is a form of benign naivety, well intended but ultimately misinformed. In this sense, *Performance in America* can be understood as a polemical project. It argues for its subject matter so that others might be persuaded to better understand the work of performance, what it does and what it achieves. The book remains unapologetic in its commitment to the arts. The work's thesis—that performance in America matters—is meant to be provocative.

Throughout *Performance in America* readers will be invited to sample different events that make the case for performance as a specific form of cultural critique and engagement. I draw my examples from the worlds of dance, theatre, and music, discussing work performed in local, regional, and national venues. The performing arts provide multiple entry points into many of the key questions and concerns that constitute and preoccupy the contemporary, questions about history and politics, citizenship and society, culture and nation. They often articulate positions that shift the current conversations already in place on these issues. The performing arts not only provide a critical space to rehearse key questions of our time; they also allow us to renegotiate the way these questions are conceived of in the first place. In this sense, the performing arts might be understood as embodied theories that help audiences restructure or, at the very least, reimagine their social selves.

Performance in America archives performances that embody what cultural theorist Raymond Williams describes as "new structures of feeling," modes of experience that begin to shift individual and communal lives. Williams takes special interest in the ways that values are dynamically experienced and felt, that particular historical meanings and values emerge. Literature and the arts play an important role in this process. He writes:

> The idea of a structure of feeling can be specifically related to the evidence of forms and conventions—semantic figures—which, in art and literature, are often among the very first indications that such a new structure is forming. . . . as a matter of cultural theory this is a way of defining forms and conventions in art and literature as inalienable elements of a social material process: not as derivation from other social forms and pre-forms, but as social formation of a specific kind which may in turn be seen as the articulation (often the only fully available articulation) of structures of feeling which as living processes are much more widely experienced.[2]

In several of his writings, it is worth remembering, Williams relied on the archive of theatre and drama to illuminate many of his most important ideas, and he devoted an entire book to the study of modern tragedy. *Performance in America* builds on Williams's work on performance, history, and politics, as well as their relation to cultural change. And it privileges performance as a charismatic cultural site that enables new forms of sociality and alternative models of being.

Performance, as Jill Dolan has argued, is uniquely positioned to do such work. "Live performance provides a place where people come together, embodied and passionate, to share experiences of meaning making and imagination that can describe or capture fleeting intimations of a better world," she writes.[3] Given its convictions about the power of theatre and performance, my work is interested in identifying performances that advocate for the theatre's capacity to shape daily life. I am drawn to texts that strive to make a difference, that promote a progressive point of view, and that engage in contemporary concerns. I am also committed to calling attention to performances that are innovative and creative, and that move their artistic medium forward. Politics and aesthetics are mutually interdependent, and my book aims to think through their relation.

The individual chapters offer case studies that provide specific readings of local performances in particular moments in time. Beyond calling attention to individual artists and productions, the chapters contextualize how performance participates in far-reaching conversations within contemporary U.S. culture and demonstrate how these performances can be understood historically. I begin with a chapter on dance and consider the choreography of two of the most interesting artists from the dance world: Bill T. Jones and Neil Greenberg. Jones and Greenberg have been creating dance since the 1980s, but I highlight the work they produced in the mid-1990s. The work of these artists, both HIV-positive, marks a shift in AIDS in light of the new drug treatments that became available in this period, while offering a radically different way of thinking about the crisis. This chapter, entitled "Not about AIDS," follows on my own earlier work, in part by insisting on AIDS as ongoing and unresolved, both in the United States and abroad. Despite the tendency to bracket AIDS from the political priorities of queer communities in the 1990s, especially in light of an increasing interest in marriage and the military, both choreographers, burdened with AIDS materially and symbolically, pushed the discussion of living with HIV forward through their own creative corporal moves.

Chapter 2, "Visa Denied: Chay Yew's Theatre of Immigration and the Performance of Asian American History," shifts the focus to Los Angeles and the new wave of immigrants who have changed the racial and cultural demographic of Southern California in recent decades. I am interested in mapping what I call the "vernacular imaginary," a mode of experience that departs from official narratives of citizenship in the United States and the nationalist myths they promote. These myths circulate globally and inspire many immigrants to abandon their homelands for what they imagine will be a better life in America. In this context, I look at *A Beautiful Country*, a collaborative production between the playwright Chay Yew and the community-based Cornerstone Theatre, that offered, according to the show's promotional materials, "one hundred and fifty years of Asian American history through dance, drama, and drag." The site-specific performance of *A Beautiful Country* in L.A.'s Chinatown district opens up new critical possibilities for thinking about migration and exile, citizenship and belonging, and the costs of each for those who traverse these borders and boundaries.

The next chapter, "Latino Genealogies: Broadway and Beyond—The Case of John Leguizamo," moves from the vernacular worlds of the Asian diaspora in America and the localized production of a community arts project in a Chinatown school auditorium to the bright lights of the Great White Way and the premiere of *Freak*, John Leguizamo's one-person show at the Cort Theatre on Broadway. I here wish to consider what Leguizamo's hugely successful Broadway debut might tell us about contemporary Latino life in the United States. I discuss the material conditions that enabled Leguizamo—and, by extension, Latino audiences—to arrive on Broadway, and the cultural implications of such a move. I also offer a reading of *Freak* that attends to the models of kinship and genealogy that Leguizamo promotes in his show. *Freak* both pays tribute to a history of pan-Latino popular mainstream performance and traces a historical trajectory that offers new models for imagining Latino identity.

The chapters on AIDS and dance, Asian American theatre and immigration, and Latino performance and cultural history each showcase centrally the ways that performance intervenes in contemporary national concerns. As such, they highlight how particular communities find in performance a means to critically engage and reconstitute the experience of living in contemporary America. These chapters thus combine to form a cluster that illustrates the gains of imagining performance as central to the national culture. But they also begin to articulate the book's interest in the contemporary's relation to history. Each of the book's chapters will examine both of these themes—the political, the historical—and address the ways in which they are related. In the chapter on AIDS and dance, for example, I situate the discussion not only in the political context of the mid-1990s but also on the performers' relationship to their own bodies, themselves an archive of lived experience, social movement, and artistic expression. The chapters on Asian American theatre and Latino performance ruminate more broadly on questions of history and genealogy, even as they attend to the specifics of the contemporary culture in which they are now posed—I point out how contemporary performances provide an archive of previously forgotten or neglected histories. The two chapters document minoritarian relations to physical places and their symbolic capital—urban downtowns, theatre districts, commercial venues—as well as the high stakes involved in claiming rights to these locations in the contested public sphere. At the same time, all three chapters archive histories of resilience, many of which are found in the history of the performing arts.

This theme of performance as itself an embodied archive becomes more prominent in the following two chapters that foreground the ways in which questions of gender and sexuality contribute to the book's larger themes. These chapters expand the book's ongoing discussion of history and performance by focusing on work that provides a glimpse of previously contemporary performances in America as recorded in theatre history, Hollywood film, and popular music. As these chapters highlight, when the book takes an archival turn, the contemporary returns us in unpredictable ways to history. Admittedly, this makes for an unexpected move for a book on the contemporary, but it nonetheless proves a critical one if we wish to more fully understand how the contemporary is constituted in American culture. Chapters 4 and 5 also begin to answer the following question: Where in contemporary American culture are the arts acknowledged?

In Chapter 4, "Archival Drag; or, The Afterlife of Performance," I consider the work of contemporary female impersonators who revive the legacy of performers from a different era and whose work within queer subcultures preserves the role of the arts. If the previous chapters moved backward in time from contemporary performances to the historical moments they recall, this chapter begins with a distant historical moment so as to move forward to the contemporary. I begin in the eighteenth century with the celebrated British tragedienne Sarah Siddons to trace the ways theatre, gender, and celebrity operated in eighteenth-century British culture, and how that cultural influence shaped the popular culture of Hollywood in the 1950s. From there I look at the influence of 1950s Hollywood film on gay popular performers of the 1980s, ending with a discussion of the legacy of this archival drag on contemporary female impersonators. I am interested in tracing a genealogy of performance that also serves as an archival system of popular performance. The chapter concludes with speculations on the potential loss of this archive, carried across the centuries through embodied performances.

"Cabaret as Cultural History: Popular Song and Public Performance in America," the fifth chapter, focuses on cabaret performance and is similarly concerned with how contemporary performance functions as an archive of a historical past. Here, I make the case that cabaret performance provides one of the few venues in public culture where American cultural history is passed on and preserved. It is also a genre in which women and, in particular, older women, emerge as the main practitioners. Looking at the anecdotal narratives that many of these performers introduce between songs, I argue that this patter serves as a form of cultural memory, both personal and national, public and private. Rather than simply dismiss cabaret as an elite genre, I approach it through the lens of its archival function of preserving the songbooks of American popular composers and the personal and professional experience of the women who have sung them. In particular, I discuss three women who arrived in New York in the 1940s and found themselves performing one-woman shows on the Broadway stage nearly sixty years later: Elaine Stritch, Bea Arthur, and Barbara Cook. But I also look at a later generation of women singers who perform in the celebrated cabaret venues of New York, including Mary Cleere Haran, Donna McKechnie, and Andrea Marcovicci. Taken together, the chapters on drag and cabaret suggest how contemporary American performance involves a serious interrogation of the past, and that the performances themselves involve a critical reassessment of American nostalgia. The legacies that these artists perform in their work rupture the primacy of patriotic history by summoning other sentiments, other trajectories, of popular culture.

My book concludes with a return to the discussion of performances embedded in overt political themes whose ongoing impact remains in effect. This final section unites the topics introduced throughout the book's other chapters while showcasing the important role the performing arts hold in the national culture. "Tragedy and the Performance Arts in the Wake of September 11, 2001," addresses the response of the performing arts to the terrorist attack of 9/11. The chapter departs from the earlier writing in the book in that it is composed in the first person and as an account of my own experiences of the events. I begin by discussing the idea of tragedy and how it structures contemporary life before considering how the performing arts, especially in New York City, became a central component to the national economic and symbolic recovery. I survey a wide range of performance events—Broadway musicals, fund-raisers for the families of fallen firefighters, and classical concerts—all in the wake of September 11. I conclude with a discussion of new work engaged with global geopolitical events including U.S. military actions in Afghanistan and the ongoing war in Iraq.

In the book's afterword, "The Time of Your Life," I take one final archival turn by discussing the 2002 revival of William Saroyan's 1939 play *The Time of Your Life* by Chicago's Steppenwolf Theatre, perhaps the most esteemed theatre company in the United States. The production was restaged in 2004 in premier regional theatres in Seattle and San Francisco. I juxtapose the play's initial contemporary moment of the late 1930s and early 1940s—the Great Depression, the eve of World

War II—with the current contemporary to see what Saroyan's work might offer us now. The book concludes in 2004, the year in which it was completed: the ten-year period between the 1994 dances of Bill T. Jones and Neil Greenberg in New York City and the 2004 performances of the Steppenwolf revival of Saroyan's *The Time of Your Life* in Seattle and San Francisco forms the book's contemporary. The chapters appear chronologically, moving forward in time sequentially before arriving at the time of the now. The chapters can also be read as an archive of this period, one that includes the historical materials summoned to enrich the book's concern with the contemporary. The same can be said for the book's collection of images, many of which are also historical. I use images less as illustrations of the performances, although they help in that regard as well, and more to expand the book's scope to include a visual component meant to complement the writing. The images help contextualize the contemporary in historical and visual terms. Performance's impermanence is challenged by its ephemera, which paradoxically can be the evidence of its loss. These remains, however, document more than simply the constraints of writing performance history even in the contemporary period. The images and other ephemera included in the book provide yet another entry point into thinking about contemporary performance in America, its contribution to the national culture, and its engagement with the historical past.

ON THE CONTEMPORARY

The book's claim for the vitality of the contemporary performing arts necessitates an interrogation of the concept of the contemporary and its relation to history. When is the contemporary? For whom does the term hold meaning? And what work does it do when it is employed? In thinking through these questions, we begin to challenge the amorphous quality of the term *contemporary*. Throughout the book, I call attention to the contemporary period's virtually instantaneous movement from the present to the immediate past, a process that shapes the historical context of the period and underlines the philosophical challenges that come with thinking about history. "The question of 'the contemporary' is," as Thomas Docherty has written, "almost by definition, a problem of representation."[4] He explains: "A presentation of the present must always involve a representing, which has the effect of marking the present moment with the passage of time." But like most scholars drawn to the "question of the contemporary," Docherty focuses on literature, philosophy, and theory. Interest in the contemporary rarely focuses on the performing arts, a regrettable omission given the temporal attributes of performance that lend themselves to discussions of representation and time. I argue that performance's own nowness, which is to say its own ephemeral nature, provides an entrance into contemplating these questions around the contemporary and the interpretive and political issues attached to them. The act of writing itself delivers the contemporary into history. *Performance in America* is interested in addressing the temporality of performance, the historiography of theatre, and the practices of theatre criticism.

Scrutinizing the idea of the contemporary enriches the discussion of both recent and current American performances. Despite its ubiquitous usage, the term *contemporary* remains surprisingly undertheorized.[5] This undertheorization allows for the term's continued usage as a shorthand for something assumed but never explained. *Contemporary* is often used interchangeably with other literary or philosophical terms such as *postmodern* that set it up as a historical period, an aesthetic category, or both at once. My interest in the contemporary moves away from these discussions and focuses on the idea of the present as a time in which an audience imagines itself within a fluid and nearly suspended temporal condition, living in a moment not yet in the past and not yet in the future, yet a period we imagine as having some power to shape our relation to both history and futurity. My thinking here is influenced by Walter Benjamin's ideas on historical materialism, where the relationship between history and the present moment is put under pressure, demystified, and fully explored. With Benjamin's practice of historical materialism, the present becomes "the time of the now." In this poetic phrase, introduced in his influential and much-quoted "Theses on the Philosophy of History," Benjamin sets out to conjure a process in which the historian breaks away from understanding history as a sequence of events and instead "grasps the constellation which his own era has formed with a definite earlier one."[6] History, therefore, does not make for a story of progress, where each period sequentially improves on the previous historical period. Benjamin's the time of the now is set in an intimate yet unpredictable relation to the historical past. I argue that performance both embodies Benjamin's time of the now and exploits it to great effect.

The undertheorization of the term *contemporary* also allows it to circulate widely but amorphously. It enables the critical derision of the contemporary as something either ahistorical or unproven. Critical efforts to theorize the contemporary are often accused of being "presentist": a focus on the contemporary is presumed to come at the expense of history, as if the contemporary could only be understood as antagonistic to the past, or in a mutually exclusive relationship to it, two positions I contest throughout the book. The charge of presentism reprimands the critic for presumably holding little interest in or knowledge of history, as if the contemporary emerged outside of history or ideology; for understanding history in ways only valid and appropriate to the current period in which the interpretation is framed, as if the contemporary were incapable of historical nuance; and for overvaluing the contemporary with positivist notions of historical progress, as if the contemporary were the culmination of history. *Performance in America* refutes these charges, providing a model for how to think about contemporary productions in both historical and political terms.

In terms of performance, the anxiety around the focus on the contemporary period as a sign of presentist bias also shapes the cultural unease around new American theatre. Since contemporary performance has yet to stand the test of time, critics import previous cultural values to assess it. But contemporary performance becomes shortchanged in this process, as do contemporary audiences who bring other interests to their theatregoing practices. The contemporary exists as neither the future nor the past, although its links to each of these frames of time define it. It raises suspicions of its relevance since it cannot be mined nostalgically for past insight or tradition, and it cannot be forecast as necessarily significant for future generations.

Throughout this project I take on the allegation of presentism in two ways. First, I demonstrate how contemporary performance is itself already embedded in a historical archive of past performances that help contextualize the work in history. In this way, the contemporary participates in an ongoing dialogue with previously contemporary works now relegated to literary history, the theatrical past, or cultural memory. Although the case studies I address are drawn from the period 1994–2004, they lead me to examine other historical periods and practices, including eighteenth-century British theatrical and visual culture, nineteenth-century American popular entertainments, the songbooks of the Great Depression in the earlier half of the twentieth century, and the 1950s and the golden age of Hollywood. Theatre and performance scholars such as Marvin Carlson, Joseph Roach, and Diana Taylor, among others, have made explicit the relationships between theatre and performance and history and memory. "Drama," writes Carlson in *The Haunted Stage*, "more than any other literary form, seems to be associated in all cultures with the retelling again and again of stories that bear a particular religious, social, or political significance for their public. There clearly seems to be something in the nature of dramatic presentation that makes it a particularly attractive repository for the storage and mechanism for the continued recirculation of cultural memory."[7] Carlson's important project on theatre and memory focuses on the material aspects of theatre production—actors, scripts, buildings—and on how these elements become repositories of meaning for audiences over time. While Carlson's ideas help dilute the binary between the contemporary and the past as specifically addressed in theatre, Roach and Taylor consider performance in the broadest sense to include a wide range of cultural practices outside of the traditional theatre, examining its relationship to cultural memory.

In *Cities of the Dead*, Roach demonstrates how performance and cultural memory are not simply linked but in fact form a genealogy indispensable to understanding the circum-Atlantic world. For Roach, "genealogies of performance also attend to 'counter-memories,' or the disparities between history as it is discursively transmitted and memory as it is publicly enacted by the bodies that bear its consequences."[8] Likewise, Taylor in *The Archive and the Repertoire* goes to great lengths to differentiate written and embodied histories, especially as they serve to commemorate a contested past, and demonstrates how performance functions as a "system of learning, storing, and transmitting knowledge."[9] The efforts of Carlson, Roach, and Taylor to understand how performance functions in relation to history and memory shape my own project's explorations of the relationship between the contemporary and the past.

While many works in contemporary theatre summon past performances in order to conjure the ghosts of previous cultural moments, other works invest little interest in anything but the present moment. My second argument against presentism offers a defense of cultural productions whose primary interests fall outside of traditional aesthetic models or social concepts of theatre. These works might intervene in an immediate social or historical problem, participate in a larger cultural inquiry where performance is one of many modes of address, or hold minimal regard for the business-as-usual standard practices of the theatre. Here, in these performances, the emphasis falls on audience relations and the politics of spectatorship.

On the contemporary

One of the reasons that the contemporary remains undertheorized is because the term seems to fold into its own hermeneutics. In other words, the contemporary cannot be explained because it is still in process. Once it passes, it is no longer the contemporary moment, but the immediate past. *Performance in America* sets out to redress this concern by theorizing the contemporary in historical and political contexts and by divesting it of its attachment to teleological time, a project that feminist theorists have already successfully undertaken. According to Robyn Wiegman, teleological time "covets the ideas of origins and succession" and follows a model that builds on what Judith Roof has described as the "generational legacy" paradigm, in which the present remains continually indebted to the past.[10] For Wiegman and Roof, the generational legacy model proves problematic given the reproductive logic it assumes. "Generation's reproductive familial narrative assumes a linear, chronological time where the elements that come first appear to cause elements that come later," Roof explains.[11] My book aligns itself with these scholars' efforts to rethink the politics of time as a relation to the past that is not causal or direct, but unpredictable and nonlinear.

Following feminist models, my book likewise refutes the reproductive mandate of the generational paradigm that sees the contemporary as indebted to the past and bound to the future, a model of history whose deference to heteronormative biases seems especially problematic. I find the power of the contemporary precisely in its nowness and argue that the significance of contemporary performance need not be based either in tradition or futurity, both biases that privilege heteronormative models of cultural reproduction. Such models value the contemporary only as the product of already legitimate cultural traditions or as the potential ideal for an imagined future. Neither of these positions prioritizes the contemporary's contribution to the time of the historical now. Rather than holding the contemporary to a standard that insists on its utility to future generations, cultural critics should consider how the contemporary speaks to its own historical moment. *Performance in America* challenges the presumption that the contemporary is obligated to recognize the past or gesture to the future. Here is where the book's indebtedness to queer theory is strongest. Queer theory has taught us to question the systems of normativity that govern daily life and culture.[12] Again, this does not mean to say that the contemporary or its study is ahistorical or outside of time. I am simply suggesting that the contemporary performing arts should not need to prove relevant to future generations in order to be valued today, nor should they be obliged to build on conventional models of tradition to be deemed significant. Rather, the contemporary should be evaluated primarily in terms of how it serves its immediate audience. Inspired by work in queer and feminist theory, *Performance in America* promotes different methods of reading the contemporary and writing theatre history.

I have organized the book around a set of related questions, each springing from my central thesis about the vitality of the performing arts to the national culture. These questions include: In what ways and at what moments does performance emerge as a progressive site of cultural production? What does performance achieve that differentiates it from other artistic practices or other forms of cultural engagement? Who invests in the performing arts and for what reasons? How do contemporary performing artists themselves understand their role in local and national cultures? How do contemporary performances engage with the historical past without replicating the norms and ideals of previous eras? What does performance tell us about American culture?

Along with its interrogation of the contemporary, *Performance in*

America demonstrates how new work in the performing arts will now and then return to past artistic practices and customs, though not in the teleological or positivist sense of exceeding, advancing, or improving on the past. Such a rehearsal of previous performances positions contemporary performance as a repository of American culture and theatre history. In this sense, contemporary performance can be understood as both an archive of past theatrical moments and an ongoing engagement with, and revival of, this history.

Much of the work I consider in *Performance in America* emerges out of minority and subcultural communities in the United States. These queer, racialized, and immigrant populations have alternative histories and often even oppositional relations to the sexual and racial normatives of conventional America, including its theatre. In *Performance in America* I am interested in publicizing the work of those artists whose commitment to the performing arts refutes the various antitheatrical discourses that permeate contemporary American culture. *Performance in America* also examines undertheorized and undervalued sites of performance including cabaret performance, the Broadway musical, and commercial theatre.

Antitheatricality in the contemporary period takes many forms, from outright efforts to stifle artistic practice to economic cuts to funding sources for the arts to efforts to censor works imagined as offensive to theatre audiences. But there also exist antitheatrical biases that trivialize the performing arts and their audiences as irrelevant or bourgeois. Such bias knows no political affiliation; it is as likely to be found among self-professed leftists as it is among conservatives. While social conservatives might prove more anxious about arts funding and are more likely to stifle alternative forms of artistic expression, progressives practice their own form of bias by devaluing and underestimating the work of the performing arts in general. Lack of engagement with the arts perhaps constitutes the Left's most subtle and prominent form of antitheatrical bias. *Performance in America* sets out to redress this problem by examining a wide range of performance practices, venues, and audiences. Despite the emphasis on community-based, alternative, and progressive performance, the book is also committed to examining mainstream theatre. Here I focus especially on traditional genres and commercial venues, and the possibilities they offer to initiate critical conversations with innovative artistic forms and not-for-profit performance spaces. Thus the book refuses to place community-based performance and commercial theatre in an oppositional or antithetical relation. *Performance in America* attends to the various forms of cultural contestation available within a rich spectrum of the performing arts. For this reason the book, while primarily focused on theatre, also discusses music and dance.

Performance in America examines diverse theatrical performances and spectatorial communities shaped by race and ethnicity, class and region, and sexuality and citizenship. The book is situated at the crossroads of the new American studies—especially in terms of the rigorous reimagining of American identity and culture that have transformed the field—and the new theatre studies—where the reconceptualization of performance has inspired a new interest in the performing arts. The book does not position performance as either oppositional or acquiescent to mainstream American cultural practices. Rather, it sets out to understand how different communities might find in performance a way to embody and articulate new social formations within contemporary American culture. *Performance in America* promotes contemporary performance both as a critical engagement with the historical past and as a fresh interrogation of, or necessary separation from, the past through new articulations of culture and identity.

The next two sections of this chapter, "The Unacknowledged Drama of American Studies," and "The Romance with the Indigenous," will address the broader issues at stake in the fields of American studies and theatre and performance studies. I argue that the critical bibliographies of both these fields reveal particular assumptions about performance in America in need of challenging. *Performance in America* sets out to revive certain debates in both these fields, debates about performance and America that often occur simultaneously and generally without the other field's direct acknowledgment. It also attempts to consider the kinds of artistic works valorized by scholars in these related fields. At first, I will look closely at some of the ways that American studies and performance studies have engaged each other, and at the limits of this engagement. At stake in this section is the tension between the two fields; on the one hand, drama pervades the critical writings about American studies as a field, yet, on the other hand, theatre and performance studies continually laments performance as overlooked. Drama offers the dominant vocabulary for figurations of conflict, narrative, and progress in American studies, yet ironically, scholarly projects in theatre and performance studies continually highlight the relative absence of theatre and performance from critical studies of American culture.[13]

THE UNACKNOWLEDGED DRAMA
OF AMERICAN STUDIES

In their introduction to *The Futures of American Studies*, a collection of essays published in 2002 that marks the intellectual and political shifts in the interdisciplinary field, the editors, Donald E. Pease and Robyn Wiegman, reconsider one of the field's central essays, Gene Wise's " 'Paradigm Dramas' in American Studies: A Cultural and Institutional History of the Movement," first published in 1977. Wise's essay attempted to assess the formation of the field and forecast its future. The essay, as Pease and Wiegman claim, positioned itself "not simply as a history of the field, but as a founding gesture."[14] Pease and Wiegman critique Wise's history of the field, especially his effort to integrate and unify American studies at a time when the field was just beginning to exceed the limited scope of its initial and dominant impulse. The field's prior interest in tracing identifiable and consistent characteristics of American culture had begun to wane in the wake of the radical political movements of the 1960s. A generation of new scholars now challenged the nationalist project of establishing an intelligible cultural, social, and intellectual history. New work on subcultures, race and ethnicity, gender, popular culture, and other emergent subjects of inquiry in the 1960s and 1970s started to make its mark on American studies, altering the way the field was composed and practiced. In his article, Wise mourns the loss of coherency in American studies and tries to steer the field toward a more homogenous movement based on his preferred genealogy and own disciplinary bias. And yet he felt that the earlier model of practicing and understanding American studies,

the "climate-of-opinion" history, was too determi[...]
and that a new paradigm attending to the dynar[...]
American culture and its study seemed in ord[...]
as follows: "Conveniently, when handling idea[...]
scholars have employed a 'climate-of-opinion' [...]
this mode, ideas are handled as surface 'reflecti[...]
forces. The social reality is seen as basic, and[...]
the ideas. Thus it is said that American scho[...]
determined by consensual forces in the culture then, new [...]
ship reflected the more radical climate of the 1960s, and so on."[15] Impatient with this model and concerned with the institutional genealogy of the field, Wise proposes a new paradigm drawn from the world of the theatre, which he understands as more involved in acts of exchange. "Where the climate-of-opinion metaphor is borrowed from observation of the weather, my working metaphor is drawn from the theatre," he explains. "It views historical ideas not as 'enveloped' by their surrounding climates," he continues, "but rather as a sequence of dramatic acts — acts which play on wider cultural scenes, or historical stages."[16] Wise's interest in securing an identifiable history of the field — including its archives, methodologies, and meanings — and his efforts to coordinate these disparate facets of the discipline rightfully suggest to Pease and Wiegman an anxiety over the field's future and Wise's inability to harness its imploding subfields.

Pease and Wiegman critique Wise's assessment of the field and unveil the senior scholar's anxiety over its status. Not only are they reluctant to endorse Wise's history of the field but they are also careful not to promote Wise's own standing within the origins and intellectual history of American studies that he constructs. Rather than secure Wise's position as a foundational figure for the field, Pease and Wiegman prefer to situate him historically within the institutional and political contexts of his writing. "We are less invested in writing continuity with his essay — and thereby founding this *Futures* [the title of their collection] as the fulfillment of that past — than in examining the various strategies of temporal management through which 'Paradigm Dramas' sought to negotiate the future."[17] Pease and Wiegman are especially critical of Wise's attempts to foreclose the field's future.

brilliant rebuttal to Wise's mission for the field, the two carefully and persuasively critique Wise's essay point by point. They leave one aspect of Wise's essay without mention and, in fact, it becomes the point of continuity that Pease and Wiegman had planned to avoid. This point has to do with the metaphor of drama. Drama enables Wise to restage the history of American studies as a sequence of interrelated and interdependent acts:

> The drama metaphor suggests a dynamic image of ideas, in contrast to the passive "reflector" role they play in climate-of-opinion explanations. It also gives to ideas a *trans*-actional quality. This is so because an act in the theatre is always an interplay with the scene around it; an actor does not simply pass on his or her lines *to* an audience, but actor and audience (at least in a play which works) are in continual dialogue, messages traveling back and forth between one role and the other.[18]

Wise's use of drama here proves revealing. He begins by speaking in terms of dramaturgy, about what makes a good play, and in this sense his perspective is traditional if not conservative. He essentially describes what in theatre studies would be understood as a "well-made play," a nineteenth-century genre where a carefully executed plot — Wise's "sequence of dramatic acts" — figured most prominently and where these acts build on one another in a chronological manner. Wise then moves to discuss the play as it would be produced in the theatre. His interest in actors and audiences also proves traditional in that it presumes the actor inhabiting and communicating discernable "messages" to an audience — "at least in a play which works," he adds parenthetically yet assuredly. This explication of the drama metaphor stands as a type of dramatic criticism that is embedded in traditional theatrical conventions and the ideological underpinnings they convey.[19] Wise introduces the drama metaphor in the opening pages of his essay in a discussion that while thoughtful, also remains brief. He soon abandons the drama metaphor, however, except to use it as a descriptive to name certain formative movements in American studies, or what he calls "representative acts," that follow sequentially and chronologically.

Pease and Wiegman find this sequential and chronological logic one of the essay's main problems in constructing a history of the field. And yet, oddly, they too invoke the drama metaphor to challenge Wise's position. At no point do they challenge Wise on the use of the metaphor of drama; instead, they allow it to stand as such. In fact, they themselves employ it to make their critique:

> But countering Wise's project at this late date is not finally the point. We are more interested in examining the implications of the unacknowledged drama we have begun to chart than in arguing with any of the essay's substantive claims. This drama involved Wise's anxieties over the recognition that the field would not reproduce any of the paradigms that he characterized as representative of the American Studies movement. The temporal crisis of his essay (and the problematic of time that his paradigmatic desire most powerfully demonstrates) provides a space for thinking about the anxiety over futurity that *America* as a nationalist icon and *American studies* as a field formation both evince.[20]

Tellingly, Pease and Wiegman use the phrase "the unacknowledged drama" to describe Wise's anxieties about the future of American studies. They preserve the language of the metaphor even as they critique the paradigm it invokes. But unlike Wise, they offer no explanation for their use of it. Neither essay is concerned with drama in any way other than as a metaphor. In fact, both essays relegate their discussion of theatre and drama to a footnote. In Wise, the footnote announces, in perhaps his most prophetic claim, the possibilities of the metaphor for the field: "I believe drama metaphors offer enormous potential for future works in American Studies, and are especially useful in bridging the long-lamented gap between humanistic and social scientific approaches to culture."[21] I find this claim particularly striking given the proliferation—and now near ubiquity—of the terms *performance* and *performativity* among the future generation of scholars Wise describes.

In a footnote to their introduction, Pease and Wiegman, too, contextualize Wise's term *paradigm dramas* within a critical genealogy based in anthropology and literary criticism. They write:

> Wise used paradigm dramas to articulate the myth-symbol paradigm with the anthropologist Victor Turner's account of the social dramas through which cultures reflected on and thereafter trans-

formed themselves. Turner has modeled his explanation of "social dramas" after Northrop Frye's description of literary mythology as educating the social imagination. Frye proposed that the literary understanding of drama might be extrapolated into an analytical category capable of representing as well as effecting social change. In placing Turner's model into the service of defining the conflicts over the future of American studies, Wise reaffirmed the explanatory power of the myth-symbol paradigm to which Turner's model was indebted—at the very moment that the paradigm had lost its epistemic authority throughout the academy.[22]

Pease and Wiegman's genealogy for Wise's paradigm drama tells only a partial history of the influence of Turner's ideas on the profession. While it might be true that the Frye/Turner model of social dramas "lost its epistemic authority" in some circles of the academy, Turner's subsequent collaborations with the scholar and director Richard Schechner in the late 1970s and early 1980s helped usher into the academy the new and interdisciplinary field of performance studies.[23] These collaborations were based on the model of social dramas that Turner had proposed in his 1974 *Drama, Fields, and Metaphors*, but because Schechner and Turner were mostly concerned with non-Western cultures and events and with indigenous traditions and rituals, their reputation in American studies remains minor and their impact on that field as yet unrecognized.

Pease and Wiegman, like Wise before them, rely on the drama metaphor to punctuate their critique, but their interest in "examining the unacknowledged drama" never extends to drama itself. So what are we to make of these unacknowledged dramas in Wise and in Pease and Wiegman? Why the continuity of the drama metaphor in a field such as American studies? What does the drama metaphor offer the field?

It would be difficult to argue drama's marginal significance to American studies given its prominence as metaphor in these state-of-the-field essays. Drama provides the underexamined current in these essays, and, as Wise predicted, it has proven incredibly fruitful as a metaphor in recent scholarship. Wise's prescient sense that drama would prove a productive metaphor for future work in American studies materialized in the early-mid 1990s when *performance* became the critical term of choice across the humanities. The word was generally used as a metaphor, as a means to differentiate and mark a contrast to anything essentialist or supposedly real. To complicate matters, the terms *performance*, *performativity*, and *performative* were invoked interchangeably without differentiating their subtle but useful distinctions and their specific intellectual traditions.[24] Moreover, the interest in performance did not necessarily inspire scholarship on theatre and performance itself.[25]

So what work does this metaphor do? How might we begin to understand the deployment of the drama metaphor? Here I want to return to Turner whose interest in metaphor is worth revisiting. "There is nothing wrong with metaphors," Turner explains, "provided that one is aware of the perils lurking behind their misuse."[26] Turner is considering the implications of speaking about what he calls "the social world" in metaphors drawn from outside of the human experience, from plants and animals, for example. The problem, as he sees it, is that these metaphors "select, emphasize, suppress, and organize" according to the logic of the metaphor and not to that of the actual object of study. However, if the metaphor, "whose combination of familiar and unfamiliar features or unfamiliar combination of familiar features provokes us into thought, provides us with new perspectives, one can be excited by them; the implications, suggestions, and supporting values entwined with their literal use enable us to see a new subject matter in a new way."[27] Turner's thoughts allow us to consider the drama metaphor in American studies as the catalyst to understand "the new subject matter" that is itself the field of American studies. It is American studies that needs to be placed relationally to something already presumed familiar; in this case, the familiar concept of drama. Drama occupies the position of the stable referent, the knowable term. Drama—and theatre and performance, used interchangeably by those working the metaphor—is therefore not just the steady metaphor that surfaces in moments of institutional or disciplinary chaos; it is the actual constant, that which is always already there. Drama is what is presumed to be known, so much so that it goes without saying. This, then, constitutes the unacknowledged drama of American studies.

Theatre and performance scholars, whose claims on the drama metaphor and the language of performance felt most earned, were quick to note that the trend for performance metaphors, although borrowed from theatre and performance studies, meant little interest in their fields except for its language. In her own 2001 state-of-the-field project, *Geographies of Learning: Theory and Practice, Activism and Performance*, Jill Dolan, one of the leading scholars in theatre and performance studies, observes of this trend:

> Theories of the performative—in feminism, gay and lesbian studies, performance studies, and cultural studies—creatively borrow from concepts in theatre studies to make their claim for the constructed nature of subjectivity, suggesting that social subjects perform themselves in negotiation with the delimiting cultural conventions of the geography in which they move. But as much as performativity seems to capture the academic imagination, and as much as performance captures the political field, theatrical performances, as located historical sites for interventionist work in social identity constructions, are rarely considered across the disciplines, methods, and politics that borrow its terms.[28]

Dolan would like to see theatre studies "visited and acknowledged" instead of "raided and discarded." Her concern that the insights and methods of theatre studies remain unacknowledged returns us to this problem of the ubiquity of performance in academic discourse even as it remains marginal, even seemingly irrelevant, to the larger intellectual communities interested in politics and social change. American studies, which Dolan does not include in her list of scholarly fields, is equally capable of this kind of raiding, as we have seen. But is American studies interested in drama in any other way than as a metaphor?

There is a near industry in theatre studies of work on American theatre and performance that bemoans drama's irrelevance and marginality to the academy and the larger national culture. Nearly every study of American drama begins as an advocacy project, one where the case for the project itself needs to be justified. The self-consciousness of the scholarship on American theatre is surprising, although it has by now nearly become the defining characteristic of the subfield. The self-consciousness is unexpected given the high number of scholarly projects on American theatre, drama, and performance. Consider two excellent books that range among the most interesting in American theatre published in the 1990s. In *The Other American Drama*, Marc Robinson's fascinating study of the American dramatic avant-garde, the author argues against the primacy of the historical genealogy of twentieth-century American drama that begins with Eugene O'Neill and works its way up to August Wilson. Robinson's alternative history challenges the plot-driven account of American drama and focuses instead on the formal innovations and influences of theatre artists such as Gertrude Stein, Tennessee Williams, and Marie Irene Fornes. Despite his enthusiasm for this work, he writes:

> Yet, in American culture, drama has been set apart from the rest of the arts, banished to a dark corner, perhaps because it's too disruptive, too unwieldy, or just too slow to catch up with the advances of the other arts. Few serious students of music, literature, or painting take an interest in drama; few cultural forums find room for spirited debates about theatrical concerns. Part of the problem, of course, is temporality. Performances disappear; productions close after only a few people see them; only a fraction of dramatic literature is part of the living repertoire—even the best contemporary writers see just a few of their plays performed more than once.[29]

Robinson's tentative explanations for why drama has been "banished to a dark corner" put the blame on drama itself ("too disruptive," "too unwieldy," "too slow"), but rather than abandon drama, Robinson sets out to recuperate it. "Theatre critics sometimes have a bathetic air, for they live in perpetual bereavement, watching the objects of their affection slip away into obscurity as the lights on stage go down," he writes. "Writing about plays, then," he concludes, "becomes genuinely restorative, in a double sense: invigorating, as exercise might be; but, more important, life restoring, setting the plays before all our minds once again and allowing a longer look."[30]

If Robinson's project is a restorative one, other projects in American theatre are about reconfiguration. In the anthology *Performing America: Cultural Nationalism in American Theater*, the editors, Jeffrey D. Mason and J. Ellen Gainor, assemble over a dozen scholars of American theatre in an effort to showcase the diversity of critical work in the area and the interdisciplinary potential of the study of American theatre and performance. In the anthology's introduction, Mason goes to great effort to place the project in the context of American literary studies and American studies more broadly conceived. His justification for expanding the study of American theatre seems compelling and persuasive:

> Underlying our overt agenda has been an interest in situating the theatre as a product, an expression, and integral constituent of its culture. Performances and para-performances persist in venues scattered throughout society, and any of them can employ and interrogate the discourse that permeates and drives the whole. The stage is only an explicit site for performing national identity, one that serves to focus the issues, rhetoric, and images found in the more general forums; its creative freedom and opportunity to take risks encourage attempts to develop, explore, test, and dispute conceptions of national character. In the performative arena, in the interchanges among artists and spectators, we can enact narratives of nation, whether ostensibly actual or openly speculative.[31]

And yet, like Robinson, Mason also laments the status of American theatre and performance studies in the academy. He is particularly concerned with the intellectual history of the field, its lack of critical tradition, and its disregard in other related fields of study:

> To so perceive the American theater is to remember a void in American theater studies. Those working in American literature can situate their work in long, rich debates over conceptualization and methodology, all in terms of the specifically American character of the experience. Yet there has been little attempt, if any, to theorize American theater or drama as such; there are no theatrical counterparts to such landmark literary studies as F. O. Matthiesson's *American Renaissance*, Henry Nash Smith's *Virgin Land*, Leo Marx's *The Machine in the Garden*, Annette Kolodny's *The Lay of the Land*, or Myra Jehlen's *American Incarnation*. . . . Plays and their productions claim only a very little space in the discourse of American studies, no matter the decade or the methodology.[32]

Robinson and Mason share a need to situate their work within a discourse of lack or neglect, or, as Mason puts it, a "void." This rhetorical move, to call attention to the lack of attention paid to American theatre, has become the standard discursive strategy for nearly every project in the field regardless of its critical methodology or its particular case studies. From Robinson's traditional study of dramatic texts to Mason and Gainor's outreach to interdisciplinarity, scholars of American theatre remain self-conscious about the object of their study, as if the field itself were either at a crossroads or a crisis. In these scenarios, the field of American theatre and performance studies either needs to be revamped so that it gains currency in intellectual circles, or it will find itself on the verge of critical extinction, such that the study of American theatre and drama itself might become obsolete. These scholarly works, fairly well known in theatre and performance studies, remain unacknowledged by, if not completely unknown to, scholars in American studies.

The reasons for these disciplinary boundaries are complicated. As Susan Harris Smith explains in the introduction to her indispensable study *American Drama: The Bastard Art*, American drama has been neglected for no one particular reason, but for the convergence of a number of conditions. Her comments are worth quoting in full, and while they primarily concern the case against drama as a literary genre, they foreground the challenges drama faces at large:

American drama has been written almost out of the American literary canon because of enduring hostile evaluations and proscriptions that themselves need to be reassessed. I argue that for several reasons American drama has been shelved out of sight: in part because of a culturally dominant puritan distaste for and suspicion of the theatre; in part because of a persistent, unwavering allegiance to European models, slavish Anglophilia, and a predilection for heightened language cemented by New Critics; in part because of a fear of populist, leftist, and experimental art; in part because of a disdain of alternative, oppositional, and vulgar performances; in part because of narrow disciplinary divisions separating drama from theatre and performance; and in part because of the dominance of prose and poetry in the hierarchy of genre studies in university literature courses and reproduced in American criticism. As a consequence, American dramatic literature has no "place" in the culture either as

a "highbrow" literary genre or, surprisingly, as a "lowbrow" popular form of entertainment. As a sociocultural product, "literature" is
not born, it is made by institutional processes, by disciplinary fiat,
and by critical assertion. In the production of an American national
literature, American drama has been a casualty of the wars of legiti-
mation fought in the academy and has been so diminished that not
even the revisionists have taken up the cause. Ultimately, however,
I am interested not as much in arguing for American drama as literature as I am in examining the phenomenon of exclusion and in
studying the tactics, discourse practices, and maneuvers employed
to deal with American drama by those who were busy dominating
and defining culture and legitimating their claim.[33]

Smith's comments above, while not directly engaged with the field
of American studies, nonetheless begin to suggest the ways in which
American studies participates in these practices of exclusion. While, on
the one hand, the field has been drawn to using drama as a metaphor
to understand its own disciplinary history, it has, on the other hand,
been complicit in many of the exclusionary processes that Smith describes. Still, as Smith notes in her study, some essays on American
theatre have appeared in *American Quarterly*, the official publication of
the American Studies Association. In fact, an early chapter of Smith's
own book project was first published as the lead essay in a critical port-
folio on American drama, which included three other theatre scholars,
in the March 1989 issue of the journal.[34]

But even in scholarship published in *American Quarterly*, work
on theatre and performance remains self-conscious and defensive.
In 1978, in somewhat of a prequel to Smith's own project, C. W. E.
Bigsby published an assessment of the field of American drama studies
from 1945 to 1978. In his opening paragraph, Bigsby immediately pro-
nounces the study of drama as worthy and important, while noting that
it has been neglected. He is taken aback that American studies has not
prioritized American theatre. "That it has failed to engage the attention
it deserves, not only from dramatic critics but from those committed
to analysis of the American temper is thus the more surprising," he
writes, "but of that neglect there can be no doubt."[35]

Nearly twenty-five years later, in the very pages of *American Quar-*

terly, the dance scholar Jane Desmond opens her review of two books on dance with virtually the same rhetorical move. American studies will be well served to pay attention to dance and performance studies, she argues, adding that American studies has been neglecting this work for too long. Theatre and drama here have been replaced by dance and performance, but the implications are essentially interchangeable: theatre, dance, and performance remain marginal to the field. Desmond writes, "As a scholarly community, American studies specialists have just recently begun to be more open to performance analyses."[36] "What I think is less the case yet," she then qualifies her claim, "is the *active* engagement of American studies scholars more broadly with the works of performance specialists: reading their works, assigning them in courses, citing them in articles, and engaging with them in print from the various locales we inhabit, whether it be literature, anthropology, history, or something more broadly connoted as cultural studies."[37] Desmond's advocacy for dance, and performance studies more generally, introduces a new factor missing in earlier accounts of performance's marginality to the field: race. In order to make her case for dance, Desmond invokes the interests of the new American studies and offers a pragmatic solution: read, teach, and cite these books. The books she reviews—Brenda Dixon Gottschild's *Waltzing in the Dark: African American Vaudeville and Race Politics in the Swing Era*, and Linda Tomko's *Dancing Class: Gender, Ethnicity, and Social Divides in American Dance, 1890–1920*—should be of interest to American studies scholars because "each engages specifically with issues at the heart of current American studies research: race and class formations."[38] Within this logic, if earlier work on theatre, dance, and performance was marginal to the field, it might be because it failed to address race and class. But, as Desmond wants to argue, now that performance studies is addressing these two issues, there is no longer an excuse for its neglect.

And yet, as Desmond is surely aware, race and class issues have been central to theatre studies for some time. Scholars such as Jorge Huerta, Yvonne Yarbro-Bejarano, Harry Elam, James Moy, Margaret Wilkerson, and others were among the first to publish work on race and ethnicity beginning in the early 1980s. Class issues, especially as they converge with gender, race, and nation, have also been foregrounded in theatre and performance studies. Books on race and class have proven central to the field of theatre and performance studies throughout the 1990s and, one could easily argue, have made the greatest impact on the field since the wave of feminist performance theory in the late 1980s. In this way, it is important to remember that theatre and performance studies do not remain exempt from the influences of the intellectual trends and innovations that inform the academy.

While I am sympathetic to Desmond's position, and while I, too, want American studies to engage more directly with the critical bibliographies, archives, and methodologies of performance studies, I cannot help but place her comments within the tradition of critical self-consciousness and anxiety I have been mapping above. *Performance in America* also, of course, locates itself in this same advocacy tradition. It, too, hopes to install theatre and performance more significantly in American studies. And while I am also interested in thinking through the antitheatrical sentiments that marginalize performance in American studies, my project also wants to trouble the way that performance is sometimes valorized within that field, broadly conceived to include ethnic studies, queer studies, and cultural studies. What are the kinds of performances that scholars in American studies and these related oppositional fields pursue and theorize? What are the implications of these choices and the omissions they foreclose? I am especially interested in exploring what I call the "romance with the indigenous," by which I mean the endorsement of community-based and often obscure cultural productions, venues, and genres that seem more rooted in the "authentic," and artists and icons who are linked to progressive social movements. The next section will unpack what I mean by these terms and will focus on the field of Chicano and Latino studies to make the point. I choose Chicano/Latino studies not to single out the field as somehow more drawn to this practice, but as representative of how this practice manifests in oppositional fields formed through identity politics and shaped by minoritarian and subcultural worlds.

THE ROMANCE WITH THE INDIGENOUS

In the fall of 1957, a relatively unknown performer in one of her first major Broadway shows broke out of gypsy anonymity to launch a career that would establish her as one of the major performers in American theatre in the twentieth century.[39] Chita Rivera's performance of Anita in *West Side Story*, in the original Broadway production at the Winter Garden, ranks among the legendary moments in Broadway history (figure 1). *Dance Magazine* placed her on the cover of its November 1957 issue and wrote glowingly of her performance:

> About the dancers, who also happen to be the singers and actors in *West Side Story*: They are, as dancers and sometimes as actors, superb. They can't sing Mr. Bernstein's complicated score, and it is his best thus far, but oh, can they dance! Each and every one of them has soloist possibilities in his own genre. Star of the piece is, indisputably, Chita Rivera. She is one of the few who can sing, can act, and, of course, dance magnificently. Here is a performer of enormous individuality with a dance approach quite uniquely her own. She has made the transition from chorus to star with seemingly no effort, shedding irritating mannerisms and replacing them with the superbly assured manner of, with luck, a future great lady of the American musical theatre.[40]

Dance Magazine's prophetic claims for Rivera as a "future great lady of the American musical theatre" were echoed in various other production reviews of the period. Rivera was consistently singled out for her performance, particularly for her lead in the Shark girls' number, "America." *West Side Story* has been written into cultural history mainly for the brilliant contributions of its artistic creative team: Jerome Robbins, Leonard Bernstein, Arthur Laurents, and Stephen Sondheim. We read little, however, about Rivera's performance except in the initial reviews, and, in fact, when discussions finally turn to the actors, it is now the Academy Award–winning performance of Rita Moreno, who starred as Anita in the film version of *West Side Story*, that is the one most often associated with the role.

Chita Rivera was born Dolores Conchita Figueroa del Rivero in Washington, DC, on January 23, 1933. She started training as a dancer at an early age. In her hometown, she studied ballet with Doris Jones, and when her family moved to New York City when she was eleven, she won a scholarship to the School of American Ballet, where she trained

1. Chita Rivera in *West Side Story* on the cover of the November 1957 issue of *Dance Magazine*. Jerome Robbins Dance Division, New York Public Library for the Performing Arts, Astor, Lenox, and Tilden Foundations

for three years. Before her breakout performance in *West Side Story*, Rivera had already appeared in a handful of musicals beginning with the 1952 national tour of the Ethel Merman vehicle *Call Me Madam* and including roles in *Can-Can* (1953) and *The Shoestring Revue* (1956). This makes for an impressive résumé for any aspiring actor, but for a young Latina working in the 1950s, Rivera's achievement was remarkable. Her roles after *West Side Story* established her stature as one of the few Broadway stars who has endured throughout the decades in shows such as *Bye Bye Birdie* (1960), *Chicago* (1975), *The Rink* (1984), and *Kiss of the Spider Woman* (1993). The fall of 2002 marked her fiftieth year as a Broadway performer. Anyone who has seen her perform can attest to her boundless energy and charisma on stage, and there is no indication that she will stop performing anytime soon. In the past few years, she has appeared in the Broadway revival of *Nine* (2003), received a Kennedy Center Lifetime Honoree Award, and was cast as the lead in *The Visit* (2001), a new musical by John Kander and Fred Ebb. She is currently working with the playwright Terrence McNally on developing a one-woman show based on her life and career.

Strange then, given Rivera's talents and professional affiliations, that so few scholars from any field—theatre and performance studies, feminist and women's studies, and ethnic and American studies—have focused attention on her work. If not for the popular press and the drama critics who review for it, and the occasional memoir of one of Rivera's collaborators or historical peers, there would be little engagement with her distinguished career in the theatre. Theatre studies seems ambivalent around the topic of stardom, as if generating intellectual energy about celebrities and the performers we admire undermines our scholarly project and reveals an uncritical embrace of fandom.[41] The fear that our love of theatre will call into question our critical capacities follows from theatre studies' efforts to credentialize itself against the charge of inconsequentiality. To indulge in our feelings of pleasure and, more to the point, to write about them, is viewed as unprofessional, a form of fandom that should be relegated to the publicists or left to our private theatre journals. Our knowledge of the history and performances of stars is information presumed to have no real cultural value, the frivolous theatre gossip of overly enthusiastic fans.

Like theatre studies, Latino studies has largely neglected to think seriously about Chita Rivera. In part, this has to do with the still heated controversy around *West Side Story* and its representation of Puerto Ricans. The resentments that continue to surround the musical's casting of non-Latinos in Latino roles, its perpetuation of Latino stereotypes as criminal and primitive, and its endorsement of American identity over Island loyalty shape the scholarship produced by Latino critics.[42] Understandably, *West Side Story*—as one of the handful of Latino representations on Broadway—ignites Latino ire. The dismissal of Broadway as a viable site for Latino scholarship results from the sense that Latinos will find little to applaud here. The late 1990s controversy over Paul Simon's *The Capeman*, a musical much maligned for its book and its representational politics of Latinos—despite star performances by Marc Anthony, Ednita Nazario, and Ruben Blades—only solidified this position. Many Latinos were upset that of all the possible stories to tell of Puerto Rico, Simon chose the sensational story of Salvador Agron, the nineteen-year-old Latino who in 1959 stabbed two teenagers in New York's Hell's Kitchen. *The Capeman* confirmed for many that Broadway was not receptive to creating positive or uplifting Latino representations and would only recycle Latino stereotypes as popular entertainment for commercial consumption. Latino scholars did little to alter this position. Except for Alberto Sandoval-Sánchez in his groundbreaking *José, Can You See? Latinos on and off Broadway*, scholars in Latino studies have not looked carefully at the industry of Broadway and what its history might contribute to our knowledge of Latino life.[43]

Chicano and Latino theatre scholars take much more interest in identifying, documenting, and advocating for community-based productions, Latino self-representations, and Latino performers who work closely within indigenous traditions and forms than in thinking about the work of a Latina Broadway star affiliated with non-Latino productions. Chicano and Latino studies prioritize the indigenous over the commercial because of the former's seemingly more direct relationship to an authentic Latino community. I do not mean to undermine this project; my own scholarship has been in concert with it for many years.[44] Its necessity must remain a priority of the field for two reasons. First, Chicanos and Latinos continue to confront many of the same structures of bias and discrimination that led to the founding of Chicano and Latino theatres in the first place. For this reason alone, Chicano and Latino theatre remains in Jorge Huerta's apt phrase a "necessary theater."[45] Second, the current work of Chicano and Latino playwrights and performers deserves our interpretive efforts because much of it is intellectually and politically engaging and emotionally and spiritually moving. A new generation of playwrights and performers are positioning themselves outside of the conventional Latino themes and structures, and their work needs to be identified, documented, and analyzed.

That said, it seems to me that the suspicion of commercial theatre endemic to the fields of both performance studies and Latino studies should be rethought. Commercial theatre offers its own pleasures and possibilities, and appreciating them should not automatically brand one as naive or politically unaware. The disdain of the commercial theatre constitutes a strain of antitheatricality that is symptomatic of larger cultural anxieties about class, capital, pleasure, and the popular. The dismissal of certain kinds of theatre as not worthwhile subjects for theatre and performance studies—or for American studies, for that matter—constitutes a variant of the antitheatrical sentiment that permeates our culture. Broadway, in this scenario, is viewed as especially problematic; not only is it seen as irrelevant but it is also imagined as lacking in artistry and talent, its audiences lacking in taste. Unable to distinguish between art and entertainment, Broadway audiences are dismissed as indiscriminate and unenlightened.

This anti-Broadway bias makes for a form of antitheatricality sanctioned by theatre scholars who do little to defend Broadway's artistic and cultural work. But it is also a form of antipopulism that needs to be rethought by progressive cultural critics. Rather than acquiesce to the anticommercial sentiment and solely endorse the indigenous, theatre and performance scholars should rethink their criteria of what constitutes a valid object of scholarly inquiry. Yet cultural critics remain more likely to champion work either obscure or unknown outside the subcultural world from which it sprang.

This model of discovery and publicity is one of the standard moves in cultural studies that focus on the performing arts. My own scholarship also participates in this practice; throughout *Performance in America*, I am interested in publicizing work that emerges out of community-based and alternative venues. Many of the artists I discuss throughout the book lack a critical bibliography and find their first extended scholarly engagement in this book. Indeed, my own romance with the indigenous, and I offer this as a self-critique, preceded this project. Nearly all of my previous academic writings and projects have promoted artists emerging out of particular subcultural communities, or what I am calling here the "indigenous." In my first book, *Acts of Intervention: Performance, Gay Culture, and AIDS*, I went to great effort to publicize the work of community-based artists whose primary interest in performance was activist based and political. I felt that many of these artists were offering the most important and effective artistic and activist responses to AIDS in their particular moment in AIDS history. Many of these artists hovered below the radar, unknown outside of the immediate communities in which they lived, worked, and sometimes died. I saw my book as an archival project that would provide an alternative history of the period between 1981 and 1996, the years that framed my study and where AIDS fatalities among gay men in the United States reached their peak.

I still am drawn to alternative performance and community-based arts. I am not out to revise my assessment of its achievement, or to brand my own endorsement of these projects as naive. In fact, I continue to seek out artists, venues, and audiences that aspire to a shared political project, one that may or may not secure them popular success or media attention. And I continue to write for community-based publications about artists with HIV, Latino performance, and queer culture. However, I no longer assume, as I was inclined to do in the past, that this work is more politically efficacious than mainstream or commercial productions. Instead, I am interested in the different kinds of politics, including the politics of pleasure, that each specific practice brings forth. That said, we must continue to demarcate the social, cultural, and material differences dividing Broadway productions from alternative or community-based theatre. My aim is not to deny these differences, but rather to challenge the uncritical valorization of alternative performance and the nearly automatic dismissal of Broadway theatre.

I name this uncritical valorization of the indigenous a "romance" to call attention to the ways that cultural critics often mystify subcultural performance. The romance with the indigenous is a bias toward the grassroots and the community-based, seen as unmediated; it can be especially problematic when it is used against work or artists whose success and achievement fall elsewhere. The case of Chita Rivera proves this point, as do the careers of others who work in the commercial theatre. But it can be equally problematic when the indigenous becomes a fetish. The indigenous is too easily extracted from a subcultural or community-based context in order to stand in for something else. Often it is burdened with the interests of the scholar or critic who is presumed to be linked with the performance due to access or membership to the community it represents. Performances can be entrapped by these identitarian or minoritarian claims. I mean to use the word *indigenous* not in the literal sense, but to refer to what is thought to be natural. By indigenous, I mean the seemingly authentic. The indigenous is presumed to have remained uncontaminated by commercialism, commodity culture, or mainstream tastes. In this way, it can refer not simply to racial or ethnic minorities, in particular Native Americans, the group that has the most immediate association with the term in the United States, but to sexual minorities and others whose relationship to the majoritarian public sphere is compromised due to their social identities or subcultural practices. But even here, disparities exist. Within queer cultures, for example, the indigenous would refer to those who reject heteronormative ideals, assimilationist goals, and commodity fetishism. In short, that would mean the sexual outlaws, radical activists, and social abjects, who are often one and the same. But the term can also then be used to differentiate among racial and ethnic minorities; the indigenous is not interchangeable with ethnic, as the case of Chita Rivera makes clear. No one would deny that Chita Rivera is Latina; however, the case for her being indigenous, at least in the way I have described it, would be less persuasive.

The romance with the indigenous presupposes access to authenticity and valorizes that which is most associated with realness. In this sense, it constitutes a type of pastoral trope. The search for the authentic marks both an escape from urbanity and a move toward the margins. For this reason, the indigenous can be located not just in the country, where it is traditionally found in conventional pastorals, but also in the ghetto, whether that ghetto is located in the Castro or in South Central. The indigenous is associated with the real, a presumption suggesting that there is much in the culture that is artificial, inauthentic, or unreal. Despite these claims to realness, others who find the work lacking in artistry or limited in scope regularly denigrate community-based performances. Let me use the example of queer performance to make this point.

Among the many dismissive responses to queer performance in the popular press and even among queer people, the accusation that queer artists are preaching to the converted is perhaps the most frequent.[46] Surprisingly, it is also the one charge that queer artists, intellectuals, and cultural workers have failed to provide with any forceful rebuttal or theorization. The ubiquity of the preaching-to-the-converted charge becomes evident with any perusal of theatre reviews or, in a more anecdotal vein, any eavesdropping on gay people's own assessment of queer theatre. Such foreclosing attitudes flow without reflection from a variety of critics and spectators alike. Mainstream theatre reviewers, for example, often dismiss queer artists who address queer issues for queer audiences as having a limited scope of address. Generally these critics see community-based work not as theatre but as propaganda; queer theatre, from this perspective, has little or no artistic value, and queer audiences have little or no critical acumen.

And yet queer spectators, too, participate in this kind of conjecture. Work that is explicitly directed toward a queer audience and performed in a community-based or queer-friendly venue remains underattended, undervalued, and mocked—by queers—for its alleged naivety or predictability. Such a contradiction—that, on the one hand, queer people harbor no critical distance from queer art, and that, on the other, queer audiences are themselves hypercritical of queer art—helps sustain the accusatory and shaming force of the preaching-to-the-converted judgment. In either case, the idea that an artist is preaching to the converted sets into motion a no-win discursive dynamic that implicates both the artist and the audience. The dismissive response assumes queer artists as didactic and queer audiences as static. Regardless of how the phrase is employed—whether it be to insist that queer artists are propagandists and queer audiences are infantile, or to insist queer artists are didactic and queer audiences bored with it all—queer performance that supposedly preaches to the converted is never understood as a valuable, indeed, vital, activity. Instead, the uncontested phrase shuts down discussions around the important cultural work that queer artists perform for their queer audiences. The result makes for yet another occasion of queer disempowerment, one that undermines the idea of building a community culture around an ongoing series of events and gatherings.

Queer artists and audiences are not the only people who must confront the idea that they are preaching to the converted. Most political artists from marginalized communities are vulnerable to this dismissal. The dialectical tension between the assumption that political artists are preaching a type of ideological redundancy to a group of sympathetic supporters and the possibility that community-based performers and audiences are participating in an active expression of what may constitute the community itself obscures the fact that these very marginalized communities are themselves subject to the continuous rhetorical and material practices of a naturalized majoritarian norm. Hegemony's performance forces its subjects to a conversion into its alleged neutrality, its claims to the true and the real. Political performers expose these coercive attempts to maintain the hegemonic norms that govern and discipline our daily life. Community-based and community-identified artists and audiences offer each other necessary opportunities to rehearse the constitutive reiteration of our own identities in light of these facts, as well as a direct, proactive resistance to, and defiance of, hegemony's own unending production of what does and does not constitute, in Judith Butler's phrase, "bodies that matter."[47] Thus the preaching-to-the-converted charge conceals yet a second, related agenda: when conservative critics dismiss community-based art projects on the grounds that this art only constitutes propaganda, they also attempt to undermine the social movements that engender these art projects. Efforts to stifle the arts are, in essence, efforts to stifle the transformative cultural movements and social actions with which community-based arts see themselves in direct relationship. At the very least, these artists reclaim the once long-standing alliance between performers and spectators as members of community who, in the enactment of collective ritual, enable the power of individuals to gather and perform the necessary constitutive rehearsal of difference.

Here, then, I want to make claims for the possibilities of community-based work and show what is most productive about this romance with the indigenous I have been describing. Subcultural work is important for the reasons I have outlined above and because these performances provide a counterpublicity to mainstream and dominant medias. Cultural theorists from American studies, queer studies, and other politicized academic locations find in these performances alternative viewpoints and practices stifled or dismissed in the broader reaches of contemporary American culture. This scholarship has called attention to the vital role of the arts in progressive social movements, and as a result it has helped move these fields forward. Nonetheless, it needs to be stated that some critics remain skeptical of scholarship that aligns itself with community-based performances. In one of the most problematic scenarios in which community-based work and the scholars who support it are challenged, David Savran, a professor of theatre, in an essay that itself stands as a rebuttal to recent trends in theatre and performance studies, writes accusingly of other scholars who "cruise East Village bars in search of performative identities" and who "hang out with Judith Butler."[48] For Savran, much of this kind of scholarly work is barely scholarly at all, for it lacks historicity and rigor; but it also falls short on the political front, for it fails to attend to the real politics of social and material culture. This form of "academic leftism," Savran claims, is largely ineffective and might be better understood as fashion. "While claiming to be radicals, many U.S. theorists instead end up advocating what [Aijaz] Ahmad styles, 'a new mystique of leftish professionalism,'" he writes.[49] Now it is no longer simply the artists who are preaching to the converted, but the critic who values their work too.

I do not want to affiliate with Savran's dismissal of the branches of theatre and performance studies that promote the subcultural or that emerge out of particular community and political struggles. Nor do I want to trivialize the work that happens in community-based venues, whether in East Village bars or elsewhere. My critique of the romance with the indigenous is not a complaint about the methodology or politics of other scholars in the field. Nor do I want to supplant or exchange a romance with the indigenous with a romance for the commercial, however seductive the allure of its spectacle. Romance can be a good thing; it stems from passion and commitment—much of the work that promotes the indigenous is exciting, smart, and timely. But these same attributes might also be found in scholarship on the commercial theatre. My aim is to encourage a more nuanced understanding of the spectrum of performances and to encourage an awareness of the broader archives available to progressive cultural critics working in American studies. Such an understanding will enrich our sense of performance in America and help counter its marginalization in the national culture. I would like to end this discussion with a few brief examples of how this might occur.

In *Topdog/Underdog*, Suzan-Lori Parks's 2002 Pulitzer Prize–winning play, two brothers named Lincoln and Booth, abandoned in childhood by their parents, strive to come to terms with their relationship in a power struggle that ends in death. The play, which premiered at the Public Theater in New York under the direction of George C.

THE YEAR'S MOST ACCLAIMED NEW AMERICAN PLAY IS NOW ON BROADWAY FOR 160 PERFORMANCES ONLY

JEFFREY WRIGHT | MOS DEF

TOPDOG | UNDERDOG

A NEW PLAY BY SUZAN-LORI PARKS | DIRECTED BY GEORGE C. WOLFE

20 WEEKS ONLY·MARCH 12–JULY 28

TELE-CHARGE: 212·239·6200/800·432·7250 OR LOG ON TO: WWW.TELECHARGE.COM GROUPS (10+): 212·302·7000/800·677·1164

⊗AMBASSADOR THEATRE, 219 W. 49TH ST.

2. Promotional flyer for Suzan-Lori Parks's *Topdog/ Underdog* on Broadway, 2002. Collection of the author

Wolfe in July of 2001, moved to Broadway in the spring of 2002 and has since toured the regional theatre circuit throughout the United States to much critical acclaim (figure 2). *Topdog/Underdog* is a two-person play; for the Public Theater run the cast consisted of Jeffrey Wright and Don Cheadle. Mos Def, the charismatic hip-hop artist, replaced Don Cheadle when the production transferred to Broadway. The play centers on the relationship between the brothers and their struggle to make a living (figure 3). One brother, Lincoln, has abandoned the lucrative but dangerous street performance of Three-Card-Monte, in which he was a resounding master, to work in an arcade where he dresses up as Abraham Lincoln so that others can reenact the president's assassination and shoot him. Booth, a brilliant thief, aspires to the older brother's former profession, and imagines the two of them working the Three-Card-Monte scam together as a team. Lincoln, however, resists and resents Booth's plan.

3. Mos Def as Booth and Jeffrey Wright as Lincoln in Suzan-Lori Parks's *Topdog/Underdog*, Ambassador Theatre, New York City, 2002. Photo by Michal Daniel.

It is easy to offer a racialized reading of the play centering on the fact that these are two brothers who traffic in petty crimes to counter the nihilism often surrounding contemporary urban life for many poor black men. The play's tragic outcome can also support such a reading, especially in a world such as ours where black-on-black crime remains a serious threat to the lives of young black men. Parks's work is often cited as a commentary on black America and race relations, and *Topdog/Underdog*, her most accessible play lends itself to such symbolic readings.[50] Parks, however, takes exception to these interpretations, as well as to facile correspondences between *Topdog/Underdog* and so-called reality. In an interview with the *New York Times*, she offers the following anecdote to make her point:

> "I've told him a hundred times, 'George [referring to Wolfe, her director] there are no metaphors!' I don't know what a metaphor is!" she said. "There are two men in a room. Just take it for that.

The meanings that people love to pull out, like slavery"—she said the word with exaggerated solemnity—"just slaver this thing with sauce. Slavery! Don't even think about slavery. Lincoln says, when he's teaching Booth cards. 'Don't think about the cards! Don't think about anything. Just watch. Just look. Just take it in.'"[51]

Parks's desire for the audience to "just take it in" challenges our interest in making sense of the play through the narrative of American cultural history that the play seemingly invokes. She resists easy analogies to history and the familiar associations that surface when discussing race in America. Despite the fact that her characters are named after mythic figures in American history, Parks insists that Lincoln and Booth are not meant to comment on the historical legacy associated with them. "It ain't about the white man," according to the playwright. "It ain't about the legacy of slavery at all. It's about these two men who are brothers and don't get along. They love each other intensely and have come through so much together, and are at each other's throats almost all the time. And that is worth talking about, too."[52] Parks's impatience with the impulse to have her work mean more than she intended is a playwright's prerogative; she is not the first artist to reject the meanings ascribed to her work. And yet, I find myself sympathetic to her dilemma. The overly quick reduction of her work to familiar racial meanings tells us a lot about our own critical investments in these issues, and it leaves little room to explore what Parks might have otherwise set out to achieve. But beyond what Parks herself might have hoped to inspire, the play provokes other conversations informed by race but not limited to it. There might be other insights that overlap or exist alongside the racial meanings that immediately surface when a play includes two young black men facing economic hardships, familial betrayals, and a loaded gun. Parks is an immensely talented playwright whose comic sensibility and dramaturgical innovations deserve a fuller scholarly engagement. And yet it would be foolish to disregard the question of race entirely. The play is about a con and a competitive one-upmanship that allows for only a sole winner. Someone will emerge the top dog, someone else the underdog. Who determines who will play which role is part of the play's dramatic tension and part of its pleasure. Like the game of cards itself, the play seduces and manipulates its audience. Parks might even be out to pull a fast one over her audiences who think they know what they see when they see two black men on stage together.

In the end, one of the characters will lose. But both of the actors will perform the roles again and repeat the scenario for the next audience in a manner not too far off the mark of Lincoln's performance at the arcade. Lincoln might get shot dead repeatedly at work, but at the end of his shift he gets up and leaves. It was only a role, only a job. The same is true of the actor in Parks's play. Though the play ends in death, both actors live to play the role the following day. The difference here is that while the brothers never get to work the cards together, the two men who play them get to work the stage together as actors in Parks's play. Such a metatheatrical commentary might still be about race, but it shifts the emphasis from the historical past to the contemporary. *Topdog/Underdog* suggests a different relationship to history than the immediate one we might expect: this is a play that summons history but is not bound to it. The narrative logic of the play is set, as Parks notes in the program, in the spatial and temporal ethos of "Here and Now." Parks's "Here and Now" does not disavow history—how could it when the characters are named Lincoln and Booth?—but brackets it in order to push the contemporary to the forefront. The playwright is interested in having us consider the immediate drama before us, the time of the now. "There's a relationship with the past, an important one," she explains. "But I think to focus on that relationship and de-emphasize the relationship of the person right in the room with you is the great mistake of American culture and the mistake of history. We have to deal with what's happening right now."[53] Parks's proposal that we deal with what is happening right now also offers an entry into rethinking the place of race in commercial theatre and in contemporary American culture at large.

Topdog/Underdog was the first play by an African American woman to win the Pulitzer Prize for drama, but it was not the only play by an artist of color recently produced on Broadway. Still, the publicity around the play marked much of its achievement as a breakthrough, as the exception to the rule, as almost an anomaly for Broadway. Despite the fact that Wolfe, the director, and Wright, one of the two actors, had already received Tony awards for their previous work on Broadway, the play was discussed as a departure from the business-as-usual of Broadway. In the review published in the *Nation*, Elizabeth Pochoda begins her appraisal by singling out the play from the standard fare of Broadway entertainments, denigrated along with their assumed audiences: "Occasionally in the murky wasteland of Broadway, where nostalgia reigns and revivals rule, the hopeful theatregoer is led to an oasis advertised as fertile enough to water the desert. Suzan-Lori Parks's *Topdog/Underdog*, which has just won the Pulitzer Prize, is one of these. Even if its success were to be measured solely by the numbers of young people and black people, both young and old, in the audience on any given night, *Topdog* could be considered a healthy sign."[54] Pochoda situates Parks's achievement in the context of the vague and confusing notion of the "oasis" that a "hopeful" spectator might "occasionally" encounter, although she never names when these other occasions have materialized, or who might had been responsible for them. While I agree with Pochoda's review, which raves about Parks's writing, the play's production values, and its racial politics, I find the introductory frame problematic in that it undermines the play's very nowness. The fact that the play is on Broadway already signals Broadway's ability to include it in its ranks and in its theatres. The play, too, is "here and now," and shifting its achievement away from this context fails to recognize one of Parks's thematic and political imperatives.

Too often, minority playwrights and performers who arrive on Broadway are discussed in this language of exceptionalism, where they are not only the exception to the standard fare of Broadway but their demographic audiences are positioned as exceptional as well. Moreover, the discourse of exceptionalism places these artists in isolation; they are the talented exceptions to the community-based artist of color whose primary achievement is presumed to be other than artistic. This discourse of exceptionalism was revealed as misdirected and downright wrong a few months after the opening of *Topdog/Underdog* when the multiracial cast of nine poets of Russell Simmons's *Def Poetry Jam* began performing at Broadway's Longacre Theatre (figure 4). Yet the alternative discourse of "authentic but untalented" did not prove an optional response for this show either. Burdened with stereotypes surrounding hip-hop culture, spoken word poetry, and community-based

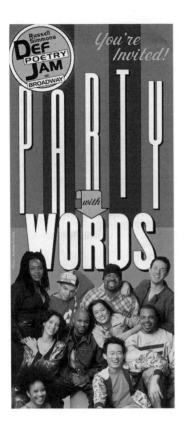

4. Promotional flyer for *Def Poetry Jam* on Broadway, 2003. Collection of the author

arts, all of which have combined to enable the performers to surface in a critical mass in the late 1990s in poetry slams throughout the United States, this group of young artists proved talented and charismatic, and their fresh perspectives a welcome addition to the 2002–2003 Broadway season.

The cast included men and women, some of whom were queer, were Latino, Asian American, African American, Jewish, and Palestinian. They performed solo monologues, duos, and large group poems together, on a range of topics from a critique of American imperialism to a love for fast foods, and from tributes to June Jordan and Tito Puente to attacks on George W. Bush and Dick Cheney.[55] With no-name actors, an unfamiliar genre—When was the last time poetry was performed on Broadway? Has it been as long as 1975 and Ntozake Shange's *For*

Colored Girls Who Have Considered Suicide When the Rainbow Is Enuf?—
and a compromised economy, it was unclear who exactly would go see
a show where young people rhyme dissent to a drumbeat. But the show
was a critical success, if not a commercial one. Despite reduced prices
and a money-back guarantee, *Def Poetry Jam* struggled at the box office.
Few shows recoup their investment, but when a minority production
fails, it becomes especially vulnerable to overinterpretation. Throughout its run, the show averaged close to 50 percent capacity of the nearly
1,100-seat theatre. Early in its run it hovered at around 35 percent, before peaking at 71 percent capacity during the final week of December 2002. These numbers might sound discouraging to some, but it is
worth noting that between three thousand and four thousand people
saw the show per week.[56]

Many people—producers, critics, and others involved in Broadway
culture—had hoped the show would bring new audiences to Broadway.
New audiences here essentially mean young people, and audiences that
better represent the racial demographic of New York City, and of the
nation at large. *Def Poetry Jam* delivered on this front, and the audience demographic differed substantially from the audiences at many
of the productions at other Broadway theatres. But the desire of producers and the press to change the demographic of Broadway seems to
me misinformed and even paternalistic. Young people as well as audiences of color will find the entertainment and venues they need in their
lives, and if it happens to be on Broadway, so be it. And, by the same
token, if older and/or whiter audiences prefer to see revivals of *Oklahoma!*, *Gypsy*, or *Nine* (with Chita Rivera), all of which were playing at
the time of *Def Poetry Jam*, that should be their choice too, and they
should not be shamed for doing so. Broadway, of course, should reach
out to as many different communities as possible, especially in terms
of accessible ticket prices. But my point is that the language of changing the demographic of Broadway audiences is too caught up in a logic
of futurity that fails to see the new audiences already attending these
shows. Perhaps Broadway is no longer something one is weaned on
from an early age, as if theatregoing were a familial inheritance, but a
place one might discover at a different moment in time, in an entirely
different context than one of generational legacy.

Rather than fetishize these events—*Topdog/Underdog, Def Poetry Jam*, and other shows by minority artists—as exceptional or as opportunities to change the demographic of Broadway audiences, why not, as Parks suggests, "Just watch. Just look. Just take it in"? What I found exciting about these shows was that they found themselves on Broadway, and that their audiences, which were diverse and contradictory, found their way there too. "Here and Now," as Parks would have it. Having sat in these theatres with these audiences it was clear that a change had already come. Parks's arrival on Broadway, and those of the young poets of *Def Poetry Jam*, might enable us to imagine Broadway differently, less as tired and ailing and needing to be revived by youth and color, and more as a place where cultural production around contemporary concerns might be found and fostered. Parks's presence on Broadway—and by extension, her audiences, and those of *Def Poetry Jam*—is not so much a "healthy sign" that an ailing Broadway is getting better, as Pochoda diagnoses it, but rather a mark of the ongoing engagement of the commercial theatre with central questions of contemporary culture of, to use Parks's words, "what's happening right now." If this is to be a sign at all, let us see it as a sign of the times.

CHAPTER ONE

Not About AIDS

Soon after the 1996 international AIDS conference in Vancouver, which officially announced the success of protease inhibitors, there was a great deal of talk in the United States about the end of AIDS, and much of it implied that the need to talk about AIDS had ended as well. Reports both in the popular media and in lesbian and gay publications suggested that the AIDS epidemic had run its course. While acknowledging that most people across the world lacked access to the new drugs, these accounts put forward the idea that the AIDS crisis was now over. In the absence of a cure or vaccine, this discourse seemed striking. In his controversial article, "When AIDS Ends," published in the November 10, 1996, *New York Times Magazine* (figure 5), Andrew Sullivan wrote: "A difference between the end of AIDS and the end of many other plagues: for the first time in history, a large proportion of the survivors will not simply be those who escaped infection, or were immune to the virus, but those who contracted the illness, contemplated their own deaths, and still survived."[1] Cover articles in other major publications of the period further demonstrated this shift in AIDS discourse and shared in its assumptions—from *Newsweek*'s "The End of AIDS?" published in the December 2, 1996, issue (figure 6) to *Time Magazine*'s selection of Dr. David Ho, a pioneer of the new AIDS treatment research, as "Man of the Year" (figure 7), which indicated that an understanding of AIDS as a manageable condition rather than a terminal one had taken shape. In late 1996, AIDS returned to the forefront of U.S. culture only to an-

The New York Times Magazine

'A difference between the end of AIDS and the end of many other plagues: for the first time in history, a large proportion of the survivors will not simply be those who escaped infection, or were immune to the virus, but those who contracted the illness, contemplated their own deaths *and still survived.*'

WHEN AIDS ENDS By Andrew Sullivan

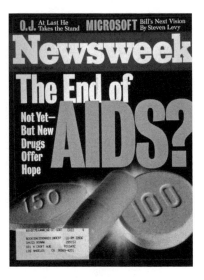

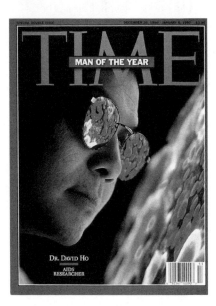

5. (top left) "When AIDS Ends" by Andrew Sullivan, cover of the *New York Times Magazine*, November 10, 1996, designed by Chip Kidd. Courtesy of the *New York Times*

6. (top right) "The End of AIDS?" cover of *Newsweek*, December 2, 1996. © 1996 John Rizzo, courtesy of *Newsweek*

7. (bottom left) "Man of the Year: Dr. David Ho, AIDS Researcher," cover of *Time*, December 30, 1996. Courtesy of Time Life Pictures/Getty Images

nounce its departure. Not surprisingly, the end-of-AIDS discourse soon led to a general lack of media interest in the disease, as well as to calls from gay figures for "post-AIDS" identities and cultures.

These developments surfacing in the late 1990s have left me wondering what it means to continue prioritizing AIDS in discussions of contemporary gay culture and politics. How might we return our critical attention to AIDS in light of the shifts in the political, cultural, and sexual climates of the late 1990s and the early twenty-first century? I wish to explore two central questions: how might the so-called end of AIDS itself be understood as an AIDS discourse, one that tells us much about our relationship to AIDS; and how did artists living with HIV/AIDS respond to calls for post-AIDS identities and cultures? The performing arts, and dance in particular, offered an alternative entry point into the national focus on AIDS that helped shift the conversation away from this discourse of an ending. Moreover, the performing arts fully participated in the efforts to rethink AIDS in light of the medical breakthroughs of the period. This chapter examines the discourse of AIDS in a number of different contexts including queer and minority communities, and the political responses these new treatment options brought forth at the time. It focuses on the artistic response primarily, however, because it is here that some of the most productive critical reassessments of the contemporary moment first emerged.

In *Dry Bones Breathe*, perhaps the most telling book of 1998, Eric Rofes, a longtime progressive gay activist, argues that contemporary gay culture needs to disentangle itself from the dated AIDS-as-crisis model that characterized the gay community's response in the first decade of the epidemic.[2] Rofes, unlike most commentators, carefully explains that he is speaking specifically about gay male culture in America and that post-AIDS does not necessarily mean the end of AIDS. "This admittedly controversial term," Rofes writes, "claims that the communal experience of AIDS-as-crisis has ended, [it] does not imply that the epidemic of AIDS is over."[3] Despite drawing such distinctions and making an overall effort to remain sensitive to those living with HIV/AIDS, Rofes suggests that "it may be time for gay men to abandon the acronym 'AIDS' altogether."[4]

While many commentators questioned the concept of post-AIDS, most of their critiques were cast as expressions of concern about a new wave of infection among the very subjects who imagined themselves living in a post-AIDS world: urban gay men. Michaelangelo Signorile's September 1998 *Out* article "641,086 and Counting" proves typical. Signorile argues that "we are headed toward an unqualified disaster."[5] This disaster, "in which a new generation of gay men become as immersed in the horrors of AIDS, disease, and death as previous generations," was taking shape because of the message and belief that AIDS was over. Signorile's title, "641,086 and Counting," invoked Larry Kramer's 1983 *New York Native* essay, "1,112 and Counting," which helped inaugurate the AIDS activist movement. Kramer's title simultaneously registered the number of AIDS cases at the time of its publication and predicted more cases in the future. The article, as Kramer put it, was meant to "scare the shit out of you."[6] In "641,086 and Counting," Signorile sounds the alarm for a new generation of gay men. "Will it take massive death and suffering for us to wake up once again?" he asks near the end of his critique of post-AIDS rhetoric.[7] He models his effort to motivate gay men on Kramer's foundational rhetoric of early 1980s AIDS activism in the hope that this time around, such rhetoric will counter apathy and denial.[8]

Surprisingly, Signorile neglected to account for the global shifts in AIDS demographics since 1983. Few critics of the end-of-AIDS rhetoric, in fact, seriously questioned the assumptions that condition the post-AIDS discourse either globally or in the context of the United States. This discourse, as Phillip Brian Harper argues in response to Sullivan's essay, invests in a specific category of "racial-national normativity," or, as Harper more bluntly puts it, in "U.S. whites," who are its implicit subjects.[9] He recasts Sullivan's speculation that for many in the United States, HIV infection "no longer signifies death" but "merely . . . illness" to mean that, for Sullivan, the deaths of "those not included in his racial-national normativity"—that is to say nonwhites and those living outside the United States—"effectively do not constitute AIDS-related deaths at all."[10]

While I completely agree with Harper on this issue, I am less interested in similarly disassociating myself from Sullivan: Harper's opening sentence, "For quite a while now, I have strongly suspected that Andrew Sullivan and I inhabit entirely different worlds," rings false for me given that my world often does literally overlap with Sullivan's, regardless of my disagreement with many of his assertions.[11] I have often seen Sullivan in the bars, vacation resorts, commercial spaces, and sexual publics that I visit throughout the United States. My point here is that we, as gay men, do sometimes share social and sexual worlds with those with whom we may politically disagree. I am thus more interested in thinking through what was meant by the end-of-AIDS discourse that began circulating in queer culture in the late 1990s. This discourse takes many forms. Claims for the end of AIDS and a post-AIDS discourse might be best understood not as markers of a definitive and identifiable moment of closure, but as the next development in the discursive history of AIDS. For Sullivan, it means putting forward his experience optimistically and naively as the normative experience of AIDS, without much concern for the effects of his rhetoric on others; it is a normalizing process that demonstrates a lack of self-consciousness, what we might call a discourse undetectable. For Rofes, who asks us to consider abandoning the term *AIDS*, it means "finding a new language that captures our experience."[12] For Signorile, concerned with HIV prevention, it means returning to the language of early 1980s AIDS activism. For Harper, who advocates a more "conscious and responsible discursive engagement," it means interrogating the social normativity that these end-of-AIDS pronouncements enforce.[13] Given these different meanings and competing claims, we might consider the language about the end of AIDS as yet another moment in what Paula Treichler terms "an epidemic of signification," the ongoing evolution of cultural meanings and values attached to AIDS that help shape how it is understood.[14] Both the so-called end of AIDS and post-AIDS discourse participate in a larger social phenomenon that encourages us to believe that the immediate concerns facing contemporary American culture, including queer culture, are not about AIDS.

We see the tension arising from the end-of-AIDS claims played out in the United States especially around the topics of race, money, and the law. In 1998, according to the Centers for Disease Control and Prevention (CDC), blacks accounted for 57 percent of all new HIV cases in the country, even though they constituted only 12 percent of the population. In Los Angeles, where I live, Latinos accounted for nearly 50 percent of new cases in 1998. Nationally, half of all new infections occurred in people under twenty-five. These statistics are no doubt what led Mario Cooper—former chair of the national AIDS lobby group AIDS Action Council and founder of Leading for Life, an organization that advocates for African American AIDS awareness—to claim that "AIDS isn't over. For many in America, it's just beginning."[15] In 1998, Leading for Life helped spur the Congressional Black Caucus to lobby the Clinton administration to declare AIDS in the black community a "public health emergency" so that the Department of Health and Human Services could allocate funds to counter AIDS where it is most prevalent. Federal funding for treatments, prevention strategies, and support services in black and Latino communities rose by $156 million. The AIDS-as-crisis model adopted by the national black leadership in the late 1990s often posits queer communities against minority communities to make its point, even though its origins are to be found in the gay community's efforts to organize around AIDS. This tactic departs from earlier understandings of AIDS in communities of color, which put forward the idea that AIDS constituted only one of a series of interrelated catastrophes affecting U.S. racial minorities and that it should therefore not be prioritized over other pressing issues.

If by 1998 the AIDS-as-crisis model was beginning to be viewed as dated and ineffective in the gay community, the new AIDS emergency or AIDS-as-crisis discourse among black and Latino leadership was proving successful in channeling political energy to fight AIDS in communities of color. In a peculiar reversal, the lesbian and gay leadership began to follow the discarded logic of the earlier AIDS discourse used by the black and Latino leadership by promoting the restructuring of AIDS service organizations (ASOs) to accommodate other non-AIDS-related health issues facing the community and by prioritizing other political issues over HIV/AIDS prevention and treatment. While white gay men who argue for the end of AIDS regularly neglect to account for increasing infection rates among racial minorities, leaders in communities of color regularly discount queer people in the AIDS emergency discourse that calls attention to AIDS in their communities. Queers of color do not fare well in these scenarios; in fact, homosexuality and race are generally imagined as oppositional.

This opposition between race and sexuality places groups in competition for funding and other resource allocations. As Cathy J. Cohen explains in *The Boundaries of Blackness*, "Often this struggle for money has been framed as a battle between resource-rich and overly indulged white gay communities and poor and largely ignored black and Latino communities. Of course, a case can be made that white gay men have received and controlled the lion's share of available AIDS funding; this simple dichotomy, however, does little to advance the interests of any group working for more AIDS funding."[16] Consider, for example, how Patsy Fleming, former White House director of national AIDS policy, in an attempt to point out the economic discrepancies between queer communities and communities of color around the issue of AIDS, inadvertently reinforces this binary when she recounts her visit to two ASOs in the same city. As reported by the *Los Angeles Times*, "One predominantly served white homosexual men and the other served low-income blacks and Latinos, and both were conducting fund-raisers at the same time. While the first group expected to raise $1 million, the second dreamed of bringing in $100, 000."[17] Fleming's attempt to call attention to the need for more and better resources in communities of color comes across as an either-or. That is, the plight of low-income blacks and Latinos affected by HIV is played against the seeming financial security of white homosexual men, even though, clearly, not all white homosexual men, or ASOs that provide services to them, enjoy this security.

The end-of-AIDS claims have contributed significantly to the decline in monetary donations, both individual and corporate, to ASOs. Despite the booming economy at the end of the twentieth century, which saw private donations to nonprofits increase by 7 percent annually during 1997 and 1998, ASOs reported disturbing decreases in AIDS funding. The main reasons for the drop in AIDS philanthropy in this period were AIDS burnout, the growth in non-AIDS-related organizations catering to lesbian and gay communities, and the sense that AIDS was over.[18]

The supposed end of AIDS, however, does not explain the legal backlash against people with HIV. Legislation has shifted the emphasis from protecting the civil liberties of people with HIV to protecting the public from people with HIV. Calls for mandatory testing, especially among prisoners and pregnant women, for name reporting and partner notification, and for the criminalization of HIV transmission are increasing. Despite the Supreme Court's 1998 ruling that people with HIV are protected by the Americans with Disabilities Act, the legislative trend shows that "we've moved from a period where civil rights and civil liberties for a person with HIV prevailed to a compulsory and punitive approach."[19] Prisoners, immigrants, pregnant women, and the poor are the most vulnerable to prosecution. This legislative trend is directly linked to cultural anxieties about the fact that new, advanced drug therapies help people with HIV live longer than previously expected. As Sean Strub, publisher of POZ, puts it: "Combination therapy, in our enemies' eyes, enables us 'AIDS carriers,' not only to 'live longer' but, more important, to 'infect more.'"[20] If this is so, how are we to understand what is meant by the end-of-AIDS pronouncements? That discourse seems to have rendered invisible the social, cultural, and medical problems that structured this moment in the late 1990s in AIDS history. This invisibility is supported by the lesbian and gay media, which in the late 1990s positioned marriage and the military as the two main political sites on which the main resources would be spent, a choice that clearly came at the expense of AIDS.[21]

Mainstream lesbian and gay political organizations and media shifted their priorities as AIDS moved more and more into the developing world and into previously underrepresented groups throughout the United States including communities of color, poor women, and the incarcerated. The rise of marriage and the military as key issues for mainstream lesbian and gay culture underscores the symbolic centrality of marital coupling and military service to the health and defense of the nation. The move to make these concerns central to a new gay politics can also be seen as an attempt to normalize gay and lesbian culture by associating it with the most traditionally recognized forms of national duty and social and civic responsibility. The discourse about the end of AIDS both helps make this possible and displaces AIDS onto the lesser-developed world. But if mainstream American lesbian and gay politics and media reassign AIDS to the shadow of gay marriage and the military, where might we find a discourse about AIDS that both marks the significant changes surfacing in the wake of the 1996 international AIDS conference in Vancouver and that also acknowledges the political necessity of foregrounding AIDS?

Historically, performance has proven a powerful means of intervening in the public understanding and experience of AIDS and of countering neglect of the disease by the larger culture. Performance is a cultural practice that does more than illustrate the social and historical context in which it is embedded. At its best, it shapes and transforms the way we understand and experience our lives. In *Acts of Intervention: Performance, Gay Culture, and AIDS*, I argue that AIDS performance constitutes both a political intervention and an embodied theorization.[22] Performance has provided a different perspective on the events reported in the dominant media, including those of gay culture. Performance's impermanence enables the people who assemble in the audience to critically engage the contemporary, and it constitutes this audience as a provisional community engaged with current political concerns. This exchange between artists and spectators often creates new forms of sociality and identifies new forms of agency. For these reasons, performance makes for a critical political and artistic resource. In the remainder of the chapter, I consider the work of two performers with HIV, Bill T. Jones and Neil Greenberg, in light of the shifts in AIDS discourse that I have described. What does it mean to live with HIV after the AIDS crisis has supposedly ended? How might we consider the relationship between AIDS and the performing arts if contemporary culture is supposedly not about AIDS? What follows is a discussion of two dancer-choreographers whose work helps us think through the contradictions and challenges of the end of AIDS. Examining the work of these artists allows us to track and affirm some of the cultural work around HIV that performance is able to represent, work that traditional print culture and media have been much less successful in accomplishing. But why privilege performance?

I focus on these choreographers and on dance studies for a number of reasons. First, the work of these artists stands out as among the most compelling work I have seen in the past decade. Their work has enabled me to think through many of the challenges AIDS continues to provoke even when the work itself might not be about AIDS at all. Second, dance provides a unique entrance into theorizations of the body, temporality, and sociality, and yet it remains marginal to debates and discussions in cultural studies, American studies, queer theory, and lesbian and gay scholarship. I therefore want to respond to recent calls in my own primary fields—theatre and performance studies and American studies—to incorporate dance and dance research into the mix.[23] Third, dance—like the rest of the arts—often enacts a kind of counterpublicity to dominant discourses, including not only those advanced by the mainstream media but also contemporary discourses about lesbian and gay life, which increasingly resist and disavow the radical politics on which the gay and lesbian movement was founded. Unfortunately, the performing arts remain marginal to most discussions of contemporary queer life, whatever one's politics. I here set out to counter that marginalization by placing the performing arts at the heart of the national culture to see what these performances might tell us about contemporary life. Finally, dance can communicate a discourse of resistance, an embodied language of cultural memory, especially for groups that have suffered oppression throughout their histories.[24]

In 1994, Neil Greenberg and Bill T. Jones each premiered an ensemble dance in New York City that has become something of a signature work. The titles of these dances, Greenberg's *Not-About-AIDS-Dance* and Jones's *Still/Here*, function as telling reminders of how AIDS was understood at that moment.[25] *Still/Here* was based on various so-called Survival Workshops Jones conducted throughout the United States with people facing life-threatening illness, including AIDS. Jones describes the participants as "of all ages, classes, races, sexual preferences, and states of health."[26] In its promotional materials, the Bill T. Jones/Arnie Zane Dance Company describes *Still/Here* as follows:

> At the heart of *Still/Here* are the "Survival Workshops: Talking and Moving About Life and Death." The first was conducted in November 1992, in Austin, Texas as an experiment to see what, if anything, could be collected from the experiences of people living with life-threatening illness that would inform a dance/theatre work. After it was completed, we realized that the participants living on the front lines of the struggle to understand our mortality are in possession of information—is their knowledge a gift or is a burden? The participants' generosity of spirit and willingness to express their experience both with words and gestures was both exhilarating and terrible. They are the essence of *Still/Here*: their gestures inform the

choreography, their words the lyrics, their images the stage. They will always be Still/Here. This work is dedicated to them.[27]

Jones, whose lover and collaborator Arnie Zane died of AIDS in 1988, often refers to AIDS in his work and in the public discourse that accompanies it.[28] *Red Room* (1987) is a dance that Jones composed during Zane's final two years with AIDS and performed at Zane's 1988 memorial service at New York City's Joyce Theater. *Forsythia* (1989) sets out, in part, to memorialize Zane and includes Jones and Arthur Aviles dancing to a tape-recorded voice-over of Zane describing his dreams. *D-Man in the Waters* (1989) is dedicated to Damien Acquavella, a dancer with AIDS who was a member of the company. As Acquavella's health deteriorated, Jones improvised ways to honor Acquavella's desire to continue to dance despite his diagnosis. In *Last Night on Earth*, Jones's autobiography, Jones explains how AIDS and dance converged in *D-Man in the Waters*: "I promised Damien there would be a place for him in the dance. As he could no longer walk by the time of the debut, in 1989, I carried him on stage, offering my legs as he executed the arm movements of what would have been the solo. When Damien could no longer perform, I chose not to replace him in the piece. Oddly asymmetrical groupings now mark his absence. Damien passed in June of 1990."[29] *Uncle Tom's Cabin/The Promised Land* (1990) included a number of AIDS references, beginning with the title, which Zane suggested from his hospital bed. The three-hour multimedia performance even incorporated a religious figure from the local sponsoring community whom Jones would ask a series of questions, ending with the provocation, "Is AIDS punishment from God?"[30] This unscripted conversation was meant to, in Jones's words, "conjure this ephemeral, unquantifiable, potentially deadly thing called Faith."[31] But it also helped set the context for how AIDS was understood by certain communities. While none of these works center exclusively around AIDS, they are each informed by the sociohistorical contexts, including the deeply personal experiences of Jones and his company members, of the late 1980s. Jones's artistic work during this period stood at the forefront of AIDS issues even as it set out to meditate on broader cross-cultural and transhistorical themes.

Although Jones had tested HIV-positive in 1985, his HIV status did not become part of the public discourse on his work until 1990, when he was interviewed for a cover story in the *Advocate*. "Somewhere in this comfortable conversation," according to Jones, "I must have mentioned that I was HIV positive—most casually, I'm sure, because I don't think we discussed it or its ramifications during the interview. This fact appeared, however, in the first column of this prominent profile. I was concerned. . . . From then on, every review that would once have said 'Bill T. Jones, tall and black, Arnie Zane, short and white' read 'Bill T. Jones, tall, black, HIV positive.' I had to deal with it."[32]

Thus the disclosure of Jones's HIV status is something that he cannot fully control or determine. Having mentioned his status to a reporter in an aside, Jones has found it presented as a major feature of his life and work by nearly everyone who has written on him since.[33] And yet despite this unintended outing of his serostatus, Jones bravely took on the burden of representation that came with this disclosure and with his increasing celebrity. For many people at the time, he was the most visible person with HIV in the performing arts. As he admits in *Last Night on Earth*, "I had to deal with it."

In *Still/Here*, Jones combines several elements: spoken text, selected from Survival Workshops dialogue and arranged by Kenneth Frazelle and Vernon Reid, who also composed the music; images, including photos and videos of Survival Workshops participants created by Gretchen Bender; and movement, sometimes based on the gestural language of the participants, that he choreographed for his dancers. Members of the company, not the actual participants from the Survival Workshops, dance *Still/Here* (figure 8). The choreographic language, as Jones explains, "frequently relies upon a lone performer who is watched, touched, tracked, or supported by the group" (figure 9).[34] At one point at the beginning of his process, Jones had considered disbanding his company and working with a company of HIV-positive dancers. He decided against this idea for two main reasons. Not only did the company prove a way to honor the memory of Zane; Jones had also assembled an extraordinary group of dancers over the years.

During its New York premiere at the Brooklyn Academy of Music, Arlene Croce, the prominent dance critic for the *New Yorker*, refused to review *Still/Here* but nonetheless dismissed it as "victim art" in the

8. (top) Gabri Christa, Odile Reine-Adelaide, and Maya Saffrin of the Bill T. Jones/Arnie Zane Dance Company performing *Still/Here*, 1994. Photo by Beatriz Schiller

9. (bottom) Maya Saffrin, Odile Reine-Adelaide, Gabri Christa, Daniel Russell, Rosalynde LeBlanc, Lawrence Goldhuber, Gordon F. White, Torrin Cummings, and Arthur Aviles of the Bill T. Jones/Arnie Zane Dance Company performing *Still/Here*, 1994. Photo by Johan Elbers

very pages where a review would have run. Croce claimed that Jones "thinks that victimhood in and of itself is sufficient to the creation of an art spectacle" and that Jones and his audiences were "co-religionists in the cult of the Self."[35] She presumed that since Jones was HIV-positive, any thoughts he might have on the time-honored theme of mortality must be narrowly understood as autobiographical, or, to use her deriding terms, "the cult of the Self." Croce's polemical and dismissive misrepresentation of *Still/Here* framed the national discussions of the dance to such an extent that virtually every review of the piece mentioned it.

Still/Here, which I saw performed in 1994 at the Brooklyn Academy of Music, had little relation to the victimhood charge that Croce had imagined. Instead of representing victimhood, the piece was a beautiful and moving meditation on mortality and on the various means people from diverse human backgrounds employ to come to terms with it. As someone who was immersed in the AIDS community, had experienced the deaths of various friends, and had witnessed the challenges of various friends living with HIV—including one of the actual participants in the Survival Workshops whose image, voice, and reflections on living with HIV had been incorporated into *Still/Here*—I found the work filled with hope and danced with creative resilience. *Still/Here*, as Marcia Siegel has noted, "evokes a sort of 1970s positivism, an almost poignant faith that supportive friends and self-awareness can help even those who are imperiled to live bravely."[36] This sentiment, that support and self-awareness might make a difference, in fact made for one of the most effective resources of hope to many of us in the 1980s and early 1990s. The performance's power, as Siegel notes, is found in this belief.

Whereas *Still/Here* received such unprecedented media attention for a contemporary dance event that it catapulted Jones into the national limelight, few people outside of the dance world are familiar with Neil Greenberg's work. Greenberg danced with Merce Cunningham before founding his own five-member company, Dance by Neil Greenberg, in 1987.[37] *Not-About-AIDS-Dance* premiered in New York City almost six months before *Still/Here* (figure. 10). It was performed at the Kitchen, one of New York City's leading dance venues, from May 5–

10. Neil Greenberg in *Not-About-AIDS-Dance*, Dance by Neil Greenberg, 1994. Photo by Alice Garik

8, 1994, and again, as an encore performance, from December 13–17, 1994 (figure 11). The *New York Times* named it "one of the year's 10 best" dance events of 1994, and it received a 1995 Bessie Award for outstanding dance and performance. *Not-About-AIDS-Dance* inaugurated a trilogy of dance pieces, the first dance followed by *The Disco Project* (1995) and *Part Three* (1998), that tracks Greenberg's experience of HIV in the context of the life changes he and his fellow company members undergo during a four-year period (figures 12 and 13). This personal information is provided by texts projected onto the back wall of the performance space. The texts always express Greenberg's point of view, regardless of who is dancing (figure 14). At no point do the dancers themselves speak. *Not-About-AIDS-Dance* refers to what David Gere calls the "silent communication" that characterizes most dances in the 1980s and early 1990s: the reluctance of choreographers to identify their work with AIDS despite the sense that the work may be about AIDS in some way.[38] Greenberg's ironic title means to call attention to this phenomenon and to distance his own work from it. The title intervenes in this silence by invoking the very rhetoric that enables it. *Not-About-AIDS-*

"...important, moving and very beautiful...
A profoundly truthful, unsentimental masterwork about illness and life."
– Jennifer Dunning, *The New York Times*

Not-About-AIDS-Dance
Neil Greenberg at The Kitchen
Encore Performances
December 13-17

11. (top) Promotional postcard for Dance by Neil Greenberg's *Not-About-AIDS-Dance* at the Kitchen, New York City, 1994. Collection of the author

THE DISCO PROJECT
Dance by Neil Greenberg

12. (center) Promotional postcard for Dance by Neil Greenberg's *The Disco Project* at Highways Performance Space, Santa Monica, California, 1996. Collection of the author

Dance By Neil Greenberg   March 31-April 5

13. (bottom) Promotional postcard for Dance by Neil Greenberg's *Part Three* at Playhouse 91, New York City, 1998. Collection of the author

14. "This is the song I danced to when I broke up with the married man. (Years ago. Before AIDS.)" Justine Lynch performing in *The Disco Project*, Dance by Neil Greenberg, 1995. Photo by Tom Brazil

Dance extends beyond this silent signification in the dance world to comment on the cultural silence and suppression of AIDS.

The dance itself begins in silence, with Greenberg paying tribute to his brother, Jon, who died of AIDS-related complications. Through projected texts the audience learns that "this is the first material I made after my brother died," while Justine Lynch, one of the dancers, performs the material. The rest of the company, dressed in white tank tops and shorts, quickly joins her, and the movements are repeated in solos and quartets. The projections introduce the company members and offer reference points for them and for the dance. "Jo is dancing that same material again" and "Ellen was a big pothead in high school" are among the first things we are told. The information given is generally personal and conversational. Short, idiosyncratic fragments pulled from popular music break the silence that forms the primary score for the dance.

In another section, Greenberg incorporates so-called found movements, the physical gestures he observed while his brother lay in a coma: rolled-back eyes, fingers pointing to the head, stillness (figure

15). He performs this section alone and without musical accompaniment. The projections state the following:

> This is what my brother Jon looked like in his coma.
> He was in a coma 2 days before he died of AIDS.
> I'm HIV+.
> But this part of the dance isn't meant to be about me.

Later Greenberg will tell his audience that he is asymptomatic. By now, even though he is memorializing his brother, he is also positioning his audience to consider his own HIV status in relation to his brother's death. Throughout *Not-About-AIDS-Dance*, text projections will mention others who died while Greenberg was creating the piece. These deaths structure and condition the dance. The list seems unending:

> I went away in August.
> When I came back I learned Ed Hartmann and Jon Falabella had died.
> On Labor Day Richard Wolcott died.
> When I came back from Richard's funeral I learned David Hagen had died.
> Within a week Donald Greenhill died.
> It was quieter then for awhile.

In this section, as Leigh Witchel aptly observes, "the projections progress faster than anywhere else in the dance, and then, like the announcement, there is a diminuendo and it does seem quieter for a while."[39] But only for a while. *Not-About-AIDS-Dance* ends with text projections that inform us of more deaths, each marking a moment in the dance's composition and thus a moment in history: "At this point in the making of the dance my friend Ron Vawter died." A quartet forms and then disbands from the stage to stand at opposite ends of the performance space. The four dancers join Greenberg, who is watching from the wings. The movement is repeated. Another slide announces yet another death: "At this point in the making of the dance my friend Michael Mitchell died." The quartet repeats the choreography. Before we hear of more deaths, the dance abruptly ends. *Not-About-AIDS-Dance* therefore

15. "This is what my brother Jon looked like in his coma," Neil Greenberg performing in *Not-About-AIDS-Dance*, Dance by Neil Greenberg, 1994. Photo by Tom Brazil

16. (this page) Promotional flyer for Bill T. Jones/Arnie Zane Dance Company's *We Set Out Early . . . Visibility Was Poor* at Royce Hall, Los Angeles, 1998. Collection of the author

17. (opposite) Members of Bill T. Jones/Arnie Zane Dance Company performing *We Set Out Early . . . Visibility Was Poor*, 1998. Photo by Beatriz Schiller

not only memorializes the dead but also calls attention to the relentless dying that occurred during the dance's making—between July 1993, when Jon Greenberg died, and May 1994, when the dance premiered.

Both *Still/Here* and *Not-About-AIDS-Dance* were created and performed in the midst of what we can only describe as the AIDS crisis, a period of deep skepticism about the possibility of survival, a period marked by the continued acceleration of HIV infections and AIDS-related deaths. Greenberg and Jones created work that reflected on mortality and was understood at the time to be—on some level and to varying degrees—about AIDS. In *Not-About-AIDS-Dance*, Greenberg, for example, shares his own experiences with HIV, but in *Still/Here*, Jones does not. In fact, *Still/Here* never mentions the words HIV or AIDS. While we need to consider these works in their particular cultural and historical context, it is equally important to recognize that both works set AIDS within a larger meditation on loss, illness, survival, and everyday life. *Still/Here*, for example, also concerns itself with other life-threatening illnesses. *Not-About-AIDS-Dance* also treats the various other issues, serious and banal, facing the members of the company. (For one dancer, Christopher, the dance is not about anything discernible. "Christopher wants his dancing to speak for itself," we are told.)

It also memorializes non-AIDS-related deaths that the company has experienced. These dances are at once about AIDS and not about AIDS, insofar as they are never reducible to, or exclusively concerned with, the AIDS crisis.

The paradox of being both about and not about AIDS becomes all the more evident when we consider the work these choreographers created at the end of AIDS or during the post-AIDS discursive moment. During the 1997–98 season, Jones premiered *We Set Out Early . . . Visibility Was Poor*, while Greenberg premiered *Part Three*.[40] Unlike Jones's earlier work, *We Set Out Early* contains no text, image, or narrative to organize its meaning (figure 16). The seventy-minute dance is performed in three sections, with music by Igor Stravinsky, John Cage, and the contemporary Latvian composer Peteris Vasks (figure 17). Much has been said of *We Set Out Early*'s abstractness; given Jones's previously emphatic addressing of social issues, his reluctance to provide a so-called message here struck many critics as noteworthy. Indeed, the work is described not only as abstract but as "non-linear, with little narrative structure"; it "luxuriates in the freedom of pure movement"—Jones, it seemed to some reviewers, "is tired of talking."[41]

Jones himself admits that the piece "started with the music, not from an idea I wanted to express." "I've been talked about so much," he explains; "it's difficult for many journalists to talk about the work because they're so busy talking about me. I made a work I really did not want to have to talk about; I truly wanted it to be a theatrical, visual experience."[42] Jones does not imply that AIDS is over simply because he does not speak about it in *We Set Out Early*. Nor do his comments constitute a disavowal of AIDS. *We Set Out Early*, unlike earlier work that secured Jones's celebrity, does not address social or cultural concerns. In fact, one might even argue that Jones's celebrity—which both arises from and exceeds his race, sexuality, and serostatus—now enables him to create work that is not about these issues. In the context of AIDS, Jones's much publicized HIV identity serves as a precondition for a post-AIDS piece of work.

While *We Set Out Early* may not address a particular social subject, Jones has plenty to say about his piece. He recognizes that dance communicates cultural meaning and that therefore *We Set Out Early* still makes a social statement. "The social messages are there, yes, but they are not overt," he explains. The piece "is about how we live and if there is subversion in it, it's by the example of the company, which is a cast of nations, touching each other, celebrating our bodies and humanity through movement."[43] For Jones, the message may be found in the image of the performing bodies of the dancers.

Given Jones's own views of *We Set Out Early*, I find his discussions of the artistic process for it especially interesting. Jones explains that he learned from the participants in the Survival Workshops preparatory to *Still/Here* that the key to survival lay in identifying what matters most and then giving oneself over to it. For Jones, what mattered was dance. "I looked around and, lo and behold, I was so glad to find out that I really loved dancing, as a primary art form. OK, I would give myself to that. Don't talk about things, because we can dance, we can see who you are, your race, your sexuality, what you're afraid of."[44] Since *Still/Here* Jones has become interested in finding a personal dance vocabulary; he works with Janet Wong, his rehearsal director, to codify his movements so that the company can then learn them. *We Set Out Early*, for example, was created first through the music: "The music became the map and I followed the map with my body and the company followed my body."[45]

The creative process began in the studio with Jones dancing to the Stravinsky score; Jones videotaped himself and then studied his movement with Wong. Together they decided which sections worked. Wong then learned the sections herself and taught the movements back to Jones and to the ten-member company. In Jones's words: "I start out alone, approaching the music purely as rhythm and texture. I work with Janet, then the company comes into it, and I respond to their personalities and shapes. . . . I choose and edit, but I also listen and see what people naturally give back."[46]

Throughout this process, Jones's body is positioned as the exemplary body, the body whose movements are studied, rehearsed, and then performed by the other dancers. His body constitutes the filter through which the dance is made. Because Jones's body, like all bodies, is marked by race, gender, age, sexuality, serostatus, and other vectors of identity, all of which he has explicitly addressed in much of his earlier work, his body helps make the meaning of the dance too. In the end, however, this is not to say that *We Set Out Early* is about Bill T. Jones. Rather, Jones's material body, along with the artistic body of his work, helps organize our responses to the dance.

Whether Jones engages in an explicit production of meaning (as in *Still/Here*, interspersed as it is with video, voice-over, and Jones's public statements about the Survival Workshops) or in a kind of resistance to meaning (as in *We Set Out Early*, with its lack of narrative or text to provide the dance with an anticipated social message; Jones's own statements about the piece almost exclusively concern artistic process), the meanings of both pieces are still in part shaped by his artistic career. In other words, the history of his work's production and reception informs how we think about his choreography in the present. *We Set Out Early* cannot but signify in relation to *Still/Here* and its reception. Yet this history should not completely determine our understanding of Jones's work; it is not productive to reduce Jones's dance work to the issue of identity, even if identity lies at the heart of many of his earlier works.

Jones himself does not dance in *We Set Out Early* (he did not dance in *Still/Here* either). However, when I saw it performed in Los Angeles in 1998, Jones performed a short solo that he had choreographed as a prologue to the evening's program. Dancing to the third movement of

Beethoven's String Quartet no. 16, Jones demonstrated with exuberant physicality and grace the possibilities for artists with HIV (figure 18). The dance was not about AIDS, but if it had anything to tell us about the disease, it was, to paraphrase Jones's own words, by the example of the dancer celebrating his body and humanity through movement. Jones, we might say, is still here.

If Jones is often read in the context of AIDS regardless of what his work might actually say about it, Neil Greenberg, whose career has generated less national media attention, remains less marked by his serostatus. But instead of obscuring his serostatus, Greenberg has continued to find it politically necessary and artistically useful to mark his relationship to AIDS explicitly. He also asks us to consider each installment of his trilogy in relation to the previous parts and to work that predates the trilogy. He has his dancers perform sections of his earlier dances in the newer pieces and informs us of doing so in text projections that accompany the performance. Thus the work builds meaning through self-referential systems that reflect on the physical process of Greenberg's HIV status and the artistic process of his choreography. The last dance of his trilogy is itself composed of three parts. In fact, Greenberg calls the dance *Part Three* and gives each section a subtitle: *Part Three (My Fair Lady)*, *Part Three (Judy Garland)*, and *Part Three (Luck)*. *Part Three (My Fair Lady)* incorporates music by Alan Jay Lerner and Frederick Loewe from the film soundtrack, as well as traces of music from Jimmy Somerville and the Communards, and from Judy Garland (figure 19). *Part Three (Judy Garland)* includes musical selections from Garland's career, including "Somewhere over the Rainbow." *Part Three (Luck)* is danced without musical accompaniment and is the only section of *Part Three* with projected texts.

In *Part Three (Luck)*, the text projections bring the lives of the company since The *Disco Project* up to date. We learn, for example, that "Ellen is moving to L.A." and that "Justine now has a boyfriend." Greenberg's own updates are presented during his three solos. "Neil's Solo 1 of 3" informs us that he is on protease inhibitors: "I started taking the pills last February"; "by March, my 'viral load' tested undetectable." From this moment on, dance and health issues intersect.[47] Consider, for example, the full text projections in "Neil's Solo 3 of 3":

18. Bill T. Jones in prologue to *We Set Out Early . . . Visibility Was Poor*, 1998. Photo by Johan Elbers

19. Christopher Batenhorst, Neil Greenberg, and Paige Martin performing in Dance by Neil Greenberg's *Part Three (My Fair Lady)*, New York City, 1998. Photo by Tom Brazil

I was sick in October.
Unexplained high fevers that sent me into the hospital—
Right when we were to start work on this dance.
I had a complete recovery but it was scary.
I think it was just the flu.
Whatever.
We lost some rehearsal time.

The work demonstrates that when the piece is about AIDS it is also about dance and its production. In Greenberg's trilogy, AIDS is not just a theme; it is a constraint placed on the dance itself. It informs and conditions the process of the dance in its creation, rehearsal, and performance.[48]

Greenberg's insistence that we not lose sight of his HIV status, or of the way in which it continues to inform his choreography, comments on the cultural tendency to relegate AIDS to the margins of cultural inquiry and expression. Like the trilogy as a whole, *Part Three (Luck)* makes public what is assumed private. It brings into the public sphere a discourse for AIDS that is not about closure or finality, or the end of AIDS, but about process, including the changing of our understanding of AIDS. Unlike the first two dances in the trilogy, *Part Three (Luck)* does not address others with HIV. Although deeply personal, the dance is not meant as a universalizing claim for new AIDS treatments. Greenberg offers the following insight:

> I had to make a new piece, because I had to update the audience. In *Not-About-AIDS-Dance*, I enacted my brother's death by showing what he looked like in a coma. By doing so, I implicitly asked the audience to imagine me dying of AIDS. Now I'm on these new drugs. My viral load is undetectable. I told my parents and the company, and I feel I have to tell the audience. If I've asked an audience to get involved with me, I have a responsibility not to just leave them dangling.[49]

Part Three (Luck) also references Greenberg's sense of loss in the face of the company's dispersal (two of the original dancers, whose lives the triology also documents, have moved on to other projects). Greenberg considers it unlikely that the complete trilogy will be performed again. "The year I made *Not-About-AIDS-Dance*, I wanted to make that moment stand still," he explains in the context of the trilogy's final performance in the spring of 1998; "[in *Part Three (Luck)*] I had to deal with the emotional trauma of not being able to hold onto the moment anymore."[50]

The trilogy memorializes Greenberg's brother, Jon; his lover, Frank; and many of his friends who died during the period in which the dances were made. It also marks the dramatic shifts that the new drug therapies have brought about for many people in the United States. At the same time, it counters the "not-about-AIDS" discourse that characterizes contemporary gay culture. Greenberg's work proves especially important in helping us think about how to address both the experience of AIDS and its erasure from the cultural landscape of gay and lesbian politics. In fact, *Not-About-AIDS-Dance*, and the trilogy it launches, forces that erasure into visibility within the space of performance. Greenberg refuses to normalize AIDS or to imagine it as "over"; he seeks instead a new creative vocabulary with which to address the continuing challenges of living with HIV.[51]

The final section of the last dance in the complete trilogy takes *Luck* as its subtitle because, as Greenberg states, "I have been lucky. For some reason the virus in my body didn't kill me before these new drugs came along, so that's luck. Or is it? To me, dancing is about delving into such questions."[52] Greenberg's comments on dance call attention to the role that the performing arts can continue to play in helping us think through the challenges of AIDS. Delving into the complex and challenging questions we face, as Greenberg reminds us, is not the exclusive domain of writers, activists, cultural analysts, or scholars. And the forces that perpetuate this divide between writers and performers and that set up a binary between theorists and artists needs to be aggressively challenged. The arts play a critical role in the culture and, in the case of AIDS, sometimes provide the means to move through the impasse of stalled rhetoric and political confusion. As we have seen, Greenberg and Jones show us ways to move forward, both in our recognition of the important historical shifts and medical breakthroughs concerning HIV/AIDS and in our need to continue to focus our energies on AIDS. These two dancer-choreographers' works ranked among the first successful attempts to think through an idea of change without lapsing into an end-of-AIDS discourse premised on either disregard or disavowal. These men offer ways of moving through the world without succumbing to the post-AIDS sentiments that surfaced in the late 1990s and shaped queer culture in the early twenty-first century.

While in this chapter we learned about New York–based choreographers able to help move the debates around AIDS in the mid-1990s forward in productive ways, in the process providing new models of living with HIV, in the next chapter we move across the country to observe how a Los Angeles–based playwright born in Singapore collaborated with a local multiracial theatre company to advance the conversation about immigration and citizenship in a high school auditorium in the Chinatown district of L.A. The chapter continues the book's emphasis on the political possibilities of contemporary performance and introduces more forcefully the role that history plays in this process. If the dancing bodies of Bill T. Jones and Neil Greenberg embody and perform the kinesthetic memory of their past lived experiences, and if these bodies carry symbolic weight as such to their audiences, the following section will show how shared geopolitical space can constitute a cultural landscape of remembering and historical revival for the Asian immigrant.

CHAPTER TWO

Visa Denied: Chay Yew's Theatre

of Immigration and the Performance

of Asian American History

But the question is still the same. Stay or go? Stay or go?

—CHAY YEW, *A Beautiful Country*

Frontiers, like borders, are understood and experienced differently depending on one's relation to them. For many people, frontiers and borders are inextricably linked with migration and exile, with the domestic and the diasporic—that is, with the politics of home. Within the U.S. context, the history of the frontier has been written as a narrative of national expansion and progress, of Manifest Destiny and American imperialism. Within the global context, America has mythologized itself as the very frontier of possibility, a myth, as Una Chaudhuri has explained, that privileges America as "the place of both literal and metaphorical openness, where the history of the future can be worked out."[1] In both these contexts, frontiers reveal much about transnational power relations and local negotiations of geopolitical space.

California in general, and Los Angeles in particular, occupy a specific position in relation to these issues. With Los Angeles now serving as the primary entrance point for new immigrants, and with minority populations increasingly shifting the racial demographics of the state, California has become the location making the apparatus of the nation-state most immediately evident and most vehemently preserved. California has historically registered as a national bellwether, and as Joseph Boone argues in his introduction to *Queer Frontiers: Millennial Geographies, Genders, and Generations*:

In the popular imagination, California has long loomed as the end point of the continental United States and the "final frontier" of the mythic Old West; and Los Angeles has become the nation's premiere psychic embodiment, unlike any other city in the United States, of racial diversity and ethnic hybridity, of mass culture and celluloid dreams, of futurism and apocalypse, of unrest and mindlessness, of sexual promiscuity and perversity, of the Pacific Rim's meeting point of Asia and America, and, as recent immigration controversies have highlighted, the meeting point of North and Central America.[2]

Given the weight of these projections, we might want to consider whose imagination constitutes the "popular" in such formulations of California as frontier. The network of associations that Boone lists in his introduction composes the primary narratives about the region and sets the foundation for official accounts of it. In order to complicate further this dominant understanding, I would like to address what might be called the "vernacular imagination" of immigrant subjects whose experiences of California or Los Angeles are often shaped by the very myths of America that exclude them. In this chapter, I am interested in unpacking the ways that the vernacular imaginary is able to construct a critical temporality that is both historical and contemporary.

The vernacular imagination stands alongside the popular imagination, which is more closely aligned with the official narratives of the region. But the vernacular differs in that it does not wield the force of the popular in its influence or its practice in the greater culture. While the popular and the official shape the vernacular imaginary, the vernacular imagination seldom shapes the popular and the official outside of market trend or commodity fetishism. The vernacular imaginary is more than simply a reflexive response to the popular or official accounts of the nation: given the large numbers of immigrants who regularly cross U.S. borders, the vernacular imaginary accounts for a wide range of responses to nationalist and populist myths of the nation. And yet the specific experiences of diasporic migration and the multiple effects of globalization also inform it.

Yet the feelings and experiences of these particular populations and communities are rarely discussed in relation to those that compose what Boone identifies as the popular imagination. Indigenous traditions and customs, local beliefs and rituals, and subcultural practices and routines are either bracketed—and therefore mainly understood in isolation—or they are discussed as the cost of assimilation to the majoritarian norm. But what might be said of the tension between these two modes of experience, between the vernacular and the official? I am interested here in precisely this tension, and in mapping out the ways in which new immigrants enter into and negotiate these longstanding and powerful myths of the nation. Performance offers the vernacular imaginary the means to embody this tension and critically assess it as a community. In this case, as also outlined in the previous chapter's focus on AIDS and dance, performance produces an opportunity for a critical reappraisal of the official culture and makes space for other modes of understanding, or what I am calling here the vernacular imaginary.

Before focusing on the specific case study that I find best articulates what I mean by the vernacular imagination, I want to turn briefly to the work of a diverse group of queer theorists—drawn from Chicana studies, social theory, art history, and performance studies—to map out the critical methodology I find most productive here. Queer theory offers the critique of normativity necessary to interrogate some of the key terms of this chapter, *American, citizenship, official,* and *history.* But I am also drawn to discuss what often remains peripheral to queer studies as it emerged in the late 1980s and was practiced throughout the 1990s. Despite its emergence at the height of the politics of multiculturalism in the late 1980s, queer studies has only recently begun to seriously address race and ethnicity, transnationalism and immigration.

My emphasis here on the social experiences of race, ethnicity, migration, and diaspora is not meant as a corrective to, or a displacement of, the social experience of sexuality foregrounded in much of what is understood as queer theory or lesbian and gay studies, especially in the 1990s. A number of scholars have already demonstrated the necessity of thinking about sexuality and race as interrelated and inextricably linked. The Chicana studies scholar Yvonne Yarbro-Bejarano, for example, in an earlier critique of queer theory, points out what would soon be understood as a basic tenant of identity formation.

Everyone's sex has a race and vice versa, just as everyone's gender identity is constructed in the interplay among race, class, sexuality, and nation. No one becomes who he or she is in relation to only one social category, and no representation of sexuality is free of racialization (even in the absence of people of color). . . . Besides considering the interplay between race and desire across and within color lines, the general task facing lesbian and gay theory is to question what the African American photographer Lyle Ashton Harris calls, "the positioning of sexuality as the transcendental signifier" in analysis of history and identity as well. The destabilization and expansion of regulatory categories of analysis will help us produce more complex imaginings of ourselves in the world and the place of race in our lived realities as gendered sexual subjects.[3]

Yarbro-Bejarano and others have led the way for exploring new ways of thinking about sexuality and race outside of the simple additive model of late 1980s multiculturalism, which explored notions of difference through the idea of inclusion.[4] "The 'additive' model of 'including' previously excluded categories in an attempt at correction maintains power in the hands of those who constitute the 'norm,' graciously inviting the 'different' in," writes Yarbro-Bejarano.[5]

Michael Warner, in his introduction to *Fear of a Queer Planet*, famously wrote the blueprint for the queer challenge to the norm, arguing that queer critique needs to be grounded in the social. For Warner, "every person who comes to a queer self-understanding knows in one way or another that her stigmatization is connected with gender, the family, notions of individual freedom, the state, public speech, consumption and desire, nature and culture, maturation, reproductive politics, racial and national fantasy, class identity, truth and trust, censorship, intimate life and social display, terror and violence, health care, and deep cultural norms about the bearing of the body."[6] Warner's grounding of queer experience in the material and political world offers a means to reject the additive model of inclusion and revise the entire constellation of political and institutional structures of daily life—the "planet" of Warner's metaphor. But if queer theory provides the language for the critique of various forms of normativity, it has not always prioritized the need to challenge the racial normativity governing queer culture and even queer theory itself. That said, it would be insufficient to simply catalogue the limitations of queer theory as it was articulated and practiced in the 1990s. Rather, what is important now, in the early twenty-first century, is to engage in more localized queer critiques that attend to the particular social and cultural formations of racialization and national identity.

Keeping in mind these political and analytical concerns, I do not wish to set the experiences of race, ethnicity, immigration, and diaspora against that of sexuality, as if one held more power than the others. Instead, I want to identify and examine contemporary cultural work that considers the interrelation among them. In part, I am interested in naming and promoting modes of performance that provide counterpublicity to the popular myths of Los Angeles. The archive for this work remains, for the most part, undocumented and unexamined. It exists in oral history, cultural memory, social ritual, communal folklore, and local performance—mediums that do not rely on print culture for their preservation. Because this archive often exists outside of official culture, it is often undervalued or even derided. So, too, are most efforts to recover it. Scholars of queer culture have been at the forefront of imagining ways to archive queer life, and many have also engaged in theorizing the status of the archive itself.

Richard Meyer, an art historian writing about queer ephemera, aptly points out that since queer culture exists on the periphery of official history, queer scholars need to imagine new and different archival methods and research strategies. In an essay titled "At Home in Marginal Domains," Meyer draws his attention to the always there but always marginal visual artifacts of minoritarian cultures. He recycles Walter Benjamin's thoughts on art scholarship, in particular Benjamin's call for the scholar to hold "the capacity to be at home in marginal domains." For Meyer, to be at home in marginal domains means to recognize the necessity of attending to what the dominant culture discards or trivializes—not to elevate it to the status of the art object, but to recognize the critical context obscured by traditional criteria of historical significance:

> When Walter Benjamin wrote "Rigorous Study of Art" in 1933, he was almost certainly not thinking of homosexuality as one of

the "marginal domains" to which the "new type" of art-historical re-searcher should attend. Yet Benjamin was thinking of various forms of visual production (e.g., architectural renderings and stage designs) that had been marginalized within the field of art history. And he was arguing for a scholarly method that would include what he called "an esteem for the insignificant," an esteem for anonymous works and overlooked details, for the obscure and non-canonical.[7]

But to be at home in marginal domains is to risk losing the credential-izing legitimacy that comes with conventional scholarship on the tra-ditional archive. José Esteban Muñoz, a performance studies scholar, writing about the archives of queer culture, explains one of the main reasons for this occurrence of dominant disdain: "Because the archives of queerness are makeshift and randomly organized, due to the re-straints historically shackled upon minoritarian cultural workers, the Right is able to question the evidentiary authority of queer inquiry."[8] Muñoz goes on to argue against this critique of queer theory, in part by advocating for the performativity of queer scholarship, or what he calls "queer acts." For Muñoz, queer acts, including the writing of queer scholarship, challenge the reactionary dismissal of queer inquiry through performative practice and honor the resilience of queer life given the restraints in which it must endure. Both Meyer and Muñoz join other queer historians interested in positioning and understand-ing ephemera as that which enables and constitutes the archives for our scholarship. Ephemera are composed of the remnants of history, and they function as a kind of critical residue. That is to say, what is either deliberately or inadvertently left behind then serves as the proof or evidence of the lost or forgotten performance. Ephemera, however, is neither interchangeable with the lost performance, nor can it fully replace it. It is the traceable remains of what had once transpired. As such, ephemera loses its status as waste or trivia to become central to the understanding of minoritarian life and culture.

Meyer and Muñoz's efforts to expand the archive and challenge the authority of official evidence open a critical space for those of us inter-ested in the alternative histories, memories, and performances of mi-nority subjects. While, in these instances, Meyer and Muñoz focus pri-marily on defending queer theory and preserving queer culture, their basic ideas extend to postcolonial and critical race studies as well. When we consider or foreground racial and ethnic minorities, the concern over the undocumented archive and the question of "evidentiary authority" often corresponds to larger cultural anxieties concerning nation and citizenship. For the immigrant, this issue of documentation is central; documentation determines access to citizenship. Mining the archives that preserve the interrelations between the social experiences of race and sexuality may in fact help us perceive more critically the ways in which citizenship has been constructed and enforced historically. Through this understanding, we may even find ways to respond to contemporary exclusionary forms of nationalist discourse in practice throughout the United States, but especially in the state of California.

Here, then, a focus on the performing arts allows for a fuller explication of these issues and concerns. The arts serve as the launching ground for the expression of many of these new social formations, and they open up an unprecedented space in the public sphere for the articulation of these concerns. A new generation of queer playwrights and performers of color have begun to call attention to the rich archives of memory that exist in the vernacular imagination of the queer immigrant subject. These new works thus participate in a larger cultural project, already underway, exploring histories and memories that exist as alternatives to those that circulate as the so-called popular imagination, or, more firmly, as official history. While this engagement of alternatives has been a long-standing project of ethnic and minority arts practices, the new artists trouble many of the foundational assumptions of earlier models of community arts practices and foreground questions of sexuality, transnationalism, and globalization in their work.

Chay Yew's saga of Miss Visa Denied, a Malaysian immigrant and drag queen, in *A Beautiful Country* (1998), stands as a case in point. The play is a collaboration between Chay Yew, a Los Angeles–based playwright and one of the most significant new voices in American theatre, and Cornerstone Theatre, a Los Angeles–based company that, according to its mission, "builds bridges between and within diverse communities." *A Beautiful Country*, written and directed by Yew, was commissioned by Cornerstone and was produced in association with the

CORNERSTONE THEATER COMPANY
IN ASSOCIATION WITH THE
MARK TAPER FORUM'S ASIAN THEATRE WORKSHOP
AND EAST WEST PLAYERS
PRESENTS

a beautiful country

by chay Yew

150 YEARS OF
ASIAN AMERICAN
HISTORY IN
DANCE, DRAMA
AND DRAG

20. Promotional flyer for *A Beautiful Country*, Cornerstone Theatre, Los Angeles, 1998. Collection of the author

Mark Taper Forum's Asian Theatre Workshop, which Yew directs, and with the East West Players, where Yew is a resident artist (figure 20). Yew's earlier plays include *Porcelain* (1992) and *A Language of Their Own* (1995); these plays helped establish Yew's career as a playwright on the national level. Both received critical acclaim for their formal innovations and their representation of gay Asian lives. Yew's theatre brings to the foreground the lives and experiences of those he calls the "hyphenated Americans," people who live at the intersection of multiple and overlapping worlds: Asia and America, citizenship and exile, migration and home.[9] The hyphenated American also describes those for whom the nomenclature *American* needs further marking by another term. In most cases in Yew's world this other term is *Asian*. While an earlier generation of Asian American playwrights, artists, and activists felt it necessary to name themselves and their work and movement "Asian American," Yew wishes to call the stability of that appellation itself into question. His theatre sets out to unsettle our comfort with the normative world of Asian America. He writes plays that while informed by the traditions of Asian American theatre, set out to move those traditions forward.[10]

Cornerstone Theatre has emerged as one of the most esteemed community-based theatres in the United States. It is composed of a company of professionals who form an ensemble that produces theatre in a wide range of communities throughout the Southern California region and the United States. Community members are invited to create theatre alongside the ensemble in order to explore issues of particular relevance to the community and region. Cornerstone was founded in 1986 in Cambridge, Massachusetts, by a group of Harvard students disillusioned by the American Repertory Theatre there, which they felt was neither representative of America nor accessible to it. Initially, for the company's first five years, the members would travel throughout the United States and make theatre with local communities, especially in rural locations outside of the regional theatre circuit. In 1991, the company relocated to Los Angeles, making it their home base since. As Sonja Kuftinec writes in her book-length history of the company, Cornerstone attends to the various elements in creating performance:

> Cornerstone's shows thus involve the community in every aspect of the production, from planning to adaptation, to publicity, rehearsal, and performance. . . . The social transactions engaged by Cornerstone's performance process animates a sense of community structurally, interpersonally, and through the process of shared meaning making—the "making things" aspect of cultural production. These interactions begin long before auditions, rehearsals, or even text selection, in some instances, as contact with collaborators reinforces leadership structures while enabling dialogue among residents of a town or members of a community.[11]

In Los Angeles, Cornerstone often embarks on bridge projects, in which a series of performances are produced throughout the city around a particular theme or issue, each involving a particular constituency or community. *A Beautiful Country* formed part of a larger cycle of plays called the B.H. project, which focused on neighborhoods in Los Angeles that had B.H. as their initials. Throughout 1997–99, Cornerstone worked with communities in Boyle Heights, Baldwin Hills, Beverly Hills, and Broadway/Hill, an intersection in the heart of L.A.'s Chinatown, where *A Beautiful Country* was staged. The idea behind the B.H. project was to expand the company's traditional outreach to lower-income and primarily minority communities to include higher-income communities such as Beverly Hills. At the end of the cycle, Cornerstone staged *Broken Hearts* (1999), which brought together artists and audiences of the four B.H. neighborhoods in a play written by Lisa Loomer and directed by one of the company's founding artistic directors, Bill Rausch, on the main stage of the Mark Taper Forum.[12]

    A Beautiful Country recovers a history of Asian American immigrant experience—150 years of Asian American history—through "dance, drama, and drag," as the program notes put it. A multimedia and multidisciplinary performance, *A Beautiful Country* chronicles multiple stories of pan-Asian immigration and exile to the United States, from Filipino migrant workers in the 1930s to Hmong refugees in the 1970s and 1980s; from the effects of the 1882 Chinese Exclusion Act to the internment of Japanese Americans during World War II; from the Negro Alley Massacre in Los Angeles in 1885, where fifteen Chinese men were hanged and four others were shot and stabbed to death during an interracial riot, to more recent hate crimes against new Asian immigrants. A multiracial cast of over twenty-five members, composed of professional actors and community members from the Los Angeles Chinatown neighborhood where the play is presented, performs these stories (figures 21 and 22).[13]

    A Beautiful Country is neither a chronological history play nor a docudrama of Asian American history. In this sense, it departs both from the traditional Asian American history play where, as Josephine Lee explains, "the personal stories of individual valor told in these plays threaten to eclipse the larger social situation," and from the conventional dramatic realism of Asian American theatre, which "promises a coherent subjectivity, an authentic voice, a truth within the stories."[14] Rather, Yew stages the various contradictions of Asian American experi-

21. (this page) Cast members of Chay Yew's *A Beautiful Country* perform "The Dance of the Migrant Workers" scene, Los Angeles, 1998. Photo by Craig Schwartz

22. (opposite) Eric Steinberg, Chris Wells, and Page Leong perform Henry Grimm's *The Chinese Must Go!* in Chay Yew's *A Beautiful Country*, Los Angeles, 1998. Photo by Craig Schwartz

ence, the ways in which racial and national identities are forged historically through—in Lisa Lowe's telling phrase—"immigrant acts," a term that at once summons forth the exclusionary practices of U.S. immigration laws and policies and the performances generated by Asian immigrants and Asian Americans who have found themselves often enmeshed within these shifting historical conditions and constraints.[15] At the same time, *A Beautiful Country* mines the official archives of U.S. culture, including the dates of specific immigration laws and the first interventions achieved by Asian Americans, presenting this information on slides projected onto the back wall of the performance space in both English and Chinese.

But other archives are also summoned forth, including the oral histories of various community members, which are interspersed throughout the performance, and the diverse cultural arts of the Asian diaspora, which are performed throughout the production. Yew enriches this fabric still further by staging earlier representations of Asian Americans in U.S. popular culture, including a scene from Henry Grimm's 1879 racist play *The Chinese Must Go!*—a theatricalization of the anti-Chinese sentiment resulting from the shifting economic conditions of U.S. labor forces in the 1870s—and a humorous dramatiza-

tion of a 1941 *Life* magazine feature that attempts to distinguish, for the white majority, the difference between the Chinese and Japanese.

Consider, for example, two scenes from the play drawn from each archive, the vernacular and the official. The first is based on the testimonial of José Casas, a Mexican American who lives in Los Angeles and whose grandfather was Chinese. The second example emerges from the text from the *Life* magazine feature. José Casas himself performs the first scene. He addresses the audience in his own voice after being introduced by a slide:

Slide: TESTIMONY
Slide: JOSE CASAS
JOSE CASAS IS MEXICAN-AMERICAN
José: Look at me.
How many of you would think Chinese?
I am,
a little bit, that is.
My grandfather,
he was Mexicano
But he was also Chinese.
He was,

as our family would say,
our Chinese *abuelito*.
Our Chinese grandpa.
His name was Marty Le Wong.
It's true.
My great-grandfather left China
at the turn of the century
with his family
because he was afraid
of getting caught in the Boxer Rebellion.
After a few years,
my grandfather's family found a home
for themselves
in Mexico,
of all places.
He would come to California
every few years for visits,
and I still remember
the last time he came to Los Angeles.
I was about eleven or twelve at the time,
and towards the end of this particular visit
my mother's *compadre* suggested
that he take me to Chinatown,
which was really good for my mom
because he didn't even know
there was a Chinatown in L.A.
It was nice
having my grandfather around.
He was different. . .
I miss him.
He was always trying to teach me
about what it meant to be Chinese,
and I never listened.
And now
I wish I had.
Being right here,

right now
in Chinatown,
how could I not?
I want to trace my Asian heritage,
maybe even go to China one day.
I think
my Chinese *abuelito*
would have loved that.[16]

Casas's testimony is meant to complicate the idea of Asian American and help revise whatever stereotypes the audience might still hold, perceptions held even among the Asian Americans in the audience. Like most testimonies, it is presented as an experience of authenticity. It is also incredibly sentimental. Casas anchors his claim to Asian Americanness in a biological genealogy of heteronormative patriarchy that has endured generational migrations across continents. In his accounting, however, the Mexicanness of his background is eclipsed by the Chinese great-grandfather who stands in for ethnic origins. Remarkably, however, Casas is able to control the narrative of his genealogy, privileging whatever he chooses to emphasize in the account of his identity. Though the slide claims he is "Mexican American," he himself troubles this labeling by claiming that he is also Chinese. Only in the vernacular archives of oral history would this seeming contradiction be allowed to stand. Casas is the agent of his identity, commanding how it will be documented in this performance. The play offers no commentary or critique of his account. It stands as his testimonial, one not open to official revisions or editorial annotations.

A scene that draws attention to cultural stereotype soon follows the Casas monologue. While "How to Tell Your Friends from the Japs" is meant to read as an authentic news story, it is performed in *A Beautiful Country* as a campy send-up of the investigative reporting that gave it its official power in the first place.

Slide: HOW TO TELL YOUR FRIENDS FROM THE JAPS

Slide: DECEMBER 22, 1941

Slide: *TIME* MAGAZINE

(Breezy forties music plays.)

A fashion runway. A very camp Truman Capote-esque MC *takes to the mike.*

MC: It's 1941
Can you tell your friends from the Japs?
Here are some helpful tips
to tell
the friend from the enemy

(A Japanese model wearing horn-rimmed glasses and a Chinese model enter.)

MC: Some Chinese are tall
Virtually
all Japanese are short.
Japanese are stockier and more broad-hipped
than the Chinese.
Japanese are seldom fat
They often dry up and grow lean
as they age
The Chinese often put on weight
particularly if they are prosperous.
Chinese are not as hairy as Japanese
Most Chinese avoid horn-rimmed spectacles
Although both the Japanese and Chinese
have the typical epicanthic fold
of the upper eyelid
(which makes them look almond-eyed)
Japanese eyes are closer together
The Chinese expression
is likely to be more placid
kindly
open
The Japanese expression
is more positive
dogmatic

arrogant
Japanese are hesitant
nervous in conversation
laugh loudly at the wrong time
Japanese walk stiffly erect
hard-heeled
Chinese walk more relaxedly
have an easy gait
they sometimes shuffle
See?
Japanese
Chinese
Japanese
Chinese
Can you tell the difference?[17]

The magazine article, actually published in *Life* and not *Time*, first appeared during World War II, only weeks after the Japanese attack on Pearl Harbor (figure 23). It meant to differentiate between the Japanese and the Chinese by presuming the Chinese as friends and the Japanese as enemies. However, in Yew's hand, the article becomes an opportunity for the two nations to have a fashion showdown on the runway. While the MC mouths the racist discourse of the article, the actors enact a counterperformance on the stage. Even here the official rendition of the article is called into question by the vernacular performance of the Cornerstone ensemble. It is precisely this tension between official and undocumented archives, between popular and the vernacular imaginations, between the *Life* magazine feature and the individual testimonial, that propels the drama of the play.

Just how these historical concerns transect with queer concerns becomes evident in Yew's decision to place at the heart of his play the figure of Miss Visa Denied, an immigrant drag queen from Malaysia meant to be, according to the program, "a metaphor of duality experienced by most immigrants: a person caught between two continents, two cultures, two languages, and two homes."[18] The play's dramatic structure, indeed, is framed by Visa's efforts to gain entrance into the United States. At first, we see Visa as a silent diva "dressed like

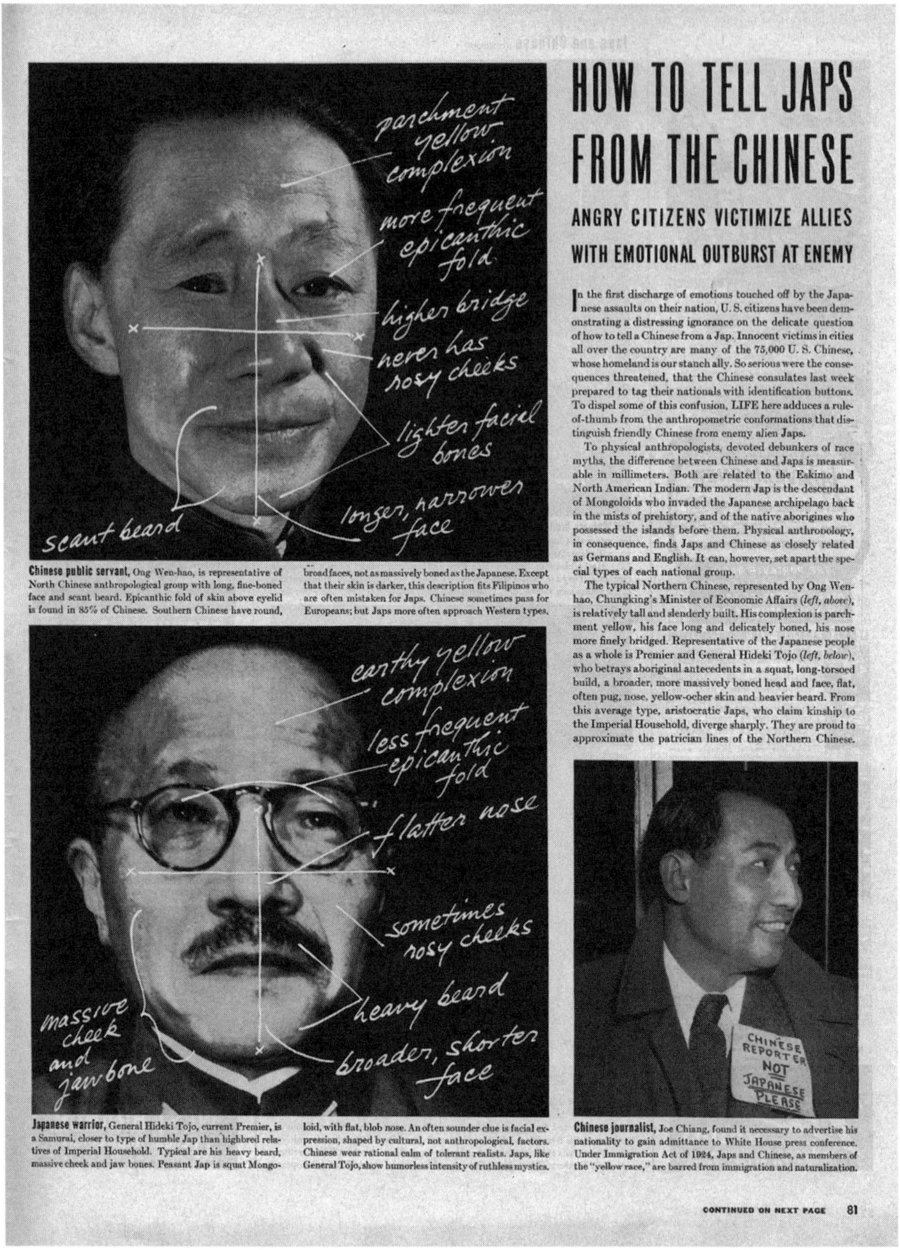

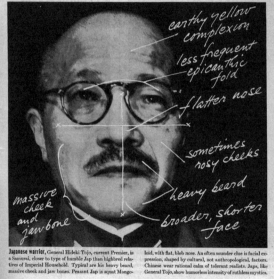

HOW TO TELL JAPS FROM THE CHINESE

ANGRY CITIZENS VICTIMIZE ALLIES WITH EMOTIONAL OUTBURST AT ENEMY

In the first discharge of emotions touched off by the Japanese assaults on their nation, U. S. citizens have been demonstrating a distressing ignorance on the delicate question of how to tell a Chinese from a Jap. Innocent victims in cities all over the country are many of the 75,000 U. S. Chinese, whose homeland is our stanch ally. So serious were the consequences threatened, that the Chinese consulates last week prepared to tag their nationals with identification buttons. To dispel some of this confusion, LIFE here adduces a rule-of-thumb from the anthropometric conformations that distinguish friendly Chinese from enemy alien Japs.

To physical anthropologists, devoted debunkers of race myths, the difference between Chinese and Japs is measurable in millimeters. Both are related to the Eskimo and North American Indian. The modern Jap is the descendant of Mongoloids who invaded the Japanese archipelago back in the mists of prehistory, and of the native aborigines who possessed the islands before them. Physical anthropology, in consequence, finds Japs and Chinese as closely related as Germans and English. It can, however, set apart the special types of each national group.

The typical Northern Chinese, represented by Ong Wen-hao, Chungking's Minister of Economic Affairs (*left, above*), is relatively tall and slenderly built. His complexion is parchment yellow, his face long and delicately boned, his nose more finely bridged. Representative of the Japanese people as a whole is Premier and General Hideki Tojo (*left, below*), who betrays aboriginal antecedents in a squat, long-torsoed build, a broader, more massively boned head and face, flat, often pug, nose, yellow-ocher skin and heavier beard. From this average type, aristocratic Japs, who claim kinship to the Imperial Household, diverge sharply. They are proud to approximate the patrician lines of the Northern Chinese.

parchment yellow complexion
more frequent epicanthic fold
higher bridge
never has rosy cheeks
lighter facial bones
longer, narrower face
scant beard

Chinese public servant, Ong Wen-hao, is representative of North Chinese anthropological group with long, fine-boned face and scant beard. Epicanthic fold of skin above eyelid is found in 85% of Chinese. Southern Chinese have round, broad faces, not as massively boned as the Japanese. Except that their skin is darker, this description fits Filipinos who are often mistaken for Japs. Chinese sometimes pass for Europeans; but Japs more often approach Western types.

earthy yellow complexion
less frequent epicanthic fold
flatter nose
sometimes rosy cheeks
heavy beard
massive cheek and jawbone
broader, shorter face

Japanese warrior, General Hideki Tojo, current Premier, is a Samurai, closer to type of humble Jap than highbred relatives of Imperial Household. Typical are his heavy beard, massive cheek and jaw bones. Peasant Jap is squat Mongoloid, with flat, blob nose. An often sounder clue is facial expression, shaped by cultural, not anthropological, factors. Chinese wear rational calm of tolerant realists. Japs, like General Tojo, show humorless intensity of ruthless mystics.

CHINESE REPORTER NOT JAPANESE PLEASE

Chinese journalist, Joe Chiang, found it necessary to advertise his nationality to gain admittance to White House press conference. Under Immigration Act of 1924, Japs and Chinese, as members of the "yellow race," are barred from immigration and naturalization.

CONTINUED ON NEXT PAGE 81

23. "How to Tell Japs from the Chinese," *Life*, December 22, 1941, detail. Collection of the author

Madonna," the international music star, being interrogated by a U.S. immigration officer. This opening scene captures the official force of nationalist surveillance as Visa, unable or unwilling to speak in return, remains mute:

> Officer: Passport please
> Passport
> Name?
> Purpose of this trip
> Purpose
> Why are you here?
> Business?
> Pleasure?
> Working?
> Vacation?
> I see
> How long will you be here?
> How long?
> Days?
> Weeks?
> Months?
> You cannot stay for more than three months.[19]

Visa's refusal to speak marks a refusal of the burden of liveness. Knowing she will be confined to a certain demand of abject performance — as immigrant, as queer, as person of color — Visa refuses to participate in the limited script available to her under these conditions. Instead, we get only one side of the conversation, the interrogation. The scene ends with Visa being led away for further questioning.

In the material world, Visa would have little agency; in the world of the play, she runs the show. Throughout the play, Visa literally oversees the 150-year history that *A Beautiful Country*'s narrative unfolds. The character of Visa is played by three actors: a male actor who embodies Visa on stage but does not speak, another male actor who speaks Visa's inner thoughts, but only from an offstage microphone, and a female actor meant to represent Visa's soul and performing only through dance. The duality assigned to Visa in the production notes is thus misleading: while she may serve as "a metaphor for the duality experienced by most immigrants," the fact that Yew chooses three actors to perform the character suggests not simply duality but multiple fragmentation. The play powerfully demonstrates how the experience of immigration not only displaces immigrants geographically but also enacts a kind of symbolic violence or fragmentation on the level of the individual subject.[20] Yew dramatizes this sense of fragmentation by distributing Visa's body, voice, and soul among three different actors.

This fragmentation of subjectivity is further echoed by the fragmentation of history that makes up the narrative: of necessity, Yew's ambitious staging of "150 years of Asian American history in dance, drama, and drag" in two hours of playing time only presents fragments from this rich and complex history. In *A Beautiful Country* history and subjectivity are always interrelated, positioned within a dialectical system of mutual exchange. Hence Visa's own story unfolds simultaneously with the play's larger historical interests. Throughout the play, Yew stages aspects of Visa's subjectivity—her memories of migration, her nostalgia for home, the erotics of her desire. The play never presents Visa in any way that asks the audience to see her as a freak or a fetish. In one scene, we witness Visa interacting with her mother; together they study an English-language phrase book, test out makeup, and plan their evening (figure 24). This banal exchange is meant to convey the intimacy of their love for one another. At the end of the scene, the mother's main affective response is one of homesickness, not homophobia (figure 25). The stage directions read: "Mother then gets up and looks at the video screen and sings a song about homesickness and a mother's love as Visa looks on. Mother then walks to the video screen looking longingly at the video. She stands in front of the video screen. Then Mother slowly caresses the screen."[21] The implication here is one of exile, displacement, and a yearning for home. Visa represents to the mother this traditional sense of belonging and connection affiliated with family and citizenship, one now all but lost to her. Rather than despair over a cross-dressing queer son, the mother accepts Visa for who she is, recognizing in her child a shared sense of loss and displacement. One result from this rather unremarkable presentation of Visa's sexuality is that the queer and Asian immigrant character is presented as a subject in

24. (top) Reggie Lee and Nancy Yee perform in Chay Yew's *A Beautiful Country*, Los Angeles, 1998. Photo by Craig Schwartz

25. (bottom) Nancy Yee performs in Chay Yew's *A Beautiful Country*, Los Angeles, 1998. Photo by Craig Schwartz

history, rather than a spectacle of history. This decision is important since Visa's own sense of self feels most complete when she herself is performing, as in her full-drag lip-synching rendition of "Vogue," Madonna's 1990 international dance hit.

"Vogue" pays tribute to classic Hollywood glamour and style, and its emphatic demand to "strike a pose" on the fashion runway beckons the performative. When it was first released, the song proved irresistible to drag queens everywhere, but it quickly played itself out in queer urban subcultural nightlife and its drag versions were shortly seen as passé and unimaginative. For Visa, however, "Vogue" still resonates with a sense of beauty and celebrity that she aspires toward and hopes to embody once in America. Her performance of "Vogue" is not meant to be ironic or camp; it is her performance of self.

While Visa's drag performance of Madonna's song announces her queerness, it also forms one of her own immigrant acts: performing "Vogue" is what she does when she arrives in the United States. Others before her participated in different forms of performative self-expression, ones informed by their historical moment of migration and arrival. Madonna's "Vogue," then, is what Visa does; it is what she brings to the "beautiful country," and it shapes how she experiences the effects of queer globalization. Her performance only makes sense within the context of the other Asian immigrant acts presented throughout *A Beautiful Country*. Visa expresses this link between queerness and diaspora in an eloquent monologue that describes her subjective experience of America:

> Room 444
> There is so much to live
> to love
> about this beautiful country
>
> Every time my feet finds this stage
> Every time the light drenches my skin
> I am strangely home
>
> My foundation
> mascara
> rouge

My new face
My lip-synch life
My makeover life in America
This theater
This is my home
My between home
between the port of Penang
and the port of Los Angeles
Forever
living in two worlds
Forever
belonging to none
I only wish
I wasn't lonely[22]

Tellingly, this monologue forms part of a series, each one told from a different room in a bathhouse. Each monologue archives Visa's erotic and affective experiences as a queer diasporic subject negotiating the sexual and social worlds of Los Angeles. Visa's efforts to find belonging lead her to sexual subcultures available throughout Southern California, where she is afforded the moments to ruminate on her new life—in what she still calls "the beautiful country"—as she awaits her next sexual encounter. "A moment is all I have," she explains. "Surely all these moments, all these pieces, add up to something," she continues before she commences on the next of her monologues in this sequence. Visa's sense of fragmentation becomes palpable in these scenes, which she compares to the stage.

The theme of fragmentation is also brought into relief by the cross-racial and cross-gendered performances of the actors and the overt theatricality of the production. Everyone here is performing a role, a point that Yew's direction does not obscure. In a debt to Bertolt Brecht's epic theatre, and the Chinese opera that inspired Brecht, Yew's actors perform on a raised platform described as the "acting area"; when they are not performing, they sit visibly on opposite sides of the platform, along with the play's musicians and dancers. Yew's actors perform across categories of race, gender, and national origin, and the cross-racial performances, in particular, exploit the theatrical medium's reliance on actors and role-playing to comment on the limited roles imagined and allowed for Asians in America. In this regard, A Beautiful Country's antirealist investments contribute to the play's larger cultural politics. Asian American performers, as Karen Shimakawa has argued, "never walk onto an empty stage." Citing the work of Robert Lee, James Moy, and others, Shimakawa explains how "that space is always already densely populated with phantasms of orientalness through and against which an Asian American performer must struggle to be seen."[23] While Yew's decision to cast non-Asians to occasionally perform Asian or Asian American roles throughout the play begins to dilute the force of these "phantasms of orientalness," his dramaturgy insists on invoking this material and representational history.

Yew also makes it evident that Visa's lip-synching performance of Madonna must be placed in relation to the social and historical forces that have shaped her sexual and racial subjectivity. Although Visa, as the program notes explain, "embodies and pursues the American Dream by wearing the mask of a pop icon and lipsynching words that aren't his," her performance asks to be historicized in the context of a long tradition of Asian immigrant efforts to pass through and into the national culture. That these attempts at passing often remain tragically unsuccessful—as the dramatization unfolding before Visa and the audience shows—only underscores the stakes involved in transnational and diasporic crossings. Therefore Visa's performance of Madonna's "Vogue" suggests that she imagines this role not only as quintessentially queer but also—and perhaps even more so—as quintessentially American.[24] Visa's performance constitutes a form of posing and even, we might say, a form of passing. It is a performance that suggests, as she states, "my makeover life in America." Through drag, Visa might be able to enter into America in the full glamour and sophistication that Madonna's song hold for her. In this sense, Visa performs "Vogue" as a disidentification with Asian normativity.[25]

At the end of the play, Visa returns to the stage in full drag, once again lip-synching and dancing to Madonna's "Vogue." As she works the runway in all her glamour, slides projected on the back wall convey her day-to-day reality and the actual world through which she must maneuver. It is a world far less enchanting than Visa has suggested so far, and one where her beauty and celebrity remain virtually unacknowledged. And it is a world much more dangerous than has been acknowledged, especially for a queer diasporic immigrant. As becomes evident, Visa's performance in this final scene takes place on two levels: on the literal level, she performs in the very same space as everything previously represented and staged in the play, and her lip-synching forms the final act in the playing time of *A Beautiful Country*; on the metaphoric level, Visa performs on the very same psychic and physical terrain of those who have historically passed before her, for she is the most recent immigrant in a long history of Asians in America. All of these past performances haunt her as she enacts her own performance in present-day Los Angeles:

Slide: 1998
Slide: Los Angeles
Slide: After my late shift at Starbucks at Pershing Square, I walked along lonely Los Angeles Street.
Slide: On the wet street pavement, I could see a blue moon dancing.
Slide: As if by command, I ventured down the same streets where the Chinese lived more than a hundred years ago.
Slide: When I reached the heart of the plaza, I felt a stirring of collective fear the Chinese had.
Slide: In front, a city on fire, eyes silent with hate.
Slide: Behind, wagons, frenzied escape, a forced passage home.
Slide: It was more than a hundred years ago.
Slide: But the question is still the same.
Slide: Stay or go?
Slide: Stay or go?
Slide: I'm staying.
Slide: I'm home.[26]

Visa's performance ends when a technical failure stops the music. Alone and in the spotlight of bright fluorescent lights, Visa is, according to Yew's stage directions, "stunned and embarrassed by being onstage and 'voiceless.'" Left alone to improvise, she summons her other selves: the male actor, who has served as her voice, and the woman actor, who has represented her soul, appear on stage and help remove her drag. If the earlier Visa imagined "this theatre" as "my home, my between home, between the port of Penang and the port of Los Angeles," Visa now questions the security of this belief. Yew cleverly detheatricalizes his central character in order to call attention to the drama inherent in Visa's material world, where the theatre provides only a temporary respite from the harshness of America. Home is no longer only "this theatre" but also "the same street the Chinese lived more than a hundred years ago, the heart of the plaza, Los Angeles."

The fragmented narrative of Visa's subjective immigrant experience, which the play has interjected throughout its presentation of Asian American history, now overlaps with the play's own need for closure (figure 26). It is in this moment that the onstage Visa finally speaks in what the stage directions describe as "broken and halting English":

Visa: My
name
is
Wong Kong Shin
I
come
from
Penang
West Malaysia
No
I
come
from
Los Angeles
California
United States of America [27]

Visa's journey from Penang to Los Angeles — that is to say, her journey from Wong Kong Shin to Miss Visa Denied and back again to Wong Kong Shin — requires a set of performances that allow him to gain entrance into the United States, however temporary.

If "queer acts," as José Muñoz argues, "stand as evidence of queer

26. "I come from Los Angeles, California, United States of America." Reggie Lee and Chris Wells perform the epilogue of Chay Yew's *A Beautiful Country*, Los Angeles, 1998. Photo by Craig Schwartz

lives, powers, and possibilities," and if "immigrant acts," as Lisa Lowe argues, "[name] . . . the *acts* of labor, resistance, memory, and survival, as well as the politicized cultural work that emerges from dislocation and disidentification,"[28] then perhaps the alliance between queer theory and Asian American studies makes possible what we might call "queer immigrant acts." Queer immigrant acts such as Visa's—and Yew's—acknowledge the alternative forms of sociality and community that these interrelated and collective efforts render possible. Queer immigrant acts make possible transnational queer subjects, transforming the social and public worlds in which these individuals travel. Although in the end Wong Kong Shin's queer immigrant act denies Visa's centrality to his sense of self, such an act reintegrates the various fragmented parts of his identity—voice, soul, and body—that have been performed separately throughout *A Beautiful Country*.[29] He speaks now for the first time in his own voice. Such an act, at once Asian American and queer, locates Kong Shin as a subject in history, and as a subject in motion. The removal of Visa's drag to reveal Kong Shin neither indicates the disavowal of the agency enabled by the drag persona nor marks a return to an authentic self that the Visa persona has eclipsed. Rather, Visa and Kong Shin can now share the stage as they have shared the body of Reggie Lee, the actor who has performed them throughout the production.

The play ends with an epilogue that revisits the initial scene with the U.S. immigrant officer. This time, after the interrogation, the immigrant officer stamps Visa's papers and allows temporary entrance: "Welcome to America. Next." The repetition of the immigration scene at the end of the play is now nuanced with the shared history of immigration, exile, and forced migration of generations of Asians to America. The play insists on the acknowledgment of this historical past as a means to contextualize the contemporary conditions that new immigrants from the Asian diaspora encounter. Other vectors of identity and experience brought forth by historical circumstance, geopolitical friction, and political struggle will also inform this migration.

Unlike most work in Asian American theatre, *A Beautiful Country* explores the interrelation between queerness and diaspora.[30] The play presents various historical and imagined dimensions of Asian

American social experience, at once expanding the representational field of Asian American theatre and demanding the critical interrogation of race, gender, and sexuality. It also goes to great effort to challenge the assumptions around the term *Asian American* in its insistence on locating Asian and Pacific Islander migration to the United States within transnational and global contexts. Here, it seems to me, Yew's work is in line with new scholarship in Asian American studies that sets out to revise the foundational logic of the field as it was prescribed in the 1960s and relevant to Asian immigration patterns up to that historical point. This "new" Asian American studies aims to contextualize U.S. imperialism in Asia and the Pacific, address the effects of global capitalism on Asian and Asian American experience, and open up the term *Asian American* to examine the social experiences of those who Lisa Lowe identifies as the "New Asian" immigrants, people who arrived in the United States after the Immigration and Nationality Act of 1965.[31]

New scholarship in Asian American studies is also engaged with putting pressure on the notion of the frontier, the concept by which I introduced this chapter and that I used as its critical frame. As David Palumbo-Liu explains, the frontier was more than a mythic space of possibility; it was also something highly racialized and, as such, a source of cultural anxiety. Moreover, he explains, this "racial frontier" linked, for better or worse, the United States with Asia:

> The very shape and character of the United States in the twentieth century — specifically, in the imaginings of modern American development in the global system — is inseparable from historical occasions of real contact between and interpenetrations of Asia and America, in and across the Pacific Ocean. The defining mythos of America, its "manifest destiny," was, after all, to form a bridge westward from the Old World, *not just* to the western coast of the North American continent, but from there to the trans-Pacific regions of Asia. This "lure" toward and across the Pacific expanse was complemented by anxiety regarding what the eminent Chicago sociologist Robert E. Park designated as America's "racial frontier." For him, the Pacific represented a formidable challenge to modern America in

terms of both race and culture. Crucially, at the same time that many Americans retreated from that challenge and held firmly to a particular narrative of nation that stopped at such frontiers in order to preserve a certain definition of the nation (as a narrative that would still cling to the old world of Europe), Park and others sketched out possible modalities in which that "frontier," perhaps marked more by race than geography, might be transsected.[32]

While Palumbo-Liu, Lowe, and a new generation of Asian American scholars have explored the implications of this racial frontier in exciting and important scholarship on Asian and American lives and cultures, the "racial frontier" and the "queer frontier" have only recently been aligned in academic and scholarly inquiry.[33]

In an important critical project that sets out to link Asian American studies with queer theory, David Eng raises a number of interrelated questions that neither Asian American studies nor mainstream queer theory have previously prioritized. He wonders, "How might we theorize queerness and diaspora against a historical legacy that has unrelentingly configured Asian Americans as exterior or eccentric to the U.S. nation-state? How might queerness and diaspora provide a critical methodology for a more adequate understanding of Asian American racial and sexual formation as shaped in the space between the domestic and the diasporic?"[34] These are also the questions that frame Yew's play and distinguish his work from earlier Asian American theatre, even including his own previous explorations of gay Asian lives.[35] *A Beautiful Country* participates in what Eng recommends at the end of his important essay: "In the late 1990s queerness and diaspora should be used not only to reevaluate the past but to orient the future of Asian American political projects and strategies whose claims on oppositional politics can be acknowledged as such. This is a moment that should be marked by our definitive shifting away from a politics of cultural nationalism to a politics of transnational culturalism."[36]

This shift toward transnational culturalism and a reorientation toward the future through an excavation of the archives of the past seems to me to be precisely what Yew's play has accomplished. It is not so much that he has queered the various archives of Asian America, although there is some of that too, as the play's campy restaging of *The Chinese Must Go!* proves. Nor is it simply that he has thematized queer Asian immigration and brought a consideration of that experience into representation, although the story of Miss Visa Denied also certainly does that. *A Beautiful Country* challenges us to consider the relationship between queerness and diaspora as a productive association, a critical alliance that puts pressure on the normative force of popular imaginations and official archives. Here, then, the play also anticipates and contributes to the productive discussions on queer globalizations currently occurring with scholars, activists, and human rights advocates. As Arnaldo Cruz-Malavé and Martin F. Manalansan IV write in their introduction to *Queer Globalizations*, scholars and others committed to the human rights of queer people throughout the world are devoted to exploring the complex dynamics of the effects of transnationalism, global capitalism, and the resulting breakdown of the nation-state on queer lives:

> Instead of providing a term or grammar that would dispel the complexity of these cross-cultural interactions, making them universally legible, the contributors to this anthology would rather open them up, and interrupt and interrogate the hegemonic logics and loves that prematurely solve them, reducing their meaning and their political potential. They would rather develop a situated knowledge of the ways global capital has routed queer cultures and lives, in the hope that these queer itineraries may also yield counterhegemonic routes that can redeploy and redirect global capital's mass dispersions, and pain, toward global cross-cultural engagements and coalitions that are more respectful of queer culture and lives.[37]

The performing arts, as *A Beautiful Country* proves, have a role to play in this project. They stand to amplify, enrich, and inform the scholarly conversations at work on these topics, as they embody the critical issues through performance and collective spectatorship. Despite the restrictions of its reach—the play only ran a limited number of weeks and in only one locale—Cornerstone's production of *A Beautiful Country* made a direct intervention into the Asian American communities of Southern California and into our understanding of their histories in

Southern California and the extended regions of the American West and the Pacific Rim.

In *A Beautiful Country*, Yew stages the past so as to historicize the present. *A Beautiful Country* presents the necessary social and political context facing Asian and Pacific Islander immigrants to the United States in the contemporary moment. After shifting the critical framework—from the national to the transnational, from the domestic to the diasporic, from the normative to the queer—the play brings us back, once again, to the politics of home. But the question remains the same: Stay or go? Stay or go?

CHAPTER THREE

Latino Genealogies: Broadway and Beyond—
the Case of John Leguizamo

Latino performance has historically been linked with the social movements of Latinos and Chicanos. From its earliest manifestations in
the religious and secular cultural rituals of the indigenous people of
the Southwest to the incorporation of many of these rituals in the na-
scent theatre conventions of the mid-nineteenth century, Latino performance has primarily functioned to rehearse and enact various Latino
cultural beliefs and customs.[1] From the itinerant Mexican players, who
performed for the communities around the early California missions
in the coastal cities of San Diego, Los Angeles, and San Francisco, to the
pan-Latino vaudeville houses of early immigrants in New York, Florida,
California, and the Southwest, Latino performance can be understood,
in the words of theatre historian Nicolás Kanellos, as "protecting the
home culture and language in exile, educating the youth in the traditional customs and mores, providing the ideological and spiritual
leadership that was needed to fend off the threat of assimilation to
Anglo-American culture."[2] From this perspective, performance functioned as a space within the public sphere to negotiate and rehearse
shifting social mores and internal conflicts. For these reasons, Latino
performance continues to be, in Jorge Huerta's apt phrase, "a necessary
theater."[3] Here, Huerta describes the Chicano theatre movement that
grew out of farmworker struggles in the 1960s, and the role that theatre and performance played to politically organize an oppressed and
exploited people. Scholars have well documented this fact but, as I have

argued, commercial theatre for the most part remains unexamined. Broadway, perhaps the country's most celebrated commercial zone for the performing arts, has generally not been imagined as a place of political possibility or Latino belonging.

If the previous chapter showcased the history of new Asian American immigrants throughout greater Los Angeles and their historical struggles to attain civil rights and national recognition, this chapter shifts to New York City and focuses on the ways that John Leguizamo's Broadway debut signaled a new moment in Latino cultural history, one where pan-Latino affiliations were proposed for political and cultural gain in the 1990s. Despite living and working in high numbers in the immediate areas surrounding Times Square, Latinos—and I am including Puerto Ricans, Dominicans, and those of other Caribbean, South and Central American backgrounds, as well as Mexicans under this term—have not found much employment, let alone a sense of home, in the neighborhood's Broadway theatres. In 1998, however, the enormously charismatic performer John Leguizamo premiered *Freak*, his latest one-person show, on Broadway, thus offering Latinos from throughout greater New York City an opportunity to reassess their relationship with one of the city's premiere cultural and commercial venues (figure 27). The results of this process, moreover, did more than alter and revise the standard business and conventional demographics of Broadway—Latinos did decide to go to *Freak*, after all—Leguizamo's show challenged the structuring tenets of Latino life and culture.

Freak played at the Cort Theatre for close to six months in 1998.[4] Leguizamo's Broadway schedule included evening performances from Tuesday through Saturday, with matinee performances on Saturday and Sunday afternoons. The Cort Theatre's seating capacity allows for 1,084 audience members—Leguizamo performed to mostly sold-out houses, and the only reason the play closed was because Leguizamo had prior film commitments that he needed to honor. Leguizamo was contracted to perform *Freak* at the Cort from February 12, 1998, to April 30, 1998. The show was twice extended and ran for twenty weeks before closing on July 6, 1998. *Freak* proved a critical success, garnering strong reviews in all national print media including the *New York Times*.[5] The show received nominations for two Tony Awards: best play and best

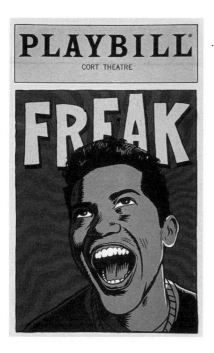

27. Playbill for John Leguizamo's *Freak* at the Cort Theatre, New York City, 1998. Collection of the author

performance by a leading actor in a play. It also proved a commercial success. *Freak*, which cost just over $700,000 to produce, grossed $1.2 million during its short run. Of the over thirty productions that opened on Broadway during the 1997–98 season, only two other plays—Yasmina Reza's *Art*, which won the 1998 Tony award for best play, and David Hare's *The Judas Kiss*, which starred Liam Neeson—had made a profit by the time Leguizamo's play closed.[6]

Leguizamo's success on Broadway is extraordinary given, as Alberto Sandoval-Sánchez reminds us in *José, Can You See? Latinos on and off Broadway*, that so few Latino self-representations have been available on a Broadway stage.[7] Broadway has historically excluded Latino theatre and, by extension, Latino audiences from its profile. Previously only three other plays by and about Latinos have ever been produced there—Miguel Piñero's *Short Eyes* (1974), Luis Valdez's *Zoot Suit* (1979), and Reinaldo Povod's *Cuba and His Teddy Bear* (1986)—and Leguizamo was the first Latino actor to perform solo on a Broadway stage. (In this context, *Freak*'s success is nothing short of freakish.)

In light of *Freak*'s success, I am interested in thinking through what Leguizamo's work tells us about contemporary Latino life and culture. However, let me say from the start that I am not out to suggest that Leguizamo's enormous success gives the actor-playwright access to some greater truth claim about Latinos than other Latino writers, performers, and artists. Rather, it is precisely because *Freak* circulates more widely within popular culture than these other performances that it becomes necessary for this question to be raised and considered seriously. (The film version of *Freak*, directed by Spike Lee, that aired on H B O in the fall of 1998 received a 1999 Emmy for Outstanding Performance in a Variety or Music Program.)[8] Despite the critical attention that cultural studies has directed toward popular and mainstream archives, and despite the renewed interest in theatre and performance studies, Broadway itself—as a site of cultural production—nonetheless remains vastly undertheorized. Scholars of theatre and performance studies have only recently begun to directly engage the rich archives of Broadway.[9] Latino studies has also ignored the significance of mainstream popular culture, except to report on the representational politics of film and television. As I argued in the book's introduction, commercial theatre constitutes both a potential site of critical possibility and a form of engaged cultural critique. My work on Leguizamo is in concert with new work in Latino studies that interrogates contemporary Latino celebrities, Latino popular culture, and Latino commercial arts.[10] Taking seriously Leguizamo's success provides an entrance into thinking critically about the arrival of Latino performance on the national level in the late 1990s (figures 28 and 29).

Leguizamo's Broadway performance proves especially interesting in what it tells us about Latino identity and history. In the following pages, I will be arguing that *Freak* presents two concurrent and at times competing Latino genealogical systems. The first is based on the traditional biological family, the heteronormative kinship structure that positions young John himself as freak. Young John does not immediately adhere to this group, and it will be his father who will mark his difference early on in the play. The second genealogical system is based on a history of pan-Latino performers whose Latino background and isolated Latino celebrity marked them as freaks within American popular cul-

28–29. John Leguizamo performs in *Freak*, Cort Theatre, New York City, 1998. Photos by Joan Marcus

ture; these artists, as we shall see, inform Leguizamo's own cultural identity. Young John forms an immediate connection with this second group when he first encounters them in his youth. The bridge between these systems will be his queer Uncle Sanny, whose loyalty to one of these groups becomes apparent early on in the performance. The play is about young John's negotiation of these kinship structures. I take seriously Leguizamo's comic performance and the ways that *Freak* addresses the nature of Latino belonging, the means by which Latinos find and express a sense of individual and collective cultural identity.

By *freak* I mean those people who stand as figures outside the norm, those who are understood not simply as unusual but as emphatically different to the point of deviance. The word is introduced early on in the performance when Leguizamo's father, in a scene in which he is drunk, asks his ten-year-old son for a kiss. The two are sitting out on the fire escape, young John on his father's knee.[11] The father, Fausto, wants the son to show him both respect and affection. "I'm your father, you little faggot. Come on give me a kiss. You kiss me or I'll punch the shit out of you."[12] Young John complies, but in the process, he misreads the codes of Latino machismo, in this case, his father's simultaneous invocation of affection and violence. As a result, the father calls young John a "freak" for kissing him inappropriately: "Not on the lips, you little freak!" In this context the word has a derogatory and dismissive sting.

This said, I also want to conjure Coco Fusco's important 1994 essay, "The Other History of Intercultural Performance," in which she describes the performance and reception of *Couple in a Cage*, her 1992 collaboration with Guillermo Gómez-Peña, in which the two performers exhibited themselves for three days in a cage as authentic indigenous people recently discovered.[13] Fusco was disturbed that many spectators perceived Fusco and Gómez-Peña as authentic ethnographic specimens, as actual natives in a cage, rather than as Latino performers aiming to deconstruct this antiquated image of the colonized other. Fusco's essay provides a useful entry into discussions of the performance of "freaks"; in her revisionist history of performance, she locates the origins of performance art and racial performance in the exhibitions of people of color in the "taverns, theaters, gardens, museums, zoos, circuses, and world fairs of Europe, and the freak shows of the United States" for "aesthetic contemplation, scientific analysis, and entertainment."[14] Fusco's own disturbing experiences in her caged performances suggest that contemporary Latino performers remain vulnerable to an ethnographic gaze that reduces progressive performance to a kind of freak show during which the artists lose the power to critique the very institutions that enforce this worldview. The ethnographic gaze becomes especially evident in performances of multiculturalism, where Fusco claims, "the central position of the white spectator, the objective of these events as a confirmation of their position as global consumers of exotic cultures, and the stress on authenticity as an aesthetic value, all remain fundamental to the spectacle of Otherness many continue to enjoy."[15] Rachel Adams has also demonstrated how the history of freak shows in America constitutes a history of negotiating the normative ideologies of race, gender, and the body. Adams's 2001 book-length study, *Sideshow U.S.A.: Freaks and the American Cultural Imagination*, tracks the shifting popularity of the freak show in American culture in order to argue their important cultural function in "allowing ordinary people to confront, and master, the most extreme and terrifying forms of Otherness they could imagine, from exotic dark-skinned people, to victims of war and disease, to ambiguously sexed bodies."[16] Adams's research demonstrates the historical and cultural contexts that promote the non-normative as spectacle, and the ways that so-called freaks have surfaced in moments of cultural stress.

While these definitions understand the word *freak* as a noun, this term circulates in yet a third way: *freak*, in an urban vernacular, is also a verb, something one does. To "freak" is to act outside socially acceptable behavior, as well as outside one's own given norms; it often holds sexual connotations. Leguizamo's title summons each of these meanings—the derogatory, the ethnographic, and the antinormative—and each contributes to the work's overall effect. With these definitions of *freak* in mind, I want to interrogate both the internal and external politics of Leguizamo's *Freak* performance. I want to first begin by briefly considering the events leading up to the show's success. How was it that Leguizamo was able to become the first Latino solo performer on Broadway?

A number of factors, I would argue, enabled Leguizamo's Broadway run. First, Leguizamo's earlier one-person shows, *Mambo Mouth* (1990) and *Spic-O-Rama* (1992) were both critical and commercial successes off Broadway, selling out their initial runs and even transferring to larger off-Broadway houses while winning prestigious theatre awards along the way. Leguizamo's gifted impersonations, energetic performances, and irreverent comic sensibilities proved enormously appealing to critics and audiences alike. I have been fortunate enough to see each of Leguizamo's solo shows, and each time the audience response was among the most enthusiastic I have seen in the theatre. These earlier shows established Leguizamo's artistic career. Second, Leguizamo's emerging celebrity in the 1990s as a film actor in such popular films as *To Wong Foo, Thanks for Everything! Julie Newmar*, and *William Shakespeare's Romeo and Juliet*, had secured enough name recognition for producers to support his performance projects in the hope of acquiring a crossover mainstream audience and turning a healthy profit. Leguizamo's appeal enabled him to sustain a Latino audience while developing a diverse non-Latino fan base. And third, by 1998, Leguizamo was in a position to finance much of his own theatre projects.

Yet none of these factors guarantee success. A main reason for Legui-

30. Promotional coupon for John Leguizamo's *Freak* on Broadway, 1998. Collection of the author

zamo's commercial success had to do with *Freak*'s marketing and outreach efforts to Latino audiences. Leguizamo's advertising campaign extended into new markets outside of Manhattan and included discounted offers in alternative media. Ads for the production appeared regularly on New York City's Spanish radio stations, and discounted coupon flyers were distributed throughout downtown venues and Latin clubs throughout the city (figure 30). Tickets for the price of $17.50 were made available for a third of the seats in the theatre. (The highest ticket price, for advanced-sale, nondiscounted orchestra seats, was $55, but even these seats were made available for $35 throughout the run.)[17] These efforts rendered Latinos an estimated average of 75 percent of Leguizamo's audience.[18] The early outreach to Latino audiences led to strong word of mouth, the free publicity Broadway needs to survive. Leguizamo wanted to allow his audiences to see his show in the way that they might go to see a movie—impulsively and spontaneously and with minimal advance planning. He encouraged walk-up sales and offered various incentives for people to come to the box office the day of the performance. So one way to answer the question of what *Freak* tells us about contemporary Latino life and culture is that contrary to conventional wisdom, Latinos will come to Broadway if the work on stage speaks to them and is made accessible to them.

While these external politics of Leguizamo's *Freak* unsettle preconceptions of Broadway demographics, as well as standard models of Broadway operations, the performance's internal politics concentrates on challenging certain foundational tropes of Latino culture. *Freak*, according to Leguizamo, is a "Semi-Demi-Quasi-Pseudo Autobiography." It tells the story of Leguizamo and his immigrant family, who left Colombia "during the big plantain famine of the late sixties"[19] when he was five years old. *Freak* focuses on Leguizamo's youth and adolescence, in this sense working as a performative *bildungsroman*. We thus witness Leguizamo's coming of age as an artist and as a Latino. *Freak* therefore also constitutes a memory play, a work that revisits the past in order to understand the present, and it is composed of a series of recollections of his childhood, youth, and adolescence. He performs earlier versions of himself, these scenes bringing the audience back in time to relive these earlier moments in his life. But Leguizamo also performs a roster of remembered characters drawn both from three generations of his family and from the diverse ethnic and racial populations of New York City. Much of the performance tracks the disintegration of Leguizamo's immediate family (composed of his two parents and younger brother), especially the deteriorating state of his parents' marriage. His father Fausto, an abusive patriarch whose familial rule terrorizes the rest of the family, features prominently in *Freak*, functioning as the source of much of the dramatic tension that fuels the play. The rest of the family is always trying to dodge the father's fury, which ignites often and with little provocation. Fausto's wife and sons must endure the husband and father's rage even as they plot means to escape it.

Leguizamo's hyperbolic performance of his father's tyranny is meant, of course, to be humorous. But it also communicates a deep ambivalence about the organizing principle of traditional Latino life, the family. In Leguizamo's world, family is neither the idealized site where he finds respite and comfort from the difficulties of daily life nor is it the reproductive site where Latino culture passes from one generation to another. In this sense, *Freak* departs from the standard literature by and about Latinos. From the creative to the sociological, from the spiritual to the economic, from the popular to the elite, literature by, for, and about Latinos tends to place the traditional biological family at the heart of Latino life. As Arlene Dávila points out, this idea of the centrality of Latino family lies at the heart of Latino marketing and advertising and forms the dominant trope for successful commercial campaigns for Latino consumerism. Despite major shifts in marketing budgets, outreach efforts, and even representational images of the traditional family over time, Dávila writes, "What has nonetheless remained consistent is the use of the family to communicate a range of values that are supposedly associated with Hispanics."[20] The family serves as a representational shorthand for tradition, spirituality, and communal solidarity. It also, as a result, discourages any form of individualism. *Freak*'s refusal to recycle these tropes given their economic success in mainstream Latino markets further removes it from the business-as-usual of Latino commercial culture.

Even among the most progressive of Latino cultural artists, this conservative notion of the centrality of the family seems inescapable. "Blood is thicker than water, family is greater than friends, and the Virgin Mary watches over all of us," chants Luis Alfaro, the Chicano poet, performer, and 1997 MacArthur fellow, in *Downtown*, his lyrical auto-performance of growing up in Los Angeles's Pico-Union district. Alfaro links the bonds of family to the bonds of Catholicism for the immigrant imaginary when he recalls how the haunting words of his family elders have now become his own despite his own reluctance to adopt them.[21] Alfaro presents this invocation of the family bond's hegemony as nearly inevitable. The family remains so deep rooted in the Latino psyche that its force cannot be constrained, regardless of one's own position within it. Alfaro gives voice to this prevalent theme in the literature by and about Latinos.

Like any other ideological framework, the preservation of the family as a system of normativity is ensured by its continued reinscription. We see this play out regularly in the national political arena. Let me cite two contemporaneous examples, the heated debates around Elian Gonzalez, the young Cuban boy whose question of citizenship became played out as a family drama, and the ongoing recruitment of Latino voters by the Republican party under the banner of "family values."[22] Let me also cite, however, what is missing in these representations of Latino life: the new social formations of queer Latinos, who have embarked on creative reimaginings of kinship, and the new social alliances of Latino migrant cultures, which have forged new models of community in response to the pressures of transnational economies and globalization.

Unlike other contemporary Latino writers who set out to recover the family model by exposing its dysfunction, Leguizamo's critique does not invest in the possibility of the family's rehabilitation. Consider, for example, the important writings of someone as critical of traditional family structures as Cherríe Moraga, whose efforts to "make *familia* from scratch"[23] are beautifully realized throughout her work. From *Giving up the Ghost*, her earliest play to *Hungry Woman: Mexican Medea*, one of her more recent pieces, to *Waiting in the Wings*, her stunning memoir of queer motherhood, Moraga's dramaturgy and prose sets out to expose the political and ideological structures of the family unit so that they might be reconfigured to improve the living conditions of all its members, especially those of women. As Yvonne Yarbro-Bejarano so astutely writes in her comprehensive study of Moraga's writings, Moraga's dramaturgy "is the vision of a theatrical practice that must delve into the festering places of Chicano culture in order to cure them."[24] The traditional family is one such festering place. In *The Last Generation*, Moraga writes, "Since lesbian and gay men have often been forced out of our blood families, and since our love and sexual desire are not housed within the traditional family, we are in a critical position to address those areas within our cultural family that need to change."[25]

Statements such as this reveal the political investments many progressive Latinos hold in sustaining the structure of the family despite the emotional costs of those "forced out," a rejection that often leaves the person vulnerable to violence, trauma, and even death. It also leads critics to romanticize the family as a site of utopic possibility. In a recent essay on Moraga's theatre, Tiffany Ana Lopez claims that while Moraga's plays are striking critiques of the family, her Chicana characters search to re-create the most fruitful emotional properties of the family, yet she/they also simultaneously engage in the process of "making" something else. Moraga's project acknowledges that family fulfills important emotional needs and, significantly, stands as a master narrative of most, if not all, social relationships. Therefore, one should not dismiss the family as an important model of community; one should instead think of it more in terms of *negotiation* and draw upon those aspects that are powerful and do work, even while discarding what is limiting and does not translate into the imagining of community as a place of liberation for *all* of its members.[26]

I quote extensively here from Lopez's account because it articulates a clear sense of this issue as it often appears in contemporary Latino cultural productions and because it foregrounds the complicity of critics who continue to invest in "master narratives" of family even as they seem to challenge them. Lopez's account also helps me differentiate the work of Leguizamo from this tradition. Even if we agree with Chicano theatre scholar Jorge Huerta's assertion that family relationships are a "recurring theme in most immigrant dramas"[27] and that dysfunctional families are themselves the norm in all plays about the family—or, as Huerta puts it, "any attempt to find a Latino play about a 'functional family' will prove futile"—Leguizamo's play marks a striking departure from the conventional representation of the Latino family.[28]

In *Freak*, familial dysfunctionality does not become exposed so that the family might rehabilitate itself or heal; rather, familial dysfunction in *Freak* is represented as that which enables the rejection of the family unit. *Freak* not only models how one might reject the family; it goes so far as to represent that rejection as a mark of power. At one moment in the play, for example, young John's mother leaves her abusive marriage to Fausto in a scene presented as her moment of triumph, of liberation even, from the constraints of the family's heteronormative structure. "'Cause I'm not about reproduction anymore, I'm about me-production," she declares to Fausto as she leaves after a particularly violent eruption. "Don't confuse the end of your world with the beginning of mine. I have awakened . . . I'm freaking out."[29] Tellingly, she describes her rebellion, freakish within the context of the traditional family, as "freaking out." While her husband thinks she is having a nervous breakdown, she brilliantly reprimands him: "No, Fausto, I'm having a breakthrough."[30]

In Leguizamo's world, the broken nuclear family does not represent a negative value; women and children benefit from its demise. In *Freak*, Leguizamo performs the breakdown of the traditional biological family; furthermore, by representing that break in his show, Leguizamo goes against the dominant representations of Latino culture. This double move begins to call into question the normative structures of Latino life and culture. With the critique of Latino patriarchy and the representation of the disintegration of the nuclear family, *Freak* opens up a space for other forms of Latino belonging to surface. If the family, traditionally seen as the place where ethnicity is constituted and validated, now fails young John, what other means become available to him? Where else might he look for a sense of what it means to be Latino?

While Leguizamo's focus on the failure of the family unit marks the primary narrative of the play, *Freak* includes two short scenes that invoke a different genealogy. Here, Leguizamo introduces performance and its history as a viable site for Latino cultural identity. The scenes introduce an alternative genealogical system based on a history of pan-Latino performers whose Latino difference marked them in their historical moments as what we might call freaks. This lineage—which includes Desi Arnaz, Rita Moreno, and Cheech Marin of Cheech and Chong—refers to Latino entertainers who paved a way for the Leguizamo we are watching perform on Broadway; they are who we might call his artistic ancestors, whose struggle against institutional racism in the performing arts informs and enables Leguizamo's own. This move from the domestic sphere to the public sphere not only shifts the play's emphasis but it enables Leguizamo to foreground one of *Freak*'s main themes. The performing arts, in Leguizamo's worldview, are a lifeline.

Young John is initiated into this alternative model of identification and community by his uncle Sanny, who, because of the various pressures in John's family, has become what young John calls his "surrogate moms." Sanny is somewhat of a freak himself. As Leguizamo explains: "Now my uncle Sanny was a little unconventional. He was what you'd call a triple threat: Latin, gay, and deaf."[31] Still, John connects with his uncle: "I loved him and I told him so," he reminisces in a surprising tribute to what Eve Kosofsky Sedgwick calls "queer tutelage," the under-theorized and undervalued role of queer aunts and uncles in the formative years of children.[32] Sanny's experience of difference forces him to find other models of affiliation outside the structure of the Latino family unit. In a revealing short scene, uncle Sanny locates himself in a historical lineage outside of the biological. "I know your father doesn't respect me," he explains to young John, "but that's bullshit. Because feature this: many highly respectable individuals of ancient and modern times have been homosexuals: Plato, Michelangelo, Disney."[33] Uncle Sanny's comments suggest the possibility of different forms of self-understanding drawn from history and popular culture, a possibility that John begins to formulate for himself. Even though John does not want to become his uncle completely—"I wanna grow up and be just like you, uncle Sanny, except for the liking men part"[34]—he admires Sanny's ability to stand up to his father and Sanny's ability to find other sources of inspiration and identification outside of conventional structures. In citing Plato, Michelangelo, and Disney, Sanny links himself to what might be called a queer genealogy, a genealogy structured not by accurate historical knowledge but by an imagined lineage of homosexual heroes, however unconventional or ridiculous.

John's opportunity to become just like his uncle "except for the liking men part" begins, somewhat reluctantly, at the theatre. It turns out that uncle Sanny has a habit of sneaking young John into Broadway shows so that Leguizamo can, in Sanny's telling phrase, "get culture." Sanny ushers John into these shows moments before the production's second act, just as the paying audience returns to their seats after the intermission. During one of these ritual "second-acting" adventures, John discovers a new world of possibility. In the performance of this scene, he moves from the Cort's stage and climbs up into the box seats on the upper left of the theatre. He takes the place of one of his own spectators and sits in the audience holding a program, as if he were a spectator to his own show. He then continues his performance from the box seat, resuming his portrayal of his younger self at the theatre with uncle Sanny and his younger brother.

I wasn't sitting with anyone I knew and I'm ascared of being clocked and I'm peeping at this ridiculous musical *Chorus Line* thing when I hear somebody called Morales on stage. There was a Latin person in the show. And she didn't have a gun or hypodermic needle in her hand and she wasn't a hooker or a maid and she wasn't servicing anybody so it was hard to tell if she was Latin and everybody's respecting her and admiring her . . . I was lost in this amazing moment, singing along as loud as I could. Then I felt a hand grab me and I was yanked up out of my seat by one of those Pilgrim ladies and beat with the flashlight. My brother got caught, too, 'cause he was still smoking his Kools, and Sanny got busted, 'cause he was lip-syncing along too loudly. And I'm still like, "she's singing to me, she's singing to me!" And Uncle Sanny's yelling, "shut the hell up and run! Run!" And that's how I got culture.[35]

Leguizamo here describes the "amazing moment" in *A Chorus Line* (1975) when the character Diana Morales sings her introductory solo "Nothing." "Nothing" tells the story of Morales, the young enthusiastic Puerto Rican acting student who feels "nothing" when asked to improvise a "bobsled ride in the snow" in one of her acting classes. "Maybe it's genetic, they don't have bobsleds in San Juan," she explains. She is taunted by other students for her inability to perform the improvs— "they called me nothing . . . they called me hopeless."[36] In a manner of speaking, she is, in this context, a "freak." Her teacher's pedagogy is, as Morales sings, "bullshit," and rather than succumbing to the oppressive conditions around her, and after praying to the Virgin Mary for support, she quits. Morales is, as Alberto Sandoval-Sánchez explains, "conscious of how mainstream culture objectifies her and how she is represented as an exotic 'other.' "[37] Her resistance to this objectification forms the basis of her character, and it enables her to succeed on her own terms in the end.

It proves significant that Leguizamo cites *A Chorus Line* as one of the transformative experiences of his adolescence. *A Chorus Line*, conceived, choreographed, and directed by Michael Bennett, stands as one of the most critically and commercially successful productions in the history of Broadway. It opened on July 25, 1975, at the Shubert Theatre and ran for 6,137 performances before closing on April 28, 1990. The book of the musical focuses on a group of young actors auditioning for a part in the chorus line of a new Broadway musical, and we watch them as they compete for these parts. Only eight actors—four men and four women of the more than twenty actors featured—will make the final cut. *A Chorus Line* is remarkable for many reasons, including the little-discussed fact that the musical features a strikingly racially diverse cast, including two principle Latino roles. There is Paul, a Puerto Rican dancer who after falling and sustaining an injury in rehearsals cannot be cast, and Diana Morales, his friend, who will succeed. The structure of the musical requires that each of the characters auditioning for the chorus perform a solo, which might be a dance, a song, or a monologue. They take turns stepping out from the audition line to introduce themselves to each other and, by extension, to the audience. Young John is transfixed by the character of Morales and her story. Here is her solo (figure 31), which Leguizamo inserts into *Freak*:

DIANA: So excited because I'm gonna go to the High School of Performing Arts! I mean, I was dying to be a serious actress. Anyway, it's the first day of acting class—and we're in the auditorium and the teacher, Mr. Karp . . . Oh, Mr. Karp . . . Anyway, he puts us up on the stage with our legs around each other, one in back of the other and he says: "Okay . . . we're going to do improvisations. Now, you're on a bobsled. It's snowing out. And it's cold . . . Okay . . . Go!"

(The line people back up, run offstage left. DIANA *sings)*

Ev'ry day for a week we would try to feel the motion, feel the motion, down the hill. Ev'ry day for a week we would try to hear the wind rush, hear the wind rush, feel the chill. And I dug right down to the bottom of my soul to see what I had inside. Yes, I dug right down to the bottom of my soul and I tried, I tried.

(Speaking)

And everybody is going "whoooshhh, whoooshhh . . . I feel the snow . . . I feel the cold . . . I feel the air." And Mr. Karp turns to me and says, "Okay, Morales. What did you feel?"

(Sings)

And I said . . . "Nothing, I'm feeling nothing." And he says "Nothing could get a girl transferred." They all felt something, but I felt nothing except the feeling that this bullshit was absurd.

(Speaking)

But I said to myself, "Hey, it's only the first week. Maybe it's genetic. They don't have bobsleds in San Juan."

(Sings)

Second week, more advanced and we had to be a table, be a sports car . . . ice-cream cone. Mr. Karp, he would say, "very good, except Morales. Try, Morales, all alone." So I dug right down to the bottom of my soul to see how an ice-cream felt. Yes, I dug right down to the bottom of my soul and I tried to melt. The kids yelled "Nothing!" They called me "Nothing!" and Karp allowed it, which really makes me burn. They were so helpful. They called me hopeless. Until I really didn't know where else to turn.

(Speaking)

And Karp kept saying, "Morales, I think you should transfer to Girls' High. You'll never be an actress. Never!" *Jesus Christ!*

(Sings)

Went to church, praying, "Santa Maria, send me guidance, send me guidance," on my knees. Went to church, praying, "Santa Maria, help me feel it, help me feel it. Pretty please!" And a voice from down at the bottom of my soul came up to the top of my head. And the voice from down at the bottom of my soul, here is what it said: "This man is nothing! This course is nothing! If you want something, go find a better class. And when you find one you'll be an actress." And I assure you that's what finally came to pass. Six months later I heard that Karp had died. And I dug right down to the bottom of my soul . . . and cried, 'cause I felt . . . nothing.

(Speaking)

I mean, I didn't want him to die or anything, but . . .[38]

31. "Nothing," Priscilla Lopez as Diana Morales in the original Broadway production of *A Chorus Line*, New York City, 1975. Photo by Martha Swope

Morales's solo returns her to a difficult moment in her past, one she has overcome but not without some struggle. The story that she tells captures her at an age more or less the same as that of young John. Moreover, at the time that he is watching her perform, he occupies more or less the same psychic space as Morales did at that time. Both need to find a way to survive tyrannical male figures of authority whose power seems inevitable and unsurpassable.

Morales's story, however, will end in triumph. The young Latina who felt nothing, and who was so discouraged by her teacher that she dropped out of the High School of the Performing Arts, has been called back to audition for the chorus of a Broadway show. By the end of *A Chorus Line*, she will be one of the few actors who actually make the final cut. Her performance is meant to affirm Latino identity in the midst of its denigration.

Young John, watching this performance in the theatre, is transformed by this moment and in his enthusiasm confuses the role for the actor. Morales is, after all, a fictional character, even if her story is based on the personal experiences of Priscilla Lopez, the original Broadway cast member who first performed the role. In fact, fifteen different actors performed the role on Broadway during its long run, and it remains unclear which of these actors young John watched perform at the time. Nonetheless, Morales's determination, and presumably the actor's convincing performance of it, pushes young John to cheer her on in a moment of cultural identification, when he "gets culture." The phrase *gets culture* does double work in this scene: it refers to a poor immigrant youth's exposure to the arts, but it also refers to his introduction to a Latino cultural lineage outside of the constraints of the family.

Watching the Latina actor perform Morales in *A Chorus Line* provides John the means to imagine for himself a life in the theatre. Inspired by Morales, he decides to become an actor. In the scene where he describes his experience of Morales, he makes much of the fact that "she didn't have a gun or a hypodermic needle in her hand and she wasn't a hooker or a maid," the predominant representations of Latinos in popular culture. But it is also worth mentioning that she was not a mother, daughter, or wife either, that she was not represented as playing any of the conventional roles that Latinas are imagined to occupy within Latino culture. The fact that Morales is an actor is central to the point. We learn nothing about her background other than that she struggled to become an actor; we see her only in relationship to her artistic peers.

By the end of *A Chorus Line*, in fact, it is Morales, the Puerto Rican, who advocates most articulately for the theatre in the showstopping number "What I Did for Love" (figure 32). Morales leads the ensemble in this song about the risks of a life in the theatre where some are cast and some are not, and no one is guaranteed success. You do it, as Morales sings, without regret and for the love of it:

> Kiss today goodbye
> The sweetness and the sorrow
> Wish me luck, the same to you,
> But I can't regret
> What I did for love, what I did for love.[39]

Morales voices this sentiment, she is the actor most aligned with this notion of a life dedicated to the theatre. After this number, the actors learn their fate. In a dramatic turn, Morales is first named in the group that seems destined to be cast, only to be asked immediately to step back into the line. The director invites eight actors to step forward into this front line. But, in fact, the front line constitutes the group that has been eliminated. Thus Morales makes the cut and is successfully cast in the chorus of the upcoming Broadway musical.

Morales embodies the sense of perseverance and resilience that lies at the heart of *A Chorus Line*, which is why Leguizamo focuses on Morales exclusively in *Freak* and makes no mention of Paul, the gay Latino dancer, whose story arguably stands as the centerpiece of the musical. In his monologue, Paul conveys the hardships he faced as an effeminate gay Latino teenager who holds an intense identification with Cyd Charisse: He drops out of school and finds work as a dancer in Manhattan's queer club scene. He auditions for the Jewel Box Revue, a drag show, and is cast as a girl (figure 33).

> PAUL: Well, I was finally in show business. It was the asshole of show business—but it was a job. . . . Nothing to brag about. I had friends.

32. (opporite) "What I Did for Love," Priscilla Lopez, Kelly Bishop, and cast members of *A Chorus Line* in the original Broadway production, New York City, 1975. Photo by Martha Swope

33. (this page) "Paul's Monologue," Sammy Williams in the original Broadway production of *A Chorus Line*, New York City, 1975. Photo by Martha Swope

But after a while it was so demeaning. Nobody at the Jewel Box had any dignity and most of them were ashamed of themselves and considered themselves freaks. I don't know, I think it was the lack of dignity that got to me, so I left. Oh, I muddled around for a while. I worked as an office boy, a waiter—But without an education, you can't get a good job. So, when the Jewel Box called and asked if I'd come back, I went.

We were working the Apollo Theatre on a Hundred and Twenty-Fifth Street. Doing four shows a day with a movie. It was really tacky. The show was going to go to Chicago. My parents wanted to say good-bye and they were going to bring my luggage to the theatre after the show. Well, we were doing this oriental number and I looked like Anna May Wong. I had these two great big chrysanthemums on either side of my head and a huge headdress with gold balls hanging all over it. I was going on for the finale and going down the stairs and who should I see standing by the stage door . . . my parents. They got there too early. I freaked. I didn't know what to do. I thought to myself: "I know, I'll just walk quickly past them like all the others and they'll never recognize me." So I took a deep breath and started down the stairs and just as I passed my mother I heard her say, "Oh, my God." Well . . . I died. But what could I do? I had to go on for the finale so I just kept going. After the show I went back to my dressing room and after I finished dressing and taking my makeup off, I went back down stairs. And there they were standing in the middle of all these . . . And all they said to me was please write, make sure you eat and take care of yourself. And just before my parents left, my father turned to the producer and said: "Take care of my son . . ." That was the first time he ever called me that . . . I . . . ah . . . I . . . ah. (He breaks down.)[40]

Paul's story is based on the real-life experiences of Nicholas Dante, one of the cowriters of the musical's book. His story is one of the earliest sympathetic portrayals of homosexuality on Broadway, and one of the very few representations of a queer Latino in Broadway's history. Paul's story constitutes the longest narrative of *A Chorus Line* and as such manipulates the spectator to rally for his success.

Paul's knee injury during the auditions for the musical seals his fate. No matter how talented, since he is injured, he cannot be cast. His fall is heartbreaking to the other actors who recognize their own vulnerability in this scene. The audience, too, experiences Paul's fall as tragic. No longer able to dance, he holds little use value for the director of the upcoming musical and so must leave. But that seems little reason to cast him out of Leguizamo's show; Paul's story is also one of Latino resilience and triumph. Why then does Leguizamo fail to endorse Paul in his tribute to Latino performing artists? Dramaturgically, it would involve an excessive amount of plot explication to tell Paul's story in *Freak*. Unlike Morales, Paul does not sing; his solo is delivered as a monologue. He is also a dancer, which makes quoting him more difficult as well. Yet these reasons aside, I would argue that the main reason Paul does not appear in *Freak* is that Paul's story is antithetical to Leguizamo's own. While Paul's narrative even summons the language of freakery— "Most of them considered themselves freaks" and "I freaked"—in the end it represents a story of familial reconciliation, of paternal acceptance, and of the family's ability to absorb what it imagines as most abhorrent. The triumph of the narrative has little to do with Paul's artistry and everything to do with the father's unconditional love for the son. Leguizamo's narrative in *Freak* refuses to mirror this trajectory and chooses to follow Morales's track instead.

In the humorous and satiric scenes that follow the Morales scene in *Freak*, we see John, the emerging actor, rejected from the Juilliard School, harangued by the director Lee Strasberg, and insulted by various racist casting agents. His experiences as a Latino actor form much of the humor in the rest of the play. Leguizamo demystifies the romantic notion of the struggling artist by showing the humiliation he has had to endure to make it as a Latino actor. By the end of *Freak*, Leguizamo has himself become an actor struggling to resist, much like Morales, the demoralization that comes with performing Latino stereotypes. But unlike Morales, who had to make "something from nothing," John has Morales for his inspiration.

I think it is for this reason that the Morales scene makes for the only moment in *Freak* during which Leguizamo moves into the audience and sits among us. He once again becomes a spectator to Morales, the one character in *Freak* whom he does not impersonate. Her voice fills the Cort Theatre as it once did the Shubert Theatre those many years ago. As we watch Leguizamo recreate a formative moment of his past, we are invited to position our own spectatorship in relation to Leguizamo's model of Latino spectatorship at the performance of *A Chorus Line*. "She was singing to me!" he exclaims as he revels in the character of Morales, "She was singing to me!" Now, however, it is Leguizamo who is singing to us, and we are his audience. The theatre, he suggests, allows for this move from spectator to performer, from audience to stage. The theatre offers not simply a potential site for Latino community but a potential site of Latino continuity.

Significantly, the play ends with the reinvocation of Morales. After an unfortunate encounter with his father that replays the taunts of his childhood and that takes place in the backstage dressing room of a theatre, Leguizamo breaks away from the intrusive and ostensibly resurgent narrative of the Latino family. But first, the father mocks young John and compares him unfavorably to his new son:

> "Dad, Hey, Dad, waz up?" I hugged him. "It's great to see ya. You never returned my calls, never wrote, nothing. It's all right. I never took it personally. What brings you here?"

"My new kid wanted to see the show," he said.

"Oh," I said, disappointed.

"My junior is so much better looking and funny, more talented, more intelligent than you ever were. That's why he's the best in his acting class," Pops beamed proudly.[41]

This backstage dressing room scene can be read suggestively against the Latino father-and-son scene in *A Chorus Line*, and it even seems like a direct refusal of it. There is no reunion, no resolution, to the father-son conflict. Rather than ending with a scene of family reconciliation, Leguizamo ends *Freak* with a tribute to Latino popular culture. Just as the father can replace one son with another through the heteronormative reproductive mandate of Latino machismo, young John manages to situate himself in a Latino tradition not reliant on the patriarchal model of kinship.

In a moment unusual for its earnestness, Leguizamo cedes the stage to his other more inspirational kin, those prior Latino actors—the Puerto Rican, Chicano, and Cuban entertainers—who have come before him.

> And all of a sudden I allowed myself to want more for myself, to be more and do more, master of my own destiny, never wait for anyone, take life into my own hands, like my father had once wanted for me and like all the Morales, Morenos, Arnazs, Puentes, Cheechs and Chongs before me; who had to eat it, live it, get fed up with it, finesse it, scheme it, even Machiavelli it, to get out from under the ills that Latin flesh is heir to and who dug right down to the bottom of their souls to turn nothing into something. I dedicate this all to you.[42]

Leguizamo ends his performance by placing *Freak* in the context of this Latino performance tradition. In the end, Leguizamo dedicates his work to both genealogical systems, the biological and the artistic. After the dedication, the performance concludes with Leguizamo walking with his back to the audience and toward a blown-up black-and-white image of his father holding him as a young boy. These final moments beginning with the dedication and extending to the image remain without irony or humor. What are we to make of the photograph of John and his father that appears at the end of the performance? Is this not the very familial reconciliation that, as I have argued, *Freak* refuses? (I found myself troubled and confused by this final image—this apparent homage to the father whose tyranny John has sought to escape throughout the performance.) The image suggests to me Leguizamo's own coming to terms with a troubled father-son relation, an acknowledgment of the force of familial bonds in shaping one's identity. *Freak*, therefore, is not about the disavowal of the family. It is about generating alternative and more expansive models of Latino relations.

At the end of the performance, Leguizamo returns to the stage dancing energetically and humorously, clearly reveling in the audience's enthusiastic reception of his work. As house music fills the Cort, and with the audience on their feet, Leguizamo returns to center stage for his final curtain call, resorting to the Leguizamo persona who first greeted the audience at the beginning of his show. The photographic image of father and son near the end of the performance points to the biological, the necessary origins of a life. But the play ends not with this image, but with the artist dancing in front of his audience. Dance here becomes the integrative form that bridges the biological genealogy that brings forth the body with the alternative genealogy of the performing arts that brings forth the actor we have watched on the Cort stage. The earlier double ending—the textual dedication and the visual image—is integrated by the end through the performer's dancing body. As we leave the theatre, the image of Leguizamo's dancing form stays with us.[43] The image is celebratory, festive, and uplifting.

Unlike the familial, defined by those related by either blood or the law, the representational legacy that *Freak* proposes accommodates people from diverse cultural backgrounds who meet under the rubric Latino. *Freak* locates itself on an ongoing trajectory of Latino performance, a historical movement that, as we have seen, helps sustain Latino culture. In many ways, this transmission of cultural identity constitutes what *Freak* is about. Thus *Freak* not only houses the archives of previous mainstream Latino performances, such as that of Morales in *A Chorus Line*, but it enables Latinos to forge new means of understanding their own cultural identity based on these very performances. Leguizamo does not simply follow in the footsteps of prior Latino mainstream entertainers; he insists on making those past footsteps visible. The historical tracks of pan-Latino performance thus resurface in the public discourse of his work. In this sense, *Freak* is also about moving away from strictly nationalist cultural politics. "I don't like the separation that nationalism creates among us," Leguizamo states, preferring the alliances made possible by a pan-Latino cultural politics.[44]

Leguizamo, born in Colombia, barely mentions his nation of origin in *Freak*. According to the 1990 U.S. census, Colombians made up 5 percent of the Latino population in New York City. While Colombians ranked third in overall highest percentages of Latino New York, they lacked the cultural and political visibility of Puerto Ricans who comprised 46 percent of the population, and Dominicans who comprised 15 percent. The 2000 census, however, marks a shift. Increasingly, new immigrants from Central and South America, the Caribbean, and Mexico are settling in New York City. While important cultural differences remain between and among these various Latino groups, this " 'new,' post-Nuyorican Nueva York," as sociologist Juan Flores describes it, suggests the potential benefits for strategic pan-Latino group associations.[45] While Flores, for example, cites how in the past Latinos have secured a sense of solidarity through civic organizations, Spanish-language newspapers, and residential neighborhoods, what is different now, he argues, is "the discursive context, the sociohistorical climate in which the (self)-naming is enacted."[46] In other words, while the range of myths and anxieties about Latinos continues to incite familiar political anxieties in the areas of labor, immigration, and education, for example, the media coverage of these issues has also increased.

Latinos, Flores and others point out, are generating more national media attention than ever before. This late 1990s sociohistorical shift in the discursive practices by and about Latinos, however, often leaves unstated what is actually at stake for the implied normative Anglo subject, as well as for those identified as Latino or Hispanic. As Flores explains: "There is an assumption that the terms [Latino or Hispanic] refer to something real or in the making, whether a demographic aggregate, a voting bloc, a market, a language or cultural group, a 'community,' or . . . a 'condition.' Given the xenophobic tenor of mainstream politics in the 1990s, of course, which perceives 'Hispanic' and 'Latino' most of all as a 'problem,' such conceptions are all necessary and contribute to the social construction of a major group identity."[47]

The challenge for Latinos, then, is to consider what progressive possibilities might open up through pan-Latino coalitions, even as we consider the limitations of such idealizations of a Latino group identity. "There is no pan-ethnic Latino identity as such," writes Román de la Campa, "and national origin will always remain crucial in any grouping of this so called 'minority.' But its presence as an identifiable entity in the United States does emerge in certain contexts, when its intrinsic diversity is fused together as a differential 'other.'"[48] This pan-Latino presence, no doubt, takes many forms, as Latino scholars and critics have recently demonstrated to great effect. But as Arlene Dávila argues in *Latinos, Inc.*, her important study of Latino media and marketing, increasingly the commercial arena—corporate markets, mainstream media, and consumer culture—becomes a primary site for debating Latino "social identities and public standing." But other commercial sites exist for this debate as well, some of them perhaps unlikely, and, as in the case of Broadway, places that have remained unexplored.

Mainstream popular culture—let alone Broadway—would not seem to be the first place one would look to find the presence of a pan-ethnic Latino identity, nor would it seem to be the site for a progressive Latino cultural politics. But from its innovative marketing and generous outreach to its critique of Latino stereotypes and its celebration of Latino popular culture, Leguizamo's *Freak* embodies and performs this new Latino cultural politics. If Leguizamo's work does cross over, the crossover is not simply about a Latino performer succeeding on Broadway, or about white audiences attending his show. It is also about Latinos from all national backgrounds crossing over from Queens, Brooklyn, the Bronx, and elsewhere to arrive on Broadway and claim their seats at his performance.

Freak fully participates in a discursive shift, and it stands as one of the most forceful and productive articulations of a pan-Latino affiliation. Leguizamo's critical and commercial success on this front seems all the more remarkable. And yet, I would argue, *Freak* does more. By forwarding new models of kinship and identification, Leguizamo challenges the normative impulses embedded in Latino culture, impulses that presume the centrality of the biological family model for the Latino imaginary.[49]

While some Latino critics might take issue with Leguizamo's performance—that it reifies traditional Latino sex and gender systems, that it panders to a crossover audience, that it traffics in ethnic stereotypes—these critiques miss out on what I find useful in this work.[50] I do not wish to dismiss these critiques; I believe they provide a necessary interrogation of what is at stake in contemporary Latino cultural production. Leguizamo cannot remain exempt from critique, but to focus solely on the above concerns seems a disservice both to his work and to his audiences. Nonetheless, whatever the force of these charges, they do not, by any means, exhaust the possibilities of how we might think about Leguizamo's work or what his work might tell us about contemporary Latino life.

Leguizamo's performance reconstitutes the contemporary as a critical temporality that Latinos can recast on their own terms, and it reimagines the commercial as a contested site that Latinos should not cede to others. Leguizamo's version of the contemporary also insists on a historical move to affirm previous performances that Latino scholars have overlooked as sites of affinity and possibility. This scholarly neglect obscures an archive of performances that, as Leguizamo demonstrates, does more than simply represent examples of Latino resilience in a national culture of discrimination and bias. The Latino archive embodied in Leguizamo's performance promotes a legacy showcasing the vital role of the popular performing arts.

The next two chapters—on female celebrity and impersonation and on cabaret performance and American popular song—extend and expand this emphasis on the contemporary's archive and address the ways that performance itself can be imagined as an archival practice. Like Leguizamo's tribute to pan-Latino cultural history, these chapters highlight the locations in which the significance of the performing arts are themselves preserved. But, as we shall see, this archival turn does much more than simply recuperate a lost tradition; it shapes the contemporary as a critical space invoking a cultural repository of alternative sites of knowledge production and collective belonging.

CHAPTER FOUR

Archival Drag; or, the Afterlife of Performance

Official archives are understood as the repositories of a national culture. It is here, presumably, that the documents central to the formation and promotion of the nation are housed. As such, they constitute the nation's official memory, the site where the story of the nation can be retrieved and retold. Archives house the records of the past, catalogue the traces of this history, and preserve them for posterity. In her 2001 book *Dust: The Archive and Cultural History*, cultural historian Carolyn Steedman suggests that

> a prosaic definition [of the archive] is useful; a definition that for the moment, is not about analogies and does not involve questions of meaning, that understands it simply as a name for the many places in which the past (which does not now exist, but which once did actually happen; which cannot be retrieved, but which may be represented) has deposited some traces and fragments, usually in written form. In these archives someone (usually from about 1870 onwards, across the Western world) has catalogued these traces.[1]

And yet archives, as Steedman writes throughout her project, do in fact reveal the operations of state power and authority through the choices made about inclusion and exclusion of documents and by the system of classification and display used to make these materials intelligible as evidence of lives lived. As various scholars have argued, archives and archival conventions are deeply politicized sites of contestation. Rather than imaging archives as the place where historians can get the facts and learn of the past, cultural theorists should consider, as Ann Laura Stoler puts it, "archives not as sites of knowledge retrieval but of knowledge production."[2] Stoler's insistence that we contemplate the ideological underpinnings of traditional archives and the systems they employ to catalogue information pushes us to challenge the impulse toward documentation in the first place. She begs the question: can there be an archival practice that alters the dominant tendencies of the official archive, which tend to be positivist narratives of the nation-state? Stoler recommends that we read the archive against the grain, that is to say, rather than abandoning the archive, we should approach it with a certain critical scrutiny, one that resists the seductive draw of facts, evidence, and knowable plots. "To understand an archive," she writes, "one needs to understand the institutions that it served."[3]

Performance studies has long engaged the archival question, a question of enormous interest to the field, especially given the pressures and constraints on live performance to constitute itself as permanent. Traditional theatre historians, for example, have done the important work over the years of reconstructing the theatrical past by mining official archives for traces of performance history. More recently, scholars in performance studies have taken on the charge of performance's impermanence in debates that have invigorated the field and generated new critical paradigms. Some of this work has also linked these debates to critiques of the nation-state. Diana Taylor, for example, links the power of the official archive to modes of state power and colonial rule. In the *Archive and the Repertoire*, she differentiates between written and embodied history and proposes that the repertoire—as opposed to the archive, which relies more heavily on text culture—be understood as the means by which cultural meanings are expressed and passed on through embodied performance. "The repertoire," she writes, "enacts embodied memory: performances, gestures, orality, movement, dance, singing—in short, all those acts usually thought of as ephemeral, non-reproducible knowledge."[4]

Taylor's project focuses on the contested cultural memory of the Americas and is particularly concerned with the effects of colonialism and state power on practices of cultural memory. She asks: "What is at risk politically in thinking about embodied knowledge and performance as ephemeral as that which disappears? Whose memories 'disappear' if only archival knowledge is valorized and given permanence?" She argues that "there is an advantage to thinking about a repertoire performed through dance, theatre, song, ritual, witnessing, healing practices, memory paths, and the many other forms of repeatable behaviors as something that cannot be housed or contained in the archive."[5] This emphasis on the limits of the archive in preserving performance is in itself not new, but Taylor's refusal to mourn the failure of the archive departs from the sense that performance can only constitute a vanishing, a loss. Taylor's promotion of the repertoire not as the archive's antagonistic opposite, but as a separate repository of cultural memory, allows for that memory to be reembodied, reperformed, and thus restored. And while other scholars such as Joseph Roach and Marvin Carlson have written on this sense of performance's return—through surrogation, through haunted stages—Taylor builds on these ideas and links them more directly with the problem of the archive. The archive, as performance theorist Rebecca Schneider has written, "is habitual to Western culture."[6] Taylor's work sets out to break that habit; in doing so, it offers other sites of possibility for retrieving cultural memory. This work Taylor calls the "repertoire."

This chapter sets out to think through these issues of the archive as they relate to contemporary American performance. The question of the archive has been one of the book's primary concerns, beginning with the ways that choreographers with HIV constructed, to use Ann Cvetkovich's useful coinage, an "archive of feelings" around new modes of living with the disease in the mid-1990s, and including the ways that Asian American and Latino artists reconstructed a past through vernacular cultural practices and popular yet idiosyncratic entertainments.[7] As my earlier chapters have demonstrated, minoritarian groups posit a different relationship to archives because of their status as marginal or subcultural. Performance, I have argued, itself constitutes an embodied archival practice, whether it houses the body's own experience of itself, the rituals of Asian American cultural resilience, or an alternative genealogy of Latino belonging. Contemporary American performance has a history, and this history can be located in any number of cultural repositories.

Here now I am interested in contemporary performances that can be understood in the context of what Carolyn Dinshaw calls "a queer historical impulse," an impulse to make connections across time and to find the significant affinities between the past and the present that cannot be reduced to positivist notions of historical progress or causal relationships of cultural change.[8] Dinshaw's interest in cross-temporal connections or "touch," as she describes it, allows us to rethink the ways in which, and the reasons that, contemporary performance brings the past forward into the present. I am inspired by Dinshaw's queer historical impulse and adapt it here to rethink the work that the contemporary achieves, what it tells us about the archive and the national culture's investments in public memory.

Both Dinshaw and Taylor provide a framework for critically reassessing contemporary performance's relationship to history. This framework proves particularly helpful given Schneider's observation that within contemporary theatre, there has been "a return to history."[9] In this chapter I, too, take a historical turn and return to the question of the archive and performance's relationship to it. If earlier chapters began in the immediate contemporary before delving into the archive, this chapter reverses the chronology and begins in the past. I make this move so as to demonstrate the ways that history and the contemporary work both ways, as it were, in constituting themselves. That said, however, I want to showcase much more than just a theme in contemporary American performance; my interest in the historical and archival aspects of contemporary performance are meant to foreground a cultural politics around memory and belonging that performance offers. We have seen how this works in various subcultural and minoritarian communities, but here I wish to focus on another realm—the queer subcultural worlds of female impersonation, or what I call archival drag, a performance that sets out to reembody and revive a performance from the past. I begin in the eighteenth century with the female celebrity of Sarah Siddons, a figure integral to the English national culture as the leading tragedienne of her time. Siddons's reputation was secured primarily through her artistic craft rather than her life, although her life, too, was of much interest to her fans. By returning to the eighteenth century, we are also able to observe a moment when theatre and performance proved central to the national culture. This moment held great interest for two highly esteemed archival sites—the J. Paul Getty Museum and the Huntington Library Arts Collections and Botanical Gardens—which in 1999 set out to revisit Siddons and her milieu. The following section begins with a discussion of these contemporary exhibits and the impulses behind them, and then moves to identify other cultural practices that suggest a different model of archival production. Performance, I will argue, is one.

Let me state early on that I am less interested in reviving the celebrity of Sarah Siddons than in thinking through what her cultural afterlife might tell us about performance and its archives. The case of Siddons also provides entrance to questions about the nature of the contemporary and its relation to history. The historical appearance, disappearance, and reappearance of Siddons beget a series of questions that I address in the following pages and that I have addressed throughout the book: How might performance enable the transmission of cultural memory from one historical moment to another? In what ways might contemporary performances, especially those in popular culture, reembody once celebrated, though now obscure, moments in theatrical history? And what might this reembodiment tell us about the relationship between the present and the historical past?

These also range among the questions that guide Joseph Roach's influential study *Cities of the Dead: Circum-Atlantic Performance*, in which Roach touches on the different ways that ritual and performance serve as cultural memory. He writes that, "the social processes of memory and forgetting, familiarly known as culture, may be carried out by a variety of performance events, from stage plays to sacred rites, from carnivals to the invisible rituals of everyday life. To perform in this sense is to bring forth, to make manifest, and to transmit."[10] Roach's work informs my own exploration of memory and performance. And, as Roach makes clear, the idea of the archive is of central importance to this endeavor. Performance archives are generally assumed to be housed in museums or libraries, a presumption at the heart of the Siddons's revival at the Getty Museum and the Huntington Library. Roach, however, encourages theatre and performance historians to broaden their understanding of the archive, to see that other cultural forms and practices might also connect us to the theatrical past. By examining a wide range of cultural practices including theatrical and ritual performance, Roach demonstrates how such public events shape and inform our sense of history and tradition. In doing so, he calls into question the power of the written word as the primary authority on and documentary record of the cultural past. "Genealogies of performance," he writes, "attend to the 'counter-memories,' or the disparities between history as it is discursively transmitted and memory as it is publicly enacted by the bodies that bear its consequences."[11] Roach's methodologies and critical insights—along with Taylor's and Dinshaw's—open up avenues of critical investigation for studies of subcultures and their relations to the official archives of the hegemonic norm. These scholars model interdisciplinary comparative studies and demonstrate all that is to be gained by putting disparate historical events and cultural practices in critical conversation.

I will admit that the archive for this chapter is itself anachronistic, perverse, and unpredictable. It begins with a once famous eighteenth-century actress and ends with a discussion of two distinguished queer performance artists, Richard Move and John Kelly, whose recreations of Martha Graham and Joni Mitchell, respectively, are legendary among a particular subculture and, as we shall see, timely to us all. My phrase *archival drag* refers to the nature of contemporary performances that draw on historical reembodiment and expertise, as well as to the possible fatigue readers may face with yet another rumination on the archive or yet another on drag performance, let alone one on both of these well-rehearsed themes. But these topics remain rich in possibility, especially when put in conversation with each other.

THE AFTERLIFE OF SARAH SIDDONS

In 1999, the eighteenth-century British stage actress Sarah Siddons resurfaced in Southern California. Two exhibitions—*A Passion for Performance: Sarah Siddons and her Portraitists*, at the J. Paul Getty Museum, and *Cultivating Celebrity: Portraiture as Publicity in the Career of Sarah Siddons*, at the Huntington Library Art Collections and Botanical Gardens—showcased the figure of Siddons as she was portrayed and publicized in late-eighteenth-century London. Prior to Siddons's reemergence via these exhibitions and the media coverage they generated, I wonder whether the late-twentieth-century museumgoing public was familiar with Sarah Siddons's name and achievements.[12] If Siddons escapes immediate recognition in our contemporary moment, it is perhaps because the genres that made her famous in her day—tragic drama, portrait painting, and theatre criticism—no longer carry the same cultural weight that they held in eighteenth-century England. Can we name, for instance, a contemporary stage actress whose fame is based on the virtuosity of her stagecraft and who is known, as Siddons was, for portraying classic roles in theatre?

Siddons's celebrated performances of famous women—Lady Macbeth, Queen Katharine, Queen Elizabeth—in plays by famous men —Shakespeare, Dryden, Sheridan—made her one of the most talked-about women of her time. Her performances were legendary and engendered a fan base that cut across the class and regional divisions of eighteenth-century British life. Contemporary eighteenth-century scholars have written extensively about Siddons and her celebrity, especially regarding the effect of her artistry on audiences. Michael Booth says, for example, that "for one thing, it was difficult even to get into Drury Lane on the nights Mrs. Siddons was acting during that [1782–83] season. Box seats were virtually unobtainable, and large crowds rushed into the unreserved pit and galleries when the doors were opened."[13] Julie Ann Carlson notes that during the summer of 1784, " 'Siddons fever' was declared an official malady in Edinburgh and 'faintings and hysterics' became so 'commonplace' that Siddons grew accustomed to playing 'amidst shrieks and groans.' "[14] And Michael S. Wilson, in writing about the centrality of Siddons to eighteenth-century British life and culture, points out how most of the major figures of this period were implicated in the Siddons fervor. "Burke, Gibbon, Fox, Walpole, Windham, and Sheridan were usually in attendance on Siddons's opening nights," he writes. Clearly, Siddons and, by extension, the theatre itself, proved a significant cultural force of the time. Wilson goes on to foreground this point when he writes: "When the press could with little exaggeration report that 'on a Siddons night, Drury Lane looked more like a meeting of the House of Lords than a theatre,' and her benefit book was referred to as 'the Court Guide,' we must recognize that the actress was an integral part of the national life."[15]

The period's Siddons fever led to the commodification of Siddons and the dissemination of her image throughout the region. The art historian Heather McPherson makes this idea apparent when she writes:

> Beginning in the 1780s a veritable Siddons industry developed which diffused the actress's image through visual artifacts ranging from paintings and miniatures to crude, inexpensive popular prints and Prattware plates. While some drawings served as models for printmakers or preparatory studies, others were independent works or transcriptions of performances. Through the extraordinary range of images of Siddons, which cut across aesthetic and economic hierarchies, we can gauge Siddons's broader impact as a sociocultural phenomenon and aesthetic artifact. By the second half of the eighteenth century, actors had become well-known public figures who were painted by the leading artists and widely chronicled in the press. What sets Siddons apart from her contemporaries is the quality and range of images depicting her which testify to the cult she inspired.[16]

Siddons's popularity led to the creation of an unprecedented number of likenesses of her in the academic and popular worlds of visual culture. Michael Booth notes that the *Biographical Dictionary of Actors, Actresses, Musicians, Dancers, Managers, and Other Stage Personnel in London, 1660–1800* records "189 portrait paintings, drawings and engravings of Mrs. Siddons, and another 152 of her in stage roles with a further number of caricatures, busts, statues, models in wax, paintings on porcelain, engravings on glass, and a chess set with Siddons as the Queen."[17] Siddons's popularity in the period and the region secured her reputation as the greatest tragic actress of her day.

And yet Siddons's celebrity extended beyond her own historical moment and became iconic for later generations that inherited the legacy of eighteenth-century British theatre culture. The fame and reputation of Sarah Siddons were sustained by the power of eighteenth-century theatre criticism and portrait painting. William Hazlitt's much-cited assessment of Siddons's acting stands as both a monumental tribute to her and as one of the foundational texts of her celebrity: "We can conceive of nothing grander. It was something above nature. It seemed almost as if a being of superior order had dropped from a higher sphere to awe the world with the majesty of her appearance. Power was seated on her brow, passion emanated from her breast as from a shrine; she was tragedy personified."[18] In his extraordinary praise for the actress, Hazlitt inserts her into the realm of the mythic, if not the supernatural. In so doing, he contributes to the already legendary status of Siddons as the embodiment of theatrical grandeur and the power of tragedy.

In reading Hazlitt, we are reminded that we have no direct access to Sarah Siddons, the stage performer. We know Siddons today only as an image, or, rather, as a series of images and textual descriptions. The primary traces of Siddons's celebrated career are the visual likenesses of her captured by painters of her day and the textual accounts of her work and life by those, such as Hazlitt, who put them down in writing.[19] Siddons preceded the media on which celebrity now depends: photography, film, television, mass-market magazines, and, increasingly, the Internet.

The two 1999 Southern Californian exhibitions at the Getty and at the Huntington situated the figure of Siddons within the traditional archival settings of the museum and the library. These two established venues rank among the most exalted sites for the documentation, preservation, and display of the historical past. As such, they generate an enormous amount of recognition and prestige. In the case of Sarah Siddons, the nearly simultaneous exhibits at these formal and influential institutions secured Hazlitt's sense of Siddons as mythic, and of Siddons's career as exceptional. Yet the very nature of Siddons's celebrity prompts us to look elsewhere as well. Siddons formed as much a part of eighteenth-century's popular culture as of the period's high arts. Her legacy might also be housed elsewhere, outside of the official documentary systems of institutional settings such as the Getty or the Huntington. Performance constitutes an alternative archive in which the afterlife of Siddons appears palpable and present. Performance and its capacity to replay a repertoire of cultural practices enable a different critical genealogy in which Siddons's career and influence might be tracked.

While both of the Los Angeles exhibitions successfully showcased the visual and material culture of Siddons's historical period, they less successfully conveyed a sense of her theatrical achievement. The Getty seemed openly aware of this challenge and the desirability of capturing Siddons's brilliance as a performer; in an effort to meet the challenge, the museum commissioned a play on Siddons from the contemporary playwright Frank Dwyer. *The Affliction of Glory: A Comedy about Tragedy*, which ran concurrently with *A Passion for Performance*, highlights the tensions between the historical past and the contemporary moment, though it never quite resolves these tensions into a convincing drama. *The Affliction of Glory* focuses on a young couple—an actress and her actor boyfriend—who are themselves staging a play about Siddons and Sir Joshua Reynolds, a friend and also the painter of Siddons's most famous portrait. The actors were cast as both the historical figures and the contemporary characters. In the program note, Dwyer ponders the relationship between visual culture, lived experience, and the performing arts:

> We're all in motion—in play, as Sarah was—in alchemical process the opposite of Art, our Present becoming our Past. But tonight belongs to us, alive, our being alive heightened as we collaborate together at a play. In the theater we watch the Past become the Present as the Present becomes the Past; and perhaps, if we concentrate, Sarah Siddons may be lured out of her long retirement, may step down from one of her frames (which one, which is the best likeness?), and join us.[20]

Like the exhibition it accompanied, *The Affliction of Glory* reveals a great deal about Siddons and her milieu. Dwyer's comments in the program suggest that he and, presumably, the Getty hoped that the play might go further, that it might summon the individual magnetism and dramatic power of Siddons, what Hazlitt called her "majesty," for a late-twentieth-century audience. Dwyer hoped to revive the aura of Siddons through her own media: performance. His play was meant to put the contemporary in dialogue with the past and foreground that dialogue so that audiences might benefit from the exchange. Instead, *The Affliction of Glory* mainly offered the museum visitors that composed its primary audience another static representation of Siddons, albeit in a form different from that of the paintings in the Getty galleries. Yet even on the level of visual stagecraft, the play could not compete with the eighteenth-century oil paintings of Siddons on display in the museum. It remained unable to make relevant Siddons's career and life to contemporary audiences. The exhibition's paintings at least had the aura of Siddons's era engrained on the canvas. The play, however, nearly undermined the Getty's unspoken investment in high culture by calling into question the entire enterprise of showcasing Siddons in the first place. What was to be gained by these exhibits? What led the Getty—and the Huntington—to excavate Siddons for contemporary audiences? In part, the exhibition resulted from the interest of curators and conservators who felt that the Siddons paintings would benefit from study and treatment in the Getty's painting conservation studio. These museum officials also felt that the career of Siddons might in fact enlighten contemporary audiences on the fleeting nature of both celebrity and performance. Organizers commissioned the Dwyer play in part to make that point.

The primary means by which Siddons's celebrity persists is a 1784 portrait entitled *Sarah Siddons as the Tragic Muse* by Sir Joshua Reynolds (figure 34). The portrait presents Siddons, an actress who secured her reputation performing tragic roles, as Melpomene, the Tragic Muse of Greek mythology. Melpomene is one of the nine Muses, the Greek goddesses who preside over the arts and sciences and serve as the inspiration for those who toil in these arenas. The daughters of Zeus, king of the gods, and Mnemosyne, the goddess of memory, the Muses bestow the gift of talent and inspire artists to excel at their craft.[21] In Reynolds's portrait, Siddons is simultaneously the embodiment of Melpomene and a contemporary materialization of the Tragic Muse. On the one hand, Siddons merely assumes the classical guise of the Tragic Muse for the purposes of Reynolds's portrait. On the other, Siddons herself inspires her contemporaries—including Reynolds—in both the visual and the performing arts.

Even as he portrayed Siddons enthroned as the Tragic Muse, Reynolds also inscribed his own physical likeness onto the portrait. The shadowy figure bearing a chalice to the right of Siddons is based on

34. Joshua Reynolds (British, 1723–92), *Sarah Siddons as the Tragic Muse*, 1784, oil on canvas, 239.4 × 147.6 cm, Courtesy of the Huntington Library, Art Collections, and Botanical Gardens, San Marino, California. Photo: ©The Henry E. Huntington Library and Art Collections

a prior study, now in the collection of the Tate Gallery, that Reynolds had made of his own face earlier that year.[22] According to the art historian Jennifer Montagu, the figure in the portrait recalls not only Reynolds's self-portrait but also the seventeenth-century French painter Charles Le Brun's drawing of the passion of fear, one of the two emotions, along with pity, that Aristotle had associated with tragedy in his *Poetics*.[23] Given the self-possessed, nearly affectless pose of Siddons, the fact that Reynolds would fashion his own likeness into a personification of fear seems particularly striking.

Certainly, the associative link between portrait and painter, between Siddons and Reynolds, increased their respective celebrity. After the painting was exhibited at the Royal Academy of Arts in London, interest in Siddons was routed through Reynolds and vice versa. Siddons, for example, was well aware of the ways that visual media could serve as publicity for her career. As Heather McPherson argues in a fascinat-

35. Bette Davis as Sir Joshua Reynolds's Tragic Muse, Thirty-fifth Pageant of the Masters, Laguna Beach, 1957. Courtesy of Festival of the Arts, Laguna Beach, California

ing account of the traffic between eighteenth-century art, commerce, and celebrity, "From the outset of her career, Siddons was cognizant of the publicity value of images in the fiercely competitive public arena of the theater. In fact, it could be argued that images played an unprecedented role in establishing and maintaining her reputation as the preeminent tragédienne on the English Stage. Siddons, who was much in demand among fashionable painters because of her celebrity, stole as much time as possible to sit for pictures."[24]

Reynolds also seemed to recognize the advantage of painting Siddons for his own career. In 1782 he suffered a stroke and, as McPherson reports, "his artistic preeminence was coming increasingly under attack." She further claims that Reynolds's portrait of Siddons set out to "reclaim his own position at the center of the artistic stage by boldly asserting the aesthetic connection linking portraiture, the theater, and the tragic sublime in a stunning demonstration that subsumed his theories about grand manner painting."[25] As McPherson suggests, the reciprocal exchanges between painting and theatre in late-eighteenth-century culture benefited both artists. Not only did actors and painters set out to explore the interdisciplinary possibilities of aesthetic collaboration; they also set out to exploit the commercial linkage between these two cultural art forms.

The 1784 painting *Sarah Siddons as the Tragic Muse* secured the artistic reputations of Siddons and Reynolds and perpetuated their publicity beyond eighteenth-century British culture. The two 1999 Siddons exhibitions revisit the cultural landscape of Siddons and her milieu in order to reconsider the mechanisms of her celebrity and to recirculate that celebrity for new audiences. However, the circuits of Siddons's fame—and, by extension, of Reynolds's—are not confined to the museum, the rare book library, or other repositories of elite culture. Siddons's celebrity also survives within the archives of popular culture and performance. It is here that we can trace the afterlife of Sarah Siddons. If the Getty's official efforts to revive Siddons—especially through its commission of the Dwyer play—were unable to conjure Siddons, this does not mean that the project itself must prove an impossible one.

In 1957, for one night only, Bette Davis embodied Reynolds's *Sarah Siddons as the Tragic Muse* in the thirty-fifth Pageant of the Masters in Irvine, California (figure 35). The pageant, which is still mounted on an annual basis, recreates famous works of art as *tableaux vivants*—or "living pictures"—with live actors onstage depicting famous figures and scenes from the history of Western art.[26] The first incarnation of the Pageant of the Masters was a publicity stunt that formed part of the larger Festival of the Arts conceived in 1932 as a means to draw people to visit and support the Laguna art community during the difficult years of the Great Depression. Given the popularity of the *tableaux vivants*, the community of Laguna decided to mount the event as a full-fledged theatrical performance in 1935 under the vision and direction of Roy Rupp, who built sets, cast the actors, and selected the images to be presented. Generally, the cast was drawn from local actors and volunteers, but the case of Bette Davis proved especially unusual. In the 1950s, Davis lived close by and served as an occasional pageant volunteer. But she only appeared once on stage and that was for that one summer night in 1957.

In her performance as *Sarah Siddons as the Tragic Muse*, Davis did not impersonate Siddons, who Davis, of course, could never have met and whose performances Davis could not have seen. Instead, Davis impersonated the Reynolds portrait of Siddons, the prior—and celebrated— embodiment of the Tragic Muse. By this time the portrait no longer signified for viewers—or even for performers such as Davis—a personification of the Tragic Muse; the concept of the personification as understood centuries earlier was largely lost to twentieth-century audiences. In effect, Davis cited Siddons as a visual object, a painted portrait, which had in the century since her death become Siddons's most famous role.

The image of Bette Davis as *Sarah Siddons as the Tragic Muse* by Sir Joshua Reynolds calls attention to the various media involved in the cultivation of fame. If portrait painting served as the primary means in the eighteenth century of capturing Siddons's celebrity, Davis's embodiment of Siddons's Tragic Muse reminds us that performance was what lay at the heart of Siddons's fame. That is to say, Siddons was an actress before she was the subject of a painting. But if, as various scholars have argued, performances as such cannot but disappear because they are constitutionally ephemeral, where are we to find the archives of past performances?[27]

Davis's *tableau vivant* of 1957 sheds light on this very question since it brings to the fore both the archives of Siddons's celebrity and of its intrinsic instability. While Davis embodied a painting rather than a theatrical role made famous by Siddons, Davis, in a particularly uncanny tribute, may have inadvertently impersonated an actual Sarah Siddons performance. Consider that in November 1785, as part of the Drury Lane revival of David Garrick's *Shakespeare Jubilee* (1769), Siddons herself staged a *tableau vivant* of Reynolds's portrait.[28] At the 1957 Pageant of the Masters, Davis demonstrated how live performance remembers not only performances from an earlier historical moment but also the prior archives of those past performances. Nearly two hundred years later, one of the most distinguished actors of the twentieth century revived both Siddons performances. Just as Siddons had assumed the esteemed role of Tragic Muse for the 1780s, and in the process supplanted her old rival, Mary Ann Yates, who originated the role at the 1769 *Jubilee* at Drury Lane and who, according to Michael Wilson, "still had exclusive claims to be the symbolic role of Tragic Muse," Bette Davis assumed the role of Tragic Muse for the 1950s.[29]

Davis's revival of Siddons's portrait and *tableau vivant* at Drury Lane positions her in direct relation to Siddons, and it also links her with the historical convention of identifying the leading tragedienne actor of the day with the muse. Rather than insisting on performance's evanescence, then, we might want to consider the possibility that contemporary performances revive past performances while past performances are manifest in contemporary ones. In this way, performance might be said to serve as its own archive. Performance constitutes a means by which past performances are not just remembered but revived. In the case of Sarah Siddons, performance—and not the library or museum—is the place where the actor's celebrity was first located—and subsequently preserved and cultivated.

This idea that performance archives its own past stands as one of the running motifs of Marvin Carlson's important study titled *The Haunted Stage*. Here Carlson joins Roach, Taylor, and Schneider in exploring the ways in which performances, rather than disappear, might, in fact, remain. Carlson's contribution to this discussion focuses on the material conditions of the theatre. He demonstrates how theatre spaces, productions, texts, and actors are recycled into future theatrical performances that then ghost the contemporary performance. This haunting constitutes a form of cultural memory, and one we see performed in the American popular culture of the 1950s. While the juxtaposition of Siddons and Davis involves a complex interplay and exchange among different ages, media, and locations, Siddons nonetheless ghosts the celebrity of Davis in this period. Davis not only revives Siddons, but Siddons haunts one of Davis's most famous roles.

For fans of Bette Davis, the irony is that her 1957 portrayal of Reynolds's painting of *Sarah Siddons as the Tragic Muse* cites not only a Siddons performance but also one of Davis's most celebrated cinematic performances from her own archive. *All about Eve*, the 1950 Hollywood film directed by Joseph L. Mankiewicz, stars Davis as Margo Channing,

36. Eve receiving the Sarah Siddons Award for Distinguished Achievement. Film still from *All about Eve*, dir. Joseph L. Mankiewicz, 1950. Collection of the author

a famous and accomplished stage actress ultimately supplanted by Eve Harrington, an aspiring and manipulative younger actress. In the process of paying tribute to Siddons, *All about Eve* demonstrates how celebrity is partially secured by the performative citation of already famous people.

The film begins and ends at an awards ceremony. Eve, played by Anne Baxter, is receiving the Sarah Siddons Award for Distinguished Achievement in the Theatre (figure 36). The published screenplay of the film foregrounds the significance of the Sarah Siddons Award to the main story of *All about Eve*, which is primarily narrated by the theatre critic Addison DeWitt. Notice how the film begins with a detailed account of the award ceremony and how the camera spotlights the Sarah Siddons Award:

> FADE IN
>
> DINING HALL — SARAH SIDDONS SOCIETY — NIGHT
>
> It is not a large room and jammed with tables; mostly for four but some for six and eight. A long table of honor, for about thirty people, has been placed upon a dais.
>
> Dinner is over. Demi-tasses, cigars and brandy. The overall effect is one of worn elegance and dogged gentility. It is June.
>
> The CAMERA, as it has been throughout the CREDIT TITLES, is on a FULL CLOSEUP
>
> Of the SARAH SIDDONS AWARD. It is a gold statuette, about a foot high, of Sarah Siddons as "The Tragic Muse." Exquisitely framed in a nest of flowers, it rests on a miniature altar in the center of the table of honor.

Over this we hear the crisp, cultured, precise VOICE of ADDISON
DEWITT:

ADDISON'S VOICE

The Sarah Siddons Award for Distinguished Achievement is perhaps unknown to you. It has been spared the sensational and commercial publicity that attends such questionable "honors" as the
Nobel Prize—and those awards presented annually by that film society . . .

The CAMERA has EASED BACK to include some of the table of
honor and a distinguished gentleman with snow-white hair who is
speaking. He is a few years either side of 100. We do not hear what
he says.

ADDISON'S VOICE

The distinguished-looking gentleman is an extremely old actor.
Being an actor, he will go on speaking for some time. It is not important that you hear what he says.

The CAMERA EASES BACK some more, and CONTINUES until it dis-
closes a fairly COMPREHENSIVE SHOT of the room.

ADDISON'S VOICE

However, it is important that you know where you are, and why
you are here. This is the dining hall of the Sarah Siddons Society.
The occasion is its annual banquet and presentation of the highest honor our Theatre knows—the Sarah Siddons Award for Distinguished Achievement.[30]

The opening sequence continues in this fashion, cultivating the significance of the Sarah Siddons Award as it introduces the film's cast of
characters, all of which are affiliated with the world of the theatre. The
film is remarkable in its avid representation of the theatre as symbolic
and material cultural capital. It demonstrates the allure of the theatre as
a repository of cultural values signifying taste, intelligence, and class,
and it foregrounds the economic behind-the-scenes machinations that
make theatrical productions possible. The film also makes the remarkable assumption that the theatre had a central part in the national conversation. In representing the world of the theatre, the film positions
theatre as more than merely a site of cultural production. Theatre, the

37. The Sarah Siddons Award
for Distinguished Achievement.
Film still from *All about Eve*,
dir. Joseph L. Mankiewicz, 1950.
Collection of the author

film seems to argue, constitutes a place where the nation's central concerns might be addressed and debated.

In many ways, *All about Eve* represents one of the last moments of a golden age in American theatre history, capturing the immediate period before Hollywood cinema would usurp the role of Broadway in the national culture. For this reason, the resurgence of a once famous but now obscure eighteenth-century stage actress in a popular Hollywood film about postwar American theatre demands our critical attention.[31] The Sarah Siddons Award, as Addison DeWitt makes perfectly clear in the film's immediate opening lines, is "the highest honor our Theatre knows." In *All about Eve*, Sarah Siddons is meant to signify not simply artistic excellence but the very best of what the theatre represents to the larger culture.

The design of the Sarah Siddons Award, a statuette of Siddons in her pose as Tragic Muse, at once memorializes and miniaturizes the Reynolds painting, adding yet another level to the citational dimension of the film (figure 37). And yet there is more. At the time of the film, no such award for distinguished achievement in the theatre existed. *All about Eve*'s attention to Sarah Siddons inspired a group of theatre aficionados in Chicago to establish a Sarah Siddons Society. The society grants an annual award to an outstanding stage actress. Helen Hayes was the first to receive the award for her 1952 performance in *Mrs. McThing*, and the award continues to be bestowed on stage actresses to this day—*All about Eve*'s homage to Siddons materialized in an actual society and an annual ritual that recirculates Siddons's legacy for contemporary audiences.

And now back to Eve. The film moves from the opening sequence at the Sarah Siddons Awards ceremony to the backstory of how Eve arrived at this triumphant moment. This narrative of Eve's success composes the rest of the film except for the end, when we return to the awards ceremony for the film's conclusion. Eve begins as Margo's most devoted fan, but soon becomes her assistant, then her understudy, and finally Margo's rival. It is Eve, we must remember, who ultimately receives the Sarah Siddons Award. Not only does she receive the award but she receives it for a role originally intended for Margo. Yet it is Margo, Bette Davis's character, who holds the associative link with Siddons. Like Sarah Siddons, Margo Channing inspires fandom.[32] And both Siddons and Channing signify artistic virtuosity. The film secures the link between Siddons and Channing in the notorious "Fasten your seatbelts, it's going to be a bumpy night" party scene in which Eve's plot to become Margo's understudy is hatched. Margo begins to realize the extent to which by now Eve has already infiltrated the world that she, Margo, has built in order to sustain her own celebrity. This is a world composed not only of Margo's lover, friends, and assistants but also of theatre critics, producers, and agents.

Margo feels threatened by Eve and sees her as a rival for her lover's affections and her friends' loyalties. Everyone at the party is praising Eve's qualities, but Margo, in an increasingly drunken rant fueled by her insecurity and jealousy, lashes out at her guests. Like Siddons before her, Margo commands the attention of her peers. Even during Margo's worst moments, her guests never doubt her talent. Addison DeWitt, the powerful theatre critic who serves as the film's main narrator, likens Margo's hosting of the party to a theatrical performance. This is evident when he delivers his impromptu review of her behavior, which he finds impressive: "You're maudlin and full of self-pity. You're magnificent."[33] The theatrical analogy becomes explicit when Karen, the best friend whom Margo has just belittled as a "happy little housewife," instructs Margo to "stop being a star—stop treating your guests as your supporting cast!" In response to Karen's recriminations, Margo retires to her bedroom, followed, a few moments later, by her lover. Addison, Eve, and the handful of other guests who have been witnessing Margo's vitriolic performance at the party are left on the stairwell.

38. Margo Channing (Bette Davis) with Joshua Reynolds's *Sarah Siddons as the Tragic Muse*. Film still from *All about Eve*, dir. Joseph L. Mankiewicz, 1950. Collection of the author

39. Joshua Reynolds's *Sarah Siddons as the Tragic Muse*. Film still from *All about Eve*, dir. Joseph L. Mankiewicz, 1950. Collection of the author

Addison opines: "Too bad. We'll miss the third act. They're going to play it offstage."

The very last shot in this, the film's most famous scene, is a close-up of a copy of *Sarah Siddons as the Tragic Muse* that adorns the wall of Margo's apartment (figures 38 and 39). Eve has just secured the intimacy of Karen, who has naively agreed to advocate to her husband Bill, the director—and against Margo's knowledge—that Eve be cast as Margo's understudy. Eve's plot to usurp Margo is now in play:

EVE: Karen . . . *(Karen pauses)* . . . you won't forget will you? What we talked about before?

KAREN: *(smiles)* No, Eve. I won't forget.

She [Eve] follows the men downstairs. CAMERA MOVES to a CLOSEUP of an old engraving of Mrs. Siddons as "The Tragic Muse" which hangs among other theatrical mementos on the stair wall. . . .

FADE OUT[34]

At precisely the moment in the narrative when Margo seems most vulnerable, the film positions her in relation to Siddons and summons a citational legacy that insures Margo's placement in a genealogy of theatrical celebrity.

The famous party scene in Margo's apartment suggests that even in the space of her own home, Margo cannot stop performing her celebrity. The presence of the Reynolds portrait of Siddons in Margo's apartment reveals Margo's own identification with the eighteenth-century actress, and it establishes Margo as her heir. And yet—Eve. What are we to make of Eve's impersonation of Margo, so successful that it allows the younger woman to usurp Margo's own claim to the Sarah Siddons Award? *All about Eve* suggests that the key to celebrity is an impersonation of stardom so aggressive that it ultimately becomes a violent displacement.

All about Eve is framed by Eve's moment of triumph as she receives the Sarah Siddons Award. Yet the logic of the film insists that we recognize Eve's honor as an injustice to Margo. While Eve displaces Margo within the narrative of the film, thus making it, at least on the level of the plot, all about Eve, we might say that Bette Davis lays claim to the role of legendary star, of diva, to which the name and portrait of Sarah Siddons refer in the film. Despite the fact that the film is framed by the presentation of the Sarah Siddons Award to Eve Harrington, it is Margo Channing who the film positions as the actual star. To be sure, it is Bette Davis and not Anne Baxter who is remembered for her performance in *All about Eve*. And it is Davis who is celebrated as an icon of her period, and who herself was imitated by other future performers.

THE AFTERLIFE OF BETTE DAVIS

If performance provides an archive of prior performances, where are the performances that cite Bette Davis's celebrity? And do these performances, like Eve's in *All about Eve*, aggressively displace the original star? With these questions in mind, I would like to summon another actor who participates in the genealogy of female celebrity and theatrical virtuosity I have been outlining—a performer who built a career on impersonating other stars, most notably Bette Davis. Charles Pierce, the most successful drag performer of his generation, considered himself a "male actress" rather than a "female impersonator." He saw himself as a man who performed female roles. Pierce performed his first female role in 1969, the year of the Stonewall rebellion, the New York City riots that marked the beginning of the modern gay and lesbian liberation movement.[35] Pierce was in his early forties at the time. Before Stonewall, Pierce wrote comic material for other performers and took male character parts at the Pasadena Playhouse where he trained as an actor. In the early 1950s, he started performing his own stand-up comedy in gay clubs, and by the end of the decade, Pierce's routine included lip-synching. Eventually he would come to impersonate the major female stars of his day. Pierce's performances can be understood as archival in two ways. First, they collect the actual performances of female popular celebrity and set out to curate them in such a way that they begin to speak to one another about the shifting ideologies of gender and sexuality over time. Second, these performances house the memories of a subculture who for any number of reasons found points of identification with these women performers. Pierce's performances of these stars collect, in Ann Cvetkovitch's phrasing, an "archive of feelings"—feelings of love, admiration, and respect that escape or elude more traditional forms of documentation. In this sense, Pierce's work marks an important contribution to the formation and preservation of gay culture.

In many ways, Pierce's career, which first took off in nightclubs and bars, mirrored the gay subculture's own increasing visibility. With the establishment of gay commercial and artistic venues—from nightclubs and bars to community-based theatres and galleries, with queer magazines and newspapers promoting these sites—queer artists such as Pierce were able to build a loyal fan base and make a living. Pierce worked the clubs of Miami and San Francisco, developing a repertoire of female impersonations and pantomimes, often with puppets. Pierce's over-the-top rendition of already outrageous female icons such as Mae West and Tallulah Bankhead established his cult status among his many gay fans. In the wake of Stonewall and in the years before AIDS, Pierce's drag performances were legendary for their wit and virtuosity. Using his own voice to conjure Hollywood icons, Pierce would appear costumed as these other icons and perform hilarious and exaggerated send-ups of their signature mannerisms and roles.

Pierce's most famous role, the role that secured his own reputation as a theatrical star, was that of Bette Davis. His Davis impersonation generally occurred in the comic camp mode that became Pierce's own signature, but at times Pierce would include a segment from *All about Eve* that was more dramatic and, according to him, even poignant. In one of the most extensive interviews he conducted, Pierce addresses this issue:

INTERVIEWER: Is there a poignant element [in your show]?

PIERCE: There's one part in the show where Katherine does "Always Mademoiselle," the number from *Coco*. That's the one dramatic number. Having done it for fifteen years, on my last engagement I went back to what I used to do, Katherine Hepburn's original "calla lily" speech from *Stage Door*. I sit on the piano in a spotlight, and that's the one poignant moment in the show. Also, if the audience is in the mood and I'm in the mood, I will do the *All About Eve* speech when Bette was in the car, as Margo, about her career: "Funny business, a woman's career, the things you drop on your way up the ladder." I'll do that dramatically, take a puff and blow it out, slow curtain, the end. It's very dramatic. The hand comes to the right as the spotlight follows me down, so you just see the hand, my pianist plays a note, blackout. And then we're right back to the comedy bits.[36]

Pierce's homage to Davis constituted both icon worship and camp parody. As the passage above suggests, Pierce took his impersonation of Davis very seriously. His performances were at once a deep identification with Davis and her roles and a major send-up of Davis's most spectacular characters. Margo Channing proved enormously popular, and he performed her to huge audience approval.[37]

Pierce's performances proved so successful that they moved from these queer subcultural venues to more established mainstream theatres. At the height of his career, in the early 1980s, Pierce performed his Davis impersonations—along with his various renditions of other stars—at the prestigious Dorothy Chandler Pavilion at the Music Center in Los Angeles. The poster for the show, billed as *Charles Pierce:*

40. Advertisement for the show *Charles Pierce: First Annual Farewell Performance* at the Dorothy Chandler Pavilion, Los Angeles, 1983. Courtesy Gay, Lesbian, Bisexual, Transgender Historical Society of Northern California

First Annual Farewell Performance, featured a photo of Pierce, cigarette in hand, coiffed and posed in classic Bette Davis style (figure 40).[38] Shortly after this L.A. performance, Pierce starred in San Francisco as Margo Channing in *Applause,* the 1970 Broadway musical version of *All about Eve* written by Betty Comden and Adolph Green.[39] Throughout his life and work, Pierce championed Davis's career. His performances were a tribute to Davis's own stardom, and as such they helped perpetuate Davis's own celebrity, much as hers helped perpetuate Sarah Siddons's.

Charles Pierce died in 1999 at the age of seventy-two. The obituaries published in the gay and mainstream press celebrated Pierce as a star, a person whose performances had achieved legendary status.[40] Pierce's death begs the question I have been asking of previous stars such as Siddons and Davis: How will his performance of celebrity be remembered and archived? Before Pierce died, he gathered together his scrapbooks, photographs, programs, recordings, and videotapes, shipping them to the New York Public Library for the Performing Arts at Lincoln Center in New York City. The staff completed cataloguing Pierce's archive only weeks before his death. But if, as I have been arguing, performance can serve as its own archive, I wonder who has been studying his work, and if it will be reembodied in the future.

THE AFTERLIFE OF CHARLES PIERCE

To recover the work of Charles Pierce through the available documentation of his career—a set of flyers and reviews, some press photographs and playbills, a few bootleg videotapes—would certainly prove a challenge. No less difficult, it seems to me, would be the project of recovering the theatrical performances of Sarah Siddons through the viewing of her painted portraits. Yet despite this challenge, nearly two years after his death, Charles Pierce resurfaced in Los Angeles. Like Sarah Siddons before him, whose Southern California exhibitions nearly coincided with the date of Pierce's death, Pierce became the subject of an exhibition. *Satirist in Sequins: The World of Charles Pierce* helped launch the grand opening of the One Institute and Archives at the University of Southern California, an extensive collection of art, ephemera, books, manuscripts, and archival materials documenting the lives of gay, lesbian, bisexual, and transgendered people.

The One Institute and Archives was founded in 1994 when it merged the One Institute—one of the oldest gay and lesbian organizations, incorporated in 1952—with the private collection of queer memorabilia that writer and activist Jim Kepner began preserving in 1942. The 2001 opening of the new space, which houses the largest research library on gay, lesbian, bisexual, and transgendered history, was itself haunted by these previous organizations and activists who made possible the archive and the collection it contains. That afternoon, many of the veterans who had motivated the gay rights movement had since died, and others were too frail to attend. Others, of course, were at hand and summoned the achievements of those unable to be present, whatever the reasons of their absence. These people began to compensate for the major difference between a material archive and a performance archive, which is the absence of the body. But the attendees also called into question this difference by their presence as surrogate bodies for the missing and the dead. Although the One Institute and Archives might

41. Charles Pierce memorabilia at *Satirist in Sequins: The World of Charles Pierce*, One Institute and Archives, Los Angeles, 2001. Photo by Richard Meyer

primarily be a paper archive, it was established by a larger subcultural movement, one out to defy the constraints of its own temporality. This larger history of political struggle informs the archive's own difficult efforts to secure firm standing as an institutional repository of queer memory. I should add that these were not the only people haunting the space. The building's previous inhabitants also ghosted the event: the archive is now housed in a former fraternity on campus.

Satirist in Sequins displayed a selection of Pierce's costumes, promotional photographs, program books, and other theatre paraphernalia related to his career (figure 41). These items were exhibited with care and concern under glass cases, and with the sense that they constituted valuable but vulnerable artifacts of a previous age and of an important historical figure. In an adjacent room, a videotape of Pierce in performance—as Bette Davis, but also as Tallulah Bankhead, Joan Crawford, and Mae West, among others—ran on a continuous loop. Bill Kaiser, the exhibition's curator, explained to me that the institution had selected Pierce for two main reasons: "One, we had the good fortune to receive a lot of his props, costumes, and artifacts from his dear ex-ecutor, Don Kobus, who I got to visit with and learn a lot about Charles Pierce's career. And two, I thought he was a very courageous figure who inspired and was out before many others were."[41] Kaiser's com-ments call attention to the good sense of Pierce's executor to preserve the documentation of his friend's career, and the coordinated efforts of Pierce, Kobus, and Kaiser to secure his legacy.

During the opening festivities of the One Institute and Archives, various friends and fans of Pierce gathered at the exhibition to share stories and recollections of his artistic life. Kaiser went on to explain that the exhibition was especially meaningful to Pierce's fans, "who got to relive the experience of seeing Pierce perform." While the exhibition enabled these friends and fans to reenact their memories of Pierce, it also invited those who had never seen Pierce on stage to revel in his theatrical persona and achievements. Pierce stopped performing in the early 1990s, and many of the younger generation of queers had never heard of him.

Some of us who had known about Pierce had never seen him per-form during his many years on the circuit. I myself had ample op-portunities to see Pierce on stage but never took advantage of them. It never occurred to me that Pierce might be someone whose work would have much meaning for me or that I would enjoy his imperson-ations of female celebrities. As a result of my own bias, I considered his work antiquated and clichéd, and his citational practices—the celebri-ties, songs, and films that populate his performances—as not immedi-ately overlapping with my own. My own version of an antitheatrical prejudice was directed against a performer and a genre—female imper-sonation—that seemed to be of an entirely different era and politics. I based this on nothing more than my uncritical perception that the work would be predictable, a more heightened version of the drag that permeated the gay clubs I frequented. How many impersonations of Bette Davis or Judy Garland can one see in a lifetime? This bias seems regrettable insofar as it foreclosed my chance to experience Pierce's per-formances firsthand and recognize the man's historical achievement.

Luckily, there exist other artists who also set out to recreate past per-formances and whose citational practices resonate more immediately with my own interest and life experience. My own tastes run more to the next generation of female impersonators, performers such as John Kelly, whose performances as Joni Mitchell, an artist whose songbook proved central to my own formative years, I find extraordinarily moving, and the choreographer and dancer Richard Move, whose tributes to Martha Graham are uncanny. I also attend and admire John Epperson's Lypsinka performances, which like Pierce's work, rely on old Hollywood citations and an expert knowledge of female celebrity, both major and minor.[42] Epperson, however, never speaks. His entire performance is a collage of recorded voices and sounds from the past that he lip-synchs to great effect. Costumed in period dress, Epperson as Lypsinka is a throwback to the glamour years of classic Hollywood. Epperson, in fact, may be the premier drag artist currently on the scene, and the primary heir to Pierce. When Pierce died, Epperson offered the following tribute: "The name 'Charles Pierce' meant 'magic' and what he would call 'madness.' People who had never seen him as Tallulah and Bette Davis—at the same time—don't know what they've missed. (People who don't know Tallulah and Bette don't know what they are missing!) People who did see Charles's act know they saw a comic mastermind."[43]

While Epperson can be more immediately placed within the tradition of Pierce, performers such as Kelly and Move are less likely to be imagined in this lineage. They are affiliated with, and arguably central to, the New York avant-garde, and they have built careers outside of the female impersonations that they perform. Both perform at alternative art spaces, established dance studios, international performance festivals, and downtown clubs, all venues that inform their status as innovative artists. Their work constitutes a kind of archival drag; they craft performances that set out to recreate the artistry of women geniuses such as Mitchell and Graham by mining their careers and reintroducing their archive for new audiences and audiences already familiar with the female artists. Like Epperson, they are embodied archival systems. While Epperson constructs a persona that is a composite of past female celebrities that may or may not be immediately recognizable to his audience, Kelly and Move reconstruct the actual performance styles of Mitchell and Graham. For audiences already familiar with the careers of these two women, these performances offer striking tributes to their artistry. For spectators unfamiliar with the women, Kelly and Move perform a pedagogical intervention and recycle Mitchell and Graham back into the contemporary. It is here that the performance is asked to do its primary cultural work. Not only do these performers comment on female talent and celebrity but they also make the case for the relevance of the arts in the national culture.

Both Kelly and Move bring to their work an expert artistry that is reverential in its deference to the original. Their performances, while full of humor and wit, have an earnestness that distinguishes their work from that of Pierce or Epperson. Richard Move studies Graham's choreography and curates full-evening performances based on her performance techniques. He recruits other dancers to perform in his famous Martha @ Mother shows. Such distinguished artists as Mikhail Baryshnikov, Yvonne Rainer, Mark Morris, and Merce Cunningham, for example, have joined Move in his evening tributes at Mother, a club in New York's meatpacking district where Move premiered the series (figures 42 and 43).

Move as Martha acts as host to the evening's performances, which are comprised of a sequence of Graham-inspired dances, sometimes even danced by members of the actual Martha Graham Company, and premieres from other contemporary choreographers showcasing original work. Move presides over the evening dressed as Martha and inserts monologues based on Graham's autobiography throughout the performance. "My whole premise is that Martha never died. It's just that now she's hosting a series in which she performs and introduces other people's work," he explains.[44] Move and Janet Stapleton curate the shows. When Move and Stapleton first premiered Martha, they were issued a cease-and-desist notice by the Graham Estate, which was not pleased with the unauthorized events. The estate would not allow Move, or any of the performers at Mother, to perform her copyrighted work. Furthermore, the estate had hoped to prohibit the use of the name Martha as well, a point that led *Village Voice* columnist Michael Musto to quip, "I'm sure it's actually based on Martha Reeves, Martha Stewart, or the woman with the vineyard."[45]

In fact, Move does not restage actual Graham choreographies. Instead, he evokes her genius in a sophisticated homage that allows for

42–43. Postcards for Martha @ Mother, New York City, 1999. Collection of the author

the humor of camp parody but exceeds it by the sheer and nonironic insistence on Graham's brilliance. Move is dead serious about Graham's significance:

> Besides of course, the technique, which is the basis for all modern and contemporary dance, her commissions are the great masterpieces of modern music—Copland's *Appalachian Spring*, et cetera. When Noguchi started making sets, it was a completely different way of looking at the dance and its relation to scenery. She paved the way for how we perceive choreography in relation to music, costume, setting. She was the first to use stretch fabrics—all these things we take as givens, she totally paved the way for. Every choreographer in the modern contemporary realm is really indebted to her, whether they care to admit it or not. On all counts, she really was the first.[46]

Move allows Graham's sentimental views of dance to surface during the monologues based on Graham's autobiography and the biographies written about her. Graham's romantic sense that art and religion are linked features throughout the performance, and Move seems to endorse this view through his own sense of commitment to the Graham oeuvre and to dance in general. The show is pedagogical in nature—we are meant to learn about Graham and her times. It includes videos by Charles Atlas, who combines historical dance footage from various sources with hysterical film footage of clips with Martha references, as in the famous Richard Burton "Martha!" scene from *Who's Afraid of Virginia Woolf?* (1966), and even actual clips of Graham herself. The performance also invokes the historical context in which Graham lived and performed. Graham, to cite one point that Move stresses, refused to perform for Hitler at the 1936 Olympics.

Move seems confident that Graham would approve of his Martha series. In an interview exchange with *Time Out New York* (TONY), he imagines what Graham, who died in 1991, would have to say: When asked by the magazine whether he ever felt guilty about spoofing Martha, Move gravely answered, "*Never*. First of all, I only show her in the most positive light. In the series, Martha is the consummate goddess. People like Stuart Hodes—who knew Martha since 1946—said,

44. Richard Move
as Martha Graham,
Town Hall, New York
City, 2001. Photo by
Richard Termine

'The only person who does this better than you is Martha herself.' I know she would be very pleased with the notion that we are educating an audience about her."[47] Move's Martha dance events reveal a genuine expertise in the life and work of Martha Graham that move the performance beyond parody or spoof. While the image of Move, a six-foot-four-inch man, impersonating the famously diminutive Graham is comically absurd, the impulse behind the impersonation is less so (figure 44). Move is interested in reintroducing Graham to a new audience and showcasing new choreographers shaped and influenced by her singular talent.

John Kelly, who has performed with Move at various Martha events, most notably as the German choreographer Pina Bausch, follows a similar track in his series of performances as Joni Mitchell, which are so extraordinary in their archival virtuosity that they also cannot be confined to the category of camp. While Kelly can be as witty as the archest drag queen, he brings to his performances a talent so obvious that his audiences know they are in the company of an artist of exquisite imagination and commitment. His interest in drag appears sophisticated and nuanced. In a short essay entitled "In Praise of Drag," Kelly voices his own investments in drag and reveals both the biases against it and the ways that drag performance shifted in the 1980s among a generation of queers in the East Village, the milieu that fostered him as an artist. He writes:

> Drag is acting. But it's not reciting a play, it's acting with my body, the whole mechanism. . . . Drag today is often perceived as a joke, easily dismissed, often relegated to an other, slightly suspect column. For me, it's never been about mere titillation. In the early eighties, there was an incredible scene in New York. Drag was nasty, the forbidden fruit, sexy and dangerous. It was punk and androgynous. It wasn't ha ha ha; it was really interesting. It was about pushing people's buttons and having them question their relationship to gender and how they judge people based purely on what they see.
>
> I have used my traditional drag craft—lip-synching and live vocal production—in my work. I regard singing in part as a way of merging the inner (personal) nature with the other (public) picture. The constant task of the vocal artist to navigate freely between the chest register and the head or falsetto register, negotiating the "break" in the voice, is an opportunity to both actually and metaphorically consider my "selves."[48]

Kelly's comments provide a context for understanding the ways that drag has shifted over time. His words also echo the bias that informed my own sense that Pierce's work should be "relegated to an other, slightly suspect column." As someone who came out in the late 1970s, I felt impatient with drag acts that recycled female celebrities such as Judy Garland, Barbra Streisand, or Billie Holliday, all icons of a previous generation. I was more open to appreciating new performers participating in the emergent scene that Kelly describes above. I would, in fact, see some of these performances at clubs such as the Pyramid, Boy Bar, and the other East Village venues in the 1980s. The older artists such as Charles Pierce and performers of his age seemed of a different era and for a different generation, suggesting to me that each queer generation produces its own iconic drag personas and performances. I should note that today my younger queer friends are familiar with drag performers completely different from those I follow. These performers populate the thriving nightlife of contemporary urban gay culture and seem ubiquitous to those who frequent this scene.

But Kelly's comments also capture the seriousness with which he approached drag performance. For him it was one more artistic possibility, another medium to express his creativity. In the Joni Mitchell performances, he plays the dulcimer, the guitar, and the piano, as well as singing her original arrangements (figure 45). The musical artistry is authentic, even if the persona is at times tongue-in-cheek. Kelly addresses his audience as Mitchell, telling stories of her life as if they were his own. Only occasionally will he alter a lyric to shift the emphasis of the song and the performance's historical context. In his stunning rendition of "Woodstock," Mitchell's anthem to the sixties generation, Kelly changes the location from Woodstock to Wigstock, the Tompkins Square celebration of drag and alternative performance—and the occasion to when Kelly first performed his Mitchell persona in 1985. Mitchell's 1969 original version, a tribute to the utopian yearnings of a generation facing the Vietnam War, is also a semihallucinogenic peace song: "By the time we got to Woodstock / We were half a million strong / And everywhere there was song and celebration / And I dreamed I saw the bombers / Riding shotgun in the sky / And they were turning into butterflies / Above our nation."[49] The original, from the album *Ladies of the Canyon*, features Mitchell singing only to the accompaniment of an electric piano. Ever the virtuoso, Mitchell would rearrange the song throughout her career to allow for different musical styles and contexts. She always honored the spirit of the song, however. Kelly's version preserves the original musical context, down to the vocal yodeling that Mitchell uses to close the song (figure 46). In his version, however, he changes the location from the subcultural hippie gathering at the pastoral setting of Yasgur's Farm to the queer subcultural gathering at the urban landscape of Tompkins Square Park. In each case—the 1960s and the 1990s, Woodstock and Wigstock—the song celebrates the subculture as the refuge from a world filled with hatred and corruption "caught in the devil's bargain." Here the links between two particular countercultural subgroups—hippies and queers—become explicit.

45. John Kelly in *Paved Paradise*, New York City, 1997. Photo by Paula Court

46. John Kelly performs "Woodstock" in *Paved Paradise*, New York City, 1997. Photo by Paula Court

Each group is idealized and imagined as utopian: "We are stardust, we are golden, and we got to get ourselves back to the garden." The tribute extends beyond Mitchell's artistry and the historical period in which she sang. Kelly's version of "Woodstock" summons the participants of Wigstock as a social movement, anchored in a history of sexual liberation, peace activism, and countercultural critique. His utopia also adjusts to the historical reality of his own era. Instead of seeing "the bombers riding shotgun in the sky . . . turning into butterflies," Kelly sings, "And I dreamed I saw the drag queens . . . and they have found the cure for AIDS for all the nations."[50] This AIDS context also valorizes the drag queen as central to the queer political landscape, with her contribution having global effects.

Those of us who know Kelly's career can also see these drag performances as an extension of his larger interests in exploring the life of the artist, whether that artist is an actual historical figure—like Joni Mitchell, Egon Schiele, the Viennese Expressionist artist, or Barbette, the 1920s trapeze performer, all of whom inspired Kelly to create full-

47. Joni Mitchell and John Kelly backstage at the Fez in New York City, 1997. Photo by Paula Court

evening performance homages in their honor—or a fictional creation such as Dagmar Onasis, who he calls "the love child of Maria Callas and Aristotle Onasis," perhaps Kelly's most famous drag role. Kelly is also famous for his vocal skills, and he has created entire performances based on the music and songs of canonical composers such as Schumann, Purcell, and Mahler. His three different full-evening performances as Joni Mitchell—*Paved Paradise, Shiny Hot Nights,* and *Get Up and Jive*—all form part of this lifelong meditation on artistic creativity.

At one performance of *Paved Paradise* at the Fez in New York City, Joni Mitchell was in the audience (figure 47). Seated at a back table with friends, Mitchell, who had not previously seen Kelly perform and was uncertain of his talents, later told him when they met backstage that she had cried four times during the show. That same night she gave him a dulcimer as a gift, which he now plays when he performs the Mitchell tributes. Mitchell rarely performs her own material anymore; for many spectators, Kelly's performances are the closest they will get to hear a full-evening recital of Mitchell's songbook sung in her style and in her persona.

This chapter has been an attempt to propose that theatrical performance lives not only in the memory of those who witness it but also in the vestiges, artifacts, and performances that survive into a later cultural moment where they may be reembodied by other actors and received by other audiences. Such performances help shape a history that exceeds the traditional archival systems of the museum, the library, or the university. This history endures and is passed on through performances that archive the past even as they restage and reimagine it. In the case of Move and Kelly—as in the citation of Sarah Siddons in *All about Eve* and of Bette Davis in the performances by Charles Pierce— their performances reject the marginal role delegated to the performing arts and conjure an archive of a time when the arts proved more central to the national culture. This kind of work exceeds the tributary, however. Move and Kelly summon the past to inspire creativity in the contemporary moment. They drag back into the public sphere artists who have either died or retired, refusing to acknowledge the finality of death—the death of the artist, of the avant-garde, of queer culture. Their archival drag reinvokes past genius, and not simply as an insider joke. The arts once mattered, they remind us, and they can matter again.

The last time I saw John Kelly as Joni Mitchell was in the spring of 2004. He was performing once again at the Fez, a nightclub basement cabaret space in the East Village. The performance, *Get Up and Jive*, was sold out, a routine occurrence whenever Kelly performs at the club. He was accompanied by Zecca Esquibel at the keyboards in full drag as Georgia O'Keefe, the famous visual artist whom Mitchell befriended. The two make quite an immediate and humorous visual impression with their wigs and frocks, but as the music begins and the performance commences, it is clear that the night will once again showcase Kelly's distinguished talents and Mitchell's brilliant music. Kelly always varies the shows; each of the three full-evening performances of Mitchell introduce new songs from the singer's oeuvre and include different anecdotes between the songs—stories based on Kelly's archival research into Mitchell's concerts and anecdotes improvised by the Mitchell persona he performs (figures 48–50).

That particular night's show at the Fez included some of Mitchell's more obscure (but still beautiful) songs, "Harry's House/Centerpiece" from *The Hissing of Summer Lawns*, for example, but also some of her

48. Postcard for John Kelly's *Paved Paradise* at the Jungle at Tropical Joe's in Provincetown, Massachusetts, 1998. Collection of the author

49. Postcard for John Kelly's *Shiny Hot Nights* at the Fez in New York City, 2001. Collection of the author

50. Postcard for John Kelly's *Get Up and Jive!* at the Fez in New York City, 2004. Collection of the author

most political work, "Slouching Toward Bethlehem," from *Night Ride Home*, equally obscure, perhaps, and equally stunning in Kelly's delivery. At one point before singing "Woodstock/Wigstock," Kelly set up the song in the context of the war in Iraq. This is an audience that takes a certain ownership of the Wigstock interpretation; the Fez is located in the same East Village neighborhood, after all, and many in the audience are Wigstock veterans and aficionados. But now the song takes on yet another poignant layer; Mitchell's song is summoned to inspire the antiwar activism that it achieved earlier on. No longer simply an endorsement of the subcultural practices of the queer underworld of New York's East Village, the song has now been recycled as a political tract meant to invoke the national sentiments of an earlier generation standing up for social change.

Kelly's insistence that "Woodstock" be heard as a repository of national feeling moves the song out of the subcultural location of the performance venue and into the heart of contemporary national debate. He sings the song to comment on the current political climate and to encourage cultural dissent. Moreover—is he speaking as Mitchell or as himself in this moment?—he encourages his audience to vote and to defeat George W. Bush, a point he has never addressed before in any of his performances that I have attended over the years. Kelly has always let his performances speak for themselves, and astute audiences could always interpret the politics of his work. But on that night Kelly was not drawn to such subtlety, indicating his impatience with Bush's presidency.

Close to the end of his performance Kelly sang Mitchell's sad and ghostly "The Fiddle and the Drum" from *Clouds*, her second album, released in 1969. It is one of the few songs in the entire Mitchell songbook that is performed a cappella. Kelly, too, sings it unaccompanied by any instruments. Mitchell's lyrics speak against American militarism, and in this context, the reality of one sole voice expressing this collective sentiment seems strikingly brave:

> And so once again
> Oh, America my friend
> And so once again
> You are fighting us all

And when we ask you why
You raise your fist and you cry and we fall
Oh, my friend
How did you come
To trade the fiddle for the drum[51]

The performance remained unmediated by technology or context, and except for the few beats of silence that frame the piece, the song had no setup; when Kelly sang the song, he was not miked. His natural voice filled the Fez with Mitchell's timely lyrics: Kelly had retrieved from the Mitchell archive yet another of her intense antiwar songs, and this time there was no possibility to hear it with the sense of irony that Kelly allows for in his rendition of "Woodstock." That said, Kelly's performance never depends on audience nostalgia to make an antiwar critique.

Kelly's renditions of Mitchell's antiwar songs, while certainly nostalgic, are meant to put the songs back in service. In this sense, he works whatever nostalgic impulses the audience might hold for the material against the grain. That is to say, the songs should not be relegated only to a particular subculture or moment in history such as hippies or the 1960s; Mitchell's songbook can still do important cultural work precisely by summoning the kinds of energies they once circulated and putting those energies back in circulation in the contemporary moment. Thus Kelly's work is not simply about revisiting the past so as to render that past romantic or ideal; Kelly revisits the past so as to put that past in conversation with the present, and in doing so places contemporary social struggles in a historical context of ongoing progressive engagement through the arts.

In "The Fiddle and the Drum," Kelly recovers a Mitchell song that while profound and beautiful, does not range among her best-known work. On *Clouds* it is followed by one of Mitchell's most famous songs, "Both Sides, Now," which closes the album. The immediate guitar chord Mitchell strums to launch the song signals a return to the comforts of musical accompaniment, and Mitchell's solemn voice appears quiet and meditative, seemingly less urgent than in "The Fiddle and the Drum." The album ends with Mitchell's anti-epiphanic insight: "I've looked at life from both sides now, from up and down, and still somehow, it's life's illusions I recall, I really don't know life at all." In *Get Up and Jive*, however, Kelly lets "The Fiddle and the Drum" stand alone. At the end of the song and following the enthusiastic applause it generates, the room remains quiet. We are left with the song's final lyric: "We have all come to fear the beating of your drum," a sentiment first articulated by a young, Canadian-born woman in her twenties, who sang it in the late 1960s as a commentary on a U.S. led war she wanted to see end. Thirty-five years later it is sung again, this time by a middle-aged gay man dressed in archival drag as this young woman, and offering it back in the form of an echo, a counterpoint to the continuing beating drum of American imperialism and militarism. His rendition is at once an archival embodiment of a previous peace performance and a contemporary practice questioning the nation through song.

The idea of addressing the nation through song lies at the heart of the next chapter, which focuses on female cabaret performance. In it, I will be drawn once again to thinking about the ways that performance might be viewed as an archive. Cabaret performance both foregrounds the national songbook constituted in the first half of the twentieth century and functions as a repository of national sentiments associated with these performances. I discuss the ways that women have used cabaret performance as a form of cultural memory, both personal and national, and how this genre begins to archive their public and private lives.

CHAPTER FIVE

Cabaret as Cultural History: Popular Song and Public Performance in America

Contemporary performance, as I have been arguing throughout this book, opens up a space in the national culture for a set of alternative sentiments and practices. It does so in a variety of ways, including, paradoxically, a return to historical source materials that are invigorated by new framings and innovative revisions. This chapter, like the previous one, foregrounds this kind of relationship between the contemporary and the past and takes what is understood as the American songbook as one of its primary case studies. The American songbook is preserved and sustained by cabaret performance, the chapter's focus. In many ways, cabaret performance constitutes a gendered genre and practice, a contested space that throughout its history has showcased the woman singer. I here examine women and cabaret to argue that cabaret becomes an embodied archive of American cultural history, a place where women, especially older women, perform the history of their lives in the theatre and, by extension, the larger culture. I consider the performers Elaine Stritch, Bea Arthur, and Barbara Cook, all women in their seventies performing on Broadway. But I also discuss mid-career and younger performers such as Donna McKechnie, Mary Cleere Haran, and Andrea Marcovicci who perform in traditional cabaret venues throughout New York City. These and other accomplished women cabaret singers often perform in cabaret venues such as Arci's Place, Joe's Pub, and Feinstein's at the Regency—all venues named after men—often between more commercially lucrative theatre jobs.

But some of these performers play the cabaret circuit exclusively, preferring the intimacy of the smaller cabaret room. I am interested in how these contemporary women artists use the practice of cabaret in a variety of settings and venues to allow for a cultural archive of alternatives to emerge through the rich and expansive repertoire of musical performance. I will also argue that these women singers do more than simply narrate their own life stories; rather, their lives also tell of the shifting ideologies of gender and sexuality throughout the twentieth century, conveying the history of American culture through song.

IN THE FALL of 1938 the songwriting team of Richard Rodgers and Lorenz Hart premiered their latest show, *The Boys from Syracuse*, on Broadway. It was their sixth show to reach Broadway in three years, and it proved to be one of the most successful of their twenty-four year collaboration, even landing them on the cover of *Time* magazine (figure 51). The musical, which ran for 238 performances at the Alvin Theatre, received mainly strong reviews, especially for its songs. The reviewer for the *New York World Telegram* announced, "I believe it will be regarded as the greatest musical comedy of its time."[1] *The Boys from Syracuse* included such songs as "Falling in Love with Love" and "This Can't be Love," songs now considered classics of the American songbook. By 1938 Rodgers and Hart had reached the top of their game, and the genre of the musical theatre was on the eve of its golden age. The two men had returned a few years back from a five-year stint in Hollywood, where they had worked on a number of films including *The Hot Heiress* (1931), *Love Me Tonight* (1932) with Jeanette McDonald and Maurice Chevalier, *Hallelujah! I'm A Bum* (1933) with Al Jolson, *Hollywood Party* (1934) with Bing Crosby and W. C. Fields, and *Mississippi* (1935). But New York was their home and Broadway their stage.

The Boys from Syracuse was the first musical adaptation of a Shakespeare play. It had been Rodgers's idea. When he had pitched the project to Hart, they quickly decided that Shakespeare's *The Comedy of Errors* would make the ideal choice. Hart was especially keen on casting his younger brother Teddy, a Broadway actor, in the role of one of the Dromio twins. The play's combination of outrageous farce, the invocation of the ancient world, and the appeal of the romance of the Shake-

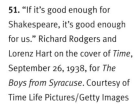

51. "If it's good enough for Shakespeare, it's good enough for us." Richard Rodgers and Lorenz Hart on the cover of *Time*, September 26, 1938, for *The Boys from Syracuse*. Courtesy of Time Life Pictures/Getty Images

spearean young lovers made a sure fire hit for them. They took the idea to the more established director George Abbott, who signed on to write the book, direct the play, and produce the musical. Abbott had worked with Rodgers and Hart earlier in the decade when he directed *Jumbo* (1935), the first production they mounted after returning from Hollywood, and the first of Abbott's many musical theatre productions over the span of the twentieth century. *Jumbo* was by all accounts a huge spectacle, produced by Billy Rose and featuring a ninety-person cast led by Jimmy Durante at the Hippodrome, the largest theatre in the world when it was built in 1905. The plot of *Jumbo* involves a romance between the son and daughter of rival circus families, and it included close to five hundred animals on stage. *Jumbo* was, in fact, a full-fledged circus with acrobats, clowns, and Big Rosie as the elephant Jumbo. It emerged as one of the largest theatrical events in the history of New York City. Audiences loved it, and it ran for nearly a year. Despite its strong reception, the musical extravaganza never turned a profit.

Shortly after *Jumbo* closed, the Hippodrome, located on Sixth Avenue between Forty-third and Forty-fourth Street, was demolished, and in its place is now a parking lot—the Hippodrome parking lot. But in the earlier part of the twentieth century, the Hippodrome, like Rodgers and Hart themselves, was emblematic of urban New York.

Rodgers and Hart quickly became a New York institution. They first met in 1919 when a mutual friend, who thought they might make a compatible songwriting team, had the good sense to introduce them. They soon began writing songs for amateur and college shows, although they did not experience their first big break until 1925, when the musical revue the *Garrick Gaieties* became the surprise hit of the Broadway season. *Garrick Gaieties* began as a two-night benefit for the Theatre Guild, a producing organization founded in 1919, which was in need of funds to finish the building of a new Broadway theatre, their first, what is now the Virginia Theatre on West Fifty-second Street.[2] The show, performed at the Garrick Theatre on West Thirty-fifth Street, was extended for six more performances that also quickly sold out. Rodgers and Hart turned overnight sensations, the darlings of the New York press, and one of their songs for the *Garrick Gaieties*, "Manhattan"— "We'll take Manhattan, the Bronx, and Staten Island too / We'll turn Manhattan into an isle of joy"—became an immediate classic. Hart's witty lyrics were reprinted in newspapers, and dance bands throughout the country quickly added the song to their repertoire. The Theatre Guild decided to continue the hit show indefinitely, and it ran for 230 performances before finally closing. The show's success proved a surprise given that it featured lesser-known members of the guild as actors and the music and lyrics of but an emerging songwriting team. Hart was thirty years old at the time, Rodgers only twenty-three.

Mary Cleere Haran, the extraordinary contemporary singer, tells these stories of Rodgers and Hart and the early years of the American musical in *Falling in Love with Love: The Rodgers and Hart Story*, her cabaret performance at the Algonquin Hotel's legendary Oak Room (figure 52). Haran's performance, which premiered during the summer of 2002, was one of many throughout the city to mark the Richard Rodgers Centenary. (Rodgers was born in New York in 1902 and died in 1979; Hart was born in 1895 and died in 1943.) At the Oak Room, one of

52. Mary Cleere Haran in performance, New York City, 2002. Photo by Richard Termine

the city's premier cabaret performance venues, Haran showcased the songs Rodgers wrote with Hart in the 1920s, 1930s, and 1940s.

Early on in the performance, she introduces her show's titular song, "Falling in Love with Love," by telling the story of her own life as the daughter of Irish Catholics who grew up in San Francisco. She also intersperses anecdotes of her own early theatre career. Although too young to have ever originated a role in a Rodgers and Hart musical, she performed as one of the courtesans in the 1974 San Francisco revival of *The Boys from Syracuse* at the Eureka Theatre. At the time, Haran was already appearing in the hit production *Beach Blanket Babylon*, and she used her earnings from that show to front the entire production costs of the Rodgers and Hart revival. *The Boys from Syracuse* turned out to be a runaway hit and one of the most enchanting theatrical experiences of her career. She was twenty-two years old at the time. Now, nearly thirty years later, Haran tells this story to her devoted audience. Haran goes on to sing "Falling in Love with Love" with the familiar care of an archivist, using her voice to highlight Hart's lyrics and compliment Rodger's music. Her crisp voice—accompanied by her longtime collaborator Richard Rodney Bennett on piano, and Linc Milliman on bass—fills the Oak Room with the sounds of history, a history at once popular and personal, national and individual. Her commitment to the Rodgers and Hart archive is obvious given the wealth of information she has about their personal lives and professional careers; her affection for the music comes across by the care with which she presents the songs. Her voice appears commanding without overshadowing the songs themselves. The Rodgers and Hart songbook enables her to showcase her talent as a singer, but it also provides her the opportunity to revisit and recirculate narratives of her own career and theirs, two distinct historical periods from the past that find their shared embodiment in the present performance. The fact that these two separate historical spheres—the 1920s, 1930s, and 1940s of Rodgers and Hart; the 1950s, 1960s, and 1970s of Haran—meet up in the contemporary seems as much a surprise to her as it does to her audiences.

Haran's impeccable delivery points to her commitment to the songs themselves. As she sees it, her role is to communicate the song, rather than embellish it; in this sense, she brings to mind the vocal clarity of Ella Fitzgerald, who first recorded the Rodgers and Hart song book in 1956.[3] Haran's interpretations are subtle and refined, her vocal delivery expressing the song's sentiment and allowing for the artistry of Rodgers and Hart to remain intact. In the patter that sets up the songs, Haran reveals herself as a scholar of the American musical. She offers an extended context for each song, serving as the bridge between her audience and the theatrical past. The intimacy she establishes through these stories also extends to her own history with the material.

Haran explains that as a young girl she was quite familiar with the work of Rodgers and Hammerstein, the famous songwriting team of *Oklahoma!* (1943), *Carousel* (1945), *South Pacific* (1954), and *The Sound of Music* (1959), among other milestones of the American musical theatre, but was completely unaware that Rodgers had had an earlier collaborator whose songs were now classics.

> I knew who Richard Rodgers was. If you grew up in the 1950s and 1960s, you had to know that he and Oscar Hammerstein wrote

very famous musicals that took place in exotic lands like Siam, Bavaria, Oklahoma, and Chinatown. And though I liked their songs a lot when I was little, I had noticed that adults really liked their shows and took them rather seriously. I had often heard my father singing all of Enzio Pinza's songs from *South Pacific* in the morning when he was shaving and didn't know anyone was listening.

And the nuns in my grammar school played selections from *The King and I* over the public address system whenever it rained. They would go on and on about what a wonderful show it was because it dealt with serious themes like East meets West. I think the real reason the nuns loved *The King and I* was because they secretly identified with the chaste yet titillating relationship between the schoolteacher, Anna, and the King.

So I was shocked when Bob [a friend] told me that before Oscar Hammerstein, Richard Rodgers had had an entirely different life with an entirely different writing partner named Lorenz Hart. "What kind of songs did they write?" I asked.

"Oh, they're really good and I bet you know a lot of them already," Bob told me.

And he started to play some on the piano: "My Funny Valentine," "My Heart Stood Still," "Where or When," "Isn't It Romantic," "I Didn't Know What Time It Was," "Little Girl Blue," "Sing for Your Supper," "Bewitched, Bothered, and Bewildered."

I finally told Bob to stop. I was dumbfounded. I knew and loved each and every single one of these songs.

"You mean to tell me that all these great songs were written by the same two people—and one of them was Richard Rodgers?" I exclaimed.[4]

Haran went on to research the career of Rodgers and Hart, and her Algonquin Hotel show was one result of her findings. Through her performance at the Algonquin—itself a New York City cultural institution famous for its roundtable of the 1920s featuring the likes of Dorothy Parker, Alexander Woollcott, Edna Ferber, and others—Haran brings to life a lost era of American history. Her cabaret performance summons past performances—those seminal and ephemeral, those legendary and forgotten—and the artists, venues, and audiences who constituted the Broadway and Manhattan of yesteryear. As Haran's work makes clear, contemporary cabaret performance raises important questions that have been central to my book project: What is the relationship of the contemporary to earlier periods in history? In what ways might performance contribute to our understanding of national identity, personal subjectivity, and cultural agency? How does performance archive its own past? What are the cultural effects of particular modes of performance?

In order to begin to answer these questions, it might prove useful to consider how cabaret itself is discussed. Generally, cabaret performance is understood in three ways. The traditional view imagines cabaret as the liminal space of urban nightlife, a location that licenses decadence and excess in periods of ideological uniformity and control. John Kander and Fred Ebb's 1966 musical *Cabaret* made this sociological position enormously popular. Its primary focus remains on cabaret's audience and venue. The second way that cabaret is discussed is in relationship to a so-called historical avant-garde emerging in Europe and tied to early twentieth-century aesthetic movements with revolutionary goals that found expression through the performing arts. This view understands cabaret as a historical genre. Laurence Senelick's important work exemplifies this approach and catalogues its participants. The third way cabaret is imagined is as a showcase for popular song— cabaret performers sing standards from someone else's songbook. This position promotes the idea of a musical canon and generally trumpets the work of male composers. I call this position the musicologist approach. However, none of these positions—the sociological, the historical, or the musicologist—account for the actual centrality of the performer herself. I argue that women performing in cabaret perform a narrative of their own careers in the theatre, that cabaret functions as a kind of autobiography of women's individual struggle in the performing arts, and that the performance of this personal narrative functions as a form of theatre history. Sometimes, as in the case of Haran's showcases for the Rodgers and Hart songbook, the performance revisits the lives of figures other than that of the performer as well. These cabaret performances serve multiple pedagogical functions to the larger culture. They keep alive a nearly forgotten history of American theatre as they provide the historical context necessary for us to understand contemporary performance. Studying these performances also helps us track the shifting ideologies of gender, race, and class in the United States. And they beg the question: How and when did cabaret emerge as a genre for women in the performing arts?

The history of cabaret performance is fraught with competing and often contradictory accounts of its origins. My interest here is not in resolving these tensions but in calling attention to them and in seeing how the genre accommodated women performers over time. Part of the challenge for theatre historians interested in cabaret has to do with sorting through the various popular performances from different historical periods and distinct cultural traditions associated with the form. Senelick, for example, has gone to great length to differentiate the various forms of cabaret performance in Europe from the 1890s to the 1940s. His important scholarship reminds us that "although it bore different names and natures at different times in the course of its development, the cabaret essentially defined the genre the Germans called *Kleinkunst* and the Russians, 'theatre of miniatures': art that is minor not in significance or intentions but reduced in scale to its essential components." [5] Senelick's two volumes of cabaret performance excerpts provide a wonderfully diverse sampling of the styles of European cabaret throughout the first half of the twentieth century. But he also provides an invaluable sense of the genre's relationship to other theatrical traditions. As Senelick writes:

> Cabaret was also inspired, to a large extent, by variety which, over the course of the nineteenth century, had evolved as a highly commercialized species of urban popular entertainment. By 1890, variety theatres had themselves become grandiose, elaborate palaces of stereotyped amusement. But the innovators of cabaret intended to distil from the vaudeville, circus, and music halls their vitality, immediacy, and vivacity; to adopt the rapid alternation of attractions; and then, to harness their demotic features in order to convey a rarified artistic style or a liberal political message or a skewed vision of the world. What proved attractive to the early cabaretists and their coteries was the play element, the sense that art did not have to be

uplifting or earnest. Most serious artists had despaired of the boule-
vard theatre, because of its commercially viable forms, the farce and
the melodrama, struck them as beneath contempt; yet the artistically serious theatre, the pilgrimages to Bayreuth and the darkened
auditoriums for versitic stagings of Ibsen, Hauptmann, and problem drama, seemed to many to be fatally dismal, crepe-draped mir-
rors of the middle-class sensibility. The first propagandists for cabaret wanted the spectator to smoke, drink, comment, and join in the
chorus as he would a music hall; they wanted to reclaim the theatre
for sensuality and mirth.[6]

Senelick's comments point to cabaret's links with both popular entertainments and elite cultural practices. But they also suggest that cabaret's history is closely tied to the problem of genre. What is cabaret, and
how is it different from other forms of performance that include songs,
sketches, and monologues?

The question of cabaret's formal qualities is inextricably linked to its
context, venue, and audience. Senelick's research allows us to see the
complexity of these issues as it relates to cabaret's early history and its
exclusive performance in Europe. Shane Vogel, on the other hand, emphasizes cabaret's sociality, especially focusing on cabaret's transgressive role in the culture. Vogel is particularly interested in charting the
relationship between the performer and the spectator, as well as the improvisational nature of the performance event itself. For Vogel, cabaret
constitutes both a historical genre and a social space. It can also function as a site of where the meanings of racial difference become am-
plified and contested. American cabaret traces its roots to black performance traditions and to locations including most significantly Harlem.
Vogel's research on the overlap and interplay between the European
traditions and the U.S. context falls more in line with the sociological
position that imagines cabaret as the space of political agitation and cultural transgression. This is also the position aligned with the cabaret
blues that Michael Denning discusses in his important study of Billie
Holiday and other singers affiliated with the Café Society cabaret club
in New York City in the late 1930s. In *The Cultural Front*, Denning uncovers the many ways that the Café Society combined political satire
with jazz.[7]

This position of cabaret as a space of political agitation and social possibility was secured with the popularization of both the 1966 Kander and Ebb Broadway musical *Cabaret* and its critically acclaimed 1972 Hollywood film version directed by Bob Fosse starring Liza Minnelli and Joel Grey, which presented the decadent milieu of 1930s Berlin during the rise of fascism. It quickly became the primary understanding and dominant image of cabaret performance. *Cabaret* was based on *I Am a Camera*, John Van Druten's 1951 stage adaptation of Christopher Isherwood's paired novels *Mr. Norris Changes Trains* (1935) and *Goodbye to Berlin* (1939), reissued in 1946 as *The Berlin Stories*, which ran on Broadway during the 1951–52 season and starred Julie Harris in her Tony Award–winning performance as Sally Bowles. Kander and Ebb's musical fixed the idea of cabaret performance as transgressive and the cabaret nightclub itself as a space for social experimentation. As Vogel writes: "From its inception, cabaret has functioned as a crucible not only for artistic collaboration but also for counterdiscourses to dominant ideologies. Inextricably bound up with notions of gender, race, sexuality and nationality, cabaret has provided an opportunity to interrogate the status quo through performance."[8] Vogel goes on to chart the various regulations against cabaret performances in the United States throughout the twentieth century, citing how "the history of cabaret is also the history of its regulation."[9] This sociological position places cabaret within the political and cultural context of its historical period.

In the United States, cabaret's history is also related to the culture and practice of the concert saloon and other indigenous popular entertainments of the nineteenth century including minstrel shows, vaudevilles, and musical revues. In Brooks McNamara's fascinating study of the concert saloon in the period from the Civil War to the beginning of the twentieth century, we get a sense of the emergence of popular theatre in New York City and its transformation from an association with criminality to one of near respectability.[10] As McNamara makes clear, in the mid-nineteenth century the role of the popular entertainer proved a source of intense cultural anxiety. Various efforts to regulate performance were standard practices of the period, and especially vulnerable were concert saloon singers, viewed as immoral and criminal. The sense that concert saloons constituted havens for prostitution, gambling, and other illicit activities led to a strong antitheatrical sentiment that pitched more legitimate theatres and their practitioners against those entertainers who worked the saloon circuit.

Women performers faired poorly in these debates. McNamara uncovers early public performances by women singers who occasionally took the stage to sing a song or two. Often these singers were also "waiter girls" who served drinks and entertained the male clients. One report, published on April 16, 1864, in the *Clipper*, a print periodical founded in 1853 to cover sports and theatre and, as McNamara explains, one that "between about 1865–1875, . . . was the only American newspaper carrying extensive news about popular performance forms such as minstrelsy, variety halls, circus, and concert saloons and their shows," provides a snapshot of women performers in the period.[11]

> At many concert saloons of the day, for example, waiter girls seemed not only to have brought drinks to customers, but to have been expected to appear onstage, if they played a musical instrument or could carry a reasonable tune. Perhaps it was a requirement for the job, and certainly many of the waiter girls also were sometimes performers. In any event, as the *Clipper* pointed out, in 1864, at the Boulevard, "on the road to [McComb's] dam, "a couple of the 'sprites,' as alike as two peas, sang a very sweet duet together, accompanied by [the versatile] Walter Smith on the violin and Piano Tom on the piano. Their names we cannot recall, but many who are cracked up as Irish Nightingales, English Thrushes, Black Swans, etc., are not a marker to these same lady amateurs. After the duet, one of them sang a pretty ballad, written by Charles McKay and set to music by H. Russell, entitled 'Sunshine After Rain,' the sentiments of which are exceedingly beautiful."[12]

The women here remain nameless, in fact, "their names we cannot recall," suggesting that the particular performers themselves were not the central attraction at these venues and that they were more or less interchangeable—"as alike as two peas," as the article describes the singers of the duet. The male musical accompanists and the male composers, however, are listed. Nonetheless, this *Clipper* profile gives us a sense of the event, and now, nearly 150 years later, a sense of its cultural reception.

While the popular press discussed some of the saloon performances, much of their documentation was made possible by the legal efforts to shut these places and performances down. The Society for the Reformation of Juvenile Delinquents, founded in the early nineteenth century and recruited by the state legislature to investigate questionable performance venues in New York City, provides McNamara with invaluable descriptions of the venues, audiences, and performers of the 1870s and 1880s. Consider, for example, the following account of an 1882 performance at the Bowery Varieties at 33 Bowery in Lower Manhattan described by McNamara based on his research on the Society:

> Although in 1882 the Society reports were calling the place [the Bowery Varieties] a theatre, it is impossible to know whether the building has actually become more or less a variety theatre or whether the Society had simply found it convenient to muddy the distinction further. Probably it was basically still a traditional male-oriented concert saloon since a note in the May 1882 Society citation pointed out that admission was free, that "some females [sat] at tables drinking and smoking with men." "Private Boxes"—possibly a code for prostitution on the premises—were mentioned in one report.
>
> The show on May 2, 1882 included an unnamed song by a female, who also sang "Pitcher of Beer," encoring it with the past part of the unnamed song. This was followed by another tune, "Awfully Awful," sung by another woman, "attired in fancy costume," who danced at the end of each verse. Then came music by the "orchestra" and another unnamed song. The show ended with another woman singing, "A Violet from My Mother's Grave."[13]

This more clinical account differs substantially from the emotional register of the *Clipper* writer who describes the songs' tone and affect: "a very sweet duet" or "a pretty ballad" or "exceedingly beautiful sentiments." And yet it gives a sense of the cultural anxiety surrounding such performances.[14] The historian Faye E. Dudden also notes that the phenomenon of the waiter girl both presumes a male audience and "made viewing women's bodies an element of commercial entertainment in the most matter-of-fact way." She goes on to document some of the advertisements in the popular press, including this one from the Bowery Gaieties: "We are fully aware that the public would not care to listen to a woman singing if she were old or ugly, no matter how fine a talent she might be."[15]

Not everyone was drawn to employing waiter girls in their establishments. Many, in fact, attempted to produce revues that provided alternative programming to the suspicious activities of the more illicit venues in the Bowery.[16] One manager, Tony Pastor, opened the Music Hall in 1864 and offered family-fare entertainment that drew large and devoted audiences who supported his more moral vision of entertainment. Many of the performers most popular in the 1870s and 1880s began their careers at his establishment. As Cecil Smith points out in his study of early American musical comedy, none was more beloved than Lillian Russell, whose celebrity ranges among the late nineteenth century's most legendary. Pastor grew a reputation for discovering new talent and introduced Russell to his audiences in 1880. By 1885, she was a star of the comic operas popular at the time. *Polly, the Pet of the Regiment* was the vehicle that provided her the means to stardom. As Smith notes, Russell introduced a sentimental ballad, "The Silver Line," in the second act, and the song became one of the most popular of the period. Russell's celebrity was secured. "To this day," Smith wrote in 1950, sixty-five years later, "Lillian Russell remains one of the most deeply beloved and widely admired prima donnas of the American popular musical stage. Such latter-day celebrities as Marilyn Miller, Gertrude Lawrence, Ethel Merman, and Mary Martin have never received quite the same unbridled adulation; nor has any of them become the single, supreme, unchallenged symbol of all that was most desirable and most glamorous in her period."[17]

Nineteenth-century women singers from the much-maligned waiter girls to the much-admired Lillian Russell provided the two poles of popular performance in the period. Their performances form much of the critical backdrop for the later women Smith cites in his quote. As the American musical began to secure its distinct form and structure in the early twentieth century, women singers benefited from the multiple roles that became available to them. While most of these other popular entertainments either fused into newer forms or dropped out of the cultural landscape completely, the woman singer's role in the culture grew substantially. Speakeasies, for example, offered women singers employment for two seemingly contradictory reasons: first, singers helped credentialize the venue as a legitimate nightclub, rather than simply a watering hole; second, the women singers helped sell the drinks. And yet, as James Gavin points out in *Intimate Nights: The Golden Age of Cabaret,* his indispensable history of New York City nightlife in the twentieth century, these women, much like the waiter girls before them, were vulnerable to any number of difficulties when performing in these venues including, among other things, barroom brawls, gangster violence, and occasional toxic moonshine.[18]

The blues tradition also featured prominently in moving women singers forward, with black women singers such as Ma Rainey and Bessie Smith finding larger public audiences. While the influence of the blues on jazz and on American popular music is a routine observation, more might be said of the role of the female singer and her growing influence.[19] From jazz and swing, which increasingly repositioned female singers or "canaries" into the front lines — and whose impact and influence was felt from Harlem to rural America — to supper clubs in posh Manhattan hotels — whose clientele expected late-night entertainments — women singers soon moved into the spotlight singing what would become the classics of the American songbook. Despite an initial reluctance to hire women to front big bands, this practice had become widespread by the late 1930s. In *Jazz Singing,* Will Friedwald's immensely worthwhile history of jazz in the United States, he pins the exact date for the emergence of the tradition of the female singer to September 15, 1931. On this date, the controversial manager and producer Jack Kapp had Mildred Bailey front the Casa Loma Orchestra for four songs. Bailey, along with Connie Boswell and Lee Wiley, surfaced in 1931 and, according to Friedwald, these three singers "invented and defined the canary tradition in the early 1930s."[20] The success of Bailey's 1931 hit song "Rockin' Chair" secured that status of the "band canary," as female singers were called at the time. Bands immediately scurried to hire female singers, and the practice nearly immediately became a standard convention of the genre.

New York nightlife benefited from these cultural transitions, and the female singer increasingly came into demand not only in the recording studios but also as a form of popular entertainment at restaurants, clubs, and hotels featuring dining and dancing. As Gavin points out, the proliferation of small clubs only increased the demand for live acts, and many of these performers began to find this work lucrative, especially as a showcase for a chance to appear in the new technology of live television and as a springboard for a role on the Broadway stage. Women moved to New York City from all over the country seeking success in the performing arts, and they were met with enthusiasm in the city's nightclubs. A few of these women became stars.

Many of the early American musicals, in fact, foreground this theme. Musicals from the 1920s, for example, combined the popular "Cinderella" musicals, where a young working-class girl gets the guy, with the "backstage" musicals, where the life of the theatre itself becomes the subject of the show. As John Bush Jones describes them, "In the 'Cinderella musicals' of the early 1920s, a working-class girl (almost always Irish-American!) works as a maid, shop girl, or secretary. Through marriage and/or good business sense, she ultimately obtains not only the man of her dreams but wealth and elevated social status. In a few shows, she achieves theatrical stardom as well."[21] In musicals such as *The Girl in the Spotlight* (1920), *Sally* (1920), and *Show Girl* (1929), the working girl triumphs, as did the women who got to play these parts.[22] The popularity of these shows, especially among Manhattan's increasing pool of working women who bought the more affordable balcony matinee tickets, provided employment for many women singers.[23] The cultural fascination with this fantasy of female victory combined with the actual success of many of these women singers on Broadway stages and on television variety shows fueled the desire of many women who moved to New York in the years to follow. Three of the young women who came to New York in the late 1940s to find success in the commercial theatre, and did so early on, found themselves back on Broadway in the Spring of 2002.

In her remarkable one-woman tour de force *Elaine Stritch at Liberty*, which premiered at New York's Public Theater in the fall of 2001 and moved to the Neil Simon Theatre on Broadway in the Spring of 2002, the veteran performer Elaine Stritch captures the feeling so typical of the time for any number of young women as she describes her own migration from the suburbs of Detroit to New York City in the 1940s and her efforts to make it in the theatre. Stritch's performance looks back at her life in the theatre, from her earliest professional experiences in the 1940s and 1950s to her more celebrated appearances in musicals such as *Sail Away* (1961) and *Company* (1970) and plays such as the revival of *A Delicate Balance* (1996). The performance constitutes an archive of her life in the theatre told through story and song. She sings songs from the Broadway musicals associated with her career, and she tells stories of the many famous people she has encountered in her life. Some of these figures are expected; given her performance vita, artists such as Ethel Merman, Noel Coward, Judy Garland, and Edward Albee frame the artistic milieu of the day. But other contemporaries, such as Marlon Brando, Rock Hudson, Gloria Swanson, and Richard Burton, are as surprising and unexpected affiliations to us as they were to her. Stritch populates her performance with these personalities and provides anecdotes of her encounters with them in between songs that showcase the talents of many of the major composers of the American musical: Irving Berlin, George Gershwin, Jule Styne, and Betty Comden and Adolph Green. The interplay between the stories and the songs could easily lead one to claim that the songs break up the narrative, as in the traditional manner of a Broadway musical, rather than the other way around, where the narrative interrupts the recital of songs, as in a cabaret performance. Stritch's nearly seamless move from song to story makes classifying *At Liberty* difficult, and it led the 2002 Tony Award committee to establish a separate category to acknowledge it.[24]

Throughout the performance, directed by George C. Wolfe, Stritch revisits her career and in the process provides an entry point to a cultural history of the twentieth century from the perspective of the performing arts. The performance is at once a chronicle of her life in the arts, a tell-all theatrical memoir, and a window into the gendered and racialized worlds of New York that enabled and/or disabled Stritch's very career and life experiences. She embodies this history and relives it through the corporal and kinesthetic moves that, while her own, allow her audiences either to relive their own spectatorial memories of Stritch's career or to encounter this legendary performer for the first time. Audiences are given the opportunity to learn about her theatre work and the cultural history in which it is embedded. When the show first premiered, Stritch was seventy-six years old. Her gritty storytelling and raspy-throated song delivery stripped the show of the nostalgic sentiments that overshadow many performances of this kind, adding to the sense of her historical embodiment. *At Liberty* is the culmination of a career; it is more than merely a presentation of Stritch's greatest theatrical hits. It charts a lifetime of performance that ends with the sense that one has, indeed and in fact, just seen the performance of a lifetime.

Stritch introduces songs to fulfill one of three functions: they capture the milieu of the time, revisit an earlier success, or convey an emotional sentiment. Early on in the show, in a segment that describes her first years in New York, she recounts what it was like to be in her late teens, living in a residential convent, and taking acting classes at the Dramatic Workshop at the New School. Full of ambition and desire but unable to fit the stereotype of either the ingenue or the leading lady, she wonders what kind of career might be available to her. And then, nearly out of nowhere, she begins to sing "Broadway Baby," Stephen Sondheim's tribute to the women of the American musicals of the 1920s, 1930s, and 1940s from *Follies* (1971):

> I'm just a Broadway baby
> walking off my tired feet
> pounding 42nd street to be in a show, oh,
> Broadway baby,
> learning how to sing and dance,
> waiting for that one big chance to be in a show [25]

The song has no setup; Stritch simply begins singing it without any accompaniment, nearly speaking the lines, as if the lyrics were her own thoughts. A piano begins to repeat the melody after she sings it, and soon serves as an accompaniment. By the end of the first chorus, Stritch is joined by the nine-piece orchestra that performs with her throughout the show. She ends the song without any commentary about the piece itself; it is used to move the narrative from one period of her life to another, and it calls attention to her feelings at the time, even though the song itself would not be written for many years. "Broadway Baby" stands in for the many girls who moved to New York, lived in women-only residencies, took acting classes, entered the workplace as single women, went on countless auditions for a spot on the chorus or a musical review, and hoped to make it big in the entertainment business. American popular culture is full of representations of these young women—itself a variation of the "Cinderella" and "backstage" musicals of the 1920s—from films and musicals such as *Stage Door* and *All about Eve* to *A Chorus Line* and *Fame*, but few if any of these representations are told from the historical perspective of the performer herself. *At Liberty* adds depth to this portrayal and provides the context for what many young white middle-class women experienced in the 1940s in New York City at the time, albeit without Stritch's success.

Although her first appearance on Broadway was at twenty-one years old in the 1946 play *Loco*, her break came when she was cast in the 1948 musical revue *Angel in the Wings*. Cast initially and, it seemed, exclusively for the comic sketches, Stritch asked the producers for a song. The producers had a meeting at the Algonquin Hotel and, as Stritch imagines, they figured they would give her a song for the Philadelphia out-of-town tryout—and then drop it before the New York opening. But, as it turns out, they did not cut it, and she sang the one song, "Civilization," eight times a week for over a year and half. In one of *At Liberty*'s most charming and amusing moments, Stritch recreates her performance, even including the original choreography, which has her taking the role of a so-called native in a primitivist sketch in the revue—"Bongo, bongo, bongo, I don't want to leave the Congo, oh no no no no no." The juxtaposition of the older performer reviving her earliest Broadway song, now nearly fifty-five years later, uncannily places the historical past in immediate conversation with the contemporary. Stritch is both the theatrical novice and the stage veteran, straddling the divide between her lived experience and her current stage performance. This mutually interdependent exchange keeps alive a performance well retired in the popular imaginary, but for Stritch, it seems as if she never stopped performing it. "Civilization," her one song in the

53. "Elaine Stritch of New York cools off after paying a one dollar fine in mid-Manhattan Court today for wearing this halter and shorts in Central Park, Sunday. The actress, understudying for Ethel Merman, got the ticket when she took off a t-shirt after a bike ride. Said the Judge: 'A beautiful girl like you could cause a riot.' Retorted Elaine: 'I was there all day and nothing happened.'" International News Photo, June 6, 1951. Photo by Stanley Hall. Billy Rose Theatre Collection, New York Public Library for the Performing Arts, Lenox and Tilden Foundations

revue, springboards Stritch to a career in the musical theatre; *Angel in the Wings* is followed immediately by a gig as Ethel Merman's standby in *Call Me Madam* (1950). While understudying Merman, who was famous for never missing a performance, Stritch auditioned for a role in the 1952 revival of *Pal Joey*, Rodgers and Hart's 1940 musical about Joey Evans, a shady, second-rate Chicago nightclub entertainer, and got the part while still committed to the other show (figure 53).

Based on the *New Yorker* stories of John O'Hara, who also wrote the musical's book, *Pal Joey* constituted a major departure from the traditional American musical in that it featured seedy characters engaging in sex, blackmail, and corruption. The original 1940 production, in fact, received mixed reviews, mainly for its unsavory themes and plot, even occasioning the *New York Times* critic, Brooks Atkinson, to write at the time, "Although *Pal Joey* is expertly done, can you draw sweet water from a foul well?"[26] Rodgers and Hart (and O'Hara) were singled out, however, for the depth of the character portrayal; these characters might be unsavory, but they were fully developed and psychologically believable (figure 54). The songs, especially, captured the nuance and

54. Rodgers and Hart rehearsing *Pal Joey*, New York City, 1940. Billy Rose Theatre Collection, New York Public Library for the Performing Arts, Lenox and Tilden Foundations

complexity of the characters. The 1952 revival, which cast Stritch in a supporting role, initially had difficulty raising money for the production given its 1940s reviews; but Jule Styne, who produced the show, persevered. In the end, the revival of *Pal Joey* turned out a critical and commercial success.

Stritch had only one number in the show, "Zip," a performance that became a critical rave and, according to *Time*, "stops the show."[27] Stritch played the part of a reporter, Melba Snyder, assigned to interview Joey, who is arrogant and cocky. The reporter decides to bring Joey down a notch by name-dropping the various important figures she has encountered in her job, the most interesting one being Gypsy Rose Lee. She then proceeds to tell the story of the interview and goes on to recreate Lee's response. The song is remarkable in that it accounts for Lee's private thoughts as she is actually working; it is an interior monologue told through music and dance. Although the song is performed by a minor character, Melba Snyder, who then herself impersonates Lee, a character not even central to the musical's plot, it is one of the highlights of the show:

I met her at the Yankee Clipper,
And she didn't unzip one zipper.
I said, "Miss Lee, you are such an artist.
Tell me why you never miss,
What do you think of while you work?"
And she said, "While I work my thoughts go something like this:
Zip, Walter Lipman wasn't brilliant today.
Zip, Will Saroyan ever write a great play?
Zip, I was reading Schopenhauer last night.
Zip, and I think that Schopenhauer was right[28]

Hart's clever and topical lyrics recreate the patter for which Gypsy Rose Lee was known.[29] But the lyrics also do more. The song at once demystifies women's labor and presents the performer's perspective of the strip as banal. Clearly, Lee's mind wanders during the strip; she simply goes through the motions because it is her job. In *At Liberty*, Stritch, too, uses the song to demystify the business of Broadway and her own preoccupations during the 1952 run. The song is introduced in *At Liberty* to convey Stritch's dilemma in being cast in two shows simultaneously. "Zip" doesn't appear until the second act of the show, leaving plenty of time for Stritch to find out if Merman would go on in *Call Me Madam* and plenty of time for the *Pal Joey* producers to notify Stritch's understudy in *Pal Joey* if Stritch would not be available to sing "Zip."

Stritch begins the song by recreating her performance of the song in the revival (figure 55). Soon, however, she begins to rehearse the random thoughts that she herself experienced during one of her 1952 performances. This running commentary is incorporated into Hart's lyrics of Lee's private thoughts. The difference is that now, in the current production of *At Liberty*, the performer is able to do what she herself could not do in 1952 and what Lee, along with countless other women performers, could not do previously—convey their actual thought processes to the audience. They did their jobs and the audience knew no better. Stritch's contemporary performance also begs the question what she herself might be thinking as she performs this number. Despite the fact that the performance is highly autobiographical—"This existential problem in tights," as Stritch describes herself near the end of her show—it nonetheless constitutes a staged representation.[30] As John

55. Elaine Stritch performing "Zip" in *Elaine Stritch at Liberty*, Public Theatre, New York City, 2001. Photo by Michal Daniel

Lahr, who worked with Stritch on the script, explains: "It took Elaine a while to absorb my suggestions that, rather than just going out there and telling stories to accompany songs, she act a character called 'Elaine Stritch' in a drama based on her life which musical numbers—some from her career, some that expressed her emotional biography—would be integrated."[31] "Zip" calls attention to this idea of the performer inhabiting a role. The seductive movements of the song's choreography are matched by the seductive intimacy of the song's interior monologue, the seemingly authentic nakedness of the actual performer, who does not actually strip, that fuels the audience's voyeuristic investments in both these aspects of her performance.

The specifics of Stritch's own biography feature prominently throughout the evening. She tells candid stories of her decades-long career as an alcoholic, leading one critic to claim that the show at times "feels like a really, really good AA meeting."[32] Stritch's drinking, in fact, represents a leitmotif of the performance; the link between alcohol and theatre is made most apparent when Stritch catalogues the particular drink she associates with a show—*Angel in the Wings*, Canadian

Club; *Pal Joey*, Beaujolais; *Call Me Madam*, white wine, *On Your Toes*, Dewar's; *Bus Stop*, Schlitz; and so on—and she confesses that drinking made her feel that she was not alone "out there," which for her means on the stage. This confessional aspect, "the really, really good AA meeting" feel of *At Liberty*, can be traced to Stritch's Catholicism, which also serves as a recurrent motif of the show and a spiritual foundation for the performer. Her Roman Catholic upbringing—she is, in fact, the niece of Cardinal Stritch of Chicago—trains her in introspection and revelation and, when combined with the alcoholism recovery narrative, pushes the performance to the pious tradition of Saint Augustine's *Confessions*, a tale of a life of indulgence and hedonism that ends in redemption. In this sense, the space of the theatre itself takes on a spiritual resonance that Stritch exploits to great effect. In demystifying the theatre with the juicy backstage stories of near disasters and misfires—misplaced props, forgotten lines, miscast actors, bitchy competitors—Stritch reveals the mechanics of the theatre, the wires that hold things together. The theatre then becomes a metaphor for her own life too. Everything is exposed, nothing remains hidden. And yet, by the end, the theatre is presented as a space of redemption and renewal.

Near the end of her show, Stritch conveys her understanding of her performance as a chance to reclaim her life and career, one that she says, "almost happened without me." But the performance does more; it revisits a history that once was, a past moment in American cultural history that while lost, is still here through her performance. *At Liberty* goes beyond simply revisiting Stritch's own career, it revisits and revives a time once lived. Stritch best exemplifies this process in her performance of Sondheim's anthem of survival, "I'm Still Here." Before she begins the song, she bemoans the fact that many singers much younger than her, some even in their forties, have already sung the song in public—"where have they been?" she wonders impatiently. Stritch decided not to sing the piece until she had reached a certain age, one that would give the song the necessary context for it to achieve its full meaning (figure 56):

> Good times and bum times
> I've seen them all and, my dear,
> I'm still here.

Plush velvet sometimes,
Sometimes just pretzels and beer,
But I'm here.
I've stuffed the Dailies in my shoes
Strummed Ukeleles
Sung the Blues
Seen all my dreams disappear
But I'm here . . .
. . . I've been through Ghandi
Windsor and Wally's affair,
And I'm here.
Amos 'n' Andy,
Mahjongg and Platinum hair,
And I'm here.
I got through Abie's Irish Rose,
Five Dionne Babies,
Major Bowes,
Had Heebie-Jeebies
For Beebe's Bathysphere,
I've lived through Brenda Frazier,
And I'm here.[33]

The song conveys an entire cultural archive of American history as seen through the perspective of an aged cabaret performer, someone whose career has fallen in and out of critical favor and commercial viability. Many of the references in the song have long since passed out of common knowledge, but while their topicality may now be obscured or forgotten entirely, the performer, who lived through these currents, is "still here." The point of the song is not so much that this history is lost, but that the performer, who remembers it, is still here to tell us about it. The song acts as a form of embodied cultural memory, a shared consciousness between performer and spectator. In its specificity of reference, the song resembles Stritch's performance itself: a return to particular shows, anecdotes, personalities, and cultural references from her life that intersect with a broader pattern of Broadway culture and, by extension, twentieth-century American history.

The song generally receives the biggest round of applause from the

56. "I'm Still Here," Elaine Stritch performs in *Elaine Stritch at Liberty*, Public Theatre, New York City, 2001. Photo by Michal Daniel

audience not because it is Stritch's signature piece—it isn't, in fact; that would probably be "The Ladies Who Lunch" from Sondheim's *Company*. When she introduces the song at the top of the second act, she even tells us that she has never sung it before. "I'm Still Here" forms the centerpiece of *Elaine Stritch at Liberty* because it captures the fundamental spirit of the show and that of the older women singers of cabaret. Stritch has lived through all the songs and stories she has shared in her performance, some familiar and some less so, and she is still here to belt out this personal and cultural history to us now. While the song thematizes the decline of a career ("First, you're another slow-eyed vamp, then someone's mother, then you're camp, then you career to career to career"), it poignantly provides the forum in which the older woman performer can again be the leading lady. In this sense, Stritch's rendition functions differently than that of the version in the original narrative context of *Follies*, where it first appeared and was performed by Yvonne DeCarlo. In *Follies*, it is sung by a secondary character, Carlotta Campion, whose only number is this song, a ghostly performance that appears and then disappears in what seems like a flash. It is a memory song that itself becomes a faded memory as the narrative plot-

57. Promotional flyer for Bea Arthur, *Just between Friends*, New York City, 2002. Collection of the author

line returns to the story of the central characters. *Elaine Stritch at Liberty* moves the singer of "I'm Still Here" from the outer parameters of the production to center stage. Not only is she finally—or again—top-billing but she reconstructs her history in her own words.

The same season that brought Elaine Stritch to Broadway included Bea Arthur's *Just between Friends*, Arthur's cabaret-like performance at the Booth Theatre (figure 57). Arthur, accompanied by Billy Goldenberg on the piano, similarly tells stories from her career in television and on stage, singing songs intermittently. While the format appears strikingly the same and while the overlap in the two women's careers is nothing short of uncanny—they are the same age, both went to the

New School nearly the same years, and Stritch auditioned for the part that won Arthur critical acclaim in the television hit series *The Golden Girls*—their performances differ dramatically in style and tone. Arthur reveals very little about her life, and her anecdotes remain casual if not trivial. She begins her show with a non sequitur: a recipe for lamb. Even her early theatrical achievements—the original role of Yenta the matchmaker in *Fiddler on the Roof* (1964), a Tony Award for her performance as Vera Charles in *Mame* (1966), a gig with Lotte Lenya in the 1954 revival of *Three Penny Opera*—are underplayed. Arthur arguably has a more impressive theatre career than Stritch, at least in the early stages of their careers, but she does not lay any claims to being a theatre legend in the way that Stritch does. Stories from her television hits, *Maude* and *The Golden Girls*, are light and casual and mainly rely on audience recognition of familiar phrases associated with her characters. Arthur's presentation is intentionally low key, and she opts for jokes full of ribaldry and vulgarity over stories full of insight and profundity. The casualness is evident in her set, which consists only of a wing chair, an end table, and arranged flowers. Billy Goldenberg is also on stage nearby, providing the sense of a cabaret performance, as he plays the piano and occasionally banters along with Arthur. Early on in the performance, Arthur explains that she needed to get outside the "little box," and *Just between Friends* reminds audiences that her origins are in live performance, not television.

Arthur's show originated in the celebrity benefit circuit, where she was asked to perform a number or two to help raise money for any number of progressive causes. As early as 1981, she and Goldenberg were asked to participate in an American Civil Liberties Union (ACLU) benefit featuring the songs of Marilyn and Alan Bergman; they performed three songs from *Queen of the Stardust Ballroom*. Once she was invited to perform at an AIDS benefit in Palm Springs, presuming that she would be on a roster with other entertainers. It turned out, however, that the organizers expected her to perform a thirty-minute set, which she then quickly proceeded to develop with Goldenberg. *Just between Friends* continued in this vein, songs and stories being added to flesh out a full-evening performance that toured throughout the United States before premiering on Broadway in the spring of 2002. To their credit,

Arthur and Goldenberg insist on keeping the politics of the show's origins up front. Arthur's show contains bawdy jokes, backstage stories, and liberal political commentary, including her endorsement of same-sex marriage. She also includes occasional tributes to other performers, even one to Charles Pierce, who was one of Arthur's closest friends. Pierce had asked Arthur to speak at his memorial service, and Arthur delivers one of the eulogies in *Just between Friends*, which included the story of "A Mother's Ingenuity," a humorous tale of a mother, her son, and his lover. Arthur's recital of the tale archives a popular joke of the closet and reveals the ease of her relationships with the lesbian and gay community. It also very poignantly keeps the name of Pierce in circulation, in this case offering him a moment on the Broadway stage. The previous chapter wondered where Pierce's legacy might find reembodiment, and strangely and surprisingly, it is here in Arthur's Broadway performance that he is summoned.

Arthur also tells stories of her collaborations with legendary figures in the performing arts such as Jerome Robbins, Tallulah Bankhead, and Angela Lansbury, but she offers little of the historical context of the period that made these figures famous, and she reveals nothing much about the influence these artists had on her career. The stories are breezy and light, meaning to entertain. One exception involves a story of her very first audition for the 1947 road company of *Call Me Mister*. Hoping for a big break, she tells of the anxiety of auditioning, and of the backstage world of young people trying to make it in show business. Her audition was scheduled at the Nederlander Theatre on Forty-first Street, and her friends got her drunk at the basement bar beforehand. Needless to say, she blew the audition, but she offers a sense of the world at that time, and of the enthusiasm and optimism of the day: "I was living in New York and what an exciting time it was to be there!"[34]

Between auditions, she and her friends—"unemployed would-be actors"—would sneak into Broadway shows at intermission, and after the show they would go out drinking and carousing in the clubs. Unemployed and between shows, these actors were among the core constituents of Manhattan nightlife. In these clubs she heard singers such as Tony Bennett, Lena Horne, and Mabel Mercer. The worlds of Broadway, cabaret, and the nightclub intersect as a snapshot of late-1940s

New York cultural history presented to the audience. Much of the evening centers on celebrity name-dropping, but on this occasion, a sense of history begins to surface as well. Arthur here segues into Cy Coleman's "Isn't He Adorable," a song made famous by Mabel Mercer, perhaps the most influential singer of cabaret performance in the twentieth century. Once renowned for her intimate performances, Mercer has slipped into cultural obscurity since her death in 1984; only in the world of cabaret does her reputation live on.

At the end of her performance, which lasts just over an hour, Arthur thanks her audience and ends the show with the line, "I want to thank you all for coming, and I am not going to sing 'I'm Still Here!' " Her nonperformance of the song seems like its own defiant differentiation from Stritch, a refusal almost to position herself under the terms that Stritch claims for herself when she performs the song nightly only a few blocks away at the Neil Simon Theatre. Arthur leaves the stage of the Booth rejecting the song and its meanings, even as Goldenberg inconspicuously incorporates the melody of the Sondheim song into the piano medley that closes the show. It makes for a fascinating and complex moment. In part, it humorously acknowledges Stritch's performance and presumes the audience's knowledge of that show and its centerpiece. But not everyone in the audience will hear the musical citation and make the connection between the song and the Stritch performance; it remains an insider's joke. In fact, the show's final lines about "I'm Still Here," might seem to many in her audience as much a non sequitur as the opening lines about the recipe for lamb.

While Bea Arthur summons the Sondheim song only to reject it as a means of interpreting her performance or her career in general, Barbara Cook makes an entire evening out of Sondheim and his oeuvre. Cook's emphatic identification with Sondheim has little to do with her own career trajectory. Unlike Stritch, who was cast in the original Broadway cast of *Company*, Cook has never originated a Sondheim role.[35] Cook's affiliation remains almost completely honorific. She is there to celebrate Sondheim's career, using her voice to do so. *Barbara Cook Sings Mostly Sondheim* was conceived as a full-evening concert in celebration of Sondheim's seventieth birthday on March 22, 2000. Inspired by the May 22, 2000, Library of Congress celebration of Sondheim, the greatest living composer of the musical theatre and, undoubtedly, one of the most influential of the twentieth century, Cook decided to devote an evening to Sondheim songs, as well as to songs he wished he had written (drawn from a list that the composer had included in a *New York Times Magazine* cover article on him and his career). *Mostly Sondheim* originated as a cabaret performance in November 2000 at one of New York City's premiere cabaret venues, Feinstein's at the Regency, under the title *Barbara Cook: In Good Company*, with musical direction by Wally Harper, also credited with the idea for the show. Cook and Harper developed the evening and presented it at Carnegie Hall on February 14, 2001, as *Mostly Sondheim*, touring before the show was presented at Lincoln Center.[36]

Cook's performance in *Mostly Sondheim* is completely traditional in that the performer, a trained soprano, sings to convey her virtuosity through the accomplished songbook of a canonical composer. *Mostly Sondheim* secures Cook's reputation as one of the great voices of American popular song and assumes Sondheim's stature as a genius (figure 58). Cook enters the stage immediately singing "Everybody Says Don't" from the 1964 show *Anyone Can Whistle*. There is no introduction to the song, to the composer, or even to the performer; Cook simply sings the song, and she does so beautifully. After the applause, Cook addresses her audience:

> Let me tell you a little about our program tonight. Last spring Stephen Sondheim celebrated his seventieth birthday, and as part of that celebration the Library of Congress did a big concert in Washington for him. Now you would think that on a night like that, the entire program would consist of songs by Stephen Sondheim, but it was his idea to have a large part of the program devoted to songs he wishes he had written. So that's what we are going to do tonight, we are going to do songs that Stephen wishes he had written, and the ones we are mighty glad he did.[37]

We hear nothing about Cook's relationship to the material, and there is little introduction to Sondheim as well. Cook's patter simply offers her a chance to catch her breath before returning to the program. Next up are three songs by Harold Arlen, a composer known for such standards

as "Over the Rainbow," "Stormy Weather," and "I've Got the World on a String" and whose influence on Sondheim, Cook suggests, becomes evident from listening. And yet again, there is little context for this comparison; it is assumed and not conveyed. The presumption is that audiences are already familiar with Arlen, Sondheim, and Cook herself. Her performance, like all exercises in the classics, never calls attention to its own virtuosity or status; everything goes without saying, nothing is explained. This sense of the performance's timelessness and universal appeal is never pitched as nostalgic or sentimental. Its formality and importance is secured through its venues. In New York, she performed the show at Lincoln Center and Carnegie Hall, perhaps the two most prestigious houses for the popular performing arts in the city. These sites are never understood as the venues of the subcultural worlds of the New York elite whose familiarity with Arlen, Sondheim, and Cook convey the vernacular knowledge that begins to grant entry into this elite subculture in the first place. This vernacular knowledge not only provides access to a particular subcultural world; it also obscures the

58. Barbara Cook in performance, London, 2003. Photo by Mike Martin

59. Barbara Cook publicity still from 1954. Billy Rose Theatre Collection, New York Public Library for the Performing Arts, Lenox and Tilden Foundations

ideological work that allows these venues and performances to pass and register not as subcultural practices but as culture itself.

This observation by no means discredits either Cook or Sondheim's achievement. *Mostly Sondheim* stands as an extraordinary concert recital; it is the performance of an artist in peak form singing some of the most celebrated songs of the American musical tradition. The combination of Cook and Sondheim, as Frank Rich writes in the liner notes to the Carnegie Hall recording, is as remarkable as it is unlikely:

> It was within only a few weeks at the end of 1957 that Barbara Cook and Stephen Sondheim both took Broadway by storm — in hit shows that could not have more aptly symbolized the opposite poles of the post-war American musical theatre. Cook was Marian the Librarian in *The Music Man*, the Meredith Wilson slice of small-town America that transported Cold War audiences back to the bygone heartland of big brass bands and innocent love stories that always turned out happily in the end. Sondheim was the new young writer whose lyrics for *West Side Story* delineated an increasingly troubled

urban America where music could be dissonant, words could be angry and young love could end in tragedy. . . . So long typed as the sunniest of Broadway ingénues, Cook finds in Sondheim's songs a whole octave of rue and heartbreak without forsaking any of her ineffable Southern warmth. So long typed as the headiest of Broadway songwriters, Sondheim finds in Cook an interpreter of pure soul as well as all the requisite urban wit.[38]

Cook, also in her seventies, began her musical career like Stritch and Arthur in the late 1940s. She moved to New York in 1948 from Atlanta when she was twenty-one years old. (In one of the evening's few personal anecdotes, Cook shares that the first Broadway musical she saw when she moved to the city was *Annie Get Your Gun* (1946), starring Ethel Merman and with music by Irving Berlin.) Within a few years she was singing at the Blue Angel, one of New York's most renowned nightclubs at the time. In *Intimate Nights*, James Gavin reports that Cook's approach was one "of one-eyed wonderment at getting to sing in such a swank place."[39] Jimmy Lyon, the pianist at the Blue Angel, explained that when Cook performed, "she didn't have an act. All she did was stand there and sing ballads in that gorgeous voice, but everybody adored her."[40] Before long, she was starring on Broadway in a series of ingenue roles that launched her professional career: *Candide* (1956), *The Music Man* (1957), and *She Loves Me* (1963). For a generation of audiences, Cook was the voice and embodiment of the innocent young girl discovering love for the first time (figure 59).

In the mid-1970s, Cook returned to the cabaret circuit of these early years in her career and began more regularly to present herself as a concert singer. Like many of her generation, Cook found in cabaret a regular venue in which to perform. The paucity of roles for older women singers, combined with the opportunity to perform a repertoire of their own choosing, positioned cabaret as a lucrative and artistic opportunity for many of these older women artists. Cook's roots in cabaret become obscured in *Mostly Sondheim*, and there seems little reason for her to revisit them given the clarity of the evening's mission to pay tribute to Sondheim and his influences.

It might still hold true that in *Mostly Sondheim*, Cook still does not "have an act," unlike Stritch, Arthur, and other singers of the cabaret circuit. She appears uninterested in using her performance as a means to uncover a cultural past, be it hers, Sondheim's, or that of her audience. Lyon's 1950 observation that "all she did was stand there and sing ballads in that gorgeous voice" still characterizes Cook more than fifty years later. This, in fact, has become her act: her performance is an act of pure virtuosity that presents itself as a classic, and in that she succeeds.

Cook ended the evening with one of the songs that Sondheim wished he had written, "The Trolley Song" by Hugh Martin and Ralph Blane and made famous by Judy Garland in the 1944 film *Meet Me in Saint Louis.* Cook's exuberant and charismatic rendition of the song returns her to the youthful persona of her earlier career as ingenue. She introduced the song by saying, "This next song is one that I loved for a long time, but I felt—and still feel—that it was the particular property of a particular singer. Anyway when it was more appropriate for me to sing the song, I wouldn't touch it. But now that we have this little conceit going here, I thought maybe I could finally sing the song." She never mentions Garland or the song's title, keeping the dramatic tension going until the song announces itself. If there is a song more suggestive of the excitement of young love, I cannot think of it:

> With my high starched collar and my high topped shoes,
> And my hair piled high upon my head,
> I went to lose a jolly hour and lost my heart instead.
> With his light brown derby and his bright green tie,
> He was quite the handsomest of men,
> I started to yen, so I counted to ten, then I counted to ten again,
> "Clang, clang, clang," went the trolley,
> "Ding, ding, ding," went the bell,
> "Zing, zing, zing," went my heart-strings,
> For the moment I saw him I fell. . . .[41]

If Stritch felt that she could not sing "I'm Still Here" until she reached a certain age, until her version of the song encapsulated a life and its context, and until her voice, now aged by cigarettes and booze, finally did the song its justice, Cook here suggests something quite different in ending her performance with "The Trolley Song." Although she claims that the moment when it was "appropriate" for her to sing it has long passed, and that her age now makes for a striking incongruity with the helpless naivety of the song's persona, she can still capture and communicate the work's essence through the sheer power of her voice. To strike this point, she returns for her encore to sing without a microphone or amplification Sondheim's heartbreaking title song from *Anyone Can Whistle*. The song laments the singer's inability to whistle—"to let go, lower my guard, learn to be free"—and underlines her yearning for the chance to live carefree.

Two songs from *Anyone Can Whistle* frame *Barbara Cook Sings Mostly Sondheim*. One would think that the pieces would be reversed, that the evening would begin with "Anyone Can Whistle," the song of constraint, and end with "Everybody Says Don't," the song of defiance. But in choosing to avoid this trajectory of liberation through performance, Cook moves the focus away from hearing her performance as autobiographical; instead it is about, well, mostly Sondheim, about Sondheim's career, his revolutionary innovations to the American musical, and the personal price he has had to pay for his artistic life:

> Anyone can whistle,
> That's what they say—Easy,
> Anyone can whistle
> Any old day—Easy.
> It's all so simple:
> Relax, let go, let fly.
> So someone tell me why can't I?
> . . . Maybe you could show me
> How to let go,
> Lower my guard,
> Learn to be free,
> Maybe if you whistle,
> Whistle for me.[42]

Cook's performance in *Mostly Sondheim* might be understood as the surrogate voice for Sondheim himself—she is the one who "whistles" for him.

In Donna McKechnie's *Inside the Music* (2001), her one-woman show that she performs in cabaret venues, performing art centers, and traditional theatres, she includes a rendition of "Everybody Says Don't" that is nearly the antithesis of Cook's version.[43] McKechnie immerses her version in autobiographical anecdote; she uses the song to foreground a sense of cultural awakening, a moment of feminist consciousness encapsulated by the song's defiant rejection of the status quo. She makes little effort to present herself as the song's interpreter; rather, McKechnie sings the song as a way to interpret her life and the choices she made as a young woman. In this sense, she reverses the standard performance of the singer's relationship to a song, one where the performer offers a personal interpretation through vocal inflection, phrasing, and tone, and exploits the song's narrative logic to punctuate her life story. In fact, if Cook's version of "Everybody Says Don't" is all about virtuosic interpretation with no personal or historical context, McKechnie's song is nearly all personal context with little effort for virtuosity. Neither singer, it should be noted, mentions anything about the song itself. The song is introduced in McKechnie's show to emphasize a long but pivotal story about the artist's feminist awakening. It marks an extraordinary section of the performance in which the performer, who has made a career as an actor playing someone else for whom the song is expressive of her character, now plays herself and uses the song to move her life story forward. Like Stritch in *At Liberty*, McKechnie follows the model of the traditional musical in her use of song. In *Inside the Music*, McKechnie's version of "Everybody Says Don't" appears to reflect the performer's own words, not those of Sondheim.

McKechnie sets up her version of the song by revisiting a passionate affair she had in her twenties with a handsome actor. The story comes midway through the performance, after a medley of songs that highlight the role theatre and cinema played in her troubled adolescence in Michigan. Young and in love, she and the boyfriend are an item. When he gets a film job in a spaghetti Western shooting in Spain, she joins him on location. The boyfriend, while "so good-looking," is a control freak; he sets up all sorts of rules for her and appears especially adamant about her not mixing with the Spanish "gypsies" serving as extras. She recalls his regulations and, as she begins to catalogue them, transitions into the song: ' "Stay away from them, don't look them in the eye,' he said, 'don't smile at them, don't wear anything low-cut around them, don't wear that red top, don't wear that blue top, don't wear those earrings, don't raise your eyebrows, don't lower your eyebrows, don't do this, don't do that.' "[44] As she moves further into the story, a piano begins to play the melody of the Sondheim song, and she starts singing the lyrics: "Everybody says don't / Everybody says don't / Everybody says don't—it isn't right / Don't—it isn't nice!"[45] After only these few lines, McKechnie quickly returns to her personal narrative and offers a larger context for her story—"My family used to say don't get attention . . . don't try to stand out"—before continuing with the story of her boyfriend, the Spanish gypsies, and her growing impatience with the regulatory constraints of gender she is expected to respect. McKechnie nicely captures the way young women in the 1960s were expected to concede to the rules of others—boyfriends, parents, the normative culture—even if they themselves had different ideas for their lives:

> Everybody says don't,
> Everybody says don't,
> Everybody says don't walk on the grass,
> Don't disturb the peace,
> Don't skate on the ice.

At the last night of the film shoot, at the wrap party, the Spanish extras were dancing Flamenco while the Americans remained seated; the film people simply watched the gypsies enjoy themselves—too uptight, too shy, or too aloof to join in the celebrations. McKechnie, however, as a dancer was drawn to the music and the festivities, even though she realized that her participation would be unacceptable to her boyfriend and the others in the group: "Make just a ripple / Come on be brave." At one point one of the Spanish dancers gets the Americans to sing and sway to the music and drink from the jugs of wine, but still none of the women from the movie would dance with the Spanish gypsies. "This time a ripple / Next time a wave." Finally, one of the Spaniards looked at her, beckoning her to join him. Despite her boyfriend's protestations— "But then 'Boyfriend' looked at me, and his face said 'don't you dare,' 'don't you even think about it,' 'don't you do it, don't, don't, don't' "— she joined the dancers. McKechnie fills the stage with movement, her dance becoming an expression of her individuality, the ripple that leads her out of the relationship and into a career in the theatre as a dancer: "Sometimes you have to start small / Climbing the tiniest wall / Maybe you're going to fall / But it's better than not starting at all." McKechnie's performance of "Everybody Says Don't" is not meant to leave the spectator awed either by her vocal abilities or by her choreographic talents. Instead, it is meant to convey an aspect of her personality and the importance of dance in her life. Dance here becomes more than a talent to showcase on the stage; it represents a form of female agency. "I literally danced myself out of a relationship!" she explains when she begins the story.

McKechnie, who won a Tony Award in 1975 for her performance in *A Chorus Line* as Cassie, the hardworking, talented dancer struggling to make a return to the stage but who everyone thinks is too good to be in the chorus, tells the story of her life through song and dance. Like Cassie, McKechnie wants to keep working; performance is her life, and the show gives testimony both to her talent and her resilience. Her cabaret constitutes a choreographic archive of her life and career, but it also offers an ongoing showcase for her talent (figures 60 and 61). Unlike the older generation of women discussed above—Stritch, Arthur, and Cook—McKechnie never found herself catapulted to lasting fame and stardom. Her celebrity was fleeting. Although she has continued to work in theatre in the post–*A Chorus Line* years, she has not returned to Broadway with any regularity or achieved national recognition in other media. What seems striking about her life and career is her refusal to acquiesce to retirement or obscurity. "Being in theatre is a brutal career choice," she explains with her characteristic wit and charm, "third maybe to boxing and prostitution. But I am very proud of it. It is amazing that I am still doing this. But it was always important for me to be a creative artist. Not to be a star, not to be rich, not to be famous. My impulse as a dancer was never just to move but rather to interpret the music. I needed meaning. It completed me."[46]

Raised in Detroit during the 1950s, she dreamed of becoming a dancer, a tough sell for her Calvinist parents. She ran away from home at fifteen to move to New York City, but her father followed her, returned her to Michigan, and "had a local judge read her the riot act."[47]

60. (this page) Promotional flyer for *An Evening with Donna McKechnie* at Arci's Place, New York City, 2001. Collection of the author

61. (opposite) Promotional flyer for Donna McKechnie *Inside the Music* at the Colony Theatre, Burbank, California, 2003. Collection of the author

But eventually her parents stopped fighting her wishes, and soon after she relocated to New York with their blessing. From her first Broadway show at sixteen, in the chorus of the original cast of *How to Succeed in Business without Really Trying* (1961), to ensemble parts in the original Broadway casts both of *Promises, Promises* (1968)—where she would work with the young choreographer Michael Bennett, who she had met and befriended on the television show *Hullabaloo* (1965)—and of *Company* (1970)—which Bennett choreographed—McKechnie revisits the high points of her artistic career in *Inside the Music*, a career that culminated in her signature role in *A Chorus Line* (1975), which Bennett conceived, choreographed, and directed. Along the way, she pays tribute to the artists who helped shape her career: Frank Loesser, Bob Fosse, Gwen Verdon, Marvin Hamlisch, and, of course, Michael Bennett. Her brief marriage to Bennett, who died of AIDS in 1986, is never explicitly addressed, and she chooses to convey instead the artistic process behind the creation of *A Chorus Line*.

McKechnie's cabaret performance is unusual in that it features dance prominently, no small feat given that the actual performance space in a cabaret room is quite limited and intimate. But McKechnie exploits the intimacy of cabaret to foreground the performing body. Her physical presence is inescapable, and the labor behind the moves,

immediate. We watch her sweat as she recreates the dances she performed nightly in the early years of her career, and we hear her breathe heavily between these dances and between the songs and patter that move the autobiographical narrative forward. McKechnie works hard and it shows. She does not rely on her theatrical vita or celebrity to carry the show. In this sense, she is an antidiva. If anything, she need not try so hard; her audiences are already behind her.

At the end of the performance she revisits the song that made her famous, the "Music and the Mirror," which she first performed over twenty-five years earlier (figure 62). In *A Chorus Line*, the song represents Cassie's audition piece. Cassie is trying to restart her career, and the director of the show, Zach, simply cannot see her in the chorus. Cassie insists, but the director will have none of it:

ZACH: I just can't see you dancing in the chorus, Cassie.

CASSIE: Why not?

ZACH: Listen, if you need some money, call my business manager.

CASSIE: Well, sure I need money. Who doesn't? But I don't need a handout. I need a job. I need a job and I don't know any other way to say it. Do you want me to say it again?

62. Donna McKechnie performing in the original Broadway production of *A Chorus Line*, New York City, 1975. Photo by Martha Swope

ZACH: No.

CASSIE: Fine, then we got that far. Look, I haven't worked in two years, not really. There's nothing left for me to do. So—I'm putting myself on the line. (She steps to the chorus line.) Yes, I'm putting myself on your line. . . . (During song, lights dim out leaving her in spot)

God, I am a dancer,
A dancer dances!
Give me somebody to dance with
Give me a place to fit in
Help me return to the world of the living
By showing me how to begin.
Play me the music.
Give me the chance to come through.
All I ever needed was the music, and the mirror,
And the chance to dance with you.[48]

By the end of *A Chorus Line*, Cassie joins Morales and the others cast in the chorus of the new Broadway show that is about to begin rehearsals.

Her triumph is bittersweet; we have witnessed the tremendous effort of will and restraint that led her to this moment, and it should not have proven so difficult for her. But her spirit is not broken, she gets to perform: "God, I am a dancer / A dancer dances!"

Watching McKechnie perform this number so many years later and in the context of the narrative logic of her show, it is difficult not to be moved by the performer's resilience and determination to keep her artistry alive. The performance summons the essence of *A Chorus Line*, which celebrated the artistry of the gypsy by allowing those in the chorus to perform their individual selves through narrative, song, and dance. McKechnie embodied the spirit of *A Chorus Line*, and now, in *Inside the Music*, she uses cabaret performance to do the same. Cabaret enables her to summon her personal and artistic past and reperform it. This rehearsal of the past exceeds mere nostalgic yearning, either hers or the audience's. In *Inside the Music*, McKechnie returns us to her past to let us see how history—personal and cultural, individual and communal—marks the body and its movements, and how the body itself has learned to move through time.

Cabaret provides a forum in which the older female performer can emerge as the principal lead of the show because the show is a retrospective of her own life and career. In contrast to the Broadway musical, which often consigns older women to character roles or to invisibility, cabaret frequently showcases veteran female singers. Cabaret performance functions as both a cultural archive and a repository of the experience and expertise of older women who may no longer have other public forums in which to narrate their lives. Cabaret performance is always a retrospective of some sort, constituting both an archive and a memoir. In this sense, cabaret performances might be understood within the context that Nancy K. Miller describes in discussing the memoir craze of the 1990s: "What memoirs do is support you in the act of remembering. The memoir boom, then, should be understood not as proliferation of self-serving representations of individualistic memory but as an aid or a spur to keep cultural memory alive."[49] The singers I have discussed go to great lengths to preserve the cultural memory embedded in popular song and often inscribed on their own performing bodies. For the older woman performer, cabaret offers a venue to

63. *If I Were a Bell: Andrea Marcovicci Sings the Songs of Frank Loesser* at the Oak Room, New York City, 2003. Photo by Richard Termine

reflect on her own participation in cultural history, as well as an opportunity to mark her endurance within the shifting cultural norms of gender and sexuality. Her performance enters into dialogue with a past at once personal and historic. It is a past that haunts the contemporary even as it enables the performer to claim her time in the now.

But cabaret is not simply the art form of an older generation of women singers whose past experiences in the theatre become the means for female agency in the contemporary moment. It is also an art form that preserves the classic American songbook. As Andrea Marcovicci, one of cabaret's most established artists, explained in the mid 1990s in an effort to publicize the genre, "To my mind, the single most important function of the cabaret singer is to preserve the legacy all Americans are heir to—the popular songs of the past."[50] Ten years later, Marcovicci would extend this point to claim that the art form itself is in need of preservation. In her exquisite and incredibly moving tribute to the composer and lyricist Frank Loesser, *If I Were a Bell*, performed at the Algonquin's Oak Room in January of 2004, Marcovicci brought to life the man by singing his songbook and retelling his life and times (figure 63). Loesser, whose works include *Guys and Dolls* (1950) and *How to Succeed in Business without Really Trying*, would seem to need little preservation; his music is a staple of community and educational theatres throughout the country. But for Marcovicci, this does not suffice enough; she believes his music must also be preserved through the intimate practice of cabaret. For Marcovicci, cabaret as an art form must be handed down from one generation to another; if not, it becomes vulnerable to cultural extinction. To ensure its continuity, Marcovicci believes in the importance of mentoring younger singers. "The music can be carried on only if we are willing to pass it on to a new generation," she explains to her audience. Then, in a surprising move, she introduces Maude Maggart, a twenty-eight-year-old singer who Marcovicci has mentored over the years. Maggart proceeds to sing "Can't Get out of This Mood," a song written in 1941 by Loesser and Jimmy McHugh. At the end of her rendition, Maggart and Marcovicci share the stage, and Marcovicci champions Maggart's talent, promoting the young performer's upcoming show at the Algonquin later in the season. It will be her first. Maggart, too, has spoken excitedly about her relationship with Marcovicci. "I saw Andrea at the Gardenia in Hollywood for the first time when I was sixteen or seventeen, and I rushed home and wrote pages and pages in my diary about how special it was," she explained in an interview. "She was like a spell caster. It was the experience of appreciating a song for its craft: how it was constructed and how it could be expressed."[51] Tellingly, Maggart says nothing about the composers and focuses her comments specifically on her mentor and the way Marcovicci interprets a song. As Marcovicci and Maggart make clear, the trajectory of cabaret is not only a history of songwriters but also a tradition of performers themselves who pass the form from singer to singer.

In the first show since her extraordinary tribute to Rodgers and Hart, Mary Cleere Haran has selected the composer Harry Warren for the Ninety-second Street Y's Lyrics and Lyricists annual series. She has been invited to curate an evening program that will run for six shows over an extended weekend. True to her signature style, Haran researched the show extensively, and the program she has selected proves a fascinating combination of songs, film clips, and stories from Warren's extensive work in film and theatre. Born in Brooklyn in 1883 to an Italian immigrant family, Warren went on to write for all four of the major film studios—Paramount, Warner Brothers, Twentieth Century–Fox, MGM—during the height of the motion-picture musical years between 1935 and 1950. He wrote over 250 songs for such classic Hollywood films as *42nd Street* (1933) and *The Gold Diggers* (1933). During her performance, Haran intersperses stories of Warren's career with those of his era, stories of the Depression, of protests where war veterans marched for their pensions and were shot by the National Guard—"my generation didn't ever hear this story," she interjects—and of the rise of fascism in Western Europe. She provides a nuanced context for Warren's work as she introduces the audience to the popular entertainments of the age as well.

In many ways, this show, which ran in February 2004, follows the format typical of Haran's work. She selects a songwriter, researches his or her career, introduces the songs within their immediate cultural context, and offers anecdotes of her own relationship to the material. But there is a difference. Near the end of her performance, Haran introduces Margaret Whiting, who takes to the stage to sing "My Intuition," one of Warren's collaborations with the great composer Johnny Mercer. All along it seems that the evening has been a tribute to Warren's career, but now the program takes a different turn. Haran begins telling stories of when she first met Whiting, a Broadway and Hollywood veteran performer whose recordings include "That Old Black Magic," "Come Rain or Come Shine," and "Moonlight in Vermont." When Haran first arrived in New York from San Francisco, Whiting helped her out. Whiting called all her friends to go see Haran's inaugural show, took her to lunch afterward to debrief her, and quickly became her mentor. It is a relationship that has endured many years and many shows. Together they sing—along with Marion Cowings, another performer on the program—"It's a Great Big World," an amusing song Warren wrote with Mercer that was first made famous by Judy Garland, Cyd Charisse, and Lucille Ball. And here it becomes clear that the women see in each other's performance and presence a history that they have either lived or inherited.

The formal program ends with Warren's ode to Times Square, "The Lullaby of Broadway," which Warren wrote with Al Dubin, and one of the great songs about New York City. It is a song that captures all that is thrilling about New York life, including the paradoxical comfort that comes when the night ends. Generally, the song is sung as a celebration of the city, and it marks a high point of *42nd Street*, the musical film in which it was introduced. But Haran slows the arrangement down, singing it as a poignant and nearly heartbreaking lullaby to the transitory nature of time, to history's passing, to the end of the show. It becomes a song of closure, but also one where the sounds of the city itself promise yet another remarkable day. In Haran's version, Broadway is both the major city street that cuts across Manhattan and the tradition that houses the music of Rodgers and Hart, Warren, and various other songwriters, playwrights, and performers who throughout the years have embodied this history. When she sings at the end of her program, "Sleep tight, let's call it a day; listen to the lullaby of old Broadway," she summons these histories and offers them to us as a form of temporary closure, knowing all along that this moment will play again and again in time and through song.[52]

Haran's version of "The Lullaby of Broadway" becomes all the more affecting when placed in the context of New York in the aftermath of September 11. In this sense it comes closer to the function of a traditional lullaby, a song meant to soothe and calm a child into sleep. Haran revives a classic from the American songbook in order to engage a contemporary audience anxious about the specific cultural and political tensions of a post–September 11 world. We have seen how this music once functioned to comment on the contemporary moment of the 1930s and provide a respite for audiences trying to survive the particular historical pressures of the period. Seventy years later the song is reintroduced to summon an archive of alternatives for our contemporary. The next chapter will address the ways in which the performing arts responded to September 11 and intervened in its immediate aftermath to provide a space for assessing the nation and contesting the ensuing nationalism that came into effect as a result of the terrorist attacks.

CHAPTER SIX

Tragedy and the Performing Arts in
the Wake of September 11, 2001

We come to tragedy by many roads. It is an immediate experience,
a body of literature, a conflict of theory, an academic problem.
—RAYMOND WILLIAMS, *Modern Tragedy*

In the summer of 2001 I was immersed in two academic projects on the topic of tragedy: a special issue of *Theatre Journal*, the academic quarterly I was editing at the time, and the preparations for my fall 2001 class titled "AIDS and the Arts in America." Both of these occasions emerged out of a long-standing interest in thinking about tragedy as a mode of understanding the world. I understood the world as tragic, not in the nihilistic sense that tragedy is inevitable and that there was nothing to be done about it, but in the political sense, in that to live in a tragic world meant to recognize the ubiquity of human suffering, to take it on, push against it, and work with others to live through it as best as possible. To understand the world as tragic does not mean to succumb to the idea of tragedy as inescapable, but rather to name and confront the systemic forces that sustain and reproduce it. I came to tragedy by many roads, and I was interested in thinking through tragedy from just as many perspectives as well. The special issue of *Theatre Journal* stemmed from my interest in tragedy as an "academic problem," and the course on AIDS and the arts focused on tragedy as both a "body of literature" in need of examination and AIDS as an "immediate experience" we were all immersed in.[1] These "many roads," as British cultural theorist Raymond Williams describes them in the epigraph for this chapter, would come together in unexpected ways in September 2001.

When I first started planning the special issue on tragedy, in the fall of 2000, I wanted to instigate a reconsideration of the traditional bibliography on tragedy. Although foundational to the field of theatre studies, this body of literature seemed over time to have fallen out of critical favor. I was curious to see whether theatre and performance scholars were currently engaging with this literature and, if so, how this work might illuminate current cultural events and social experiences that might be loosely understood as tragic. Taking into account the seismic shifts in literary, cultural, and performance studies over the past several decades, I wanted to return to the literature of tragedy and see how it might be reimagined in light of recent critical insights and methods.[2] Certainly, I felt, the relevance of tragedy was as pressing for the contemporary moment as it had been fifty years earlier, in the immediate postwar years. In fact, I was struck by the incommensurability between the reality of the world in which we lived—a world of terrible suffering and loss, a world that seemed at times evacuated of hope, a world in which these feelings have been normalized as, well, simply life—and the theatre criticism of our era. How was it that we had come to abandon thinking about tragedy as intellectuals and scholars of the performing arts in the midst of world struggles? Was the idea of tragedy—as an aesthetic, as an ideology, as a philosophy, as an "immediate experience"—outdated? Did the work of such philosophers as G. W. F. Hegel, Friedrich Nietzsche, Walter Benjamin, Jean-Paul Sartre, and Raymond Williams, all of whom wrote on tragedy and theatre, exhaust our own thinking on the topic? If this was the case, how had tragedy, as a way of thinking about theatre, let alone the world, fallen out of critical favor? What might be gained by revisiting the world and its theatre through the perspective of tragedy?

At one point in my planning, I approached a colleague I admire at an academic conference about a possible contribution to this special issue. She was surprised that I would be interested in reviving what had been, for her, endlessly rehearsed to very little gain in post–World War II criticism. From her perspective, another round of questions about tragedy seemed regressive and irrelevant. Such current critical reservations about tragedy were produced no doubt by the reservations about genre studies more generally. Various people with whom I spoke to about this special issue voiced the sense that genre studies, a critical endeavor whose history since Aristotle has been inextricably linked with formalism, might itself be the problem.

A second anxiety associated with the study of tragedy, especially the classics, was the presumption that it was embedded within a neoliberal humanist tradition that espoused universal truths about the human condition found in so-called great literature. Liberal humanism presumes that individuals act according to how they think and that their choices are solely based on their character. As the literary theorist Catherine Belsey writes in her critique of this tradition: "The common feature of liberal humanism, justifying the use of the single phrase, is a commitment to man, whose essence is freedom. Liberal humanism proposes that the subject is the free, unconstrained author of meaning and action, the origin of history. Unified, knowing, and autonomous, the human being seeks a political system which guarantees freedom of choice."[3] Critics of liberal humanism insist on foregrounding the historical, political, and economic factors that structure human life and argue against this idea of an essential, which is to say ahistorical and cross-cultural, truth about the human condition.

While I understood, and to an extent even shared these anxieties about the formalist insistence on genre and the liberal humanist insistence on the universal, I still felt it might be possible to rehabilitate the discourse on the tragic to see how it could speak to us now. My own interest in tragedy stemmed in part from my academic training in comparative literature and the emphasis that my PhD program at the University of Wisconsin–Madison placed on genre studies and literary history. But there were other unanticipated events that also led me to the literature of tragedy. My college education took place side by side with the onslaught of AIDS. The bibliography of tragedy, especially the work of Raymond Williams, informed not only my intellectual growth but also offered me a philosophy that would structure my worldview in light of the suffering and loss of a generation of gay men who were my peers. Under these conditions, tragedy seemed less a descriptive device to help structure the world and more a political term that might help me critically engage it. Tragedy, as Williams argues, is neither an inevitable human condition nor a mere body of literature. The literature of tragedy informs what Williams famously calls the "structure of feelings" that shape human life. Rather than accept tragedy as a universal truth, Williams was interested in placing tragedy within its political and historical contexts. "We are not looking for a new universal meaning of tragedy," he states clearly and early on in *Modern Tragedy*; "we are looking for the structure of tragedy in our culture. Once we begin to doubt, in experience and then in analysis, the ordinary twentieth-century idea, other directions seem open."[4] Since tragedy is historically contingent, it is open to revision; the critical engagement with tragedy serves as a catalyst for actions that might revolutionize the way we live. Williams believed in the agency of individuals to restructure the social and understood that this ambitious struggle against suffering and despair, what he calls "the long revolution," began with the acknowledgment—not the disavowal—of the particular tragic realities of history.[5]

In "Tragedy and Revolution," the concluding section of "Tragic Ideas," part 1 of *Modern Tragedy*, Williams makes a persuasive case for the critical engagement of tragedy:

> The tragic action, in its deepest sense, is not the confirmation of disorder, but its experience, its comprehension and its resolution. In our time, this action is general, and its common name is revolution. We have to see the evil and the suffering, in the factual disorder that makes revolution necessary, and in the disordered struggle against this disorder. We have to recognize this suffering in a close and immediate experience, and not cover it with names. But we have to follow the whole action: not only the evil, but the men who have fought against evil; not only the crisis, but the energy released by it, the spirit learned in it. We make the connections, because that is the action of tragedy, and what we learn in suffering is again revolution, because we acknowledge others as men and any acknowledgement is the beginning of struggle, as the continuing reality of our lives. Then to see revolution, in this tragic perspective is the only way to maintain it.[6]

Williams's belief that death and suffering are not in vain proved enormously helpful to me in the 1980s in forming my response to AIDS. My own conviction that tragedy shapes contemporary life stems from my training in world literature and philosophy, as well as from my own life experience as someone who came into adulthood during the terrible decade of the 1980s, when AIDS fatalities and infections were escalating out of control in the United States.

I also found that Williams's ideas infused and informed my undergraduate teaching, including the course on AIDS and the arts. Since 1989, I have been teaching courses on contemporary American literature, art, and culture, especially on the work of racial and sexual minorities. At various institutions—Macalester College, Pomona College, the University of Washington–Seattle, Yale University, and the University of Southern California—I have been hired to help diversify the curriculum as well as the faculty. However, rather than teach what I call "feel-good multiculturalism," where students are asked to endorse cultural diversity for the better social good, my courses trouble the utopian impulse of multicultural politics and pedagogy. Instead of celebrating difference, I am interested in having my students recognize what is at stake in being marked as other. This steers far clear from the idea that minorities are necessarily victims, a facile stereotype and standard dismissal that refuses to recognize the nuances of social oppression and systemic injustice. I want to equip my students with skills to consider the ubiquity of violence in the world, the disregard for human life, and the nihilism that sometimes results from these realities. But I also want my students, as they are immersed in these materials, to see the ways individuals and communities have responded to such social conditions. Tragedy, in other words, was not only about suffering; it was also about the efforts to end it—"not only the evil, but the men who have fought against evil."[7]

In structuring the syllabus for my course titled "AIDS and the Arts in America," a course designed for first-year undergraduates with little to no experience in the study of the arts and humanities, I selected works that demonstrated the capacity for human resilience without compromising the ability to sustain social critique. I read these works as tragic, not because they might be about tragic villains and heroes, or because they might provide some sense of emotional catharsis for us—the two most popular ways to think about tragedy and, in my estimation, two of the most impoverished—but because they highlight strategies for change and offer resources of hope in the face of terrible loss and suffering. The class syllabus is organized as a series of case studies from different artistic genres—film, literature, photography, performance, music—that showcase the role the arts play in thinking about AIDS in the context of tragedy in the fullest sense of the word. If we understand the times we live in as tragic, how then might the literary, performing, and visual arts foreground the tragic so as to critique and engage it?

I had just finished rereading *Modern Tragedy* a few weeks before September 11, 2001, in preparation for writing my introduction to the special issue on tragedy and the beginning of the academic year. And then history happened in an unexpected, all but unimaginable way. Like most people, I found the terrible deaths of so many and the immeasurable suffering of countless others on September 11 simply insurmountable in terms of sadness and grief. "Mourning, fear, anxiety, and rage," writes Judith Butler cataloguing our emotions. "And in the United States," she continues, "we are everywhere now surrounded with violence, of having perpetrated it, having suffered it, living in fear of it, planning more of it."[8] How does one intervene in this cycle of violence? How does one respond to the news of September 11? How does one acknowledge and honor the dead? How does one respond to the bravery and courage of the firefighters, police officers, rescue workers, and assorted volunteers whose dedication to the dignity and preservation of life led them to their own deaths? In short, how does one mourn the totality of such an event when what is to be mourned is not yet fully known?

For me the massive destruction of human life appeared the most unbearable. While I was aware of various and complex global dynamics and geopolitical factors that helped shape the events of September 11, and that a large part of this context remained unknown to me, I nonetheless focused on processing the deaths of so many people on that one morning on the East Coast. Despite a growing sense of helplessness, a response that, while humbling, also proved insufficient, I tried to follow the national impulse to resume the regularity of day-to-day life. That day I taught my classes, two sections of a course on AIDS and the arts for incoming students needing to fulfill their general education requirements. On the eleventh we had been scheduled to discuss Carolyn

Jones's remarkable photography exhibit *Living Proof: Courage in the Face of AIDS* and the film documentary of the same name directed by Kermit Cole. The film version of *Living Proof* is a talking-heads documentary about people in New York City living with HIV in the early 1990s. Both the exhibit and the film set out to show a diverse range of people living with HIV on their own terms. *Living Proof* formed part of a larger AIDS activist project mounted in the late 1980s to transform the dominant images of people with HIV in the media. Instead of perpetuating the image of the lone, suffering, emaciated AIDS "victim," AIDS activists advocated for a much more representative range of images of the experiences of people living with HIV.[9]

The book comprises a collection of Jones's photographs, and the film documents her project. Jones photographed her subjects in the spring of 1992; she, along with Michael Liberatore, whose lover George De-Sipio Jr. conceived of the project, invited those photographed to pose with "whatever or whomever kept them going strong."[10] The exhibit included photos of people with HIV with friends, families, and lovers, as well as people with HIV surrounded by personal items whose meanings were often symbolic or obscure. DeSipio, who was struggling with HIV at the time, was furious that so few positive images of people living with HIV circulated in the media. According to Liberatore, "George felt that without a life-affirming view of how individuals deal with this illness, many people with AIDS might give up hope for ever living a full life."[11] Over seventy people with HIV posed for Jones; the portraits capture the changing demographics of HIV in the United States in the early 1990s without obscuring the fact that gay men had been dealing with AIDS since the early 1980s.

Living Proof conveys two main points, both profound in their simplicity. First, we have agency in the midst of tragedy, and that means that we do what we can to live life fully. Second, we have the possibility of community in the midst of tragedy, and that means seeking and offering support from and to others whose lives are also affected by suffering and loss. Jones's photographs capture these sentiments, and Cole's documentary brings them to life once again. The film shows the behind-the-scenes action of the shoots. People, meeting for the first time during the shoot, share information about drug treatments, alter-

64. George DeSipio Jr. and Carolyn Jones from the Living Proof Project at the opening gallery exhibit at the World Trade Center, World AIDS Day, December 1, 1992. Collection of the author

native therapies, and side effects. Friendships form, support structures strengthen, and the individuals having their portraits taken by Jones convey their subjective experience of HIV and AIDS.

Cole's documentary ends when the various people living with HIV participating in the project gather for the opening night of the exhibit at the World Trade Center (figure 64). We witness the subjects of the exhibit arrive one by one to see their portraits hanging on the walls of the World Trade Center lobby. They congregate here to celebrate their survival and the community they have forged through this shared project. DeSipio on entrance announces with complete theatrical hyperbole, "Here we are at the Center of the Universe!" In *Living Proof,* the World Trade Center represents a space of life and possibility, and it signifies a form of cultural arrival. It is the venue that first houses the evidence of their survival, the living proof that they are alive and together. The subjects of the portraits enter the World Trade Center with friends and loved ones, and we watch them watch themselves together in this towering space of seeming strength and invulnerability.

For some of my students—a combination of local Southern Californians, students from the Midwest and the Southwest, as well as international students—this video footage constituted their first encounter with the World Trade Center prior to the terrorist attacks. Only a few of my students hailed from the East Coast, and none came from New York. The students had screened the video the weekend before September 11, and while all of them had obviously heard of the twin towers, most had never visited them—or New York City, for that matter. If the World Trade Center was the venue that first housed Carolyn Jones's

Living Proof photography exhibit, Kermit Cole's *Living Proof* documentary now archived the subjects of the exhibit as well as the building itself.

I went to my classes on September 11 uncertain about who, if anyone, would arrive and what, if anything, we would discuss.[12] Nearly all of my students showed up. Even as we spoke about the events on the East Coast, we decided to proceed with our planned curriculum. *Living Proof*, after all, concerned the resilience of life in the midst of tragedy, and we felt collectively drawn to that impulse in light of the day's events. We shared our anxieties and concerns about the world as we made the effort to think through the ways that people with HIV had challenged the dominant understanding of AIDS at the time of the documentary. It seemed that what was needed in this moment was some structure to the day, some comforting, perhaps even banal ritual to combat the unsettling rupture of the morning's shocking news.

Two nights later, on the thirteenth, I accompanied a group of the University of Southern California's queer undergraduates to see the Los Angeles premiere of Terrence McNally's *Corpus Christi* at a small theatre in Hollywood. I have never found the play, a retelling of the story of Jesus and the twelve apostles set in 1950s Texas, as compelling as the scandals it has provoked. When the play was first presented in 1998 by the Manhattan Theatre Company, it sparked protests and demonstrations for its homoerotic depiction of Christ and his apostles. Following numerous threats of violence, the theatre balked and considered canceling the production. This, in turn, provoked a second series of demonstrations by those in favor of artistic freedom. The L.A. production had also come under protest by members of the Religious Right who picketed on the street outside the theatre's main entrance. We struggled over whether we should attend the theatre so soon after the events of September 11, and wondered, too, if the play would even be staged that night. Various events throughout Los Angeles had already been canceled or postponed, and it was uncertain if *Corpus Christi*, already under protest, would be performed that night.

Given these conditions, the September 13 performance of the play proved enormously and surprisingly satisfying. Sitting in a performance space and moderating a postshow discussion with a roomful of young people from different cultural and religious backgrounds about tragedy, theatre, and faith felt right to me. I was struck by the intensity of the response of the students and the actors, all in their early to mid-twenties, and the determination by which they performed as actors and audiences that evening. The theatre gave us a secular place to assemble so we could observe a performance of faith and its effects. The performance, moreover, provided us a space where we could constitute a provisional public to mourn together. The fact that the theatre itself constituted a vulnerable site of contestation threatened with violence and protest was not lost on us, especially within the context of the past forty-eight hours. The theatre enabled us to discuss and debate with each other the role of the arts and the role of citizens in the midst of difficult times. While the students and actors looked to me for leadership, I found in them a resource of hope. Together we were able to create an alternative community of mourners resistant to the growing nationalist fervor taking shape across the country, a version of which informed the protest outside the very theatre where we had gathered that night.

One of the things I appreciate most about being a professor is the chance to interact with any number of people to discuss and debate the world of art and ideas. While I was grateful for the opportunities to interact with my local community and my students, I found myself wanting to do more. But what? In a moment of both awkward civic pride and native East Coast loyalty, I left California for New York City, the place that in spite of my affection for Los Angeles, has been my symbolic home for most of my life. I had moved from New York to Los Angeles in 1995 but went back with frequent regularity. In fact, my partner and I had already planned to return in mid-October for our next visit. But I could not wait that long. The need to go to New York City, to fly cross-country and get that over with already, to see friends and support the New York economy, to visit my old neighborhood and local haunts, and to witness the tragedy for myself unfiltered by television, newspapers, and other media had become increasingly urgent in the days since the eleventh. I left Los Angeles on September 27 for the first of a sequence of long weekends in New York.

In a sense, I took to heart mayor Rudy Giuliani's September 16 plea for support: "To people from all over the country who want to help,

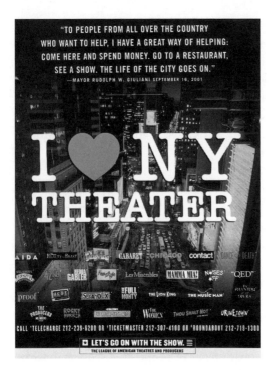

65. Advertisement for the 2001 "I Love New York Theater" campaign. Collection of the author

I have a great way of helping: Come here and spend money. Go to a restaurant, see a show. The life of the city goes on" (figure 65). This seemed easy enough for me to do. I had, after all, wanted to do something active in response to the terrorist attacks. Donating blood was not an option. Gay men are not welcome at blood banks; we are forbidden from giving blood because of our associations with HIV, regardless of our serostatus. But the theatre, well, that was another story. I could certainly do that. In fact, I do it all the time. Theatregoing, which for me is routine and familiar but which is so often perceived by others I know as frivolous and compulsive, was now sanctioned by the state.

I cannot remember the last time elected officials advocated for the theatre. It is unusual for the theatre to enter into the national public discourse in any way that does not already play into the tradition of antitheatrical prejudice. As Jonas Barish argues, the theatre has historically constituted a site of cultural anxiety and antipathy, leading various politicians, moralists, and philosophers to attack it, if not actually attempt to shut it down.[13] The culture wars of the late 1980s and early 1990s were the last time that theatre and performance found themselves at the heart of national debate. And even then, community-based performance, solo performance, and performance art, rather than Broadway shows, came under attack. Nonetheless, these debates resulted in the closure of venues, the diminishment of fiscal support for the arts, the scapegoating of particular performers, artists, and playwrights, and the implementation of various forms of direct and indirect acts of censorship.[14] And while the theatre continues now and then to incite controversy, as the *Corpus Christi* protests prove, it has long been seen as a marginal cultural practice with little relevance to the larger political realities of the nation, a view held even by some of its own practitioners. Given its predisposition toward commercial entertainment, Broadway, in particular, is seen by many as irrelevant. The anticommercial prejudice of the intellectual elite, especially among leftist critics, also includes a strong anti-Broadway bias. And yet, now, Broadway suddenly became viewed as central to the survival of the city. If I had any reservations about Giuliani's call to "see a show," it had to do with the concern over what was being understood as theatre in the moment. Did this advocacy for theatregoing include attending the various other theatres besides Broadway that were vulnerable economically? Or was Broadway prioritized over the many other venues and locations where theatre happens in New York City, including the smaller downtown theatres closer to the World Trade Center?

The fact that Giuliani, himself a controversial figure when it came to both Times Square and the arts in New York City, was placing the theatre at the center of a campaign to regenerate New York City seemed striking. Despite his highly publicized interest in opera, Giuliani's record on the arts had become increasingly fraught due to his moralistic fervor against any work he found offensive. Instead of relying on the taste and judgment of curators and presenters, or allowing the public to decide for themselves what did or did not constitute art, Giuliani seemed determined to turn the vibrant international New York art scene into a provincial and predictable market reflecting his own conservative tastes. Moreover, his determination to enforce the antiquated cabaret laws that prohibited dancing in smaller clubs seemed not simply ill-informed but, in fact, hostile. His record on Times Square was also controversial.[15] Giuliani's efforts to sanitize the theatre district and demolish the sexual subcultures to make Times Square a more lucrative location for corporate financial investors did not just shut down sex venues, as progressive critics have argued.[16] It also meant that many of the local businesses and small, owner-run establishments that catered to the neighborhood and had nothing to do with the sex industry were themselves forced to close or sell. As a result, the new Times Square that emerged under Giuliani's term of office lost much of what made the location distinct in the first place, a neighborhood vital not just to tourists but also New Yorkers. As Frank Rich noted, "It is the paradox of the Times Square comeback in the late 1990s that the neighborhood that epitomizes New York to the world is no longer on the map of many of its own residents."[17] In this sense, Giuliani's insistence on securing Broadway and the theatre district of Times Square in the immediate aftermath of September 11 seemed to me more than simply a means to stimulate the New York economy. It summoned a sense of the historical role the district has played over the years in shaping New York life for both New Yorkers and the many visitors who come from all over the United States and the world to experience for themselves its ongoing allure.[18] And even if his main motivations were driven by economic interests, they seemed justified given the serious financial losses affecting the thousands of people employed by the New York theatre industry and its related businesses—hotels, restaurants, transportation, and so on—that needed an economic boost.[19]

Like many people critical of Giuliani's conservative positions, I found myself impressed by his bold leadership on September 11. I was not all that interested in second-guessing the motivations of Giuliani's call to the theatre, especially after being in New York and hearing firsthand from various tourist-industry employees how scared they were to lose their jobs and how many of their colleagues had already been let go. Spending money in theatres, restaurants, hotels, taxis, and other related tourist industries seemed to have little to do with Giuliani, and everything to do with the people whose livelihood was on the line. The snowballing effect of the economic downturn in New York City proved a reality for many of the people I spoke with that weekend and during the various trips I took to New York in the following months. If Giuliani's call helped people boost this economy, well, then, I was all for it. And if it encouraged people to support and value the performing arts, all the better. I was struck by this unusual advocacy for the theatre, and I was drawn to endorse it. Attending the theatre, and especially Broadway, was positioned early on after the attacks as a therapeutic antidote to the suffering of the city, and as means of preserving the continuity of the city's history and traditions as well. Even more unusual, going to see a show was linked with "getting back to normal," as if theatregoing constituted a routine daily activity.

The recurrent prediction of the death of Broadway over the years, while generally referring to the decreasing relevance of Broadway to the national imaginary and to the decreasing number of new shows and plays to open in its theatres, suddenly seemed real as well.[20] For the first few weeks after the attacks, it was uncertain how many of the twenty-three shows then running on Broadway would remain open. Giuliani's own efforts of the past decade to clean up Times Square and make it safe for tourists suddenly seemed beside the point when the imagined threats to tourism and the economy were no longer sex workers, drug dealers, and the homeless, but foreign terrorists with bombs. Despite the resurgence of Forty-second Street and Times Square in the mid-1990s, the theatre district felt particularly fragile. Given the uncertainty of the immediate terrorist threat and in observance of the tragedy at the site of the World Trade Center, Broadway went dark on the eleventh and was relit on Thursday, September 13, mainly due to Giuliani's urging.

How, then, did the theatre emerge as a viable response to the events of September 11, and so much so that it became the symbolic cornerstone of the city's own survival? What was at stake in the survival of the theatre? There was a strange sense that if Broadway, that historically vulnerable New York cultural institution, could make it through this, perhaps the rest of us could too. But in the first few days after the attacks, the situation was grim. Four of the twenty-three Broadway shows running posted closing notices within a week of September 11. While none of these were bona fide hits and some of them had already been in trouble beforehand, the September 18 closing announcements of *Stones in His Pockets, A Thousand Clowns, If You Ever Leave Me,* and *The Rocky Horror Show* dealt a demoralizing and frightening blow to the industry. The critically acclaimed revival of *Kiss Me, Kate* at the Martin Beck Theatre posted its closing on the following day, and it was uncertain if such long-running shows as *Les Misérables, The Phantom of the Opera, Chicago,* and *Rent*—all dependent on the tourist market—could remain open for long. The situation proved so grave that the producers of these shows—along with those for the musical *The Full Monty*—met with guilds and unions in order to salvage their runs by renegotiating contracts for actors, stage managers, musicians, and others in the trade, who agreed to accept concessions for the next four weeks, a 25 percent cut in their paychecks. Moreover, for the next month, playwrights, designers, and directors of these works all decided to waive their royalties.

The situation for downtown theatres and arts organizations was also distressing. The Lower Manhattan Cultural Council, which supports many off-off-Broadway venues, was located at the World Trade Center and thus destroyed, as was the TKTS discount theatre tickets booth, which operated in tower 2's lobby. *InTheatre*'s archive of over thirty thousand photographs of Broadway plays was also lost in the destruction of the twin towers. Nearly every day came news of some other archive lost, theatre closed, or fiscal crisis hitting the performing arts. Of course, none of this compared to the growing knowledge of the losses of life and the ramifications of these losses to the individuals and communities involved. But the theatre's losses and vulnerabilities were also included in the reportage of the attacks, suggesting their significance and relevance to the culture at large.

Giuliani's plea to get audiences to attend a Broadway show got a serious endorsement on September 21 by the *New York Times,* which issued a rave review for *Urinetown: The Musical,* the first Broadway show to open after the attacks:

> Can we laugh and thrill to a musical at a time like this? When every individual spirit as well as the national one can use all the bolstering it can get, *Urinetown* is not just a recommended tonic. There is simply no show I've ever seen that gives off such a sense that the creators and the performers know what it takes to make the world a

better place. And did I mention that *Urinetown* is hilarious? Its reopening under the glare of lights on Broadway places it beside *The Producers*, another great musical that makes us laugh at tyranny, as a stanchion of pure American vibrancy. Watching *Urinetown* is simply the most galvanizing theatre experience in town.[21]

Urinetown, perhaps the most unlikely show to arrive on Broadway in recent years, was set to open on Broadway on September 13, with press nights on the tenth and eleventh. This surprise hit was developed by Greg Kotis and Mark Hollman and premiered at New York City's Fringe Theatre Festival in 1999. A musical satire about corporate greed, it seemed destined for obscurity. Its creators never considered the possibility that the work, whose main plot has to do with the government ban on private toilets, would have a run, let alone one on Broadway. Irreverent and absurd, the musical seemed like an inside joke. But it proved a crowd favorite at the festival and soon found investors who moved it off Broadway, where it proved a critical and commercial success. The musical's Broadway run was especially exciting given that it was a production that had originated downtown and that had introduced a new creative team. *Urinetown* was not the business as usual of Broadway, either in terms of its subject matter, its artistic team, or its immediate demographic. It promised to be, at the very least, something different.

On September 11, critics from the *New York Times*, *Variety*, *Newsday*, and the Associated Press were scheduled to attend but the performance was, of course, canceled and the opening, scheduled for two days later, postponed. While the musical did not open on the night of the thirteenth as planned, that evening nonetheless proved a milestone performance for the company and the show. Greg Kotis, who wrote *Urinetown*'s book and lyrics, explains:

> Times Square was relatively empty that night, itself an anticipated target, as it still is. Our audience was small, anxious, but eager, I think, to be in one another's company. Our director, John Rando, walked onstage and said simply that another word for life is creativity. Theatre, he said, could not save lives, nor could it put out fires, but it could offer creativity and life, which is what we hoped to offer that night. . . . Whatever fears the group of theatergoers had,

for themselves or for their city, the actors and the musicians and the crew had them also. But those fears were shushed away for the evening by the choice to be together, in that place, at that time.[22]

Thanks to the *New York Times* review, *Urinetown* quickly became a hit and joined *The Producers* and *The Lion King* as one of the hottest tickets on Broadway. On the day I saw the show, it was sold out with a long cancellation line. Given its unrivaled powerful cultural influence, the *New York Times* not only helped move *Urinetown* into the must-see category of theatre but it also gave people permission to go to the theatre and enjoy themselves. This became the campaign for various Broadway shows struggling to find an audience in the weeks following the terrorist attacks. My favorite: *Rent*'s campaign, which featured the lyrics, "The opposite of war isn't peace, it's creation."[23]

Admittedly, I got caught up in the *Urinetown* hype too. Half-curious about the hoopla, and recognizing my own need for some "spirit bolstering," I joined the crowds at the Henry Miller Theatre. I found *Urinetown* an appealing but largely overrated production that could not live up to the hype it had generated. Certainly, it was enjoyable, but was it really "the most galvanizing theatre experience in town"? What was most galvanizing for me about the performance was the readiness of its audience to enjoy the show. *Urinetown*'s strengths are its terrific cast and its clever choreography. This is a high-energy show, and the audience responded accordingly (figure 66). The critical and popular response seemed less inspired by the merits of the show itself and instead appeared indicative of a shared need to support a New York cultural institution such as Broadway, and in particular the unexpected success of an underdog such as *Urinetown*.[24]

At the previous day's matinee of the long-running musical *The Full Monty*, the audience with whom I sat appeared even more ecstatic. People were out to have a good time, and it seemed that nothing could stop them, not even the threat of terrorism or its aftermath. One group of about thirty or so elderly women bought out two center aisles of the orchestra, hooting and hollering whenever one of the cast members did anything suggestive, which, in a show about male strippers, was often. Another group of older women literally wore their national pride on their sleeves, their patriotic American flag scarves smartly

66. Jennifer Laura Thompson, Nancy Opel, and the cast perform in *Urinetown: The Musical*, New York City, 2001. Photo by Joan Marcus

draped over their shoulders. While hyperbolic performances of patriotism were quickly becoming routine throughout the country, and despite my own misgivings about these displays, which seemed to buy into the simplistic binarism of the "you are either with us or against us" mentality, there was something powerful about seeing this group of women theatregoers entering a Broadway house en masse in the aftermath of September 11. The theatre enabled audiences to constitute an alternative public quite different from the officially choreographed rites of national mourning arising in the initial weeks after the attacks.

At first, I was not sure about my relationship to this audience, a confusion familiar to me whenever I attend a mainstream production. What were the shared values or desires that would bring so many different people together—including me—at a matinee performance of the musical adaptation of the film *The Full Monty*? While these questions also surface at community-based and alternative performance venues, the very words *community* and *alternative* already help to resolve the matter, at least for me. This generally is not the case at a Broadway production where I often do not fit the audience demographic, despite my ubiquitous presence at these productions over the years. Earlier in my life I used to differentiate myself from mainstream Broadway audiences, noting my age, cultural, and economic differences. But I no longer take any satisfaction in such disidentifications, which now appear to me a foolish move since I already am, in some way, part of this group: I am there with them in that audience, after all. Quite frankly, not only was this a group I consented to join freely; I, in fact, paid money to do so. What did I share, then, with this random assemblage of people at the Eugene O'Neill Theatre who composed the audience? I went to *The Full Monty* to see Patrick Wilson—perhaps the strongest male lead performer of his generation, and one of my favorite young actors—before he left the show to begin rehearsals for the upcoming Broadway revival of *Oklahoma!* (figure 67). But I also went to join those who also felt moved to be in a Broadway house that afternoon. My sense of needing to become part of this collective setting was motivated by a need for belonging, driven by empathy to surround myself with strangers so that I might, in sharing this experience in the theatre, begin to see the mourning of others and not just my own.

On one level, *The Full Monty*'s premise that a group of working-class men in Buffalo, New York, had lost their jobs, lived in a depressed economy, and were at wit's end to make a buck—so much so that they would strip for cash—did not seem too far off the possible reality of some of the cast and other aspiring Broadway actors in the post–September 11 economy. In fact, my friend José and I had spent the previous night at the Gaiety, a male burlesque club in the heart of Times Square where young men from throughout the region strip naked for a paying, mostly gay male, audience. The Gaiety was packed that night, leaving José and me to joke that whatever else was going on in the world, the Gaiety, and the extended sex industry business, would endure.[25] *The Full Monty*, on the other hand, seemed less secure. The week before the terrorist attacks, the show was performing to nearly 90 percent audience capacity at the Eugene O'Neill, a venue that seats 1,088. During the week of September 11, the musical played to only a 32 percent capacity audience.

67. Patrick Wilson in *The Full Monty*, New York City, 2001. Photo by Craig Schwartz

The following week (September 17–23) improved considerably, but the audiences were still only at 68 percent.[26] It was uncertain the weekend I attended if the musical would regain its momentum and return to its pre–September 11 audience numbers.

And yet what struck me most about the production given this economic backdrop was the sheer virtuosity of the performers—including the musicians in the pit—their professionalism, their sense of purpose in performing for us.[27] In the end, I, too, joined the standing ovation so effortlessly offered to the company by the theatre's full house. I was very pleased to be in this audience, and the next day's *Urinetown*'s audience, even if the actual shows themselves did not prove completely satisfying or memorable on their own. Perhaps it did not really matter what show I was attending that weekend. Most likely, I would have experienced the same feelings of audience connection and inflated enthusiasm at any production that had not closed in the theatre district in the wake of September 11. These performances felt like little triumphs for all of us, a slight shift in the mood and tone of the city. That they were occurring within a space itself immediately threatened by potential terrorism—the commercial theatre district of Manhattan—only added to the sense that performance was creating temporal spectatorial communities thinking about the nation during a heightened moment of the contemporary. These shows took place in the temporal space of the contemporary threatened as much by nationalist hyperpatriotic manipulation as by possible acts of terrorism. These audiences, many, like the flag-draped group of elderly women, performing visible citizenship, gathered in a location and time deeply impacted by grief and destruction. Going to the theatre meant participating in a collective but fleeting effort to create a counterpublic space of emotion and affect that differed from the violent rhetoric of nationalism increasingly evident in the aftermath of September 11.

Not too far from *The Full Monty*, on Eighth Avenue and Forty-eighth Street, if you are walking on the east side of Eighth Avenue, you will run into the firehouse that serves Midtown and the theatre district. Fifteen of the firefighters from Battalion 9, affectionately known as the Broadway Firehouse, perished at the World Trade Center. Outside the station an impromptu memorial honoring these men surfaced soon after the attacks (figure 68). Flowers, votive candles, and condolences from all over the world, many from children, covered the outer walls of the station and extended into the street. The hush of the endless crowd that stopped to pay its respects proved as moving a tribute as the actual tokens and messages left behind. This urban altar constituted both a spontaneous sacred space and a type of improvisational environmental performance open to anyone who happened to walk by it. Its location on Eighth Avenue guaranteed a wide and ever-changing audience. Different levels of participation were invited, even encouraged. Some people absorbed as much as they could as they walked by, others stopped and lingered, taking it all in piece by piece. Guest books were available for those of us walking by to write our feelings and sign our names, and they, too, became part of the memorial as people read to

68. The Broadway Firehouse, Eighth Avenue at Forty-eighth Street, New York City, October, 2001. Photo by Richard Meyer

see the signatures from all over the world. Photos of the fallen men, "Our Brothers," filled an entire half wall of the station. These head shots paid tribute to the performance of their heroism and invited us to acknowledge that the depth of their lives could only be suggested, never captured, by these images.

Cameras are and were forbidden in most theatres, but they were everywhere else in midtown Manhattan. To be in this neighborhood was to participate in a photo shoot. Someone was always taking a picture, and it was no different there at the firehouse, where the photos of the fifteen firefighters formed the centerpiece of the memorial. The photos begot more photos; taking a picture constitutes one way of marking the moment and our participation in time, one way of memorializing the dead. "Inundated in images, we created our own," Diana

Taylor observes in her reflections on September 11.[28] Taylor is interested in thinking through the role of photography in the immediate aftermath of the attacks, especially this impulse to take pictures of the burning towers, the rubble, and the memorials. "Photography was evidence," she writes, "proof not so much of the object of the photograph but of our own existence."[29] That the search for this evidence played out in the public sphere seems significant; not only did it involve and necessitate the participation of others but it enabled us to witness each others' processes. The Broadway Firehouse was not the only fire station in the New York City region to undergo a transformation, nor were firehouses the only venues where this sense of embodied memorialization occurred. And while these sites of public gatherings collectively expressed a need to honor the missing or the dead, each site had its own sense of purpose and style.

In Chelsea, the neighborhood where I used to live, the local firehouse is located near the Joyce Theater, one of New York City's premier dance venues. On the weekend I first returned to New York after the attacks, the Joyce held a two-night benefit for the New York Police and Fire Widows' and Children's Benefit Fund, a nonprofit organization established in 1985 to assist the families of those who had died in the line of duty (figure 69). Fifteen different dance companies that often showcase their work at the Joyce performed that weekend to raise money for the fund and to honor the five members from Ladder 12 and Battalion 7 who had been missing since September 11, as well as the twenty-three members of the NYPD's Tenth Precinct. These units are long-standing members of the neighborhood and protect and look out for the Joyce throughout the year. The event billed as "Dancing for the Bravest and Finest" included longtime veteran companies such as the Limón Dance Company, the Paul Taylor Dance Company, the Lar Lubovitch Dance Company, and the Trisha Brown Dance Company to younger companies such as Ronald K. Brown/Evidence. David Gordon, Valda Seterrfield, and Desmond Richmond were among the artists who danced in a diverse program that showcased both the incredible range of the contemporary dance scene and the commitment of the dance community to mobilize for this cause. "Tonight, we want to pay respects to those who have perished in the rescue effort," wrote

DANCING FOR THE BRAVEST AND FINEST

A Benefit for
The New York Police & Fire Widows' & Children's
Benefit Fund

THE JOYCE THEATER

FRIDAY, SEPTEMBER 28

69. Program for the Joyce Theater's *Dancing for the Bravest and Finest* benefit, New York City, September 28, 2001. Collection of the author

Linda Shelton, the executive director of the Joyce in the evening's program note; "we hope that this evening's performance and the creative spirit of the artists will provide some solace and comfort to everyone gathered here."[30] Tickets for the benefit were fifty dollars and quickly sold out. As I waited in line at the Joyce box office earlier that day with others hoping to attend, we spoke of the importance of events like this—and there were many throughout New York and the country— to provide us a place to go and share a sense of belonging somewhat outside of the increasing nationalist fervor shaping public gatherings. As David Eng has noted, the noise of nationalism quickly replaced the silence of mourning that had characterized New York right after the attacks. "Yet in all that noise," he writes, "the language of mourning is no less impoverished for it has become the language of an unyielding nationalism, one that brooks no internal dissent—indeed legitimates the suppression of dissent."[31] Events such as the Joyce benefit constituted community-driven, counterpublic occasions that allowed for alternative expressions of collective mourning and remembrance to the

70. Peggy Lyman dancing Martha Graham's *Lamentation* at the Joyce Theater benefit, New York City, September 28, 2001. Photo by Richard Termine

insistent call for nationalist displays of patriotism. Here at the Joyce, artists were invited to contribute in whatever capacity made sense to them; there was no mandate for a particular type of dance or movement, no suppression of creative expression. Rather than demanding a uniform language of mourning, these artists showcased a wide range of emotion and response to September 11.

The evening began with a stirring rendition of Martha Graham's 1930 solo *Lamentation*, danced by former Martha Graham principal dancer Peggy Lyman (figure 70). Graham described the dance, which centers on a woman dressed in a sheath of purple jersey creating abstract shapes and designs, as the personification of grief itself, not the representation of the experience of an actual person or character.[32] Grounded in Graham's modernist formalism, Lyman's rendition of *Lamentation* presented the emotional sorrow at the heart of the work, suggesting that modern dance had a history of addressing tragedy that would be summoned this evening. While not all of the work in the program provided such a clear response to tragedy, much of it did. Parsons

Dance Company, for example, presented *Union*, an ensemble piece highlighting the tactile links among bodies sharing space and time. The beautifully choreographed Parsons artists, dancing to a score by John Corigliano, moved across the Joyce stage in lyrical union (figure 71).

Near the end of the program, the composer and singer Philip Hamilton, accompanied by a pianist, took the stage with a drum to sing "Sokolo: a Prayer." Hamilton's rich voice filled the Joyce with the incantatory sounds of mourning, a stunning break from the evening's emphasis on dance and movement (figure 72). Hamilton's musical interlude was immediately followed by Doug Varone's intensely felt *Nocturne*, a solo he choreographed and danced to Chopin's Nocturne in D-flat Major. His careful and thoughtful movements set to the quiet, meditative piano music of Chopin offered a poignant meditation on the body's physical limitations and the labor involved in bodily movement. It also served as a testament to the evocative power of dance to convey the solemnity of the September 11 tragedy. Other companies who performed offered dances from their repertoire, or they shared with the audience current works in progress. Whether or not the work itself evoked the tragic seemed, in many ways, beside the point. This was a benefit designed to raise money for the fund and to honor those who had died. No one anticipated or expected that these artists would create new work in response to the terrorist attacks; their mere presence at the Joyce already constituted the artistic response to September 11. The Joyce that weekend was filled with members of the extended dance community, Chelsea neighbors and friends, as well as local firefighters, police officers, and their families.

I went to one final performance that weekend. On the Sunday evening before my departure, I joined close to three thousand others at Carnegie Hall for "A Concert of Remembrance: Honoring the Victims of the Tragedy of September 11," which featured Yo-Yo Ma, the cellist, James Levine, the pianist and artistic director of the Metropolitan Opera, and Leontyne Price, the soprano, who came out of retirement for the event (figure 73). Amazingly, this event was free. Tickets were distributed on a "first come, first served" model. The line for tickets began forming early that morning, and once the box office opened, they went quickly. Hundreds of people had to be turned away. (The

71. *Union* by Parsons Dance Company at the Joyce Theater benefit, New York City, September 28, 2001. Photo by Richard Termine

72. Philip Hamilton with Peter Jones performing "Sokolo: A Prayer" at the Joyce Theater benefit, New York City, September 28, 2001. Photo by Richard Termine

concert was broadcast live on the radio.) Ma opened the program with two cello solos: Mark O'Conner's "Appalachia Waltz," followed by J. S. Bach's Cello Suite no. 5 in C Minor. Levine, accompanied by members of the Met Chamber Ensemble, performed selections from Mozart and Bolcom next. These performances were formal and masterly. The highlight of the evening was the appearance of Price, who, at seventy-four, had not sung in public for many years. After a thunderous ovation, Price sang only two songs; first, the old spiritual "This Little Light of Mine," accompanied by Levine on piano; and second, a solo rendition of both verses of "America the Beautiful" that closed the evening's one-hour program. Standing tall in a formal black gown and turban, and singing in front of an enormous American flag that hung over the stage, Price's commanding performance was unabashedly moving and powerful (figure 74). She was met with an immediate standing ovation that continued for a number of minutes. Visibly moved by such expressions of gratitude, Price left the stage escorted by the other artists who had joined her for the concert of remembrance. But what were we applauding in this moment? Certainly her performance had been impressive, but the thunderous ovation seemed directed at the largeness of the event itself, the occasion's solemnity, and the gratitude of an audience thankful for the space to share in their mourning.

I do not want to idealize these events, artists, and audiences as somehow the meaningful responses to the events of September 11, but I do want to highlight the extraordinary generosity of these people—all affiliated with the performing arts on some level—and the unquestionable significance of these gatherings. Events such as these were performed in theatres and performance venues throughout New York City and the nation, many of which have received little to no publicity for their efforts. What I have offered here constitutes an archive of what I witnessed; others will have participated in other events at different locations. Nor do I mean to suggest that in the midst of tragedy, the arts thrive in some kind of cultural renaissance that somehow compensates for the suffering and loss, as if tragedy ennobles the performing arts and gives them relevance. Instead, I am interested here in spotlighting the critical role that the performing arts—theatre, music, and dance—might play in a contemporary culture already infused with the

73. (this page) Program for "A Concert of Remembrance: Honoring the Victims of the Tragedy of September 11," Carnegie Hall, New York City, September 30, 2001. Collection of the author

74. (opposite) Leontyne Price with James Levine performing at "A Concert of Remembrance," Carnegie Hall, New York City, September 30, 2001. Photo by Richard Termine

tragic. Liveness lay at the core of these events. The performing arts offered people the chance to be with others and experience themselves together. In this sense, we were as much audiences for ourselves as for the performances.

This sense of being together—however random the "we" and however fleeting the "together"—proved a critical priority for many people, and it took various forms of public gathering in the weeks following the attacks. The tragedy of the terrorist attacks, however, was not what created this temporal we; it was the performances themselves, some not tragedies at all, that encouraged and enabled an alternative community of mourning participants to assemble and mark a different kind of response. Tragedy needs an audience to live through its enormity, to mourn its intensity, to witness its effect. The need to grieve was necessary and ongoing, and it was especially welcome in displays throughout the public sphere. Despite calls to move on and move forward, as President Bush announced less than two weeks after the eleventh, mourning could not be restrained and contained within a limited time frame. Theatre and other live performance events played an important role in this process. As theatre scholar Alice Rayner has noted, "without an audience susceptible to grief and willing to mourn, tragedy has no place."[33] In New York in the early weeks after September 11, the theatre offered one such place for tragedy and its audiences.

Tragedy's main location, however, was at Ground Zero, the site where the twin towers had once stood, and the place where most went to mourn and grieve. In part, people went to Ground Zero to see for themselves what had occurred, but they also went to support the various crews who worked to search for human remains, clean up the mess, and restore safety. I was not sure if I was going to go to Ground Zero that weekend. That was the question posed most often by nearly everyone I encountered before, during, and after this trip and the other visits to New York in the months that followed. It was also the question I most asked myself, always postponing the decision to another day. In the end, I decided against it; I did not think I could witness any more of the tragedy. I was not confident I would know how to process the images of the wreckage and take in the gravity of the loss. Mine was a different pilgrimage. I went to New York not to go to Ground Zero and see the devastation, but to go to the theatre and see live performance. In *Modern Tragedy*, Raymond Williams recommends that we follow the whole action of a tragedy — "not only the crisis, but the energy released by it, the spirit learned in it." I went to New York to try to follow that observation through.

The events I have discussed all occurred within weeks of September 11, in the immediate aftermath of the terrorist attacks. They ranged among the initial artistic responses to September 11, and should be acknowledged as such. But historians, artists, and critics tend to undermine the significance of these events by promoting the idea that the artistic response will come later, at some future date, in some time other than the contemporary moment. This idea that artists need time to absorb the events before any important creative works can emerge seems to me misguided. It also disregards the important contributions of those who act or perform in the work of others. When Broadway reopened on September 13, actors and musicians were called to perform in what many might regard as trivial entertainments inappropriate for the time. These actors needed to suspend their own ambivalence about performing during a period of profound mourning. "How could I smile at a time like this?" explained Tamlyn Brooke Shusterman, a chorus girl in the revival of *42nd Street*. Shusterman, writing in an op-ed piece in the *New York Times*, provided a backstage view on what many of these performers were experiencing as they took to the stage on September 13, 2001. But Shusterman recalls *42nd Street*'s initial historical intervention during the difficult times of the 1930s:

> The original 1933 movie version of *42nd Street* was a musical created to help raise the spirits of Americans during the Depression. And it seemed extremely important to do the same that night. I even understood the value of the American chorus girl. Sometimes wearing patent-leather shoes and girlie costumes has made me feel frivolous. But that night was not about what I might want to say as a woman. It was about escaping reality. About beauty, music and comedy. And it worked. The laughter that Thursday was so rewarding. It was not disrespectful; it was necessary.
>
> At the end of the show, we waved the American flag. Hearing the applause, seeing the uplifted faces, the flag rippling in the air, was

immensely moving. What the audience applauded was not our talents but our attempts to help in any way possible. That this gave them some comfort made me very proud to be a performer.[34]

Shusterman's account captures and records the role that even "frivolous" performances began to offer their audiences in the immediate aftermath of September 11. These performances might not themselves register as the most insightful artistic responses to September 11, given that they do not thematize or address the tragic events of the day directly or that their audiences were so limited. (Only nine hundred people came to the Ford Center for the Performing Arts to see Ms. Shusterman perform with her colleagues on September 13.) But both individually and collectively, these performances need to be acknowledged for the important cultural work they achieved at the time.

The performing arts already play a role in the national culture, and it would be a mistake to assume that we must wait several years before witnessing a profound artistic response to September 11. The relevance of the arts can be immediate and, I would argue, must be understood as such if we are to take seriously their role in the culture. This notion of the "immediate experience" of tragedy, as Williams describes it, proves significant for our understanding of the role of the arts in response to the tragic. This chapter therefore concerns itself not with tragic drama but with tragic history and the way that the arts intervened in a particular moment in time. Its main interest lies not in works that thematize September 11, but in how the theatre and other forms of performance either responded to this tragic history or could be read alongside it as it occurred and took shape. Live performance involves so much more than simply the script and thematic content of particular works performed; it is about historical context and the gathered audience as well.[35]

The artistic response to September 11 was both immediate and ongoing. This sense of an immediate response is important in many ways. First, it begins to valorize what is already in the world rather than what will some day be introduced. The idea that the future will bring profundity and clarity to the contemporary undervalues the role of the arts to make an immediate intervention in history as it takes shape. We do not have to wait several years for the great play about September 11 before we can claim that the arts have fulfilled their mandate to illuminate the world in which we live and engender discussions about it; the artistic response to September 11 took shape in the weeks that followed as actors, dancers, and musicians all responded to the tragedy by going back to work. Second, by focusing on what transpired in the initial weeks and months, a more nuanced history emerges, one that recognizes how the arts served the needs of the moment. The critical investment in futurity—the idea that the future will bring forth the perspective that will enable an insight unavailable in the present—disregards the work that the arts achieve in their contemporary moment. This model of history is one of deferral, and it runs the risk of obscuring the archives most relevant to the historical record. Finally, history's practice of deferral undercuts the necessity to document and evaluate the time of the now, and it undercuts the needs of contemporary audiences for immediate engagement and participation through the arts. This idea that the future arts will illuminate the present for us retroactively, that only later will we understand what has happened now, seems to be of service primarily to a future audience, not the audience currently in place. This notion of the future comes at the direct expense of the present. As such, it effects artists who are told it is too soon to engage, too exploitive to address, and too early to consider how they might respond to history as it unfolds. Placed in a holding tank, artists are forced to speak in a language of deferral.

The cultural investment in—if not insistence on—futurity overvalues what has yet to appear, what is not yet in the world, and it directs our attention away from what is already present in anticipation of that which will later become available. But to question the cultural investment in the future is not to suggest that the future does not matter. On the contrary, a stronger engagement with the present moment can only enhance the futures that the contemporary will produce. My aim is to trouble the normative impulse to accept the future as the goal of all contemporary practice. The contemporary does not need to be held up by future generations to decide its political or cultural relevance. In terms of the arts, this practice also places its bets on some sense of future artistic achievement that will be at once classic and profound, the idea that the great work of art will offer future audiences insight into the recent past. I am less drawn to this kind of thinking because it forecasts relevance and profundity for a future time and a future audience, and it suggests that the arts can only be relevant retroactively and not in the immediate time of the now.

This sense of timing was underlined by the world premiere of Tony Kushner's *Homebody/Kabul* in the fall of 2001 at the New York Theatre Workshop. Widely described as "eerily prescient" for addressing the historical encounters between the West and Afghanistan, Kushner's play generated enormous publicity for its political topicality and the playwright's uncanny ability to anticipate history. The *New York Times*, for example, ran a front-page profile on Kushner in the Sunday "Arts and Leisure" section on the eve of the play's New York opening with a headline that announced "For Tony Kushner, an Eerily Prescient Return." [36] The profile explains the origins of the play as first a monologue written in 1997 in response to a request from a friend, the actor Kika Markham. Kushner, who had long cultivated an interest in Afghanistan, chose it for the topic of the piece. The fifty-minute monologue, *Homebody*, first performed in London in 1999, became the basis for the play *Homebody/Kabul*. The profile, while drawn to explaining the play's history, goes to great length to address Kushner's timing:

> The piece he would create for Ms. Markham would eventually become the opening scene of what easily qualifies as one of the most timely—even eerily prophetic—plays ever to have landed in New York at a moment of national tension and emergency. *Homebody/Kabul*, a three-hour-plus, 12-character drama that Mr. Kushner completed last winter and that is now in rehearsal at New York Theatre Workshop in the East Village, reads at times as if it had been written in response to September 11, not in advance of it. The parallels to current events—the play takes place in 1998–2000—were so uncanny that after the terrorist attacks, some cast members thought Mr. Kushner should cut several lines, for fear that audiences would think he was taking advantage of the tragedy. [37]

Many other reporters also dwelt, quite understandably, on the play's "prophetic" quality, singling out especially a line during which an Af-

75. Kelly Hutchinson and Rita Wolf perform in Tony Kushner's *Homebody/Kabul*, New York Theatre Workshop, 2001. Photo by Joan Marcus

ghani character admonishes a British one in the midst of a diatribe against U.S. foreign policies in the regions in and around Afghanistan (figure 75):

> MAHALA: You love the Taliban so much, bring them to New York! Well, don't worry, they're coming to New York! Americans!
>
> PRISCILLA: I'm English.
>
> MAHALA: English, American, no difference, one big and one small, same country, American say, British do, women die, dark-skin babies die, land mine, stinger projectile, British American so what, so what you say?![38]

The scene seems to forecast the events of September 11, as well as the political alliance forged between U.S. and British governments in the war against Afghanistan. For many, Kushner's dialogue reads as brilliant insight, as if the playwright had access to greater knowledge about world events than others.

Even critics who frown at Kushner's progressive politics single him out for daring to write about contemporary world events. One writer, for example, goes so far as to bemoan Kushner's politics and his artistry, finding the play "longwinded," but praises Kushner's career-long ambition to engage world events. "Put aside for a moment his views on the grand issues of our time and give him credit for being engaged with the world in a way few other dramatists are," writes Mark Steyn in the *New Criterion*. Steyn goes on to bemoan American playwrights for their failure to address big themes in their work, especially ones that would be relevant to the current state of global affairs and that might even offer an option to Kushner's unapologetic leftist perspective.

> It's not his fault that there's no alternative view on the New York stage: the fact is that, in the years since the Soviet retreat and the Taliban's rise and Osama's opening forays, no other working playwright thought any of these themes worth writing about. What a place New York theatre would be if more writers could raise their eyes from their navels to the world, to embrace, the big sweep of history. . . . Only Tony Kushner was curious enough to want to write a play about Afghanistan.[39]

In offering Kushner a backhanded compliment, Steyn misses the larger point. It is not that Kushner is the only playwright curious enough to write a play about Afghanistan; most likely he is the only playwright who will have a play about Afghanistan produced in a major theatre.

Kushner himself rejects these forms of exceptionalism that laud him for being "prescient" or "engaged with the world." "The play was written before 9/11," Kushner answers back in the afterword to the published play; "I'm not psychic. If you choose to write about current events there's a good chance that you'll find the events you've written to be . . . well, current."[40] *Homebody/Kabul* reminds audiences that the tragic events of September 11 have an origin well before that date, and that the aftermath of September 11 effects more than only the lives of Westerners. Kushner mainly paid attention to current geopolitical events that led to the terrorist attacks, and the play provides an entry point into thinking about a complex history of social struggle and political conflict. Kushner is therefore not "eerily prescient" but, instead, engaged with our contemporary moment. His work provides an alternative to the official national discourse on the events in Afghanistan and their relationship to September 11.

And yet as these disparate critical responses suggest, Kushner's play and its timing invites a discussion about the nature of the performing arts and the contemporary, especially one that examines the role the arts might play in illuminating the current in *current events*. The play begins in the summer of 1998 with the Homebody—a middle-aged white British woman living in London and fascinated by Afghanistan—

speaking about her life. Soon, however, we find ourselves in Kabul, Afghanistan, where the woman's husband and daughter are searching for her amid rumors of her brutal murder. The play takes place during the period of the U.S. military bombing of suspected training camps for terrorists in Afghanistan.

The combination of the play's contemporary setting, Kushner's name recognition as one of the most important living playwrights, and his exhaustive research on Afghani history and culture, along with the larger unfolding geopolitical context in which the play was viewed, made *Homebody/Kabul* one of the most significant events of the 2001–2 season. Not only did the play have a successful run at the New York Theatre Workshop but it also had noteworthy productions that same season at Trinity Repertory Company in Providence, Rhode Island, under the direction of Oskar Eustis, and at Berkeley Repertory under the direction of Tony Taccone. On each of these occasions *Homebody/Kabul* generated substantial press. Reviews were generally favorable, excusing whatever formal or artistic shortcomings the play or the production might have suffered and emphasizing instead the play's ambition, relevance, and timeliness.[41] Some reviews, including Ben Brantley's in the *New York Times*, underscored a sense of the play as a work in progress, as if the contemporary setting and the unfolding political contexts counterbalanced whatever the critic might have found fault with in the play. It was not merely the play that was a work-in-progress but also the political scenario. As Brantley put it, the play was full of "potential" and might in the future become more fully realized.

When I first saw the play, early on in its New York Theatre Workshop run, Kushner was still, as is his process, making cuts and sharpening scenes. Like others, I found the production exciting and invigorating; and this sense that the artistic process was exposed to revision and rehearsal in the public eye suggested to me the hard work attached to creative practice. I did not see the play as necessarily flawed because the playwright was still working things out. It did not seem to me that Kushner was necessarily prescient either, but the fact that the world and time of the play so immediately spoke to the current geopolitical scenario was unavoidable, if not obvious, to those of us who saw the play in those initial weeks. Still, the immediacy of the production's premiere in New York so soon after the collapse of the twin towers would not last indefinitely.

Some critics even raised this issue of the play's topicality in their response to *Homebody/Kabul*. Michael Phillips, in his review of the New York Theatre Workshop production for the *Los Angeles Times*, rightfully claims that the play "is the cultural artifact of the moment," but worries that the play's immediacy might limit its relevance. "Like any theatrical event blessed or cursed by topicality," Phillips writes, "[*Homebody/Kabul*] faces a question: can it outlive its moment?"[42] While this question remains for Phillips a rhetorical one, the logic behind it implies that for the play to be successful, it will need to prove meaningful for future audiences. Phillips ends his review by quoting from an interview he conducted with no one less than Arthur Miller, then perhaps the most important living playwright in the world, and one whose own plays had been championed for their topicality as well as their universality. In fact, a revival of Miller's now classic 1953 play *The Crucible*, about the Salem witch trials and inspired by the McCarthy hearings of the early 1950s, was to open only a few months later on Broadway. "I don't think that being topical needs to limit a play's longevity or enhance it either," Miller explains; "there's something else involved, and that is whether there are some basic human truths in the play, deeper than the passing moment. If that's the case, maybe a play will last." Miller doesn't comment on the significance of addressing the audience of what he calls "the passing moment," and the quote is set up to respond to the idea of future productions in a later moment in time. Miller keeps his remarks general, and Phillips uses them to conclude his review on this open-ended note, one that only time will be able to resolve. The question—"Can *Homebody/Kabul* outlive its cultural moment?"—is picked up by other critics who spin it a bit differently.

Peggy Phelan, in her joint review of the New York Theatre Workshop and the Berkeley Repertory productions, is less interested in what Miller names as "basic human truths" and focuses instead on how the staging, reception, and context of *Homebody/Kabul* has shifted since its New York Fall 2001 premiere. She begins by noting the changes in the play's length and staging:

In the production at the Berkeley Repertory Theatre, *Kabul* had been cut substantially, and Tony Taccone's direction was more aggressive and faster paced than Donnellan's. Moreover, in the eight months between the opening of the play and its Berkeley run, the situation in Kabul had been radically altered, making the political urgency of some of Kushner's comments dated, rather than "eerily prescient." Finally, the psychological terrain between downtown New York twelve weeks after the destruction of the World Trade Center and Berkeley forty weeks later was also dramatically different. In New York, the play was seen primarily in terms of the attack on the city—there's a line in the play about the Taliban coming to New York—while in Berkeley, the reception of the play concerned Kushner's love affair with language.[43]

Phelan remains interested in the play's politics and form, and her main critique of the play follows accordingly. Rather than worry about Kushner's relevance to future audiences, Phelan wants to engage the politics presented by the play in these productions. Her concern that Kushner "falsifies the history of the world" by portraying the United States as the once and always superpower culpable for what has happened in Afghanistan is a direct and immediate response to Kushner's ideas. Her comments allow for the play to resonate more effectively in the present moment as it continues to unfold.

The response to *Homebody/Kabul* demonstrates how critics begin to read the contemporary, and how the contemporary is often dismissed as merely topical. These reviews also begin to dramatize the tension between the present moment and what Miller calls the "passing moment" as they question the play's future relevance. Strangely, the central character of the *Homebody* section herself ruminates on the idea of the contemporary in her stunning reflection on history, which opens the play (figure 76). In the world of the play it is 1998, and the Homebody is reading from an outdated guidebook to Afghanistan from 1965. She interrupts her reading to speak aloud her thoughts on the present period and offers that "these are awful times." The Homebody continues in what will become her characteristic discursive excess, a rhetorical style in which what seems like an aside will offer poignant and

76. Linda Emond as the Homebody in Tony Kushner's *Homebody/Kabul*, Mark Taper Forum, Los Angeles, 2003. Photo by Craig Schwartz

often humorous insight. In this moment, the Homebody riffs on the idea of the present and its reception in its own historical moment:

The Present is *always* an awful place to be. And it remains awful to us, the scene of our crime, the place of our shame, for at least Oh, let's say three full decades of recession—by which word, recession, I am to be taken to mean recedence, not recession as in two consecutive quarters of negative growth in gross domestic product. For a three-decades regnum of imperceptible but mercifully implacable recedency we shudder to recall the times through which we have lived, the Recent Past, about which no one wants to think: and then, have you noticed? Even the most notorious decade three or four decades later is illumined from within. Some light inside is switched on. The scenery becomes translucent, beautifully lit; features of the landscape glow; the shadows are full of agreeable color. Cynics will attribute this transformation to senescence and nostalgia; I who am optimistic, have you noticed? attribute this inner illumination to understanding. It is wisdom's hand which switches on the light within. Ah now I see what that was all about. Ah, now, now I see why we suffered so back then, now I see what we went through. I understand.[44]

The Homebody's recognition of the antipathy toward the present buys into this notion that the contemporary can be rehabilitated by time, or by the wisdom that comes with time. But it does not completely address the problem inherent in her monologue: what is so awful about the present? She tells us that which characterizes the present is that "the private is *gone*. All must be touched. All touch corrupts. All must be corrupted."[45] Here, she offers not only a discourse on the present but one that could equally be understood as a discourse on the tragic. In many ways, the Homebody overinvests in the future, a symptom of anticontemporary sentiment. She forecasts her own revision of the moment of the now, which she describes as awful, when she implies that she will reach some "understanding" of her present fate later, as everyone does, as is the process of history, at least history as she understands it. But this later never comes for her, for as we learn, she soon disappears. She is denied a future.

Perhaps, as some believe, she has finally made her move, leaving behind her awful present to find love with the Afghani hat merchant she encounters during one of her excursions in London. Here, in this scenario, she survives and her future is simply unknowable to us. In this sense, we are denied her future. More likely, she is dead, as her family, who travels to Kabul to seek some answers to her disappearance, begins to believe. The play does not resolve this mystery for us. But Kushner moves us to question the Homebody's thinking. Even though she is an optimist who loves the world—"Oh I love the world, I love, love, love, love the world!"—she is, like Harper in *Angels in America*, a hysteric on antidepressants detached from her husband and daughter. Like Harper, she makes a choice to leave. The tragic underpinnings of her world are unbearable and must be changed. In a moment of what might be called wisdom, she describes herself and her condition: "Where stands the homebody, safe in her kitchen, on her culpable shore, suffering uselessly watching others perishing in the sea, wringing her plump little maternal hands, oh, oh. Never joining the drowning, her feet neither rooted nor moving. The ocean is deep and cold and erasing. But how dreadful, how unpardonable, to remain dry. Look at her, look at her, she is so unforgivably dry. Neither here nor there."[46]

In the second part of the play, *Kabul*, we meet her husband and daughter and a larger cast of characters affected by the Homebody's disappearance. For some, their "awful times" involves poverty, oppression, and death. Forced to confront such tragic conditions, many of these characters make dramatic and life-changing choices. While these other characters all remain within the narrative trajectory of the play's unfolding drama, and while we watch them as they move forward in time, the play ends with the Homebody locked forever in the first act; she never returns. She remains in the end precisely in the place of the tragic (for her): "Neither here nor there."

Homebody/Kabul gives the lie to the idea that there is a necessary time lapse between contemporary culture and artistic response. While it was not written in response to September 11, its themes and issues immediately resonate. But not only the critics brought this point to the forefront. The artistic directors of the two theatres mounting the initial productions of the play each spoke eloquently of the need to present the play despite concerns that it might prove incendiary or inappropriate given the recent tragic events. Both Oskar Eustis, of Trinity Repertory Company in Providence, and Jim Nicola, of the New York Theatre Workshop, decided against canceling their productions of the play and chose instead to see the shows as catalysts for a better understanding of world events. "It's exactly appropriate for the theatre to be presenting Afghanis on stage, to be presenting a very complicated view of Islam, of Afghani history, of the history of Afghanistan's treatment by both the West and the former Soviet Union, and trying to understand the politics of the situation in a considerably more dimensional way than seems fashionable since September 11," explained Eustis.[47]

While Eustis's comments point to the role that the theatre can play in the life of its audiences, Nicola emphasizes the role the theatre must play in the life of its artists, especially in a time of nationalist fervor. "We require the artists in our midst to make a dismal, treacherous journey, searching for the illumination we lack," he writes. "In such a time of need for vision and clarity," he continues, "I find a great satisfaction in being able to create a harbor from which a writer like Tony can set forth well-fortified on his imaginative quest, hoping that he returns safely home."[48] Both theatres, as well as Berkeley Repertory, took risks in staging the play as a topical and important work that would have something to say to its contemporary audiences, something challenging the official narratives of the nation. Rather than postpone or cancel their productions, they decided to produce the play, thereby enabling audiences in each of these communities to engage the work as the current events around Afghanistan occurred. These theatres allowed local audiences to constitute a counterpublic where space for cultural dissent was possible and cultural debate was encouraged. In refusing to delay their productions of Homebody/Kabul to some future time or season, these directors made the case for the importance of the theatre to immediately enter into a dialectical discussion between history and the present. The uncertain future that this discussion might produce will result from such an encounter; this is the role of the theatre, these artistic directors suggest. Theatre holds the potential to shape history as it unfolds.

Performance also, as I have argued throughout this book, offers a form of counterpublicity to the dominant discourses of the nation-state. It puts forward alternative viewpoints, showcases emerging perspectives, and allows for cultural dissent. The charisma of live performance enables cultural interventions in ways more successful than those possible in other media. But it can also cohere to positions already widely held, and in fact serve to promote them. Performance in itself does not constitute a counter-hegemonic practice; it can be put to use for various political campaigns and ideological positions. Whatever the case, we should not underestimate its power. Despite its temporal and spatial constraints, factors that differentiate it from other forms of mass entertainment such as film, radio, and television, performance matters and can make a difference. And while its effects are not always identifiable or even self-evident—indeed, might be localized to the point of seeming cultural obscurity—within minor zones its power often takes hold. Consider, as a final example of theatre and tragedy in the wake of September 11, the work of Reno, whose Rebel without a Pause: Unre-

strained Reflections on September 11th emerged among the most immediate responses to the terrorist attacks and has remained, for me, one of the most enduring.

Reno, a native New Yorker, is a performer so peculiar that she defies any easy description. She is at once a stand-up comedian, a performance artist, a cultural provocateur, an autobiographical monologist, and a political activist. A downtown personality since the mid-1980s, Reno has experienced a series of bumps and starts in her artistic career. Although she has occasionally been championed as the next big thing on the order of a Whoopi Goldberg or a Lily Tomlin, Reno's celebrity remains located in the national circuits of the alternative performance scene, where she commands a loyal and consistent fan base. She is a tour de force; simply put, there is no one else quite like her. Her *Rebel without a Pause* stands as one of the most exciting performance events I have seen during the period of writing this book, and it remains one of the most powerful cultural interventions into our contemporary national debates.

Rebel without a Pause was developed at La Mama, the East Village performance space known for presenting innovative and experimental theatre and for its commitment to progressive causes, world arts and culture, and local artists. Reno was already scheduled to open a new show on the Religious Right—"the other fundamentalist religious terrorist group," as she describes them in her show—at La Mama in early October, but the events of September 11 inspired her to change the focus of her performance.[49] Beginning on October 4, 2001, Reno used the stage to respond nightly to the day's events and the increasingly complex and often confusing contemporary political landscape. Already known for her hilarity and spontaneity, Reno's post–September 11 performances found an immediate audience who welcomed her humorous commentary and unapologetic leftist politics. These improvisational rants—or "unrestrained reflections"—soon became the full-evening show that eventually moved uptown to the Zipper Theatre for a commercial run in the spring of 2002 (figure 77). *Rebel without a Pause* has since been filmed by director Nancy Savoca and has screened at various film festivals.[50]

Rebel without a Pause begins with Reno walking onstage with her dog

Lucy, who she lets out into the audience at the beginning of each show.
Once onstage, she starts listening to her answering machine, which
plays messages left for her on the morning of September 11. Notorious for her vampiric hours, Reno occupies a time zone all her own. All
of her friends knew better than to call her before the early afternoon,
when she generally greets the day, but on this morning, her friends felt
that an exception was in order and that Reno, who lives blocks from
the World Trade Center in TriBeCa, should be alerted. She had spent
the previous evening working all hours of the night on material for the
new show, but was awakened by the persistent messages. One friend,
fully aware of Reno's particular sleep patterns, humorously added to her
message, "Listen, Reno, there's something happening outside, right in
your neighborhood; if it were happening uptown, I would never have

called you." Reno wakes up to join her neighbors outside their building as they put every effort into making sense of the day's events. Even Reno, who generally thrives on chaos, comes unhinged. She proceeds to provide a blow-by-blow eyewitness account of her morning and the subsequent days and weeks that followed the destruction of the twin towers.

Uncertain what to make of the day's events, she and her neighbors go back and forth from their street-level perspective of witnessing the towers aflame to needing to watch the same image on television. Reno mimes a look of double take: Is the image on the screen the same as what she sees outside? And if so, why then turn to the television for its validation? They are hoping, like everyone else that day, for some explanation, wishing for a second that the events might simply be the latest David Copperfield staging. But, of course, that is not the case. The need to have some confirmation of their reality authorized by the news media drove some of them to watch the news on television. Some chose to flee; she names these people "the nouvelle refugees from Tribekastan" running uptown with "their YSL luggage." Considering what she herself must pack, Reno goes first for her vibrator—"that was a no-brainer," she admits. Her humor, while irreverent and often vulgar, is winning. Her audience warms up to her stage persona quickly, in part because it seems so clearly linked to the actual performer. It is not that she is simply hilarious, which, of course, she is; rather, her humor comes across as honest and direct. In this sense, she wins our trust. In a time of great skepticism around the news media, Reno's performance is, as she describes it, "unrestrained" (figures 78 and 79).

Reno's show captures many of the sentiments experienced on September 11, but rather than only emphasize the solemnity and heroism associated with the day, Reno opts for a fuller archive of feelings, including many that are less righteous or gracious. She calls attention to the hierarchy of experience people claimed, noting how people were quick to state their proximity to the World Trade Center tragedy. This bragging of what she calls "pain and knowledge" took many forms; it was competitive in spirit and driven by the need to feel part of the day's tragedy. She provides a sample of these claims: "I was just there last month!" as if the speaker were in imminent danger or had some-

78–79. Reno performs in *Rebel without a Pause*, New York City, 2001. Photos by Lisa Sylvestri

how managed to trick death; or "I saw the first plane approaching," as if that in itself amounted to anything insightful. But it is topped by someone claiming more experiential proximity in the competitive one-upmanship of "I heard the first plane take off from Logan!" And here she raises her eyebrows, shrugs her shoulder, and shakes it off. This behavior, which Reno freely admits to having taken part in as well, is matched by the sudden expertise that people have about foreign affairs, national security, and terrorist insider knowledge. One of her favorite rumors claims that machete-armed terrorists had taken over Souen, a trendy macrobiotic restaurant on the corner of Prince Street and Sixth Avenue, for their headquarters, a possibility Reno finds simply absurd—"They don't even have hot sauce!" she shouts incredulously.

But soon Reno's humorous anecdotal account takes a turn. Now that she has brought us into her world, she will share her worldview. A cultural gadfly, Reno is Aristophanic in her satire as well as in the raunchiness of her rants. And she is explosive and unforgiving. Her main critiques are directed at Bush and his administration, and here Reno is relentless. Her knowledge of current affairs is considerable and impressive; her interest in placing the events within a global context comes as a rebuttal of the nationalist tendency to isolate the U.S. perspective as the only legitimate one, a provincialism that she finds emblematic of the president's regime. Stunned by Bush's simplistic cowboy mentality, which she sees as clueless to the global crisis, she admonishes him for his imbecility—"when he's not rehearsed, he's like a drunk trying to act sober"—and goes on to indict those in his cabinet who seem to be calling the shots. She scolds Condoleezza Rice, who sees no problem in changing civil liberties in the name of national security. "We have rules and laws!" Reno warns, and these are in place to guide us especially in moments of heightened national crisis, she insists. And she is especially critical of John Ashcroft, whose undermining of the law she finds to be an immoral abuse of power, one made all the more offensive since he, like Bush, was not even elected:

> Oh, and Ashcroft—this guy who is making life-shattering decisions not only for Americans but for people all over the world—Ashcroft, the appointee of an appointee president, remember, this is a

guy who lost an election to a dead man, folks! During Ashcroft's re-election campaign—Ashcroft, the incumbent, which means he *already had* the job—his opponent died. The people of Missouri decided to vote for the dead guy! And now *he's* in charge? This is democracy? Come on people!

In these moments, Reno's rant is uninterruptible. Like the Homebody in Kushner's *Homebody/Kabul*, Reno offers a showcase of discursive excess, of ongoing verbal pyrotechnics, of surprising narrative moves and turns. While the Homebody revels in the joy of language, Reno revels in freedom of expression. Reno's monologue makes explicit the need for alternative perspectives in the national public sphere. In the climate of cultural suppression of anything seemingly "unpatriotic," especially in the immediate aftermath of September 11, Reno will not shut up. She moves from one topic to another, raising her voice in anger, in incredulity, in exasperation, and builds to an unstoppable crescendo. Even when she reaches for a glass of water, perched on the little nightstand to the side of her relatively unadorned stage, Reno continues ranting.

There is only one moment when Reno pauses, when she shows restraint. At one point in the show, after a scathing critique of cheap-and-easy displays of patriotism, she asks us to listen with her to Celine Dion's version of "God Bless America," a typically over-the-top rendition that reeks of overblown sentiment and hyperbolic patriotism. As the songs plays over the sound system, we see Reno's face twitch and turn, her eyes swell, her movements abrupt as she shifts her weight from side to side, listening intently and clearly holding back her response. The song follows a section in which Reno has interrogated what it means to be patriotic, one of the performance's key concerns. Reno is not "proud" to be an American, she explains. How can she be proud when she had nothing to do with it? She was merely born in the United States, and it took no effort on her part to become a citizen. She is, instead, "happy" to be an American, "ecstatic" to be an American, and for Reno these word choice makes all the difference. Nationalist pride, she makes clear, is the excuse people use to license racism, erode civil liberties, and stifle cultural dissent. But now, in this context, what will she say about the Celine Dion song? Will she rip it apart too?

When the song ends, Reno turns and faces her audience and asks: "Do you feel anything, does that song get to you?" She proceeds to tell us how she cannot help herself but be moved. Completely aware of its manipulative power, Reno nonetheless allows the song to take its effect, and in doing so enables us to observe and acknowledge the nuanced and often contradictory responses we share in the wake of September 11. There is so much to lose if we do not uphold the Constitution, if we scapegoat immigrants, if we allow the Bush administration to continue its policies without voicing our dissent, she quietly explains. In Reno's view, critique and dissent are the best forms of patriotism. She sees her work in this context too. "I believe in myself and in my reaction to things," she told the *New York Times*. "Since September 11, we can go in either direction, toward or away from our democratic convictions. This show is my lobbying effort to influence us in one of those directions, and laugh like hell as well."[51] Reno believes not only in herself but also in the work that performance can do to influence and shape her audiences. Aware that many will be upset by her critiques, she takes the risk of audience rejection, unwilling to compromise her integrity for our applause.

Granted, many in her audience share in her political viewpoints and are grateful for the public forum to have them voiced and heard, but Reno never settles for the easy identifications sometimes assumed within community-based productions. If there are affinities to be had, they, too, will be hard earned. Her work remains controversial and unsettling, and not everyone sits comfortably in her audience. But many surprisingly do. Among those who have found Reno's work important and a source of great comfort have been Marian Fontana, the widow of one of the firemen who perished at the World Trade Center who quickly surfaced as an advocate for the families of the victims, and the father of John Walker Lindh, the young Bay Area man whose life got entangled with the Taliban and who was captured in Afghanistan and held for treason. After seeing Reno perform in San Francisco, Lindh's father went backstage to thank her, amid his tears, for speaking out publicly about his son with empathy and concern.

Reno's show offers an ongoing engagement with the world as it unfolds; it is a performance without closure, a continuous rant with no end in sight. She adjusts her show depending on the day's news and her sense of the audience's needs. While the performance follows a familiar format, it is designed to accommodate last-minute changes, off-the-cuff improvisations, and unrestrained reflections. *Rebel without a Pause* is deeply entrenched in the topical, a characteristic that Reno will neither relinquish nor change. Hers is a performance so intensely engaged with current events that any question of posterity or universality entirely misses the point. Reno is an artist for now; her work is the best example of how contemporary artists have responded to the tragic events of September 11 and helped shape our responses to them.

A queer performance artist abandoned by her Latina birth mother and raised by an elderly white Episcopalian couple, Reno shows little interest in or patience for heteronormative models of kinship and time. Her sense of identity is understandably complicated. She did not learn she was Latina until fairly recently. In *Reno Finds Her Mom*, her 1998 HBO film, she searches out her cultural identity by looking for the woman who gave her up for adoption. Finding her birth mother did not end in reconciliation. Finding her audience, while no compensation, seems to have brought forth a different sense of belonging, one less clearly marked by set relations based on blood, law, or shared cultural lineage. She is driven to live in the now, and her contribution is directed to others living through these times too. "Look, I am a lesbian," she explained to the *New York Times*, "I'm not having any kids. I'm not close to my family, so for me there is no history, there's no posterity. This is my era. This is my time." As these comments reveal, Reno's queerness goes beyond identitarian claims of merely being a lesbian. Her queerness is found in the refusal to adhere to the reproductive regimes of heteronormativity that invest in history, posterity, and the future at the expense of the now. The show itself defies traditional theatre's habit of reproducing itself nightly. Instead, each show, so deeply entrenched in the immediate reality, differs. Reno's insistence that "this is my time" allows for a new model for the alliance of political commentary, artistic achievement, and communal possibility to surface. Discarding the solemnity surrounding September 11, Reno's performance loosens tragedy's hold on the contemporary. "What we learn in suffering is . . . revolution," Raymond Williams explained in *Modern Tragedy*. Reno's work stands as a testimony to the arts' ability to witness tragedy and name it. In that naming, we begin to rethink our relationship to the world.

PERFORMANCE IN AMERICA has set out to demonstrate all that is to be gained by thinking seriously about the role of the performing arts in contemporary U.S. culture. Throughout the book, I have chosen to address a historical archive that has been either summoned or embodied by contemporary performances. The relationship of contemporary culture to this historical archive has stood at the heart of the book's interest, as has performance's often urgent goal to reshape the current moment in which we live, a moment that we might call "the time of your life." This last chapter, on work produced in the immediate aftermath of September 11, focused on performances that were either already scheduled for production before September 11, designed as public benefits or memorials in response to the events of that day, or, as in the case of Reno's *Rebel without a Pause*, were improvised within weeks of the terrorist attacks. In each case, these performances enabled audiences to constitute themselves as a provisional public gathered in a particular space and time I call the contemporary in order to rethink their relationship to the official national performance of mourning and patriotism.

In the following afterword, I want to offer yet another model for how contemporary performance might intervene in the political sphere, one also drawn from work produced in response to September 11. But in this case, as we shall see, the creative team behind the production made deliberate choices about how their performance might function in a post–September 11 America. I consider the 2002 revival of William Saroyan's 1939 play *The Time of Your Life* by Chicago's Steppenwolf Theatre, a performance that then toured to Seattle and San Francisco in the spring of 2004. Early on, the creative team made a conscious decision to produce the play in direct response to September 11 and had specific intentions for how it might reshape the national sentiments evoked by the terrorist attacks and the subsequent wars it has engendered. Here the relationship between the current contemporary and Saroyan's contemporary is brought to the forefront. But we can also see how Reno's "this is my time" echoes Saroyan's earlier credo to "in the time of your life—live" as a politic determined to shape the contemporary. Like Reno who set out to challenge our responses to September 11, Saroyan set out to revise the national psyche during the troubled period of the late 1930s and early 1940s. Steppenwolf retrieves Saroyan from the obscured archives of American theatre in order to revive the politics of optimism and hope that his play promotes. His 1939 play, staunchly antiwar and antinationalist, recirculates for our contemporary a repertoire of sentiments that have been obscured by more dominant national impulses and agendas. In reviving Saroyan, Steppenwolf revives the debates his work engendered, including the question of the role of the arts in America.

The Time of Your Life

"There are those who believe art cannot do anything about history. I am not one of those. I believe art can do a good deal about history"— so wrote William Saroyan in 1940 to introduce the publication of his 1939 Pulitzer Prize–winning play *The Time of Your Life*.[1] Saroyan believed that art played an integral role in the public sphere and that its necessity was all the more pressing in times of national crisis. His conviction about art's centrality to the national culture fueled a career that lasted throughout most of the twentieth century until his death in 1981 at seventy-two, but it proved especially poignant in the late 1930s when the United States was coping with the terrible effects of the Great Depression and Europe found itself ravaged by war and the rise of fascism. "In a time of war if art abandons its labor, war wins its victory, and cheap history tells the fable of the world," Saroyan continued. "If it is impossible for art to reach the soldier who is on the verge of killing or being killed, it can get ready for the soldier's son. If art cannot improve the tone and meaning of the statesman's radio speech, it can anticipate his burial and be ready for his successor. If the world is amuck and there is no one for art to talk to, it can prepare itself for the next generation."[2] Sixty-some years later, if Saroyan is remembered at all, it is for the optimism of such commentary and the traumatic historical context within which it was produced.

Saroyan's philosophy of art and his insistence on art's generational legacy seem to counter my claims throughout this book that the contemporary performing arts need not rely on posterity for their value. However, I find Saroyan's comments on art and the contemporary as rich in complexity as conviction. In fact, the case of William Saroyan enables us to rethink the work of the contemporary precisely in light of this tension between the time of the now, that is, the time of your life, and that of "the next generation." Given this claim, I want to return to the time of Saroyan before addressing his possible relevance for us now. Saroyan's interest in what he names the next generation did not come at the expense of his own contemporary moment, a temporality that for him lay at the heart of political life. His invocation of generationality primarily meant to keep the possibility of art's provocation alive. Art, he believed, did not have merely one shot to make its cultural impact; its effect might prove stronger at a later moment in time. War, in other words, could not stifle art's power; art would agitate yet again. "War is tentative," he explained, but "art is not tentative."[3] This sense that art—either the work of a prior period or the future work of the next generation—would continue to challenge the logic and practice of war was less about locating art's universal greatness than about identifying its political and social role in history. Saroyan, known for his boldness, would in fact take out a full-page ad in *Variety* on August 6, 1941, selling the rights to the film version of *The Time of Your Life* to any studio that would match his offer to donate the profits to the war effort (figure 80). "Every penny of the proceeds shall go to National Defense," he challenged.[4] "I believe that art, in its way, is as great a weapon for the defense of right as a strong army and a strong navy," he continued. At the time he felt that he did not need the money, nor, he thought, did the studios.

Saroyan's belief in art's ongoing relevance and in its capacity for political agitation, along with his unwavering trust in human goodness, showcases the romantic sentiments that helped promote his success in the early years of his career and that led to his subsequent obscurity. His was a politics of optimism fueled less by naivety and blindness than by the sense that art and politics could make a difference in people's daily lives. For these reasons, I am interested in returning to Saroyan and his time to see how we might learn from his example and profit from his experience. I want to revisit his contemporary moment, especially that surrounding the 1939 premier of *The Time of Your Life* on Broadway, and the debates his play brought forth at the time, debates about

• *A Message from* WILLIAM SAROYAN *to the Moving Picture Manufacturers*

❦ ATTENTION! ❦

METRO-GOLDWYN-MAYER, RKO, PARAMOUNT, WARNER BROTHERS, TWENTIETH CENTURY-FOX, UNITED ARTISTS, and others

● Let's do some war-time business, as follows:

● Thanks to the American people and the American way of life you don't need money and I don't need money.

● *I hereby offer any of you absolutely free of charge all motion picture rights to my play "The Time of Your Life."*

● My terms are the simplest and most equitable:

● Everybody connected with the making of the picture, including the studio — its equipment and executives—shall donate free of charge his time, talent, or technical services.

● Every penny of the proceeds shall go to National Defense.

● I believe in this emergency, and I believe you believe in it.

● You and I both need the American way of life even more than the millions of men in the military and naval services.

● We owe these men, their families, and our government something more than mere dislike of the enemy, and we have no right to be any less personally involved in the present emergency than they.

● I believe that art, in its way, is as great a weapon for the defense of right as a strong army and a strong navy.

● Let's not get richer in material things until the day after tomorrow, and let's not be poverty-stricken in spirit at a time which so graciously invites generosity.

● You can reach me at 1821 15th Avenue, San Francisco.

Yours truly:

William Saroyan

80. "A Message from William Saroyan to the Moving Picture Manufacturers," *Variety*, August 6, 1941. Courtesy of the Academy of Motion Picture Arts and Sciences, Los Angeles

the theatre and the national culture. I am interested in how Saroyan, so easily dismissed by many of his contemporary critics as sentimental and naive, imagined political intervention through the arts, and how this manifested in his signature piece, *The Time of Your Life*. My interest in Saroyan does not understand itself as a recovery project, but is based instead on a sense that his work provides us an opportunity to think through the main themes of the book, mainly the relationship of the performing arts to the national culture, and that of the contemporary to the historical past. Saroyan also enacts one of the more productive and impassioned defenses of the efficacy of optimism in the twentieth century.

Optimism, a sentiment mystified as a fundamental characteristic of the American experience, finds in Saroyan a more nuanced presentation, one that goes against the grain of American individualism and exceptionalism. His brand of optimism, one can in fact argue, surfaced in spite of these national myths, not because of them. *The Time of Your Life* brought forward a new, although fleeting, sense of possibility when it premiered in the late 1930s. And yet Saroyan's success and popularity did not carry over in time. In fact, his own historical peers even questioned it. Already by 1940, during the height of Saroyan's success with *The Time of Your Life*, Larry Hart would pen the line "Will Saroyan ever write a great play?" in the song "Zip" from *Pal Joey*, and his contemporary Clifford Odets would write in his 1940 journals with a certain satisfaction how "Saroyan was referred to the other day by some Hollywood wit as 'the only permanent flash in the pan I ever met.'"[5] The unnamed Hollywood wit's assessment of Saroyan that Odets finds so amusing paradoxically captures a certain truth about Saroyan's place in American cultural history. "Today he is out of fashion," his biographer John Leggett wrote in 2002, "young people never heard of him. 'Styron?' they ask, or 'Steinbeck, you mean?' He used to be taught in the schools, read on the beach, talked of earnestly among aspiring writers."[6] Saroyan's current critical obscurity may now even play to our advantage; unburdened by fixed critical and political meanings, Saroyan's nearly blank slate enables fresh and unencumbered engagements.

Saroyan was born in 1908, the son of poor Armenian immigrants who had ranged among the thousands to seek exile in the United States in the early 1900s to avoid their mass genocide by the Ottoman Turks. Although the family originally migrated to Jersey City, where the American Presbyterian Church sponsored them, they soon went west to Fresno, California. Fresno became a refuge for many Armenians who found affinities between the San Joaquin Valley and their homeland and where the promise of work was real. Many of Saroyan's earliest writings are set here and chronicle the Armenian experience of the time. Intensely prolific, he made his reputation as a fiction writer before turning to theatre in the 1930s. By the time of *The Time of Your Life*, Saroyan had already established a name for himself with the success of his short story collection *The Daring Young Man on the Flying Trapeze*, published in 1934.

His first play, *My Heart's in the Highlands*, was produced on Broadway in 1939 by the Group Theatre, an organization founded in early 1931 by Harold Clurman, Cheryl Crawford, and Lee Strasberg in order to present serious plays by writers engaged with contemporary concerns, and most famously associated with the work of Clifford Odets. Based on one of Saroyan's short stories, *My Heart's in the Highlands* is a pastoral exploration of a family of poor Armenians in Fresno in 1914 and the role of poetry, performance, and music in their lives. The play's simple premise is that the creative arts constitute crucial expressions of the human spirit that deserve to be cultivated and preserved. Saroyan felt that his play was the first play ever to convey what was real about America. "To say that there is no American theatre at all is false, and to some degree silly. To say that there is not yet an American theatre equal to the dramatic materials provided by the American environment and people, however, is very true, and to a small degree, profound," he explained.[7] Such an Emersonian view led Saroyan to see his first work for the stage as already a classic play that was inaugurating a new and vital American theatre. Known for his confidence and self-aggrandizing, Saroyan was often baffled when others did not recognize the achievement of his work. The majority of the critics, however, did not share his view that *My Heart's in the Highlands* constituted a milestone in American theatre. In fact, some critics found the play tedious; "The collusion between the most completely undisciplined talent in

American letters and the actors of the Group Theatre bored me nearly to distraction and I would advise you to stay away from it," wrote Wolcott Gibbs in the pages of the *New Yorker*.[8]

While many critics shared this perspective on the play's shortcomings, Saroyan found two important advocates: Brooks Atkinson, the theatre critic for the *New York Times*, who recommended the play, and George Jean Nathan, who championed the play in *Newsweek*. Nathan and the critic John Mason Brown, in fact, voted for it as the best American play of the season at the annual New York Drama Critics' Circle meeting. Nathan, who served as president of the influential critics' circle, encouraged Saroyan to continue writing for the theatre. He lobbied the group to present Saroyan a citation as the most promising young playwright of the season, which it did. At the award ceremony held at the Algonquin Hotel, Nathan sat Saroyan near Eddie Dowling, an important producer, who immediately promised to buy the rights to Saroyan's next play. Inspired but also broke and in need of fast money, Saroyan wrote the entirety of *The Time of Your Life* within a week of their meeting. ("I didn't begin to write the play the next morning because at the time I was living a social life," Saroyan explained. "I began not living a social life the next day, and by Monday, May 8th, I was ready to be a writer again.")[9]

The Time of Your Life is set on a single afternoon and evening in October 1939. It takes place in San Francisco at Nick's Pacific Street Saloon, Restaurant, and Entertainment Palace at the foot of the Embarcadero. It covers a day in the life of a wide range of characters who assemble at the bar. Some of these characters are regulars who find a sense of community at Nick's, but the saloon welcomes anyone who needs respite from the day-to-day grind of urban life. Nick's is a safe haven for the unemployed, the down-and-out, and those who work the streets of the neighborhood. "Out of a warm heart and a lively fancy Saroyan has written a paean to the essential goodness in life and people, a chant of love for the scorned and rejected," wrote Louis Kronenberger in *Time*.[10] "He has filled a San Francisco waterfront dive with prostitutes, sailors, cops, bums, drunks, slot-machine addicts, hoofers, young men in love, old men in rags," Kronenberger continued in his review, offering a catalogue of types that begins to suggest the world of the play and its emotional register. These characters come in and out of Nick's to drink, dance, find work, seek companionship, or just simply hang out, suggesting how open public gathering places such as saloons functioned to provide solace and a sense of belonging in the Depression-era years. The bar's utopian communal ideal, as a place where anyone can stop and join in the scene, stands in direct contrast to its immediate exterior, where striking longshoremen have gathered. Their looming presence is palpable throughout the play and is deliberately evoked by Saroyan to capture the historical context and nuance the play's reception.

Saroyan's invocation of the strikers would instantly conjure for his 1939 audiences memories of San Francisco's labor tensions and the casualties of what is referred to as the city's Bloody Thursday. On May 9, 1934, the International Labor Association (ILA) called a strike of all West Coast dock men from Seattle to San Diego until their union was acknowledged. As the art historian Anthony Lee writes, "The 1934 Big Strike is one of the key moments in the labor history of depression-era San Francisco, perhaps of the entire country."[11] Workers stopped unloading cargo and the labor dispute continued until the strike erupted in terrible violence on Thursday, July 5. On this day, Bloody Thursday, two San Francisco strikers met death when police opened fire on the striking workers in a violent encounter that left many on both sides injured. As a result, the city shut down for three days in a general strike finally called off by labor organizers concerned about the welfare of the city. Saroyan's play is set in the historical context of labor unrest, police violence, and mounting social tension. The play valorizes the affiliations workers made in an effort to improve their lives, suggesting this model of forged alliances might benefit those inside Nick's bar as well. Nick underlines this historical backdrop early on in the play when he stresses the importance of joining the union. When Wesley, a young black man, walks into the saloon and first asks him for a job, Nick's instant response is, "Do you belong to the union?" Their exchange is telling of both the labor politics of the period and the sentiments surrounding them:

NICK (to WESLEY): DO you belong to the union?

WESLEY: What union?

NICK: For the love of Mike, where've you been? Don't you know you can't come into a place and ask for a job and get one and go to work, just like that? You've got to belong to one of the unions.

WESLEY: I didn't know. I got to have a job. Real soon.

NICK: Well you've got to belong to a union.

WESLEY: I don't want any favors. All I want is a chance to earn a living.

NICK: Go to the kitchen and tell Sam to give you some lunch.[12]

Rather than sending Wesley back into the streets, Nick offers him a meal. Soon, Wesley and Harry, a white vaudevillian hoofer also eager to earn a living and who had moments earlier offered to perform free for Nick's clientele, are improvising a song and dance routine, filling the bar with music and performance (figure 81). Nick, the bar's proprietor, himself remains uncertain why his place is so popular. Early in the play and shortly after some of the key characters are introduced, Nick comments on the bar's surprising appeal. Wesley's and Harry's performances set the tone and backdrop for the scene. Saroyan writes:

> By now Wesley is playing something of his own which is very good and out of this world. He plays about half a minute, after which Harry begins to dance.
>
> NICK (Watching): I run the lousiest dive in Frisco, and a guy arrives and makes me stock up with champagne. The whores come in and holler at me that they're ladies. Talent comes and begs me for a chance to show itself. Even society people come here once in a while. I don't know what for. Maybe it's liquor. Maybe it's the location. Maybe it's my personality. Maybe it's the crazy personality of the joint. The old honky tonk. (Pause) Maybe they can't feel at home anywhere else.
>
> By now Wesley is really playing, and Harry is going through a new routine.[13]

Nick watches these artistic improvisations, whose origins are found in the vaudeville entertainments of the past, and he observes the community formation they foster with a sense of wonder and astonishment. He is a surrogate for the spectator who also witnesses the actions of

81. Gene Kelly, center, as Harry the Hoofer, with Reginald Beane, Henry Jones, and Julie Haydon in the original Broadway cast of William Saroyan's *The Time of Your Life*, Booth Theatre, New York City, 1939. Billy Rose Theatre Collection, New York Public Library for the Performing Arts, Lenox and Tilden Foundations

these characters at the bar and must contemplate their presence on the stage. The play thus models community formation through the efforts of the characters, as well as through the labor of the actors who together enact these scenes.

The play is neither realistic nor plot-driven, which concerned many reviewers, but stands as a collage of character studies. In Saroyan's worldview, people are essentially good and will act honorably, even, and perhaps especially, in times of crisis and confusion. Institutions and authority figures function as the corrupting forces that need to be kept in check. Saroyan believed that the disenfranchised, the very people who would seem to have little reason for joy, will in particular rise to the occasion, and not merely because they have been drinking. Saroyan endowed these characters with kindness and dignity; the play shows them building bonds of trust and affection despite the world's efforts to set them apart in isolation. In a wire that he sent out early in the play's development to Eddie Dowling, who not only produced the play but performed the role of Joe, the play's central protagonist, Saroyan explained: "There's simplicity, innocence, goodness, and potential greatness in the American people, particularly the lowest of them. Their worst trouble is defense against the world. If they are left alone and have a chance, they're good people. There's good in all people."[14]

While Saroyan's writing—in his plays as well as his fiction—risks representing the poor in overly romantic ways, a charge that many of his critics made in his day, these representations might be better understood within the context of Michael Denning's discussion of ghetto pastorals, a form of proletarian writing of the period that proved enormously influential in shaping twentieth-century American literature. Denning's concern is primarily directed to the ghetto pastoral's relation to the novel. He writes: "The ghetto pastoral was, then, a curious hybrid: it combined the dream of a new proletarian literature nurtured by the cultural politics of the left, the ethnic and racial modalities through which the relations of class were lived, the recurring obsession with working-class childhood, and the struggle with the most prestigious and lucrative literary form, the novel."[15] But as Denning himself points out, many writers remained ambivalent about the novel, and, as in the case of Saroyan, explored other literary genres as well. Saroyan, given his near over-the-top sentimental representations of the poor and his insistence of their goodness, is, as Denning claims, more pastoral than not. "One could indeed," Denning writes, "arrange the ghetto pastorals along a spectrum from pastoral to naturalism, from the sentimental human comedy of William Saroyan to the visions of hell of Nelson Algren."[16] This framework offers an entry point into thinking of Saroyan's work in the historical context of the literature and politics in the 1930s and of the role that theatre played during the period.

In *The Time of Your Life*, Saroyan argues against nihilism and defeat, promoting instead a vision of hope and possibility that forms the core of the play's message. "In the time of your life, live—so that in that good time there shall be no ugliness or death for yourself or for any life your life touches," Saroyan proclaims in the play's credo.[17] *The Time of Your Life* embodies this sentiment, developed in the full text of the credo:

> In the time of your life, live—so that in that good time there shall be no ugliness or death for yourself or for any life your life touches. Seek goodness everywhere, and when it is found, bring it out of its hiding-place and let it be free and unashamed. Place in matter and in flesh the least of the values, for these are the things that hold death and must pass away. Discover in all things that which shines and is beyond corruption. Encourage virtue in whatever heart it may have been driven into secrecy and sorrow by the shame and terror of the world. Ignore the obvious, for it is unworthy of the clear eye and the kindly heart. Be the inferior of no man, nor of any man be the superior. Remember that every man is a variation of yourself. No man's guilt is not yours, nor is any man's innocence a thing apart. Despise evil and ungodliness, but not men of ungodliness or evil. These, understand. Have no shame in being kindly and gentle, but if the time comes in the time of your life to kill, kill and have no regret. In the time of your life, live—so that in that wondrous time you shall not add to the misery and sorrow of the world, but shall smile to the infinite delight and mystery of it.

These words were initially intended to be delivered over a loudspeaker to the audience at the beginning of the performance, but as the *New York Times* reported when it published the credo in its entirety on October 28, 1939, the idea was dropped before the play's tryout in Boston.[18]

The credo to *The Time of Your Life* constitutes as much a time piece as the play itself, and while it provides the foundation for Saroyan's belief system, it also conveys sentiments that he would later reject. He regretted the line about killing—"if the time comes in the time of your life to kill, kill and have no regret"—and he would later make great efforts to comment on his rejection of that statement, written on the eve of American involvement in World War II. The context for the line had everything to do with standing up to tyranny and fighting against oppression, something that as an Armenian whose family survived a mass genocide he felt compelled to address.

While he regretted the line about killing, he had no interest in revising some of the more sentimental commentary found in the credo. Saroyan was convinced that feelings such as hope and optimism needed to appear in representation and that these representations would engender social change. Perhaps no one more than Harry the Hoofer, the young energetic dancer and comedian, embodies this belief. The role was performed by a young Gene Kelly, whose talent and charisma were perfectly suited for the part. In fact, it was Saroyan who cast Kelly for the New York run, replacing an earlier actor who had performed the role in the out-of-town tryouts. Saroyan was so impressed with Kelly that he agreed to have him choreograph his own dances throughout the production. The performance helped launch Kelly's long and influential career in theatre, dance, and film.

Harry summons the passing world of vaudeville, which he hopes to revive once more for his contemporaries, a point he stresses when he pitches his talent to Nick early in the play:

> HARRY: Nick, you've got to see my act. It's the greatest thing of its kind in America. All I want is a chance. No salary to begin. Let me try tonight. If I don't wow 'em, O.K., I'll go home. If vaudeville wasn't dead, a guy like me would have a chance.

> NICK: You're not funny. You're a sad young punk. What the hell do you want to try to be funny for? You'll break everybody's heart. What's there for you to be funny about? You've been poor all your life, haven't you?

> HARRY: I've been poor all right, but don't forget that some things count more than some other things.

NICK: What counts more, for instance, than what else, for instance?

HARRY: Talent, for instance, counts more than money, for instance, that's what, and I've got talent. I get new ideas night and day. Everything comes natural to me. I've got style, but it'll take me a little time to round it out. That's all.[19]

Throughout the play, Harry will break into impromptu dances, monologues, and set pieces that he tries out on Nick's patrons. He uses Nick's saloon as a rehearsal space for his new routines. On his arrival, Harry's performances and his optimism in general begin to challenge the sense of tragedy that shadows the world of the play. As a result, Harry begins to circulate a new structure of feelings for those in the bar and, by extension, for Saroyan's contemporary audience.

In one scene, he tries out a new monologue for Krupp and McCarthy, two lifelong friends who are regulars at Nick's. Krupp is a policeman whose beat is the waterfront and whose ambivalence about his job leaves him questioning himself throughout the play. McCarthy is a longshoreman who Saroyan describes as "intelligent and well-read." They are introduced in the play in the beginning of act 2, and after their lengthy philosophical exchange on politics, writing, and even love, Harry begins his routine and arouses Krupp's suspicions:

HARRY *gets up from his table suddenly and begins a new dance.*

KRUPP (*Noticing him, with great authority*): Here. Here. What do you think you are doing?

HARRY (*Stopping*): I just got an idea for a new dance. I'm trying it out. . .

KRUPP (*To MCCARTHY*): Has he got a right to do that?

MCCARTHY: The living have danced from the beginning of time. I might even say, the dance and the life have moved along together, until now we have——(*To HARRY*) Go into your dance, son, and show us what we have.

HARRY: I haven't got it worked out completely yet, but it starts out like this.

He dances. . . .

MCCARTHY *(To HARRY)*: Splendid. Splendid.

HARRY: Then I go into this little routine. (*He demonstrates.*)

KRUPP: Is that good, Mac?

MCCARTHY: It's awful, but it's honest and ambitious, like everything else in this great country.

HARRY: Then I work along into this. (*He demonstrates.*) And this is where I really get going. (*He finishes the dance.*)

MCCARTHY: Excellent. A most satisfying demonstration of the present state of the American body and soul. Son, you're a genius.

HARRY (*Delighted*): I go on in front of an audience for the first time in my life tonight.

MCCARTHY: They'll be delighted. Where did you learn to dance?[20]

This snapshot of Harry's performance and McCarthy's response offers an insight in how to understand Saroyan's firm belief in the arts. The performing arts, as McCarthy explains, showcase "the present state of the American body and soul," even if the work itself fails traditional aesthetic criteria. For this reason alone, the performing arts must be encouraged. McCarthy's response, moreover, is not simply directed at the artist but at the figure of authority who has the means to censure the work. McCarthy's exchange with Krupp enables Harry to keep dancing without police interference. Harry is encouraged by McCarthy's interest, which leads him to try out more controversial material. The scene continues:

HARRY: Never took a lesson in life. I'm a natural-born dancer. And comedian, too.

MCCARTHY (*Astounded*): You can make people laugh?

HARRY (*Dumbly*): I can be funny, but they won't laugh.

MCCARTHY: That's odd. Why not?

HARRY: I don't know. They just won't laugh.

McCarthy requests that Harry try out his comedic routine, and Harry is happy to oblige. Harry's monologue, a seemingly nonsensical riff on life's absurdity, turns out to be a rant against fascism, what McCarthy will call "a new kind of comedy." The piece comments on American isolationism in the face of mounting global pressures, but places this isolationism in the context of the economic hardships challenging Americans on the domestic home front. Saroyan was suspicious of nationalist discourse, which he found stifling and coercive, and was drawn instead to expressions of the self that were anarchistic, creative, and deeply felt.

> HARRY: This is it. (*Goes into the act, with much energy.*) I'm up at Sharkey's on Turk Street. It's a quarter to nine, daylight saving. Wednesday, the eleventh. What I've got is a headache and a 1918 nickel. What I *want* is a cup of coffee. If I buy a cup of coffee with the nickel, I've got to walk home. I've got an eight-ball problem. George the Greek is shooting a game of snooker with Pedro the Filipino. *I'm in rags.* They're wearing thirty-five dollar suits, made to order. I haven't got a cigarette. They're smoking Bobby Burns panatelas. I'm thinking it over, like I always do. George the Greek is in a tough spot. If I buy a cup of coffee, I'll want another cup. What happens? My *ear* aches! My ear. George the Greek takes the cue. Chalks it. Studies the table. Touches the cue-ball delicately. Tick. What happens? He makes the three-ball! What do I do? I get confused. *I go out and buy a morning paper.* What the hell do I want with a morning paper? What I *want* is a cup of coffee and a good used car. I go out and buy a morning paper. Thursday, the twelfth. Maybe the headline's about *me.* I take a quick look. *No. The headline is not about me.* It's about Hitler. Seven thousand miles away. I'm here. Who the hell is Hitler? Who's behind the eight-ball? I turn around. *Everybody's behind the eight-ball!*

> (*Pause.* KRUPP moves toward HARRY as if to make an important arrest. HARRY moves to the swinging doors. MCCARTHY STOPS KRUPP.)

> MCCARTHY (*To HARRY*): It's the funniest thing I've ever heard. Or *seen,* for that matter.

> HARRY (*Coming back to MCCARTHY*): Then, why don't you laugh?

> MCCARTHY: I don't know, *yet.*

HARRY: I'm always getting funny ideas that nobody will laugh at.

MCCARTHY (*Thoughtfully*): It may be that you've stumbled headlong into a new kind of comedy.

HARRY: Well, what good is it if it doesn't make anybody laugh?

MCCARTHY: There are *kinds* of laughter, son. I must say, in all truth, that I *am* laughing, although not *out loud*.

HARRY: I want to *hear* people laugh. *Out loud*. That's why I keep thinking of funny things to say.

MCCARTHY: Well. They may catch on in time. Let's go, Krupp. So long, Joe.

MCCARTHY AND KRUPP go.[21]

Not surprisingly, the play proved enormously controversial on both the artistic and the political front. Brooks Atkinson, in one of the several pieces he wrote on the play in the *New York Times*, calls attention to these debates and defends *The Time of Your Life* as a play that breaks out of the constraints of the well-worn realist drama and invigorates familiar theatre tropes. "Although the delight that theatregoers are taking in Saroyan's *The Time of Your Life* testifies to the sanity and flexibility of public taste, some of the grammarians are less convinced," he writes. "They complain, on the one hand, that it is not a play because it does not have a plot; and, on the other hand, that it is old hat because the characters are familiar in the theatre."[22] Atkinson goes on to argue for Saroyan's dramaturgical innovations, which he finds poetic—even while promoting contemporary traditional well-made plays of the same season such as Lillian Hellman's *The Little Foxes*, which he writes, "can provide superlative excitement in the theatre by proposing a theme, working it out in terms of characters and events and arriving at a concrete conclusion." Atkinson's piece appeared a month after his rave review of the play in which he wrote that Saroyan had written "a dance in praise of life."[23] A week after his initial review, Atkinson would write in a lengthy special feature appearing on the front page to the Sunday edition arts section that *The Time of Your Life* is "an original, breezy, and deeply felt play . . . it is the freshest thing in the theatre just now."[24]

Atkinson's multiple affirmations of the play begin to display the rise of American theatre criticism and the role that it played in the popular press. Beginning in the mid-1920s, a new brand of critics who professed some knowledge of theatre and drama had begun to write for daily and weekly print media. Critics such as Atkinson, who began writing for the *New York Times* in 1925, George Jean Nathan, and John Mason Brown ranked among the most prominent of theatre critics whose reviews and profiles were readily found in newspapers and magazines. They helped educate an audience of readers on the merits of theatre. By the time Saroyan began his career as a playwright, these critics had already established their reputations and their influence, and Saroyan was one of the earliest beneficiaries of their critical engagement and support. Atkinson, Nathan, and Brown wrote extensively in defense of the play's artistic and cultural merits, overriding many of the critics and spectators who did not appreciate either Saroyan's style or his politics.

While these critics championed Saroyan as a new American playwright of enormous potential, other reviewers, including the writer Mary McCarthy writing in the *Partisan Review*, questioned the play's political agenda, especially its representation of America. Writing on both *My Heart's in the Highlands* and *The Time of Your Life*, McCarthy begins by comparing Saroyan with two other prominent figures of the period—Clifford Odets and John Steinbeck—known for their political works. "If you compare him with his contemporaries, Odets and Steinbeck, the purity of his work is blinding. Puerile and arrogant and sentimental as he may be, he is never cheap," she writes.[25] Nonetheless, she worries that Saroyan's love for America is problematic in that it promotes a sense of the nation that is "innocent" and out of touch with contemporary concerns. "This excessive, rather bumptious patriotism has created a certain amount of alarm," she explains; "it has been suspected that Saroyan has joined the propagandists of the second crusade for democracy."[26] She ends her commentary with the claim that Saroyan, rather than being timely, is instead nostalgic: "The America Saroyan loves is America-Was-Promises, and the plays he weaves around it are not so much daring innovations as legends."[27] McCarthy's reservations about Saroyan's work speak to the complexity of the period's response to the changing national landscape, the growing concerns about the war in Europe, and the role that literature might play in such times. *The Time of Your Life*, as we have seen, generated enormous press that addressed key concerns of the period. Saroyan, too, had his own firm opinions about art, America, and war, and about how these connected in the late 1930s. While he aspired to lasting significance, he very much remained grounded in his period. "My work has always been the product of my time," he explained in the introduction to the play.[28] What this meant, in part, was that Saroyan believed that writers needed to engage and fully immerse themselves in the world around them. In fact, he concludes his introduction to *The Time of Your Life* with a challenge to other writers to rise to the occasion and do their part to challenge the war. "The world now provides art new and more difficult material," he writes; "art has no alternative but to accept this material and to remove it from all foolishness, all feebleness, and all foolish and feeble fantasy."[29] It was a credit to Saroyan's artistic vision that his contemporaries engaged him and his work so seriously, revealing their own passions about the immediate issues of their day. Saroyan was—if nothing else—a truly contemporary writer conveying much about the cultural and national politics of his time.

At first glance it might seem that to revisit Saroyan and the late 1930s at the end of a book about contemporary performance makes for an eccentric choice. But the case of Saroyan allows us to think through the relationship between topicality and posterity, between then and now. It lets us consider how artists and critics addressed these concerns in a particular and distant moment in American cultural history. "Whether or not these [*My Heart's in the Highlands* and *The Time of Your Life*] are immortal plays is something that need not worry us at the present moment," Brooks Atkinson wisely wrote in 1939.[30] But now, over sixty years later, and given that Saroyan's "present moment" has passed, what are we to gain when we revisit this material other than the knowledge that it once constituted an important cultural text?

This question emerged for me when I saw the Steppenwolf Theatre Company's stunning revival of *The Time of Your Life* in 2004 (figure 82). I had never seen a production of this play, which is rarely revived, so I was curious to see what Steppenwolf, perhaps the country's premiere

82. Promotional flyer for the Steppenwolf Theatre's production of William Saroyan's *The Time of Your Life*, Chicago, 2002. Collection of the author

theatre company, would do with it. I was not thinking about Saroyan beforehand, and in fact was in the process of revising the final draft of this book before sending it off to the press when I went to see the Steppenwolf production, running at the Seattle Repertory Theatre while I happened to be visiting the city. Seattle Rep and San Francisco's American Conservatory Theater (ACT) coproduced the play and mounted the Steppenwolf production in their respective theatres during the spring of 2004 (figures 83 and 84). I had been aware of the great reviews of the original Chicago production when it opened there in 2002, but it did not occur to me to fly to Chicago to see it at the time. But in checking out the performance events running in Seattle, I noticed that Seattle Rep would be hosting the Steppenwolf production during my visit. The combination of Steppenwolf and Seattle Rep guaranteed high production values and worthwhile performances, even if the play itself, as I had remembered from reading it years ago in college, did not prove especially meaningful or memorable to me. While I appreciated Saroyan's aims on an academic level, I was not emotionally drawn into the world he had created in the play. It seemed so much about the time of his life that it appeared irrelevant to mine. But that was nearly twenty years

83. Promotional flyer for the Seattle Repertory Theatre's production of Steppenwolf's *The Time of Your Life* by William Saroyan, Seattle, 2004. Collection of the author

84. Promotional flyer for the American Conservatory Theater's production of Steppenwolf's *The Time of Your Life* by William Saroyan, San Francisco, 2004. Collection of the author

ago, and in 2004, I could not even recall what the play was about anymore. I, too, had obscured Saroyan and failed to remember much about him other than the fact that he was the playwright who wrote a play called *The Time of Your Life*.

Seattle, like Chicago, is a great theatre town. I was eager to view the Seattle Rep's collaboration with Steppenwolf, two theatres I had long respected. I was not actually craving to see a production of *The Time of Your Life*; I went to the performance because of the theatre companies involved and the stellar reviews it had received. So I was shocked when I learned that Saroyan's thesis for the role of the arts in the national culture mirrored my own. The production—beautifully directed by Tina Landau, a first-rate director and artist whose previous work I much admired, and featuring members of the Steppenwolf ensemble alongside local Seattle actors—proved extraordinary. Landau's production spoke to me in ways that confirmed many of the themes of this book—that the arts matter, that communal energies make a difference in the world, that hope makes for more than a naive sentiment, that the present deserves immediate address—while provoking me to expand my thinking about the book's aims. Seeing the play at the end of my writing challenged me to consider the work that revivals do in the contemporary period, which is to say, in a time that is not their own, and forced me to open this book to an archive I had initially assumed irrelevant to the book's mission, if not to my own worldview. How, then, did the play resurface and what were the historical and material conditions that enabled its revival?

Steppenwolf's artistic director, Martha Lavey, had been thinking of mounting a revival of Saroyan's play for many years. A high school drama teacher had presented to her a framed copy of Saroyan's credo as a gift. For over twenty years, Lavey lived with this epigraph on her walls. In the program to the Steppenwolf production she writes:

> Funnily enough, I'm not certain I actually read the play until years after reading the epigraph. When I did, finally, I regarded it as a valuable but difficult proposition. I understood something about its dramatic and theatrical challenge and recognized that for the play to convey the vital and immediate urgency of its epigraph, it required a director who felt the play's timeless heart, but respected the play's

specific historical moment and place. I knew I really wanted to see a production of the play—and I knew I really didn't want to see a quaint production of the play.[31]

Lavey's concerns about not wanting "to see a quaint production" signal the play's vulnerabilities and the potential problems presented in the staging of revivals. Saroyan's plays, as Mary McCarthy had speculated decades earlier, promote a sentimental view of America that seems excessively patriotic, even if Saroyan himself felt otherwise. While Saroyan himself deeply opposed nationalist discourse and overt patriotism, McCarthy's concerns are valid. The play could easily be misinterpreted to stand in for exactly what Saroyan was out to critique. Too often revivals of American classics are in fact "quaint" and old-fashioned, stripping away the political intervention the plays might have achieved in their time. Instead, audiences are offered nostalgic slices of cheap Americana that promote conservative ideological feelings in a time when the nation would benefit most from the presentation of an alternative archive of sentiments. Saroyan's political optimism and his draw to communal affiliation, both presented throughout *The Time of Your Life*, could clearly be abused to serve the interest of a growing neonationalist ideology in a post–9/11 world. While this holds true of cultural productions in general, Saroyan's work, as Lavey worries, appears especially vulnerable to such expropriation.

Despite these reservations, Steppenwolf decided to stage the play as the inaugural production of its 2002–3 season. Lavey felt that the play might have something to offer audiences in the wake of September 11. She asked Tina Landau to direct it. As Lavey describes their decision to do the play, the relationship between their production and the contemporary moment becomes clear. "I guess it was at that cultural moment that neither of us any longer felt shy about supporting a play that declared, so baldly, 'Seek goodness everywhere, and when it is found, bring it out of its hiding place and let it be free and unashamed.'"[32] Landau, too, echoes this revelation when she writes in the notes to the Seattle Rep production that Saroyan has helped her "reaffirm my belief in the potential of groups—collectives, communities, ensembles," and has encouraged her "to stand unashamed of optimism."[33] I find these comments telling in that they admit to the reservations many of us have around publicly acknowledging certain feelings that might be dismissed as sentimental or naive. Both Lavey and Landau respond on the level of affect; their imperative for the play is based on their belief in the feelings that the play promotes and evokes. What I appreciated most about this production—beyond the exquisite production values, impeccable acting ensemble, and daring intelligence—was that Lavey and Landau put back into circulation the sentiments of *The Time of Your Life* that had been so widely debated in the late 1930s in order to see how they might inform contemporary concerns. Saroyan's insistence, for example, that we "encourage virtue in whatever heart it may have been driven into secrecy and sorrow by the shame and terror of the world," could easily lend itself to neonationalist sentiments, religious fundamentalism, and liberal pluralism, if not quaintness.[34] How, then, to allow Saroyan's conviction in the goodness of people to stand side by side with his equally intense drive for an anarchic individualism? Saroyan's work, which also praises the collective efforts of individuals, could easily be called into the service of an unquestioned patriotism, a form of Americana valorized as normative citizenship. Steppenwolf was faced with the challenge, as Lavey recognizes, to honor the historical specificity of the play, as well as the play's big heart.

In part, the reason that the production managed to succeed had to do with the historical contextualization of the play itself. The Steppenwolf production of Saroyan's *The Time of Your Life* showcases three historical art forms associated with the 1920s and 1930s: jazz, murals, and vaudeville. These movements not only inspired Saroyan but also provide the interpretive frame that Landau as the director brought to the production. As she explains:

> The play is a vaudeville, a mural, and a piece of jazz that our ensemble plays every night. I've asked them to jam, to riff, to be in the moment. Because what I am learning most from Saroyan is not about form (although his experimentation is certainly inspiring and ahead of his time); it is also the values that are implied by the form. What is valued above all is inclusion, the embracing of all people and styles in a non-hierarchical vision.[35]

This jazz component allows the actors to be spontaneous, and it invites them to play off of each other's performances. Saroyan, who codirected the 1939 production, encouraged his actors to do something similar. Gene Kelly was asked to choreograph the movement and improvise his own dances as Harry the Hoofer, and Reginald Beane, the musical accompanist to Ethel Waters at the time and who performed the role of Wesley, was asked to compose his own music.

The design of the Steppenwolf production includes an actual muralist painting of the back wall of the stage throughout the production, a tribute to the many Works Progress Administration (WPA) murals commissioned during the New Deal, especially the urban landscapes of Thomas Hart Benton. Landau and her design team, however, also took to heart the politics of the murals in shaping the production. "We attempted to try to create the experience of the panorama and the murals of the period, and when we started working on the design, we approached it literally as a mural," she explains; "the notion that the meaning of the play comes not from following one person going through a series of whys and actions. The meaning comes from the juxtaposition of characters as a conglomerate of things American."[36] The mural-

85. A scene from the Seattle Repertory's production of William Saroyan's *The Time of Your Life*, 2004. Photo by Chris Bennion

86. Guy Adkins as Harry the Hoofer in the Seattle Repertory's production of William Saroyan's *The Time of Your Life*, Seattle, 2004. Photo by Chris Bennion

inspired design provides the environment that allows for the third component, vaudeville, to emerge as the highlight of the production. If jazz and murals combine to create an atmosphere of spontaneity and diversity, vaudeville provides the production's structure. The play is composed of a series of set pieces expressed through music, dance, and spoken word. Sometimes these are solo pieces for Saroyan's characters, maximized to great effect by the acting ensemble, at other times these set pieces involve a cluster of performers who together make the scene. There are moments as well when the entire twenty-four–actor ensemble fills the stage.

The idea that the play could be staged as a form of variety theatre, where different performance modes are included, is implicit in Saroyan's text but made explicit through Landau's direction. Landau especially foregrounds the musical elements of the play mentioned in Saroyan's stage directions (figures 85 and 86). In Landau's production, not only does Wesley play the piano onstage with Harry the Hoofer dancing along to the music and occasionally breaking out into song, as Saroyan notes, but at key moments, the entire ensemble will perform standards from the American musical songbook of the Depression. Songs such as "We're in the Money," performed with vigor and enthusiasm, underline with striking irony the economic hardships of the characters. Other songs such as "I Won't Dance," and "It's Only a Paper Moon," also drawn from Hollywood musicals, convey the romantic longings of the characters and, of course, of the times. Landau's use of period music highlights the sentiments of the play, provides a commentary on what is happening inside Nick's saloon and outside of it, and, more tellingly, accentuates what is happening onstage and off for contemporary audiences. The production ends with a haunting rendition of the Irving Berlin ballad "Let's Face the Music and Dance" from *Follow the Fleet* (1935), the film musical starring Fred Astaire and Ginger Rogers. The song, which begins with the words "there might be trouble ahead, but while there's moonlight and music and love and romance, let's face the music and dance," is introduced by Harry, played perfectly throughout the production by Guy Adkins, who is then joined by the other members of the ensemble. It ends with a spotlight on an American flag, a commentary on the play's role in the national culture, but also on the country's role in global matters and its insistence on war. The song's affirmation of dance in the face of a foreboding future perfectly underscores Saroyan's credo that "in the time of your life, live."

The Steppenwolf production, staged in three premiere regional theatres of the nation, suggested the role that performance can play in heightened moments of crisis. Performance creates provisional communities of audiences who gather in their contemporary moment to rethink their sense of the now. Performance thus becomes a space in which a critical reassessment of the contemporary and the nation is made possible. This held true for *The Time of Your Life* in 1939 and it held true for the play in 2002 and 2004. While Chicago audiences who attended the 2002 Steppenwolf production saw the play in the context of September 11, the Seattle and San Francisco audiences who saw the Landau production at the Seattle Rep and ACT in 2004 saw it in the context of the war in Iraq and the escalation of violence, death, and destruction that have increasingly characterized it. The sentiments that Saroyan put in circulation in his day return in Landau's production and recirculate in this contemporary context. What may speak to our contemporary moment is not necessarily or exclusively art that overtly thematizes either September 11 or the war in Iraq, but historical works that when juxtaposed inform our present situation. As Marvin Carlson explains, this practice of using revivals of classic plays to make "contemporary political statements" is typical in Europe, but "rarely encountered in America," although he speculates that this might change in the political climate of terrorism and war.[37] In this light, the revival of *The Time of Your Life* is neither an exercise in nostalgia, nor an effort to canonize the play or the playwright as a classic, but an effort to expand the archive of political and artistic alternatives available to us now. And it marks a revival of the sentiment that Saroyan put forward in the quote that opened this epilogue, a belief that "art can do a great deal about history."

Nostalgia's impulse—as is the impulse for canonicity—is conservative, and it undermines the feelings produced by the contemporary in favor of what was once imagined to be true and real. As Susan Bennett explains, "Nostalgia is constituted as a longing for certain qualities and attributes in lived experience that we have apparently lost, at the same time it indicates our inability to produce parallel qualities and attributes which would satisfy the particularities of lived experience in the present."[38] Rather than yearning for another moment in a time long gone, or grieving the loss of certain modes of existence that are either no longer accessible or possible, the Steppenwolf production of *The Time of Your Life* promotes a structure of feeling that might now benefit our times. The question, as Bennett reminds us in discussing the politics of revivals, changes from "What have they done to the original?" to, in her words, "How can this material be useful to us now?"[39] The audiences at each performance must decide for themselves the answer to this question.

And critics and scholars must decide on it too. As I hope to have demonstrated, the revival of Saroyan's *The Time of Your Life* constitutes a revival of the debates and discussions the play inspired in its day. The play's critical reception forms part of the archive that is also open to revival and even revision. The question of posterity, which Atkinson had put on hold in 1939, resurfaces in our contemporary moment. It relates to not only the play but to the entire archive in which it is embedded, an archive that includes not only the period's historical events, popular entertainments, and artistic movements but the era's theatre and cultural criticism as well. "Who, then, will judge the critic's judgment?" wonders Robert Brustein in *The Siege of the Arts*, his polemical collection of writings on the theatre published in 2001.[40] "Posterity perhaps," he offers, "assuming that the future will continue to have any interest in our hasty scribblings."[41] As Brustein suggests, it is impossible to predict what will prove of use to future generations, who may or may not have any interest in the "hasty scribblings" of the contemporary critic engaged in the time of the now. Predicting what will endure is an exercise in futility as foolish as it is arrogant. The task for the critic is to engage the work as it is produced in the context of its historical specificity, and to leave the question of posterity unresolved; as Atkinson suggests, "it need not worry us in the present moment." Brustein calls this engagement the theatre's "secular life," by which he means "the reputation of plays and productions in their own day," and he advises critics to direct their energies accordingly.[42] I agree with these critics, who wrote under extremely historically different circumstances—one when theatre was assumed to lie at the heart of the national culture, the other when theatre is thought not to at all.

I had no idea that Saroyan and his time would have anything to say to me in mine. That our emotional and political registers would align across time and circumstance was surprising and unknowable to me in advance. And yet the lesson here is not that we must all now read and revive Saroyan, as I have done, but that we remain open to the many surprises that characterize the contemporary, including the obscure and eccentric revival of performances from a different era. This seems to me the idea behind the play's title: at once an invitation to understand the contemporary as a transient moment of personal experience and to recognize the potential for great joy and profound pleasure in such an ephemeral temporality.

"The world now provides art new and more difficult material," Saroyan wrote in 1940, and this remains the case in 2004, the time of this chapter's writing. Steppenwolf, like Saroyan—and like the other artists I have addressed throughout this book—saw "no alternative but to accept this material" and create a critically engaged response to the contemporary's challenge. I have followed suit, as is the job of the critic, and responded accordingly. Criticism, too, must play a role, part of which may be to champion and support the daring of artists. This book set out to acknowledge the achievement of the performing arts in the contemporary moment. Whether these works will speak to other audiences at a later time is not necessarily my concern, although I hope the book's archive begins to suggest the ways that performance shapes and informs the national culture. Nor can I predict the book's own critical legacy. Its main aspiration has been to engage contemporary American performance through an interpretive model informed by and yet not bound to history. Let it stand as a document of its time and a testament of a belief in the vitality of performance in America.

NOTES

INTRODUCTION: HERE AND NOW

1   See Schechner, *Performance Theory*.
2   Williams, *Marxism and Literature*, 133.
3   Dolan, *Utopia in Performance*, 1.
4   Docherty, "Now, Here, This," 50.
5   The contemporary is often used interchangeably with the postmodern. And while there is a formidable bibliography on postmodernism, one informed by rigorous debate, the term *contemporary* is generally left untroubled by critics. For a helpful introduction to this problem, see Luckhurst and Marks, "Hurry Up Please, It's Time." Sometimes, the contemporary refers to the decades following the postwar years—the 1950s, 1960s, and 1970s. But in the early twenty-first century, those decades can no longer stand as current or even perhaps as recent.
6   Benjamin, "Theses on the Philosophy of History," 263.
7   Carlson, *The Haunted Stage*, 8.
8   Roach, *Cities of the Dead*, 26.
9   Taylor, *The Archive and the Repertoire*, 16.
10 Wiegman, "Feminism's Apocalyptic Futures," 810; Roof, "Generational Difficulties."
11 Roof, "Generational Difficulties," 71.
12 Michael Warner's introduction to *Fear of a Queer Planet* remains the most articulate and persuasive position on queer theory's intellectual and political project.
13 I am indebted to Rebecca Lemon for helping me articulate this tension.
14 Pease and Wiegman, "Futures," 2.
15 Wise, "'Paradigm Dramas' in American Studies," 168. The essay originally appeared in *American Quarterly* 31, no. 3 (1979): 293–337.
16 Ibid., 169.

17 Pease and Wiegman, "Futures," 1.

18 Wise, ' "Paradigm Dramas' in American Studies," 169.

19 On the issue of theatre and ideology, see Reinelt and Roach, *Critical Theory and Performance*.

20 Pease and Wiegman, "Futures," 3.

21 Wise, ' "Paradigm Dramas' in American Studies," 169.

22 Pease and Wiegman, "Futures," 39.

23 See Phelan, "Introduction," 3: "One potent version of the history of performance studies is that the field was born out of the fecund collaborations between Richard Schechner and Victor Turner. In bringing theatre and anthropology together, both men saw the extraordinarily deep questions these perspectives on cultural expression raised."

24 For the particular meanings and specific genealogies of these words, see Carlson, *Performance*.

25 Among the essays collected in *The Futures of American Studies*, only one essay addresses theatre, Dana Heller's account of teaching Arthur Miller's *Death of a Salesman* in Russia—"*Salesman* in Moscow"—although two others address performance, Ricardo L. Ortíz's work on a Gloria Estefan concert in Montreal—"Hemispheric Vertigo: Cuba, Quebec, and Other Provisional Reconfigurations of 'Our' New America(s)" and José Esteban Muñoz's essay on male strippers in Queens—"The Future in the Present: Sexual Avant-Gardes and the Performance of Utopia."

26 Turner, *Dramas, Fields, Metaphors*, 30–31. But see also Lisa Lowe's important forthcoming book project, *Metaphors of Globalization*.

27 Turner, *Dramas, Fields, Metaphors*, 30–31.

28 Dolan, *Geographies of Learning*, 65.

29 Robinson, *The Other American Drama*, 8.

30 Ibid., 9.

31 Mason, "American Stages (Curtain Raiser)," 1.

32 Ibid., 4.

33 Smith, *American Drama*, 3.

34 The other scholars participating in the forum were Michael Cadden, Joyce Flynn, and C. W. E. Bigsby.

35 Bigsby, "Drama as Cultural Sign."

36 Desmond, "Making American Studies Dance," 527.

37 Ibid., 526.

38 Ibid., 526.

39 A version of this discussion of Chita Rivera appeared in "Theatre Journals," my editor's column in *Theatre Journal* 54, no. 3 (2002): .

40 Leo Lerman, "At the Theatre: West Side Story," *Dance Magazine*, November 1957, 13.

41 One important exception is Stacy Wolf's book-length project on leading women of the American musical, *A Problem Like Maria*.

42 See Negron-Muntaner, "Feeling Pretty." The author, it needs to be noted, focuses exclusively on the 1961 film version.

43 Sandoval-Sánchez, *José, Can You See?*

44 See my "Latino Performance and Identity."

45 Huerta, *Necessary Theater.*

46 The following discussion first appeared in *Theatre Journal* 47, no. 2 (1995): 169–88, in an essay entitled "Preaching to the Converted" that I cowrote with the performance artist Tim Miller.

47 Butler, *Bodies That Matter.*

48 Savran, "Choices Made and Unmade," 92.

49 Ibid., 91.

50 The critical discussion on Parks's work has remained the exclusive domain of theatre and performance scholars who have been engaging her plays since the late 1980s.

51 Suzan-Lori Parks, quoted in Don Shewey, "This Time the Shock Is Her Turn toward Naturalism," *New York Times,* July 22, 2001.

52 Suzan-Lori Parks, quoted in Aaron Bryant, "Broadway, Her Way," *Crisis,* March/April 2002, 44.

53 Suzan Lori-Parks, quoted in Joshua Wolf Shenk, "Beyond a Black-and-White Lincoln," *New York Times,* April 7, 2002.

54 Pochoda, review of *Topdog/Underdog.* Pochoda's review offers an excellent discussion of the play's race politics, but see also Una Chaudhuri's illuminating review of the Public Theater production in *Theatre Journal.*

55 For an excellent discussion of the political and artistic achievements of *Def Poetry Jam,* see Dolan, *Utopia in Performance.*

56 All data provided by the League of American Theatres and Producers.

1 NOT ABOUT AIDS

1 Andrew Sullivan, "When AIDS Ends," *New York Times Magazine,* November 10, 1996, 1. The title of Sullivan's essay shifts from the magazine's cover title, "When AIDS Ends," to an internal publication title, "When Plagues End: Notes on the Twilight of an Epidemic." Further confusion results from the magazine's cover graphic, which highlights Sullivan's text and the phrase "the end of AIDS." Chip Kidd, who designed the cover, explains that "the prose was so strong that it became key." See Janet Froelich, "Cover Boy: Interview with Chip Kidd," *New York Times Magazine,* November 10, 1996, 51. My reference to Sullivan's essay follows the magazine's cover title and the byline " 'When AIDS Ends' By Andrew Sullivan." For a full discussion of the cover image and Sullivan's essay, see Phillip Brian Harper, "Gay Male Identities." Eric Rofes also discusses Sullivan's essay and the discrepancies in Sullivan's title in *Dry Bones Breathe,* 50–53. Rofes points out that yet another phrase, "After AIDS," is used in the layout of the printed pages of the

essay. Rofes also includes a discussion of *Newsweek*'s "The End of AIDS?" cover image and article, as well as responses to these essays from gay and lesbian writers whom I do not discuss in this essay.

2 See Rofes, *Dry Bones Breathe*. This book is marked by a vision of gay culture much more expansive than that of most contemporary gay male commentators. Rofes considers the experiences of many of those often left out of the profile of what passes for the gay male community: queer youth and queer elders, gays who live outside of urban centers, and gay men of color.

3 Ibid., 75.

4 Ibid., 72.

5 Michaelangelo Signorile, "641,086 and Counting," *Out*, September 1998, 72.

6 Larry Kramer, "1,112 and Counting," *New York Native*, March 14, 1983, 1. See also Kramer's own account of this essay in *Reports from The Holocaust*, 50–51.

7 Signorile, "641,086 and Counting," 188.

8 While fear might force people to pay attention to AIDS in the short run, it has not proven very successful as the basis for an HIV-prevention campaign (see Odets, *In the Shadow of the Epidemic*). Nevertheless, Signorile argues for the return of fear in a prevention campaign directed at gay men in "Don't Fear the Fear," *Advocate*, April 13, 1999, 51–55.

9 Harper, "Gay Male Identities," 8. But see also Cathy Cohen's important book, *The Boundaries of Blackness*, in which she argues that a new racist discourse emerged in the popular media around the question of access with the arrival of protease inhibitors: "In the case of reports on protease inhibitors, a troubling discourse has already developed. It seems that protease inhibitor therapies require great discipline, since a patient's medication must be taken, in some cases, every eight hours on an empty stomach. Further, without strict adherence to the defined regime with regard to the medication, it is possible that a virus resistant to these drugs might develop and spread. Thus the question of which patients or people with AIDS have 'enough discipline' to receive these new therapies is now a central part of new generation of AIDS reporting. Journalists are openly discussing and writing about who should be allowed such treatment" (184).

10 Harper, "Gay Male Identities," 8.

11 In *Love Undetectable*, Sullivan revisits his earlier essay, admitting that the hostile public response from many gay men "took my breath away." In an effort to clarify his "When AIDS Ends" claims, Sullivan writes: "But this end, of course, was laden with paradox. As the plague relented in one world, it was busy redoubling its might in another, in countries far away, and against people who had nothing with which to counter it" (33).

12 Rofes, *Dry Bones Breathe*, 72.

13 Harper, "Gay Male Identities," 27.

14 Treichler, *How to Have Theory in an Epidemic*.

15 Mario Cooper, "Two Nations under Plague," *POZ*, January 1999, 20.

16 Cohen, *The Boundaries of Blackness*, 113.

17 Elizabeth Shogren, "Clinton to Boost Minority AIDS Funding," *Los Angeles Times*, October 28, 1998.

18 See Liz Galst, "Check in the Mail?" *POZ*, December 1998, 42. Galst provides accounts from various ASOs on the decline in AIDS philanthropy.

19 Lawrence O. Gostin, director of the Georgetown University/Johns Hopkins University Program on Law and Public Health and a member of the advisory committee of the CDC, as quoted in Lynda Richardson, "Wave of Laws Aimed at People with HIV," *New York Times*, September 25, 1998.

20 Sean Strub, "s.o.s." *POZ*, December 1998, 13.

21 The cultural repercussions of this shift in the lesbian and gay movement as it relates to gay marriage are detailed by Michael Warner, for whom the most urgent concerns include attacks on queer sexual culture and the isolation of queer counterpublics from "national organizations, magazines, and publics." Warner ends his essay with the claim that "any argument for gay marriage requires an intensified concern for what is thrown into its shadow." Warner, "Normal and Normaller," 159. AIDS, I argue, is one of the issues thrown into this shadow.

22 Román, *Acts of Intervention*.

23 See, for example, Desmond, "Embodying Difference." See also Delgado and Muñoz, *Everynight Life*, and Foster, *Choreographing History*.

24 Alberto Sandoval-Sánchez and I write on this process in "Caught in the Web."

25 In part, my discussion of these works is based on performances I saw of *Still/Here* in 1994 at the Brooklyn Academy of Music and of *Not-about-AIDS Dance* in 1994 at New York City's Kitchen. I also saw Dance by Neil Greenberg's *The Disco Project* at Highways Performance Space in Santa Monica in 1995, and his complete trilogy at Playhouse 91 in New York City in 1998. I saw the Bill T. Jones/Arnie Zane Dance Company perform *We Set Out Early . . . Visibility Was Poor* at Royce Hall in Los Angeles in 1998. I am indebted to the Bill T. Jones/Arnie Zane Dance Company for photographs and press packets and to Dance by Neil Greenberg for photographs, videos, and press packets.

26 Jones with Gillespie, *Last Night on Earth*, 252.

27 Bill T. Jones/Arnie Zane Dance Company, promotional material.

28 Identity issues, as Gay Morris points out, have been evident throughout Jones's career. See Morris, "What He Called Himself."

29 Jones with Gillespie, *Last Night on Earth*, 194.

30 *Uncle Tom's Cabin/The Promised Land* was performed in over thirty-five cities, and Jones was never quite sure how these questions would be answered in advance.

31 Jones with Gillespie, *Last Night on Earth*, 220.

32 Ibid., 250. The actual *Advocate* quote reads as follows: "Even now, I would like to have straight men in my company, but I worry if I could trust them. There's a stigma associated with our company because someone in it died of AIDS and because I'm HIV-positive. I want to get on with my life and deal with my artistic

collaborators, but I still expect someone to scorn me. I find that most people are curious to know what AIDS is like, but they are scared too." Douglas Sadownick, "The Dancer Speaks Out," *Advocate*, February 27, 1990, 38.

33 Some critics have gone so far as to suggest that Jones's artistic success is due to his HIV status and race. In a *New Yorker* profile, Henry Louis Gates Jr. quotes a critic who states that "the reason he's getting so many awards so soon is that people aren't gambling on his surviving: they're giving it to him now." Gates further reports that "it is clearly a commonplace, albeit usually an unspoken one, that the fact that Jones is both HIV-positive and black has more than a little to do with his having received so many laurels so early in his career." Gates, "The Body Politic," *New Yorker*, November 28, 1994, 124. The fact that Jones continues to thrive more than a decade later renders these claims ironic at best. In 1994, however, they conveyed the sense of urgency surrounding HIV/AIDS, even if the claim about Jones's success makes little sense. If HIV-positive black gay artists are the new darlings of the elite media, how is it that no other artists are named in Gates's essay or in the larger cultural discourse of the period? Leaving aside the implications of tokenism, such comments displace attention from the artistic work and set up Jones—and other artists with HIV—as undeserving of whatever critical acclaim they may receive.

34 Jones with Gillespie, *Last Night on Earth*, 259.

35 Arlene Croce, "A Critic at Bay: Discussing the Undiscussable," *New Yorker*, December 26, 1994, 54–60. For responses to Croce's condemning rhetoric, see Richard Goldstein, "The Croce Criterion," *Village Voice*, January 3, 1995, 8; Deborah Jowitt, "Critic as Victim," *Village Voice*, January 10, 1995, 67; Frank Rich, "Dance of Death," *New York Times*, January 8, 1995; and, last but not least, letters from Tony Kushner, bell hooks, and others published in the *New Yorker* itself, January 30, 1995, 10–13. For a context in which to place *Still/Here*, see my collaboration with Tim Miller, "Preaching to the Converted." The bibliography on Bill T. Jones is impressive. For the dance context, see Siegel, "Virtual Criticism and the Dance of Death"; Brody, "Opening Sequences"; and Morris, "What He Called Himself." For studies that place Jones's work in African American cultural contexts, see Wallace, "The Autochoreography of an Ex-Snow Queen," and Holland, *Raising the Dead*.

36 Siegel, "Virtual Criticism," 249.

37 For an excellent introduction to Neil Greenberg's career, see Rick Whitaker and Don Daniels, "A Conversation with Neil Greenberg," *Ballet Review* (spring 1997): 1–12.

38 Gere, *How to Make Dances in an Epidemic*. Gere's introduction makes explicit the need to interrogate "this phenomenon that runs throughout choreography made by gay men in the age of AIDS" (23), and his book models this kind of critical practice.

39 Leigh Witchel, "Neil Greenberg's Trilogy: A Survival's Tale," *Ballet Review* (fall 1998): 8.

40 Both choreographers remain prolific. Shortly after the premier of *Part Three*, Greenberg choreographed for Mikhail Baryshnikov's *White Oak Dance Project* and premiered *This Is What Happened*, a dance-noir trio, set to Hitchcock film music by Bernard Herrmann at New York's PS 122 in the spring of 1999. Soon after *We Set Out Early . . . Visibility Was Poor*, Jones collaborated with Jessye Norman in *How! Do! We! Do!* as part of the New Visions series produced by New York's Lincoln Center in the summer of 1999, and he premiered *Out Some Place*, a full company dance, at the American Dance Festival in Durham, North Carolina. Both Jones and Greenberg danced at these events, and both artists continue to premier new work throughout the United States and abroad.

41 Karen Campbell, "Dance: Choreographer Jones Sheds New Light On 'Visibility,'" *Boston Herald*, May 31, 1998; Lewis Segal, "Clarity of Vision in *Visibility Was Poor*," *Los Angeles Times*, May 11, 1998; Elizabeth Zimmer, "The Word from Bill T. Jones: He's Moving beyond Words," *New York Times*, October 4, 1998.

42 Zimmer, "Word from Bill T. Jones."

43 Rohan Preston, "Bill T.'s Exultant Adventure," *Minneapolis Star Tribune*, September 25, 1998.

44 Jennifer Fisher, "Q & A: Bill T. Jones; Moved to Seek a Connection," *Los Angeles Times*, May 6, 1998.

45 Preston, "Bill T.'s Exultant Adventure."

46 Fisher, "Q & A."

47 AIDS is not the only topic that Greenberg addresses in his solos. The second solo, for example, announces that "last summer I fell in love."

48 Greenberg has explained to me that he was running a fever during the final performances of the trilogy in 1998.

49 Ann Daly, "A Chronicle Faces Death and Celebrates Life," *New York Times*, March 29, 1998.

50 Ibid.

51 Others in the performing arts are also exploring this new creative vocabulary. While this chapter concerns itself specifically with only two artists, I do not mean to present them as normative in terms of their health issues, artistic concerns, or even their public responses to AIDS. Nor do I intend to position them against each other, as if the response of one were to be valued over that of the other. Instead, I am interested in the work that artists with HIV are creating. I've written on other recent work by artists in "On the Unfashionability of AIDS-Arts Today." I also discuss another dancer-choreographer, Paul Timothy Diaz, whose work *Día de los vivos* (1996) both conjures and revises traditional Day of the Dead rituals, in my essay "Latino Performance and Identity." For a full-scale study of AIDS and performance, see my book *Acts of Intervention*; for a complete study of AIDS and dance, see David Gere's excellent book *How to Make Dances in an Epidemic*. Finally, my research focuses on gay male artists and AIDS; for new literature on women and AIDS, see the important anthology by Roth and Hogan, *Gendered Epidemic*.

52 Mike Steele, "Prolific Dancer Greenberg Comes with New Work," *Minneapolis Star Tribune*, March 1, 1998.

2 VISA DENIED

1 Chaudhuri, *Staging Place*, 213.
2 Boone, *Queer Frontiers*, 13.
3 Yarbro-Bejarano, "Expanding the Categories of Race and Sexuality," 130, 133.
4 See also important work by Phillip Brian Harper, one of the first scholars in African American studies to pursue these concerns. In a number of strategically placed essays throughout the late 1980s and the early to mid-1990s, Harper probed the dynamics among race, sexuality, and nation. These essays are collected in his book *Private Affairs*.
5 Yarbro-Bejarano, "Expanding the Categories of Race and Sexuality," 127.
6 Warner, *Fear of a Queer Planet*, xiii.
7 Meyer, "At Home in Marginal Domains," 19.
8 Muñoz, "Ephemera as Evidence," 7.
9 Yew, *The Hyphenated American*.
10 I have written an extended introduction to Yew's work in my introduction to *The Hyphenated American*. The following paragraph is pulled from that collection. See also my interview with Chay Yew, "Los Angeles Intersections," in Uno, *The Color of Theater*.
11 Kuftinec, *Staging America*, 62.
12 For more on this production, see Sonja Kuftinec's informative review of *Broken Hearts*.
13 The play ran from June 5 to June 21, 1998. Admission to all performances of the production was pay-what-you-can. For more on the history and style of Cornerstone Theatre, see Kuftinec, *Staging America*.
14 Lee, *Performing Asian America*, 158–59. These are two separate thoughts from Lee's book that I have brought together to emphasize my point.
15 Lowe, *Immigrant Acts*. Lowe writes: " 'Immigrant acts' [name] the *agency* of Asian immigrants and Asian Americans: the *acts* of labor, resistance, memory, and survival, as well as the politicized cultural work that emerges from dislocation and disidentification. Asian immigrants and Asian Americans have not only been 'subject to' immigration exclusion and restriction but also have been 'subjects of' the immigration process and are agents of political change, cultural expression, and social transformation" (9).
16 Yew, *A Beautiful Country*, in *The Hyphenated American*, 212–15.
17 Ibid., 216–18.
18 Peter Tamaribuchi and Amy Vaillancourt, "*A Beautiful Country*: A Brief History of Asians in America," program notes for Cornerstone Theatre production, June 5–21, 1998.
19 Yew, *A Beautiful Country*, 172.

20 For non-English speaking immigrants, or for those for whom English is not a primary language, this fragmentation is also experienced through language.

21 Yew, *A Beautiful Country*, 233–34.

22 Ibid., *A Beautiful Country*, 258.

23 Shimakawa, *National Abjection*, 17.

24 For some audiences, "queer" is imagined as only American. During rehearsals, for example, some Asian community members were upset by the inclusion of drag and homosexuality in a play about Asian American history.

25 This idea of disidentification is best theorized by José Esteban Muñoz in *Disidentifications*.

26 Yew, *A Beautiful Country*, 272.

27 Ibid., 273–74.

28 Muñoz, "Ephemera as Evidence," 6; and Lowe, *Immigrant Acts*, 9.

29 While Visa's seeming denial of her drag persona may appear to some people as a phobic response to drag, such a view misrepresents the impact of Wong Kong Shin's self-declaration and Yew's overall point here. When I posed the issue to the playwright in conversation, Yew claimed that Wong Kong Shin was not abandoning drag completely and that he imagined the character to return to drag in the very near future. While the playwright's projections for his character's future life might relieve some level of anxiety for those concerned, I think the play itself—as it is already written and directed—suggests that drag is much more than just a theatrical trompe l'oeil.

30 David Henry Hwang's *M. Butterfly* (1988), perhaps the most celebrated play in Asian American theatre, for all its important cultural interventions, cannot be said to fully address this issue. Consider John Clum's comments in this context: "It is ironic that the best-known play about a gay Asian male, David Henry Hwang's *M. Butterfly*, was written by a heterosexual and used a male-male relationship to comment on white men's attitudes to Asians in general and Asian women in particular." Clum, *Staging Gay Lives*, 345. In fact, *A Beautiful Country* ironically comments on *M. Butterfly*'s spectacularization of the drag queen through its matter-of-fact representation of Visa. For the historical interventions achieved by Hwang's play, see Kondo, *About Face*. Since Hwang's *M. Butterfly*, queer Asian American playwrights and performers such as Han Ong, Denise Uyehara, Alec Mapa, and Hung Nguyen are, along with Chay Yew and others, more forcefully exploring the interrelation between queerness and diaspora, although the critical bibliography on queer Asian American artists is lacking.

31 Lowe, "The New Asian Immigrant." See also Chuh and Shimakawa's indispensable introduction to *Orientations*.

32 Palumbo-Liu, *Asian/American*, 2.

33 I recommend here two excellent projects in Asian American studies that track the shifts in the field and make the case for a critical reinvigoration of its intellectual and political mission. See Nguyen, *Race and Resistance*; and Chuh, *Imagine Otherwise*.

34 Eng, "Out Here and Over There," 32.

35 Chay Yew's earlier plays include *Porcelain* (1992), *A Language of Their Own* (1995), and *Half Lives* (1996). The three plays comprise the *Whitelands* trilogy. For an excellent discussion of this trilogy, see Michael Reynolds's review of their production at East West Players in Los Angeles. *Half Lives*, the third play in the trilogy, has been substantially revised and is now titled *Wonderland*. In 1997, Grove Press published the first two plays of the trilogy as *Two Plays by Chay Yew*. While these three plays can each be said to explore queerness and diaspora on some level simply by their representation of queer Asian gay men, Yew is more interested in tracing the internal dynamics between Asian gay men and their sexual partners, lovers, and families in these three plays, respectively, than in forcefully positioning these characters as subjects in history. This critique is not meant to slight the plays but to further underline the significance of *A Beautiful Country*.

36 Eng, "Out Here and Over There," 43.

37 Cruz-Malavé and Manalansan, *Queer Globalizations*, 4.

3 LATINO GENEALOGIES

1 These ideas were first presented in my essay "Latino Performance and Identity."

2 Kanellos, *A History of Hispanic Theatre in the United States*, 199–200.

3 Huerta, *Necessary Theater*, 5.

4 *Freak* was originally produced in March 1997 at the Goodman Theatre in Chicago. It was then presented at the Theatre on the Square in San Francisco, where it ran from May to June. An earlier New York version was performed in New York at PS 122 in August 1997. *Freak* was written and performed by John Leguizamo and directed and developed by David Bar Katz. Douglas Stein served as the production's scenic designer, Jan Kroesze as the lighting designer, and Wendall K. Harrington designed the production's projections.

5 Ben Brantley's review in the *New York Times* mainly champions Leguizamo's performance. He writes, "That the evening remains so compellingly watchable is partly because Leguizamo is not so much a stand-up comic as a jump-up, lie-down, throw-yourself-against-the-wall comic." Brantley finds the writing less successful, however: "The electric energy and physical precision with which he invests every movement takes the performance into realms the script doesn't go." Ben Brantley, "*Freak*: A One-Man Melting Pot Bubbling Over with Demons," *New York Times*, February 13, 1998.

6 Michael Riedel, "A 'Freak' Success Story: How Leguizamo's Show Became a Rare B'way Hit," *New York Daily News*, July 7, 1998. Riedel reports that *Freak*'s weekly overhead ran between $120,000 and $150,000, depending on advertising, with Leguizamo making more than $50,000 a week.

7 Sandoval-Sánchez, *José, Can You See?*

8 *Freak* was also nominated for Outstanding Variety, Music, or Comedy Special.

9   See, for example, Most, *Making Americans*; Wolf, *A Problem Like Maria*; and Burston, *Megamusicals*.

10 See, for example, publications on Latino celebrities in television, film, and the performing arts published since the late 1990s: Deborah Paredez on Selena in "Remembering Selena, Re-membering Latinidad"; José Quiroga on Ricky Martin in *Tropics of Desire*; José Esteban Muñoz on Pedro Zamora in *Disidentifications: Queers of Color and the Performance of Politics*; and Frances Negron-Muntaner on Jennifer Lopez in "Jennifer's Butt."

11 In order to differentiate the performer from the role, I will refer to John Leguizamo the performer and actor as "Leguizamo" and John Leguizamo the character as "young John."

12 Leguizamo with Katz, *Freak*, 25. All quotes are taken from the published version of *Freak*, which appeared in print before the 1998 Broadway run. "Because we are in the midst of the show's developmental process, this version represents where the show is at the exact moment, June 19, 1997," Leguizamo and Katz write in their prefatory comments to the edition. The video of *Freak* that aired on H BO differs from the published version, which is based on an earlier performance script.

13 Coco Fusco ranks among the most interesting Latino artists on the contemporary scene, and this collaboration with Guillermo Gómez-Peña is already from well over a decade ago. To learn more about Fusco's creative and cultural work since *Couple in a Cage*, see my entry on her in *Encyclopedia of Latinos and Latinas in the United States*. But see also Fusco's *The Bodies That Were Not Ours*.

14 Coco Fusco, "The Other History of Intercultural Performance," in Fusco, *English Is Broken Here*, 41.

15 Ibid., 47.

16 Adams, *Sideshow U.S.A.*, 2.

17 In order to appreciate these prices, it might help to remember that during the 1997–98 season, many Broadway productions charged $55 for their balcony seats and up to $75 for orchestra seats.

18 See Luisita Lopez Torregrosa, "Latino Culture Whirls onto Center Stage," *New York Times*, March 26, 1998.

19 Leguizamo with Katz, *Freak*, 3.

20 Dávila, *Latinos, Inc.*, 94–95.

21 Alfaro, *Downtown* in *O Solo Homo*, 323.

22 See Rodriguez, "Latino Republicans and the 1998 Election."

23 Moraga, *Giving Up the Ghost* in *Heroes and Saints*, 35.

24 Yarbro-Bejarano, *The Wounded Heart*, 151.

25 Moraga, *The Last Generation*, 159.

26 Lopez, "Performing Aztlán," 173.

27 Huerta, "Negotiating Borders in Three Latino Plays," 157. But see also his *Chicano Drama*.

28 Ibid., 181.

29 Leguizamo with Katz, *Freak*, 97.

30 Ibid.

31 Ibid., 53.

32 Sedgwick, *Tendencies*.

33 Leguizamo with Katz, *Freak*, 53.

34 Ibid.

35 Ibid., 54–55.

36 Kirkwood and Dante, *A Chorus Line*, 65.

37 Sandoval-Sánchez, *José, Can You See?* 92.

38 Kirkwood and Dante, *A Chorus Line*, 64–67; ellipses original. *A Chorus Line* was conceived, choreographed, and directed by Michael Bennett, the musical's book was cowritten by James Kirkwood and Nicholas Dante, Marvin Hamlisch composed the music, and Edward Kleban wrote the lyrics. The artistic contributions of each man, however, have been debated and contested since the musical's origins. See, for example, Flinn, *What They Did for Love*; Mandelbaum, *A Chorus Line and the Musicals of Michael Bennett*; and Stevens and George, *The Longest Line*.

39 Kirkwood and Dante, *A Chorus Line*, 138.

40 Ibid., 102–3; ellipses original.

41 Leguizamo with Katz, *Freak*, 123.

42 Ibid., 124–25.

43 I am indebted to Susan Manning at Northwestern University for asking me to consider Leguizamo's final movements in *Freak* as part of the actual performance when I presented an earlier version of this chapter on her campus.

44 John Leguizamo, "New Voices from Latinolandia Whisper in America's Ear," *New York Times*, July 14, 1991.

45 Flores, *From Bomba to Hip-Hop*, 142.

46 Ibid., 148.

47 Ibid., 150.

48 Campa, "Latinos and the Crossover Aesthetic," xv.

49 On the Latino imaginary, see Flores, *From Bomba to Hip-Hop*, where he writes, "Latino identity is imagined not as the negation of the non-Latino, but as the affirmation of cultural and social realities, myths and possibilities, as they are inscribed in their own human trajectory" (200).

50 See Ed Morales, "Spic Nation," *Village Voice*, November 3, 1992, 109, where Morales describes one incident where a Latino television producer could not bring himself to attend a Leguizamo performance because of its title.

4 ARCHIVAL DRAG

1 Steedman, *Dust*, 68.

2 Stoler, "Colonial Archives and the Acts of Governance," 90.

3 Ibid., 107.

4 Taylor, *The Archive and the Repertoire*, 20.

5   Ibid., 36.

6   Schneider, "Archives Performance Remains," 100.

7   Cvetkovich, *An Archive of Feelings.*

8   Dinshaw, *Getting Medieval*, 1.

9   Schneider, "Driving the Lincoln," 101.

10 Roach, *Cities of the Dead*, xi.

11 Ibid., 26.

12 Christine Nipe provides a very helpful survey of the Sarah Siddons exhibitions and the other cultural events surrounding them in "Mrs. Siddons' Currency."

13 Booth, "Sarah Siddons," 18.

14 Carlson, *In the Theatre of Romanticism*, 172. Carlson is quoting from Kelly, *The Kemble Era*, 42, 22–33.

15 Wilson, "The 'Incomparable' Siddons as Reynolds's Muse," 134.

16 McPherson, "Searching for Sarah Siddons," 283.

17 Booth, "Sarah Siddons," 36. For the primary source, see Highfill, Burnim, and Langhans, *Biographical Dictionary*, 37–67.

18 William Hazlitt, "Macbeth," in Hazlitt, *Selected Writings*, 339–40.

19 For a bibliography on Sarah Siddons, see West, "The Public and Private Roles of Sarah Siddons"; and Asleson, " 'She Was Tragedy Personified.' " See also Ellen Donkin's interesting work on Siddons and her reception among eighteenth-century theatre audiences, "Mrs. Siddons Looks Back in Anger." The question of Siddons's effect on audiences has generated an interesting discussion among scholars of the period. See also Backscheider, *Spectacular Politics*; Cox, "Baille, Siddons, Larpent"; and Carlson, *In the Theatre of Romanticism*.

20 Frank Dwyer, "Searching for Sarah," program note for *The Affliction of Glory: A Comedy about Tragedy*, 3. The play was written by Frank Dwyer, directed by Corey Madden, and produced by the J. Paul Getty Museum and the Center Theatre Group/Mark Taper Forum at the Harold M. Williams Auditorium at the Getty Center, Los Angeles, California. The play ran at the Getty from August 14, 1999, through September 5, 1999.

21 "In ancient Greek myth, Mnemosyne (Memory), the mother of the Muses, is said to know everything, past, present, and future. She is the Memory that is the basis of all life and creativity. Forgetting the true order and origin of things is often tantamount to death (as in the case of Lethe, the river of death in Greek mythology, which destroys memory)." see Encyclopedia Britannica Online, s.v. "Myth," *http://www.britannica.com* (accessed January 8, 2002).

22 See Montagu, *The Expression of the Passions*, 90, 210 n. 17.

23 Ibid., 90.

24 McPherson, "Picturing Tragedy," 406.

25 Ibid., 409.

26 The Pageant of the Masters is now held annually in Laguna Beach, California.

27 Phelan, *Unmarked.*

28 See Asleson, "A Sarah Siddons Chronology": "1785, 18 December: Drury Lane re-

vives Garrick's Shakespeare Jubilee. Siddons, eight months pregnant, appears as the Tragic Muse in a re-creation of Reynolds's painting" (xv).

29 Wilson, "The 'Incomparable' Siddons as Reynolds's Muse," 123. Wilson makes the interesting point that Siddons and Yates were not the only rivals in this regard. Sir Joshua Reynolds's rival George Romney had painted Mary Ann Yates in the role of the Tragic Muse ten years earlier than Reynolds's portrait of Sarah Siddons. Yates originated the role at the 1769 *Jubilee* based on her portrait by Romney. Siddons supplants Yates—and, by extension, Reynolds supplants Romney—in Garrick's 1785 revival of the *Jubilee* at Drury Lane.

30 Carey, *All about Eve*, 115–16.

31 For an excellent critical review of the historical reception *of All about Eve* that outlines the various interpretations of the film, see Shingler, "Interpreting *All about Eve.*"

32 On Siddons and her fans, see West, "The Public and Private Roles of Sarah Siddons," 17–20, where she describes the behavior of Siddons's audiences in the theatre, especially women spectators, and the consumer culture around souvenirs, especially Siddons miniatures that stemmed from her performances.

33 The following lines are quoted from Carey, *All about Eve*, 228–29.

34 Ibid., 233.

35 For a fascinating study of the Stonewall riots, see Duberman, *Stonewall.*

36 "Charles Pierce Interview," by unknown interviewer, Los Angeles, July 22, 1989, available at the Charles Pierce Web site, *http://www.bochynski.com/charlespierce/inter.htm.* It is telling that the interview is without a byline and proves to be a key reminder of the fragility of queer performance archives. According to Keith Bochynski, who runs the Web site, "this transcript was submitted by a friend of Charles but we do not know the name of the interviewer or if this has appeared in print."

37 Vito Russo has written about *All about Eve*'s appeal to gay men and lesbians in his now classic *The Celluloid Closet.* But see also Shingler, "Interpreting *All about Eve,*" 56–58.

38 The Playboy Channel televised a one-hour version of Charles Pierce's show called *Legends of the Silver Screen* in 1982.

39 *Applause,* with a book by Betty Comden and Adolph Green, music by Charles Strause, and lyrics by Lee Adams, opened on Broadway at the Palace Theatre on March 30, 1970. It starred Lauren Bacall as Margo Channing. *Applause* won four of its eleven Tony Award nominations including Best Musical and Best Actress. *Applause* had a very successful 896-performance run on Broadway. When Bacall left the Broadway cast to launch the North American tour, the producers cast Anne Baxter, who played Eve Harrington in *All about Eve,* as her replacement. For a fascinating account of the making of *Applause,* as well as of the film *All about Eve,* see Sam Staggs, *All about "All about Eve."*

40 Many of these obituaries are available at the Charles Pierce Web site, *http://www*

.*bochynski.com/charlespierce*. Michael Kearns, a Los Angeles–based actor and a pioneer in Southern California queer and AIDS activism, wrote a moving tribute to Pierce in the *Los Angeles Times*. See Michael Kearns, "Behind the Masks Was a True Actor: In a Storied Career Impersonating Famous Women, Charles Pierce Remained Daring to the End," *Los Angeles Times*, June 7, 1999.

41 Bill Kaiser, personal communication with author, May 29, 2002. My thanks to Bill for his support of this writing.

42 I have written about John Epperson's work in *Acts of Intervention*, 95–104.

43 Peter Mintun, "Charles Pierce Dies at Seventy-six," *Bay Area Reporter*, June 3, 1999, 17.

44 Quoted in Jennifer Fisher, "Moved by Martha," *Los Angeles Times*, July 25, 1999.

45 Michael Musto, "La Dolce Musto," *Village Voice*, November 19, 1996, 26.

46 Quoted in Sara Wolf, "Divine Martha: Richard Move as the Bette Davis of Dance," *LA Weekly*, May 26, 1999, 53.

47 Quoted in Gia Kourlas, "Martha's Moves," *Time Out New York*, January 29, 1998, 64.

48 John Kelly, "In Praise of Drag," in Kelly, *John Kelly*, 55.

49 Joni Mitchell, "Woodstock," *Ladies of the Canyon*, Reprise Records, 1970.

50 Kelly's version of the song has not been recorded or published. I base the quote on my recollection of the song in performances I have attended over the years.

51 Joni Mitchell, "The Fiddle and the Drum," *Clouds*, Reprise Records, 1969.

5 CABARET AS CULTURAL HISTORY

1 Sidney B. Whipple, *New York World Telegram*, 1938.

2 The Theatre Guild is the oldest producing organization in the United States. For more on the guild, see Ken Bloom's indispensable *Broadway*.

3 The first Rodgers and Hart songbook was published in 1951 when Simon and Schuster published *The Rodgers and Hart Song Book*, which contained the words and music of forty-six of their songs.

4 Mary Cleere Haran, "Hart's Heart and Rodgers's Glorious Soul," *New York Times*, June 23, 2002.

5 Senelick, *Cabaret Performance*, 1:8. But see also his companion to this volume, treating the years 1920–40.

6 Senelick, *Cabaret Performance*, 1:8.

7 Denning, *The Cultural Front*.

8 Vogel, "Where Are We Now?" 35. But see also his dissertation, " 'When the Little Dawn Was Grey': Cabaret Performance and the Harlem Renaissance" (PhD diss., New York University, 2004).

9 Vogel, "Where Are We Now?," 35.

10 McNamara, *The New York Concert Saloon*.

11 Ibid., xiv.

12 Ibid., 88.

13 Ibid., 31.

14 Of course, women actors in the legitimate theatre of the nineteenth century were also under intense cultural scrutiny. The bibliography on this topic is considerable, ranging from actors as established as Charlotte Cushman, the subject of Lisa Merrill's important biography, *When Romeo Was a Woman*, to the actors in the popular courtesan plays of the period. For the latter, see Katie Johnson's forthcoming "Sisters in Sin: The Image of the Prostitute on the New York Stage," and her article, "*Zaza*."

15 Dudden, *Women in the American Theatre*, 143.

16 See Kibler, *Rank Ladies*, for an important history of these strains at the turn of the century.

17 Smith, *Musical Comedy in America*, 49.

18 Gavin, *Intimate Nights*.

19 See, for example, the work of Gary Giddins (*Weather Bird*) and, more recently, of Angela Davis (*Blues Legacies and Black Feminism*) and Eric Porter (*What Is This Thing Called Jazz?*) for this position and for the extensive bibliography on the topic.

20 Friedwald, *Jazz Singing*, 69–70.

21 Jones, *Our Musicals, Ourselves*, 58.

22 See ibid. for a fascinating discussion of these musicals.

23 This theme soon became a staple of the American musical and continues to inform American popular culture, from *Maid in Manhattan*, the appealing 2002 Jennifer Lopez film vehicle, to the 2002 Tony Award–winning adaptation of *Thoroughly Modern Millie*, the American public continues to indulge this narrative.

24 *Elaine Stritch at Liberty* won the Tony Award for Special Theatrical Event. Also nominated in the category that year were Bea Arthur's *Just between Friends* and Barbara Cook's *Mostly Sondheim*, both of which I discuss in this chapter, as well as John Leguizamo's *Sexaholix: A Love Story*.

25 Stephen Sondheim, "Broadway Baby," *Follies*, 1971.

26 Quoted in Richard Rodgers, *Musical Stages*, 201.

27 Review of *Pal Joey*, *Time*, January 14, 1952, 62. Wolcott Gibbs, reviewing *Pal Joey* in the *New Yorker*, claims that Stritch "gets and deserves, the greatest ovation of the evening for her rendition of a number called 'Zip.'" Gibbs, "Fine Low Fun," *New Yorker*, January 12, 1952, 38.

28 Richard Rodgers and Lorenz Hart, "Zip," *Pal Joey*, 1941.

29 I am grateful to Stacy Wolf for this observation about Lee's own patter in performance. See also Frederick Nolan's *Lorenz Hart* for more on "Zip," *Pal Joey*, and the musicals of Rodgers and Hart.

30 *Elaine Stritch at Liberty*, constructed by John Lahr, reconstructed by Elaine Stritch, and directed by George C. Wolfe, at the Public Theatre in 2001. I base my remarks on performances I attended at the Public Theatre, the Neil Simon Theatre, the

Ahmanson Theatre, and on the DVD and original cast recordings of the performance.

31 John Lahr, "Stritchiosity," program note for *Elaine Stritch at Liberty*, 2001.

32 Marc Peyser, "A Stritch in Time," *Newsweek*, February 11, 2002, 58.

33 Stephen Sondheim, "I'm Still Here," *Follies*, 1971.

34 Bea Arthur, *Just between Friends*, created by Bea Arthur and Billy Goldenberg, Booth Theatre, 2002. I base my remarks on the performance I saw at the Booth in the spring of 2002, as well as on the original soundtrack recording.

35 Cook participated in the 1985 concert version of *Follies*.

36 The concert also featured the actor and singer Malcolm Gets, who sang from the Sondheim canon, as well as duets with Cook.

37 This is a quote from the live recording of *Barbara Cook Sings Mostly Sondheim: Live at Carnegie Hall* (DRG Records 91464, 2001). I base my comments on my attendance of Cook's performances at the Lincoln Center, the Ahmanson Theatre, and the DVD and CD of the event.

38 Frank Rich, liner notes to *Barbara Cook Sings Mostly Sondheim: Live at Carnegie Hall*.

39 Gavin, *Intimate Nights*, 106.

40 Quoted in ibid., 107.

41 Hugh Martin and Ralph Blane, "The Trolley Song," *Meet Me in St. Louis*, 1944.

42 Stephen Sondheim, "Anyone Can Whistle," *Anyone Can Whistle*, 1964.

43 McKechnie has been performing a version of this show since as early as 1996. I saw her performance at Arci's Place, a cabaret venue in Manhattan in the fall of 2001, and then again at the Colony Theatre in the summer of 2003. I base my comments on these performances and on the 2002 original cast recording distributed by Fynsworth Alley.

44 Donna McKechnie, *Inside the Music*, transcribed from the original cast recording. Text by Christopher Durang and adapted from original material by Donna McKechnie, 2002.

45 Stephen Sondheim, "Everybody Says Don't," *Anyone Can Whistle*, 1964.

46 Quoted in Barry Singer, "Broadway to Park South: A Trouper Keeps Trekking," *New York Times*, July 22, 2001.

47 Christopher Durang, "About the Show . . . ," liner notes to the original cast recording of *Inside the Music*. Text by Christopher Durang and adapted from original material by Donna McKechnie, 2002.

48 Kirkwood and Dante, *A Chorus Line*, 95–96.

49 Miller, *But Enough about Me*, 14.

50 Andrea Marcovicci, "Cabaret Is Where You Go for Tenderness," *New York Times*, October 16, 1994.

51 Quoted in Adam Feldman, "Cabaret à la Maude," *Time Out New York*, March 4, 2004, 18.

52 Warren and Dubin, "The Lullaby of Broadway," *42nd Street*, 1933.

1   The special issue of *Theatre Journal* appeared in March 2002. The introduction
     I wrote for that issue serves as the springboard for this chapter. See Román,
     "Tragedy." I have been teaching courses on AIDS and the arts throughout my
     career; for more on this topic and my pedagogy, see Román, "Teaching AIDS
     Activism."

2   There are, of course, some excellent book-length studies that have in fact already
     launched this project, including Belsey, *The Subject of Tragedy*; Dollimore, *Radical
     Tragedy*; Diamond, *Unmaking Mimesis*; and Butler, *Antigone's Claim*.

3   Belsey, *The Subject of Tragedy*, 7.

4   Williams, *Modern Tragedy*, 62.

5   Williams, *The Long Revolution*.

6   Williams, *Modern Tragedy*, 83–84.

7   Of course, I would amend Williams's use of "men" to the "men and women" or
     the "people."

8   Butler, "Global Violence, Sexual Politics," 202.

9   See Patton, *Inventing AIDS*, for a full discussion of this topic.

10   Michael Liberatore, introduction to Jones, *Living Proof*, 9.

11   Ibid., 8.

12   The forum titled "Theatre and Tragedy in the Wake of 11 September 2001," also
     published in the special issue of *Theatre Journal* on tragedy, includes a number of
     responses from scholars who discuss the challenges of teaching in the days follow-
     ing these events. But see also Karla Jay, "Teaching as Healing, at Ground Zero,"
     Chronicle of Higher Education, October 11, 2001, B20.

13   See Barish, *The Antitheatrical Prejudice*.

14   See Meyer, *Outlaw Representation*, for an informed discussion of the culture wars
     of the late 1980s and early 1990s.

15   See Smith, "Giuliani Time." Unfortunately, despite Smith's cogent critique of
     Giuliani's policies during the 1990s, he makes little to no mention of Giuliani's
     campaigns against the arts here.

16   See Samuel Delany's excellent *Times Square Red, Times Square Blue* for the best
     accounting of this phenomenon.

17   See Frank Rich, "Manifestoes for the Next New York," *New York Times*, Novem-
     ber 11, 2001.

18   For a lively discussion of Broadway, Times Square, and the national imaginary, see
     Charyn, *Gangsters and Gold Diggers*.

19   Mike Wallace offers an insightful perspective on the economic crisis brought forth
     by September 11. See his "New York, New Deal."

20   All of New York City's art venues faced difficult financial challenges in the months
     following the events of September 11. This held true on the national front as well.
     For a survey of the immediate effects of the terrorist attacks on American theatre,

see Trav. S. D., "9/11: America's Theaters Respond," *American Theatre*, November 2001, 16–18.

21 Bruce Weber, review of *Urinetown: The Musical*, *New York Times*, by Greg Kotis and Mark Hollman, September 21, 2001.

22 Greg Kotis, introduction to Kotis and Hollman, *Urinetown*, xxvi.

23 The ad campaign was based on a lyric from *Rent*'s life-affirming anthem "La vie bohème," which closes the show's first act.

24 The wide support for the New York Yankees in the 2001 World Series championship also suggests a similar response.

25 While the Gaiety, made popular by Madonna's *Sex* book, had indeed endured, it had substantially changed during the Giuliani years. No longer could spectators actually tip the dancers; tips were left on the stage during the dancer's performance. Surveillance employees also insured that no sexual activity, including masturbation, occurred on the premises.

26 These figures and all Broadway grosses are available at www.playbill.com.

27 This was also a company that had suffered its own recent losses. The director Jack O'Brien's partner died while he was working on this production, and one of the show's original leads, Kathleen Freeman, nominated for a Tony Award earlier in the season, died in August 2001.

28 Taylor, *The Archive and the Repertoire*, 256. But see also Eng, "The Value of Silence," on the photographs of those missing on September 11.

29 Taylor, *The Archive and the Repertoire*, 255.

30 Linda Shelton, "Dear Friends," program note for *Dancing for the Bravest and Finest*, Joyce Theater, September 28–29, 2001.

31 Eng, "The Value of Silence," 89.

32 See Franco, *Dancing Modernism/Performing Politics*.

33 Rayner, "Contribution to the Forum on Theatre and Tragedy in the Wake of 11 September 2001," 131.

34 Tamlyn Brooke Shusterman, "Performers and Audience Join Hearts," *New York Times*, September 30, 2001.

35 For readers interested in learning more about plays and performances produced in New York that thematize the events of September 11 and their aftermath, I recommend Carlson, "9/11, Afghanistan, Iraq."

36 Peter Marks, "For Tony Kushner, an Eerily Prescient Return," *New York Times*, November 25, 2001.

37 Ibid.

38 Kushner, *Homebody/Kabul*, 83–84.

39 Mark Steyn, "Goin' to Afghanistan: Review of *Homebody/Kabul*," *New Criterion Online*, February 20, 2002, 2, *www.newcriterion.com*.

40 Tony Kushner, "An Afterword to *Homebody/Kabul*," in Kushner, *Homebody/Kabul*, 146.

41 But the play's reception was not the only news associated with it. At one point

in December 2001, Berkeley Rep nearly lost a grant from the National Endowment for the Arts (NEA) to help mount its spring 2002 production due to the play's politics. In the end, however, the NEA contributed $60,000.

42 Michael Phillips, review of *Homebody/Kabul*, by Tony Kushner, *Los Angeles Times*, December 20, 2001.

43 Phelan, review of *Homebody/Kabul*, 167.

44 Kushner, *Homebody/Kabul*, 11.

45 Ibid.

46 Ibid., 28.

47 Oskar Eustis, interview by John J. Hanlon, *Theater* 32, no. 1 (2002): 2.

48 Jim Nicola, interview by Alexis Soloski, *Theater* 32, no. 1 (2002): 9.

49 All quotes from Reno's *Rebel without a Pause: Unrestrained Reflections on September 11th*, are based on my notes from the various performances of the show I have seen in New York and Los Angeles, as well as the film version of *Rebel without a Pause* (2002), directed by Nancy Savocal. The text itself is not published, and the wording or phrasing might alter nightly.

50 For current information on Reno and her show, see her Web site http://www.citizenreno.com

51 Quoted in Robin Finn, "Public Profiles: Reno," *New York Times*, May 16, 2002.

AFTERWORD: THE TIME OF YOUR LIFE

1 William Saroyan, "An Introduction," in Saroyan, *The Time of Your Life*, 12.

2 Ibid.

3 Ibid.

4 Advertisement, *Variety*, August 6, 1941, 12.

5 Odets, *The Time Is Ripe*, 15.

6 Leggett, *A Daring Young Man*, xii.

7 Saroyan, preface to *My Heart's in the Highlands*, 22.

8 Quoted in Leggett, *A Daring Young Man*, 61.

9 Saroyan, *The Time of Your Life*, 117–18.

10 Louis Kronenberger, Review of *The Time of Your Life*, by William Saroyan, *Time*, November 6, 1939, 32.

11 Lee, *Painting on the Left*, 137

12 Saroyan, *The Time of Your Life*, 41.

13 Ibid., 44.

14 Quoted in Jack Gould, "The Times of Their Lives," *New York Times*, November 12, 1939.

15 Denning, *The Cultural Front*, 240.

16 Ibid., 251.

17 Saroyan, *The Time of Your Life*, 22.

18 *New York Times*, October 28, 1939.

19 Saroyan, *The Time of Your Life*, 43.

20 Ibid., 66–67.

21 Ibid., 68–69.

22 Brooks Atkinson, "Rulebook for Saroyanesques," *New York Times*, November 26, 1939.

23 Brooks Atkinson, Review of *The Time of Your Life*, by William Saroyan, *New York Times*, October 26, 1939.

24 Brooks Atkinson, "Saroyan at the Bar," *New York Times*, November 5, 1939.

25 McCarthy, "Theatre Chronicle," 135.

26 Ibid., 137.

27 Ibid., 138.

28 Saroyan, *The Time of Your Life*, 4.

29 Ibid., 12–13.

30 Atkinson, "Saroyan at the Bar."

31 Lavey, "Artistic Director's Preview," 2.

32 Ibid.

33 Tina Landau, "Director's Notes," Encore Arts programs for the Seattle Repertory Theatre production of *The Time of Your Life*, 7.

34 Saroyan, *The Time of Your Life*, 22.

35 Tina Landau, "Director's Notes," Encore Arts programs for the Seattle Repertory Theatre production of *The Time of Your Life*, 6.

36 Quoted in Seattle Repertory Theatre's study guide for *The Time of Your Life*, 4.

37 Carlson, "9/11, Afghanistan, Iraq," 14–15.

38 Bennett, *Performing Nostalgia*, 5.

39 Ibid., 56.

40 Brustein, *The Siege of the Arts*, 57.

41 Ibid., 57.

42 Ibid., 62–63.

BIBLIOGRAPHY

Adams, Rachel. *Sideshow U.S.A.: Freaks and the American Cultural Imagination.* Chicago: University of Chicago Press, 2001.

Asleson, Robyn. "A Sarah Siddons Chronology." In *A Passion for Performance: Sarah Siddons and Her Portraitists,* ed. Asleson et al., xii–xvii. Los Angeles: J. Paul Getty Museum, 1999.

———. "'She Was Tragedy Personified': Crafting the Siddons Legend in Art and Life." In *A Passion for Performance: Sarah Siddons and Her Portraitists,* ed. Asleson et al., 41–95. Los Angeles: J. Paul Getty Museum, 1999.

Backscheider, Paula R. *Spectacular Politics: Theatrical Power and Mass Culture in Early Modern England.* Baltimore, MD: Johns Hopkins University Press, 1993.

Barish, Jonas A. *The Antitheatrical Prejudice.* Berkeley: University of California Press, 1981.

Belsey, Catherine. *The Subject of Tragedy: Identity and Difference in Renaissance Drama.* London: Methuen, 1985.

Benjamin, Walter. "Theses on the Philosophy of History." In *Illuminations: Essays and Reflections,* 253–64. Ed. Hannah Arendt. Trans. Harry Zohn. New York: Schocken, 1969.

Bennett, Susan. *Performing Nostalgia: Shifting Shakespeare and the Contemporary Past.* London: Routledge, 1996.

Bigsby, C. W. E. "Drama as Cultural Sign: American Dramatic Criticism, 1945–1978." *American Quarterly* 30, no. 3 (1978): 331–57.

Bloom, Ken. *Broadway: An Encyclopedic Guide to the History, People, and Places of Times Square.* New York: Facts on File, 1991.

Boone, Joseph Allen, et al. *Queer Frontiers: Millennial Geographies, Genders, and Generations.* Madison: University of Wisconsin Press, 2000.

Booth, Michael R. "Sarah Siddons." In *Three Tragic Actresses: Siddons, Rachel, Ristori,* ed. Booth, John Stokes, and Susan Bassnett, 10–65. Cambridge: Cambridge University Press, 1996.

Brody, Jennifer. "Opening Sequences." In *Dancing Desires: Choreographing Sexualities On and Off the Stage*, ed. Jane Desmond, 391–401. Madison: University of Wisconsin Press, 2001.

Brustein, Robert. *The Siege of the Arts: Collected Writings, 1994–2001*. Chicago: I. R. Dee, 2001.

Burston, Jonathan. *Megamusicals*. Durham, NC: Duke University Press, forthcoming.

Butler, Judith. *Antigone's Claim: Kinship between Life and Death*. New York: Columbia University Press, 2000.

———. *Bodies That Matter: On the Discursive Limits of "Sex."* New York: Routledge, 1993.

———. "Global Violence, Sexual Politics." In *Queer Ideas: The David R. Kessler Lectures in Lesbian and Gay Studies*, ed. Center for Lesbian and Gay Studies, CUNY, 197–214. New York: Feminist Press, 2003.

Campa, Román de la. "Latinos and the Crossover Aesthetic." Foreword to *Magical Urbanism: Latinos Reinvent the U.S. City*, by Mike Davis, xi–xviii. London: Verso, 2000.

Carey, Gary, and Joseph L. Mankievicz. *More about* All about Eve. New York: Random House, 1972.

Carlson, Julie Ann. *In the Theatre of Romanticism: Coleridge, Nationalism, Women*. Cambridge: Cambridge University Press, 1994.

Carlson, Marvin. *The Haunted Stage: The Theatre as Memory Machine*. Ann Arbor: University of Michigan Press, 2001.

———. "9/11, Afghanistan, Iraq: The Response of the New York Theatre." *Theatre Survey* 45, no.1 (2004): 3–17.

———. *Performance: A Critical Introduction*. 2d ed. New York: Routledge, 2003.

Charyn, Jerome. *Gangsters and Gold Diggers: Old New York, the Jazz Age, and the Birth of Broadway*. New York: Four Walls Eight Windows, 2003.

Chaudhuri, Una. Review of *Topdog/Underdog*, by Suzan-Lori Parks. *Theatre Journal* 54, no. 2 (2002): 289–91.

———. *Staging Place: The Geography of Modern Drama*. Ann Arbor: University of Michigan Press, 1995.

Chuh, Kandice. *Imagine Otherwise: On Asian Americanist Critique*. Durham, NC: Duke University Press, 2003.

Chuh, Kandice, and Karen Shimakawa, eds. *Orientations: Mapping Studies in the Asian Diaspora*. Durham, NC: Duke University Press, 2001.

Clum, John M., ed. *Staging Gay Lives: An Anthology of Contemporary Gay Theater*. Boulder, CO: Westview, 1996.

Cohen, Cathy J. *The Boundaries of Blackness: AIDS and the Breakdown of Black Politics*. Chicago: University of Chicago Press, 1999.

Cox, Jeffrey N. "Baille, Siddons, Larpent: Gender, Power, and Politics in the Theatre of Romanticism." In *Women in British Romantic Theatre: Drama, Performance, and Society, 1790–1840*, ed. Catherine B. Burroughs, 23–47. Cambridge: Cambridge University Press, 2000.

Cruz-Malavé, Arnaldo, and Martin F. Manalansan IV. *Queer Globalizations: Citizenship and the Afterlife of Colonialism*. New York: New York University Press, 2002.

Cvetkovich, Ann. *An Archive of Feelings: Trauma, Sexuality, and Lesbian Public Cultures*. Durham, NC: Duke University Press, 2003.

Dávila, Arlene M. *Latinos, Inc.: The Marketing and Making of a People*. Berkeley: University of California Press, 2001.

Davis, Angela Y. *Blues Legacies and Black Feminism: Gertrude "Ma" Rainey, Bessie Smith, and Billie Holiday*. New York: Pantheon, 1998.

Davis, Mike. *Magical Urbanism: Latinos Reinvent the U.S. City*. London: Verso, 2000.

Delaney, Samuel R. *Times Square Red, Times Square Blue*. New York: New York University Press, 1999.

Delgado, Celeste Fraser, and José Esteban Muñoz, eds. *Everynight Life: Culture and Dance in Latin/o America*. Durham, NC: Duke University Press, 1997.

Denning, Michael. *The Cultural Front: The Laboring of American Culture in the Twentieth Century*. New York: Verso, 1997.

Desmond, Jane C. "Embodying Difference: Issues in Dance and Cultural Studies." In *Meaning in Motion: New Cultural Studies of Dance*, ed. Desmond, 29–54. Durham, NC: Duke University Press, 1997.

———. "Making American Studies Dance." *American Quarterly* 53, no. 3 (2001): 526–34.

Diamond, Elin. *Unmaking Mimesis: Essays on Feminism and Theater*. New York: Routledge, 1997.

Dinshaw, Carolyn. *Getting Medieval: Sexualities and Communities, Pre-and Postmodern*. Durham, NC: Duke University Press, 1999.

Docherty, Thomas. "Now, Here, This." In *Literature and the Contemporary*, ed. Roger Luckhurst and Peter Marks, 50–62. New York: Longman, 1999.

Dolan, Jill. *Geographies of Learning: Theory and Practice, Activism and Performance*. Middleton, CT: Wesleyan University Press, 2001.

———. *Utopia in Performance: Finding Hope in the Theatre*. Ann Arbor: University of Michigan Press, forthcoming.

Dollimore, Jonathan. *Radical Tragedy: Religion, Ideology, and Power in the Drama of Shakespeare and His Contemporaries*, 2d ed. Durham, NC: Duke University Press, 1993.

Donkin, Ellen. "Mrs. Siddons Looks Back in Anger: Feminist Historiography for Eighteenth-Century British Theater." In *Critical Theory and Performance*, ed. Janelle G. Reinelt and Joseph R. Roach, 276–90. Ann Arbor: University of Michigan Press, 1992.

Duberman, Martin B. *Stonewall*. New York: Dutton, 1993.

Dudden, Faye E. *Women in the American Theatre: Actresses and Audiences, 1790–1870*. New Haven, CT: Yale University Press, 1994.

Eng, David. "Out Here and Over There: Queerness and Diaspora in Asian American Studies." *Social Text*, nos. 52–53 (1997): 31–52.

———. "The Value of Silence." *Theatre Journal* 54, no. 1 (2002): 85–94.

Eustis, Oskar. Interview by John J. Hanlon. *Theater* 32, no. 1 (2002): 2.

Flinn, Denny Martin and Martha Swope. *What They Did For Love: The Untold Story behind the Making of A Chorus Line*. New York: Bantam, 1989.

Flores, Juan. *From Bomba to Hip-Hop: Puerto Rican Culture and Latino Identity*. New York: Columbia University Press, 2000.

Foster, Susan Leigh, ed. *Choreographing History*. Bloomington: Indiana University Press, 1995.

Franko, Mark. *Dancing Modernism/Performing Politics*. Bloomington: Indiana University Press, 1995.

Friedwald, Will. *Jazz Singing: America's Great Voices from Bessie Smith to Bebop and Beyond*. New York: Da Capo, 1996.

Fusco, Coco. *The Bodies That Were Not Ours: And Other Writings*. London: Routledge, 2001.

———. "The Other History of Intercultural Performance." In *English Is Broken Here: Notes on Cultural Fusion in the Americas*, 37–63. New York: New Press, 1995.

Gavin, James. *Intimate Nights: The Golden Age of New York Cabaret*. New York: Grove Weidenfeld, 1991.

Gere, David. *How to Make Dances in an Epidemic: Tracking Choreography in the Age of AIDS*. Madison: University of Wisconsin Press, 2004.

Giddins, Gary. *Weather Bird: Jazz at the Dawn of Its Second Century*. Oxford: Oxford University Press, 2004.

Gottschild, Brenda Dixon. *Waltzing in the Dark: African American Vaudeville and Race Politics in the Swing Era*. New York: St. Martin's, 2000.

Harper, Phillip Brian. "Gay Male Identities, Personal Privacy, and Relations of Public Exchange: Notes on Directions for Queer Critique." *Social Text*, nos. 52–53 (1997): 5–29.

———. *Private Affairs: Critical Ventures in the Culture of Social Relations*. New York: New York University Press, 1999.

Hazlitt, William, and Jon Cook. *Selected Writings*. Oxford: Oxford University Press, 1991.

Highfill, Philip H., Kalman A. Burnim, and Edward A. Langhans, eds. *A Biographical Dictionary of Actors, Actresses, Musicians, Dancers, Managers, and Other Stage Personnel in London, 1660–1800*. Vol. 14. Carbondale: Southern Illinois University Press, 1991.

Holland, Sharon Patricia. *Raising the Dead: Readings of Death and (Black) Subjectivity*. Durham, NC: Duke University Press, 2000.

Huerta, Jorge A. *Chicano Drama: Performance, Society, and Myth*. Cambridge: Cambridge University Press, 2000.

————. "Negotiating Borders in Three Latino Plays." In *Of Borders and Thresholds: Theatre History, Practice, and Theory*, ed. Michal Kobialka, 154–84. Minneapolis: University of Minnesota Press, 1999.

————, comp. *Necessary Theater: Six Plays about the Chicano Experience*. Houston: Arte Publico, 1989.

Hughes, Holly, and David Román. *O Solo Homo: The New Queer Performance*. New York: Grove, 1998.

Johnson, Katie. "*Zaza*: That 'Obtruding Harlot' of the Stage." *Theatre Journal* 54, no. 2 (2002): 223–43.

Jones, Bill. T., with Peggy Gillespie. *Last Night on Earth*. New York: Pantheon, 1995.

Jones, Carolyn. *Living Proof: Courage in the Face of AIDS*. New York: Abbeville, 1994.

Jones, John Bush. *Our Musicals, Ourselves: A Social History of the American Musical Theater*, Hanover, NH: Brandeis University Press, 2003.

Kanellos, Nicolás. *A History of Hispanic Theatre in the United States: Origins to 1940*. Austin: University of Texas Press, 1990.

Kelly, John. *John Kelly*. New York: 2wice Arts Foundation, 2001.

Kelly, Linda. *The Kemble Era: John Philip Kemble, Sarah Siddons, and the London Stage*. New York: Random House, 1980.

Kibler, M. Alison. *Rank Ladies: Gender and Cultural Hierarchy in American Vaudeville*. Chapel Hill: University of North Carolina Press, 1999.

Kirkwood, James, and Nicholas Dante. *A Chorus Line*. New York: Applause, 1995.

Kondo, Dorinne K. *About Face: Performing Race in Fashion and* Theater. New York: Routledge, 1997.

Kotis, Greg, and Mark Hollman. *Urinetown: The Musical*. New York: Faber and Faber, 2003.

Kramer, Larry. *Reports from the Holocaust: The Making of an AIDS Activist*. New York: St. Martin's, 1989.

Kuftinec, Sonja. Review of *Broken Hearts: A B.H. Mystery*, by Lisa Loomer. *Theatre Journal* 52, no. 3 (2000): 397–98.

————. *Staging America: Cornerstone and Community-Based Theater*. Carbondale: Southern Illinois University Press, 2003.

Kushner, Tony. *Homebody/Kabul*. New York: Theatre Communication Group, 2002.

Lavey, Martha. "Artistic Director's Preview." *Backstage*, no. 1 (2002): 2.

Lee, Anthony W. *Painting on the Left: Diego Rivera, Radical Politics, and San Francisco's Public Murals*. Berkeley: University of California Press, 1999.

Lee, Josephine D. *Performing Asian America: Race and Ethnicity on the Contemporary Stage*. Philadelphia: Temple University Press, 1997.

Leggett, John. *A Daring Young Man: A Biography of William Saroyan*. New York: Knopf, 2002.

Leguizamo, John, with David Bar Katz. *Freak: A Semi-Demi-Quasi-Pseudo Autobiography*. New York: Riverhead, 1997.

Lopez, Tiffany Ana. "Performing Aztlán: The Female Body as Cultural Critique in the *Teatro* of Cherríe Moraga." In *Performing America: Cultural Nationalism in*

American Theater, ed. Jeffrey D. Mason and J. Ellen Gainor, 160–77. Ann Arbor: University of Michigan Press, 1999.

Lowe, Lisa. *Immigrant Acts: On Asian American Cultural Politics.* Durham, NC: Duke University Press, 1996.

———. "The New Asian Immigrant." In *Orientations: Mapping Studies in the Asian Diaspora*, ed. Kandice Chuh and Karen Shimakawa, 267–76. Durham, NC: Duke University Press, 2001.

Luckhurst, Roger, and Peter Marks. "Hurry Up Please, It's Time: Introducing the Contemporary," in *Literature and the Contemporary*, ed. Luckhurst and Marks, 1–11. New York: Longman, 1999.

Mandelbaum, Ken. *A Chorus Line and the Musicals of Michael Bennett.* New York: St. Martin's, 1989.

Mason, Jeffrey D. "American Stages (Curtain Raiser)." In *Performing America: Cultural Nationalism in American Theater*, ed. Mason, and J. Ellen Gainor, 1–6. Ann Arbor: University of Michigan Press, 1999.

McCarthy, Mary. "Theatre Chronicle: An Innocent on Broadway." *Partisan Review* 7, no. 2 (1940): 135–38.

McNamara, Brooks. *The New York Concert Saloon: The Devil's Own Nights.* Cambridge: Cambridge University Press, 2002.

McPherson, Heather. "Picturing Tragedy: Mrs. Siddons as the Tragic Muse Revisited." *Eighteenth-Century Studies* 33, no. 3 (2000): 401–30.

———. "Searching for Sarah Siddons: Portraiture and the Historiography of Fame." *Eighteenth-Century Studies* 33, no. 2 (1999): 281–87.

Merrill, Lisa. *When Romeo Was a Woman: Charlotte Cushman and Her Circle of Female Spectators.* Ann Arbor: University of Michigan Press, 1999.

Meyer, Richard. "At Home in Marginal Domains." *Documents*, no. 18 (2000): 19–32.

———. *Outlaw Representation: Censorship and Homosexuality in Twentieth-Century American Art.* New York: Oxford University Press, 2002.

Miller, Nancy K. *But Enough about Me: Why We Read Other People's Lives.* New York: Columbia University Press, 2002.

Mitchell, Joni. "The Fiddle and the Drum." *Clouds*, 1960.

———. "Woodstock." *Ladies of the Canyon*, 1970.

Montagu, Jennifer. *The Expression of the Passions: The Origin and Influence of Charles Le Brun's Conférence sur l'Expression Générale et Particulière.* New Haven, CT: Yale University Press, 1994.

Moraga, Cherríe. *The Last Generation.* Boston: South End Press, 1993.

———. *Heroes and Saints and Other Plays.* Albuquerque, NM: West End, 1994.

Morris, Gay. "What He Called Himself: Issues of Identity in Early Dances by Bill T. Jones." In *Dancing Desires: Choreographing Sexualities On and Off the Stage*, ed. Jane C. Desmond, 243–63. Madison: University of Wisconsin Press, 2001.

Most, Andrea. *Making Americans: Jews and the Broadway Musical.* Cambridge, MA: Harvard University Press, 2004.

Muñoz, José Esteban. *Disidentifications: Queers of Color and the Performance of Politics.* Minneapolis: University of Minnesota Press, 1999.

———. "Ephemera as Evidence: Introductory Notes to Queer Acts." *Women and Performance: A Journal of Feminist Theory* 8, no. 2 (1996): 5–16.

Negron-Muntaner, Frances. "Feeling Pretty: *West Side Story* and Puerto Rican Identity Discourses." *Social Text*, no. 63 (2000): 83–97.

———. "Jennifer's Butt." *Aztlán* 22, no. 2 (1997): 181–94.

Nguyen, Viet Thanh. *Race and Resistance: Literature and Politics in Asian America.* Oxford: Oxford University Press, 2002.

Nicola, Jim. Interview by Alexis Soloski. *Theater* 32, no. 1 (2002): 9.

Nipe, Christine. "Mrs. Siddons' Currency." *Theatre Survey* 40, no. 2 (1999): 70–77.

Nolan, Frederick. *Lorenz Hart: A Poet on Broadway.* New York: Oxford University Press, 1994.

Odets, Clifford. *The Time is Ripe: The 1940 Journal of Clifford Odets.* New York: Grove, 1988.

Odets, Walt. *In the Shadow of the Epidemic: Being HIV-Negative in the Age of AIDS.* Durham, NC: Duke University Press, 1995.

Palumbo-Liu, David. *Asian/American: Historical Crossings of a Racial Frontier.* Stanford, CA: Stanford University Press, 1999.

Paredez, Deborah. "Remembering Selena, Re-membering Latinidad." *Theatre Journal* 54, no. 1 (2002): 63–84.

Patton, Cindy. *Inventing AIDS.* New York: Routledge, 1990.

Pease, Donald E., and Robyn Wiegman. "Futures." In *The Futures of American Studies*, ed. Pease and Wiegman, 1–42. Durham, NC: Duke University Press, 2002.

Phelan, Peggy. "Introduction: The Ends of Performance." In *The Ends of Performance*, ed. Phelan and Jill Lane, 1–19. New York: New York University Press, 1998.

———. Review of *Homebody/Kabul*, by Tony Kushner. *Theatre Journal* 55, no. 1 (2003): 167.

———. *Unmarked: The Politics of Performance.* New York: Routledge, 1993.

Phelan, Peggy, and Jill Lane, eds. *The Ends of Performance.* New York: New York University Press, 1998.

Porter, Eric. *What Is This Thing Called Jazz? African American Musicians as Artists, Critics, and Activists.* Berkeley: University of California Press, 2002.

Quiroga, José. *Tropics of Desire: Interventions from Queer Latino America.* New York: New York University Press, 2000.

Rayner, Alice. "Contribution to the Forum on Theatre and Tragedy in the Wake of 11 September 2001." *Theatre Journal* 54, no. 1 (2002): 129–31.

Reinelt, Janelle G., and Joseph R. Roach, eds. *Critical Theory and Performance.* Ann Arbor: University of Michigan Press, 1992.

Reynolds, Michael. Review of *Whitelands Trilogy*, by Chay Yew. *Theatre Journal* 49, no. 1 (1997): 75–79.

Roach, Joseph. *Cities of the Dead: Circum-Atlantic Performance.* New York: Columbia University Press, 1996.

Robinson, Marc. *The Other American Drama*. Baltimore, MD: Johns Hopkins University Press, 1997.

Rodgers, Richard, *Musical Stages: An Autobiography*. New York: Da Capo, 1995.

Rodgers, Richard, and Lorenz Hart. "Zip," *Pal Joey*, 1941.

Rodriguez, Gregory. "Latino Republicans and the 1998 Election." *Aztlán* 24, no. 1 (1999): 175–84.

Rofes, Eric. *Dry Bones Breathe: Gay Men Creating Post-AIDS Identities and Cultures*. New York: Haworth, 1998.

Román, David. *Acts of Intervention: Performance, Gay Culture, and AIDS*. Bloomington: Indiana University Press, 1998.

———. "Coco Fusco." In *Encyclopedia of Latinos and Latinas in the United States*, ed. Suzanne Oboler and Deena J. Gonzalez. New York: Oxford University Press, forthcoming.

———. "Latino Performance and Identity." *Aztlán* 22, no. 2 (1997): 151–68.

———. "On the Unfashionability of AIDS-Arts Today: A Symposium on AIDS and the Arts." Artery: The AIDS-Arts Forum, www.artistswithaids.org/artery/symposium/symposium_roman.html (accessed December 2001).

———. "Teaching AIDS Activism." Artery: The AIDS-Arts Forum, www.artistswithaids .org/artery/centerpieces/centerpieces_index.html (accessed December 2000).

———. "Tragedy: An Introduction." *Theatre Journal* 54, no. 1 (2002): 1–18.

Román, David, and Alberto Sandoval-Sánchez. "Caught in the Web: Latinidad, AIDS, and Allegory in *Kiss of the Spider Woman, the Musical*." *American Literature* 67, no. 3 (1995): 553–85.

Román, David, and Tim Miller. "Preaching to the Converted." *Theatre Journal* 47, no. 2 (1995): 169–88.

Roof, Judith. "Generational Difficulties; or, The Fear of a Barren History." In *Generations: Academic Feminists in Dialogue*, ed. Devoney Looser and E. Ann Kaplan, 69–87. Minneapolis: University of Minnesota Press, 1997.

Roth, Nancy L., and Katie Hogan, eds. *Gendered Epidemic: Representations of Women in the Age of AIDS*. New York: Routledge, 1998.

Russo, Vito. *The Celluloid Closet: Homosexuality in the Movies*. New York: Harper and Row, 1981.

Sandoval-Sánchez, Alberto. *José, Can You See? Latinos on and off Broadway*. Madison: University of Wisconsin Press, 1999.

Saroyan, William. Preface to *My Heart's in the Highlands*. In *The Time of Your Life and Other Plays*, 19–23. New York: Bantam, 1967.

———. *The Time of Your Life*. New York: Samuel French, 1941.

Savran, David. "Choices Made and Unmade." *Theater* 31, no. 2 (2001): 89–95.

Schechner, Richard. *Performance Theory*. Rev. and exp. ed. New York: Routledge, 1988.

Schneider, Rebecca. "Archives Performance Remains." *Performance Research* 6, no. 2 (2001): 100–108.

———. "Driving the Lincoln 'Cross History' Viewing History, Almost, Not Quite."

In *Un-Sichtbarkeiten der Differenz: Beiträge zur Genderdebatte in den Künsten*, ed. Annette Jael Lehmann, 101–16. Tübingen, Germany: Stauffenburg, 2001.

Sedgwick, Eve Kosofsky. *Tendencies*. Durham, NC: Duke University Press, 1993.

Senelick, Laurence. *Cabaret Performance*. Vol. 1, *Europe 1890–1920: Sketches, Songs, Monologues, and Memoirs*. New York: Performing Arts Journal Publications, 1989.

———. *Cabaret Performance*. Vol. 2, *Europe 1920–1940*. Baltimore, MD: Johns Hopkins University Press, 1993.

Shimakawa, Karen. *National Abjection: The Asian American Body Onstage*. Durham, NC: Duke University Press, 2002.

Shingler, Martin "Interpreting *All about Eve*: A Study in Historical Reception." In *Hollywood Spectatorship: Changing Perceptions of Cinema Audiences*, ed. Melvyn Stokes and Richard Maltby, 46–62. London: British Film Institute, 2001.

Siegel, Marcia. "Virtual Criticism and the Dance of Death." In *The Ends of Performance*, ed. Peggy Phelan and Jill Lane, 247–61. New York: New York University Press, 1998.

Smith, Cecil Michener. *Musical Comedy in America*. 1950. New York: Routledge, 1991.

Smith, Neil. "Giuliani Time: The Revanchist 1990s." *Social Text* 16, no. 4 (1998): 1–20.

Smith, Susan Harris. *American Drama: The Bastard Art*. Cambridge: Cambridge University Press, 1997.

Sondheim, Stephen. "Anyone Can Whistle." *Anyone Can Whistle*, 1964.

———. "Everybody Says Don't." *Anyone Can Whistle*, 1964.

———. "Broadway Baby." *Follies*, 1971.

———, "I'm Still Here." *Follies*, 1971.

Staggs, Sam. *All about "All about Eve": The Complete Behind-the-Scenes Story of the Bitchiest Film Ever Made*. New York: St. Martin's Press, 2000.

Steedman, Carolyn. *Dust: The Archive and Cultural History*. New Brunswick, NJ: Rutgers University Press, 2002.

Stevens, Gary, and Alan George. *The Longest Line: Broadway's Most Singular Sensation, "A Chorus Line."* New York: Applause, 1995.

Stoler, Ann Laura. "Colonial Archives and the Acts of Governance." *Archival Science*, no. 2 (2002): 87–109.

Sullivan, Andrew. *Love Undetectable: Notes on Friendship, Sex, and Survival*. New York: Knopf, 1998.

Taylor, Diana. *The Archive and the Repertoire: Performing Cultural Memory in the Americas*. Durham, NC: Duke University Press, 2003.

Tomko, Linda J. *Dancing Class: Gender, Ethnicity, and Social Divides in American Dance, 1890–1920*. Bloomington: Indiana University Press, 1999.

Trav. S. D. "9/11: America's Theaters Respond." *American Theatre* 18, no. 11 (2001): 16–18.

Treichler, Paula A. *How to Have Theory in an Epidemic: Cultural Chronicles of AIDS*. Durham, NC: Duke University Press, 1999.

Turner, Victor Witter. *Dramas, Fields, and Metaphors: Symbolic Action in Human Society*. Ithaca, NY: Cornell University Press, 1974.

Uno, Roberta, ed., with Lucy Mae San Pablo Burns. *The Color of Theater: Race, Culture, and Contemporary Performance*. London: Continuum, 2002.

Vogel, Shane. "Where Are We Now? Queer World Making and Cabaret Performance." *GLQ: A Journal of Lesbian and Gay Studies* 6, no. 1 (2000): 29–60.

Wallace, Maurice. "The Autochoreography of an Ex–Snow Queen: Dance, Desire, and the Black Masculine in Melvin Dixon's *Vanishing Rooms*." In *Novel Gazing: Queer Readings in Fiction*, ed. Eve Kosofsky Sedgwick, 379–400. Durham, NC: Duke University Press, 1997.

Wallace, Mike. "New York, New Deal." In *After the World Trade Center: Rethinking New York City*, ed. Michael Sorkin and Sharon Zukin, 209–23. New York: Routledge, 2002.

Warner, Michael. "Normal and Normaller: Beyond Gay Marriage." *GLQ: A Journal of Lesbian and Gay Studies* 5, no. 2 (1999): 119–71.

———, ed. *Fear of a Queer Planet: Queer Politics and Social Theory*. Minneapolis: University of Minnesota Press, 1993.

Warren, Harry, and Al Dubin. "The Lullaby of Broadway." *42nd Street*, 1933.

West, Shearer. "The Public and Private Roles of Sarah Siddons." In *A Passion for Performance: Sarah Siddons and Her Portraitists*, ed. Robyn Asleson et al., 1–39. Los Angeles: J. Paul Getty Museum, 1999.

Wiegman, Robyn. "Feminism's Apocalyptic Futures." *New Literary History* 31, no. 4 (2000): 805–25.

Williams, Raymond. *The Long Revolution*. Orchard Park, NY: Broadview, 2001.

———. *Marxism and Literature*. Oxford: Oxford University Press, 1977.

———. *Modern Tragedy*. Stanford, CA: Stanford University Press, 1966.

Wilson, Michael S. "The 'Incomparable' Siddons as Reynolds's Muse: Art and Ideology on the British Stage." In *So Rich a Tapestry: The Sister Arts and Cultural Studies*, ed. Ann Hurley and Kate Greenspan, 116–50. London: Associated University Presses, 1995.

Wise, Gene. " 'Paradigm Dramas' in American Studies: A Cultural and Institutional History of the Movement." In *Locating American Studies: The Evolution of a Discipline*, ed. Lucy Maddox, 166–210. Baltimore, MD: Johns Hopkins University Press, 1999.

Wolf, Stacy Ellen. *A Problem Like Maria: Gender and Sexuality in the American Musical*. Ann Arbor: University of Michigan Press, 2002.

Yarbro-Bejarano, Yvonne. "Expanding the Categories of Race and Sexuality in Lesbian and Gay Studies." In *Professions of Desire: Lesbian and Gay Studies in Literature*, ed. George E. Haggerty and Bonnie Zimmerman, 124–35. New York: Modern Language Association of America, 1995.

———. *The Wounded Heart: Writings on Cherríe Moraga*. Austin: University of Texas Press, 2001.

Yew, Chay. *The Hyphenated American: Four Plays*. New York: Grove, 2002.

INDEX

Abbott, George, 181

Acquired Immune Deficiency Syndrome (AIDS), 5–6, 172, 226, 314 n.11, 315–16 n.32, 317 n.51; in African Americans, 53–54; aids-as-crisis model, 54; decline in research funding for, 55; end-of-AIDS discourse, 50–51, 52–56; federal funding for, 54; in Latinos, 53–54; legal backlash against people with, 55–56; in people under the age of twenty-five, 53; "post-AIDS" identities, 51–52; Román's courses on, 229–31; use of fear in prevention campaigns, 314 n.8

Acts of Intervention: Performance, Gay Culture, and AIDS (Román), 35–36, 57

Adams, Rachel, 114–15

Affliction of Glory, The: A Comedy about Tragedy (Dwyer; 1999), 146

Ahmad, Aijaz, 40

AIDS Service Organizations (ASOS), 54, 55

Albee, Edward, 195

Alfaro, Luis, 118

Algonquin, 182, 185, 222

Algren, Nelson, 290

All About Eve (1950), 152–58, 174, 197, 324 n.39

Alternative performance, valorization of, 36

American Drama: The Bastard Art (S. Smith), 27–28

American Quarterly, 27–28

American songbook, the, 179–80, 222. *See also* Cook, Barbara; Haran, Mary Cleere; Marcovicci, Andrea; McKechnie, Donna; Stritch, Elaine

American studies, 18–30, 39; disciplinary boundaries and, 27–28; feminist performance theory and, 30; performance analysis and, 29; "place" of in American culture, 27–28; unacknowledged theater studies and, 24–26

American Studies Association, 28

Americans with Disabilities Act, 56

Angels in the Wings (1948), 197, 201

Anthony, Marc, 33

Antitheatricality, 16–17, 35

Anyone Can Whistle (Sondheim; 1964), 209, 214

"Anyone Can Whistle," 214

Applause (1970), 161, 324 n.39

Fitzgerald, Ella, 184
Fleming, Patsy, 55
Flores, Juan, 134
Follies (Sondheim; 1971), 196, 204
For Colored Girls Who Have Considered Suicide When the Rainbow is Enuf (Shange), 46–47
Fornes, Marie Irene, 25
Forsythia (B. Jones; 1989), 59
42nd Street (1933), 224–25; revival of, 257–58
Fosse, Bob, 189, 218
Frazelle, Kenneth, 60
Freak (Leguizamo; 1998), 6, 320 n.4, 321 n.12; advertising campaign for, 116–17; critical reaction to, 110–11; Latino genealogical systems and, 112–13; Latino performance history and, 121–23, 132–36; portrayal of Latino family life in, 117–21
Freak (film version), 112
Freaks/freak shows, 113–15
Friedwald, Will, 193
Frontier(s), the, 78; America as, 78; California as, 78–79; racial, 105–6
Frye, Northrup, 22
Full Monty, The, 242–46
Fusco, Coco, 114, 321 n.13
Futures of American Studies, The (Pease and Wiegman), 18, 312 n.25

Gaiety, the, 244, 329 n.25
Gainor, J. Ellen, 25, 27
Garland, Judy, 72, 195, 213, 224
Garrick, David, 151
Garrick Gaieties (Rogers and Hart; 1925), 182
Gates, Henry Louis, Jr., 316 n.33
Gavin, James, 193, 194, 212
Gay marriage, 315 n.21
Genre studies, 228
Geographies of Learning: Theory and Prac-tice, Activism and Performance (Dolan), 24
Gere, David, 63
Gershwin, George, 195
Get Up and Jive (Kelly; 2004), 173, 174, 178
Gets, Malcolm, 327 n.36
Ghetto pastoral, 290–91
Gibbs, Wolcott, 285–86
Girl in the Spotlight (1920), 194
Giuliani, Rudy, 235–36, 237–39
Gold Diggers, The (1933), 224
Golden Girls, The, 206
Goldenberg, Billy, 205, 206–7, 208
Gómez-Peña, Guillermo, 114
Goodbye to Berlin (Isherwood), 189
Gordon, David, 248
Gottschild, Brenda Dixon, 29
Graham, Martha, 165–68, 250
Green, Adolph, 195
Greenberg, Jon, 65–66, 68, 75
Greenberg, Neil, 5–6, 10, 57, 62–69, 75, 317 n.40; comments on dance, 77; relationship to AIDS and, 72, 74–77
Grey, Joel, 189
Grimm, Henry, 88

Hallelujah! I'm A Bum (1933), 180
Hamilton, Philip, 251
Hamlisch, Marvin, 218
Hammerstein, Oscar, 184–85
Haran, Mary Cleere, 9, 182–86, 223, 224–25; cabaret performance style of, 185–86
Hare, David, 111
Harper, Phillip Brian, 52, 53, 318 n.4
Harper, Wally, 209
Harris, Julie, 189
Harris, Lyle Ashton, 81
"Harry's House/Centerpiece," 174
Hart, Lorenz ("Larry"), 180, 182, 185, 198, 284

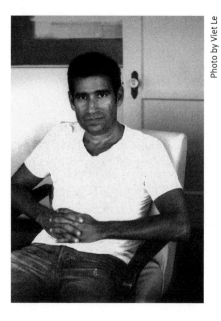

Photo by Viet Le

David Román is Professor of English at the University of Southern California
and teaches in the Program in American Studies and Ethnicity.

Library of Congress Cataloging-in-Publication Data

Román, David.

Performance in America : contemporary U.S. culture and the performing arts /
David Román.

p. cm. — (Perverse modernities)

Includes bibliographical references and index.

ISBN 0-8223-3675-8 (cloth : alk. paper)

ISBN 0-8223-3663-4 (pbk. : alk. paper)

1. Performing arts—Social aspects—United States. 1. Title. 11. Series.

PN1590.S6R66 2005

791'.0973—dc22   2005012086